TELEVISION BROADCASTING

TELEVISION BROADCASTING

An Introduction

EDITED BY

ROBERT L. HILLIARD

COMMUNICATION ARTS BOOKS

Hastings House ● Publishers ● New York

First Published, 1964
as Understanding Television
Second Printing, June 1969
Third Printing, September 1970
Fourth Printing, May 1972
Fifth Printing, October 1974
Sixth Printing, December 1976

Library of Congress Cataloging in Publication Data
Hilliard, Robert L   1925-   ed.
    Television broadcasting.

    (Communication arts books)
    Published in 1964 under title: Understanding
television.
    Includes bibliographies and index.
    1.   Television broadcasting.   I. Title.
PN1992.5.H54   1978.   791.45   77-10158
ISBN 0-8038-7169-4
ISBN 0-8038-7170-8 pbk.

Published simultaneously in Canada by
Copp Clark Ltd., Toronto

Printed in the United States of America

To Erik Barnouw and Bob Shayon, writers, creators and critics of communications in order to breathe into the living of life something better for every human being; I respect their teaching, appreciate their inspiration and value their friendship.

CONTENTS

FOREWORD

MANY OF YOU READING THIS are students, taking a course in television broadcasting to prepare you for the professional field. Some of you know me from my position with the FCC. Others of you know me, as well, from my years as general manager and vice-president of WJR, Detroit. But many years before that I stood where you are now: a student studying, working and planning to become a professional broadcaster.

Recently, while being honored by my alma mater, Michigan State University, with a Doctor of Humanities degree, I thought of the time on the same campus when I began my career in broadcasting on the staff of MSU's radio station, WKAR. It was this practical experience, combined with studies in as many broad areas as I could manage, that I feel gave me my best preparation. It was this kind of preparation that I looked for in later years when I interviewed young people seeking jobs. It was this kind of learning experience I tried to instill in students when I taught courses in broadcasting at the University of Detroit.

It is because *Television Broadcasting* takes this kind of approach that I am pleased to write the Foreword to it: from the point of view of the student, broadcaster, teacher and FCC Commissioner. This book deals with the practicalities of television broadcasting. It not only presents necessary basic theory, but it concentrates on how-to-do-it; and, importantly, on doing it with the responsibilities of the good broadcaster to the community and to the public interest.

Television Broadcasting is the kind of book I would have liked to have had when I was teaching, the kind of book I would have given my new employees at the station to use as a reference and as a guide.

To those of you planning a career in broadcasting, my encouragement, my best wishes and this advice: prepare well, be practical and be responsible.

JAMES H. QUELLO
Commissioner
Federal Communications Commission

PREFACE

IN MANY OF THE SPEECHES I have given during the past dozen years I have stressed that the mass media, particularly television, are the most powerful forces in the world today affecting the minds and emotions of humankind. And in the decade just past, the increasing number of books that describe television's potential for modifying our behavior indicate that what I've been saying has been accepted widely enough that it may now be on its way to becoming a cliché.

I would be tempted to believe that the power and importance of television have finally been recognized, except for the fact that such recognition is still paid largely by lip-service. True, more than 200 colleges and universities in the United States offer degree programs to some 20,000 students majoring in broadcasting. These students are being given an opportunity to prepare themselves to work with—if not to cope with—the significant media influences in their current and future lives. But what about the other 12 million people enrolled in institutions of higher education? What about the 50 million students enrolled in elementary and secondary schools who spend up to 12 years taking courses in print reading and writing? Very few of them ever take a course in those forms of communication that they will be dealing with far more frequently throughout their lives and which, given the statistics on people's television viewing and radio listening habits, will have much greater impact on them than will the print media.

One of our motives in writing this book is the hope that it will help to move educational purposes and practices somewhat closer to the 20th century—if not to the 21st century, in which most people now in school will live most of their lives. We hope that this book will not only help students at all levels to learn to use television effectively but will also help professionals working in the field and citizens in all walks of life to better understand, criticize and govern the television medium. Unless the schools of America begin to introduce curricula in mass media at least to the extent that they have done so over the years for print, we shall have a nation of uncritical visual and aural illiterates whose thoughts and actions will be easy prey for those who control the mass media.

This book is an outgrowth of an earlier publication, *Understanding Television*. Although it follows the same basic form, it has been completely rewritten and we have updated it to the extent that the lead time for the publishing of any book permits—in this case into the late 1970s. We have attempted to be responsive to the many comments received over the years from professors who have used the book, changing where we fell short and strengthening those areas which worked well in the classroom. One of the letters we most appreciated was from a student, Michael Booze, who wrote that "The explanations of everything from the technical to the organizational aspects of television . . . are very clearly, simply and yet thoroughly done . . . everyone in our class appreciates the fact that the authors of the book do not at any time . . . lose the student in the technicalities of television; they . . . present the material in a forthright manner." We have tried to keep this approach. We have also tried to anticipate some of the changes in the fast and ever-changing field of television and to allow a flexibility for future techniques and interpretations.

I offer my appreciation to the other contributors to this book, some of whom, because of delays not of their doing, found it necessary to revise material several times to keep it as current as possible close to the publication date. I appreciate the interest and support of FCC Commissioner James H. Quello and his graciousness in writing the Foreword to this book. And, as always, I am grateful for the patience and encouragement of Communication Arts Books publisher Russell F. Neale, his assistant James Moore, Al Lichtenberg, Lee Tobin and the other members of the Hastings House staff.

ROBERT L. HILLIARD

Washington, D.C.
February, 1978

TELEVISION BROADCASTING

WESLEY HERNDON WALLACE

Professor of Radio, Television and Motion Pictures,
University of North Carolina at Chapel Hill

● Dr. Wallace received the B.S. degree from the North Carolina State University of North Carolina at Raleigh, the M.A. from the University of North Carolina at Chapel Hill and the Ph.D. from Duke University, all in history. He has been active in commercial broadcasting since 1929 as a staff musician, announcer, copywriter, traffic manager, assistant program director, production manager and station manager. From 1943 through 1946 he served first as Officer-in-Charge of Armed Forces Radio stations WVTI, Bougainville, in the Northern Solomons and WVTM, Manila, and subsequently supervised 14 stations as Officer-in-Charge of the Armed Forces Radio Service in the Western Pacific. From 1947 to 1950 he was General Manager of the Manila Broadcasting Company in the Philippines. Since 1952 he has been a member of the Department of Radio, Television and Motion Pictures at the University of North Carolina and served as Chairman for more than 13 years. He has taught courses in the history and development of broadcasting, station management, broadcasting public relations and promotion, creative programming, social aspects of mass communication and a seminar in mass communication. He has contributed articles to historical journals and is active in various regional and national professional associations. In 1975 he received the Earle J. Gluck Distinguished Service Award from the North Carolina Association of Broadcasters and in 1976 he was inducted into the Association's Hall of Fame.

1

GROWTH, ORGANIZATION, AND IMPACT

BY WESLEY H. WALLACE

THE MANY-FACETED INSTITUTION that is television broadcasting plays a number of different and sometimes conflicting roles. These roles are assigned by society and are only partly inherent in the electronic nature of the device. Since society itself constantly undergoes change, it is not surprising that society's expectations of television and television's responses to those expectations are also undergoing change. Thus, what is apparent today in television's growth, organization and impact may not be so obvious tomorrow.

MULTIPLE ROLES OF TELEVISION

For some important voices in society, television broadcasting is a part of the institutionalism of education: a method of transmitting knowledge; a device for spreading cultural richness to culturally arid areas; a modern "school without walls" which presents both perils and rich vicarious experiences for the toddler up through the maturing teens; a mechanism for increasing the effectiveness of the more conventional school, the library and the teacher. For the world of business and industry, television broadcasting is an advertising device assisting in moving goods and services from central supplying points to the outermost limits of the United States and capable of popularizing brand names of toothpaste, cereals, soaps and beer. For the audience—a vast cross-section of America's population—television is entertainment, a pastime, a creator and sustainer of moods, a companion, a source both of vicarious experience and of topics of conversation, a formulator of our social, political and economic agenda—what we think and talk about—and sometimes, for some people, a time-waster and an addictive soporific. For those who regulate broadcasting, television is seen as a user of the electromagnetic spectrum—a natural resource—under federal license requiring operation in the public interest. To those who see this as television's role, any conflict between private and public interest must naturally be resolved in favor of the public.

For the broadcaster-owner-licensee, television's roles are multiple, somewhat confused, and sometimes contradictory: telecasting is a business, with all the usual pitfalls of business and some special ones reserved for broadcasting; telecasting is also *show* business, catering to the vagaries of public whims and tastes; telecasting is an occupation, a profession or a source of income from investment, a livelihood, or an outlet for the energies and interests of the frustrated side-show barker or the would-be "con" artist, a status symbol, a way to power, an opportunity to serve. To the licensee-operator, telecasting is part theatre, part school, part newspaper, part church and part town meeting—with many of the same problems found in each of these. To the broadcaster, the television station and its transmission channel also are frequently thought of as private property which must be protected from the always threatening—to the broadcaster's way of thinking—encroachments of government, the gibes of the critics and covetous activities of other business or public interest groups who want for themselves this valuable "property"—the license to telecast.

For some critics television frequently plays an anti-social role. The most recently developed medium of mass communication, television is accused of creating mass responses to stereotyped stimuli, of robbing the populace of its will to *do* by persuading it just to sit and absorb, of engendering "bad" social behavior through its power of persuasion, and of damaging the personalities of individuals—especially the young—in their capacities to exercise judgment and discrimination.

The role of television which dominates all others through sheer numbers of its adherents is supplying entertainment. It seems clear that the general viewing public expects and demands that television amuse, divert and titillate hour after hour. These viewers will agree grudgingly that television may sometimes play its other roles, but most viewers insist that the station owners must recognize that their primary responsibilities are to the viewing public which owns receiving sets and which takes for granted the fact that television entertainment will be *there* when the switch is snapped on.

Americans should not be surprised that the institution of television broadcasting, faced with these multifarious demands, requirements and expectations on the part of various elements of society, should frequently appear to fall short of carrying out any of its roles.

Television's Relation to Radio Broadcasting

Although it is assumed that most of the public is aware that television and radio are somewhat related, a better understanding of television is fostered if we know what elements were derived from radio broadcasting.

The emergence of radio broadcasting in the United States in the early 1920s pioneered such programming concepts as formal time periods for programs (e.g., quarter-, half- and full-hour), the continuous program dissemination from morning sign-on to evening sign-off, the brief station identification period at the end of each program as a device for accommodating commercial advertisements or public service announcements, and the program syndication concept of a network with a single origination point for programs distributed by wire and radio links to hundreds of stations for national audience consumption. The commercial aspects of radio broadcasting—the sponsored program and the spot announcement advertising goods and services—were transferred intact to television, which at least initially followed the example of radio in relying almost entirely on advertising revenues to support its operations.[1] Telecasting took advantage of established radio audience habits that included staying at home—and even rearranging living styles—to receive entertainment, to absorb information and to share a kind of participation in community, national and world affairs. The patterns of control and regulation—the broadcaster as trustee required to operate in the *public* interest, convenience, and necessity, under the eye of the federal (not state) government[2]—were well established for radio broadcasting when television was still an engineer's dream or a laboratory experiment. Radio broadcasting conditioned the public to consider that its home entertainment should be free of direct cost once the set was purchased and that it was the audience's *right* to be entertained and informed with no admission charge; television continued to cater to these ideas.[3] Finally, from an electronic point of view, radio and television have many common antecedents and in a technological sense it is not wrong to describe television as "sound" radio to which pictures, electronically separated into bits of energy, are added.

HISTORICAL DEVELOPMENT OF TELEVISION

Scientists in the 19th century were convinced that, since voice could be transmitted over wires (i.e., the telephone), pictures could also be sent. At the same time, other scientists were investigating James Clerk Maxwell's 1873 "ether" theory that something we now call electromagnetic energy traveled through space (i.e., the "ether") in wave-like form and that through the application of mathematical principles we could control and direct these "waves."

Control of electromagnetic energy was achieved earlier than success in transmitting pictures over wires. Work of such men as Heinrich Hertz, Gug-

[1] Notes may be found in a separate section at the end of each chapter of this book.

lielmo Marconi—popularly known as the "father of radio"—Lee DeForest, Reginald Fessenden, Ambrose Fleming, Edwin Howard Armstrong and many others resulted in rapid development of wireless transmission, first in telegraphic and then in voice or telephonic form. By 1920, just a quarter-century after Marconi's demonstration of wireless telegraphy, development of radio telephony had advanced to such a degree that broadcasting was technologically feasible.[4]

Early Experimentation

The evolution of picture transmission was much slower. Picture transmission, either through the medium of wires or by "wireless," could be done only after the solving of two problems: how to convert varying intensities of light energy into comparably varying electrical currents, and how to "photograph" (analyze "scan" or "read") each minute portion of the picture sequentially and not simultaneously as in the chemical photographic process. In 1873 Andrew May, an Irish telegrapher, discovered that selenium reacted to light, passing electrical current through it more easily in sunlight than in darkness. A decade later a German scientist, Paul Nipkow, invented a whirling disc that "scanned" the object being observed by letting light shine through holes in the disc in a carefully structured sequential pattern. Although the principles of one kind of television were thus established quite early, the techniques were too crude to be of great practical value.

Experiments in refining these principles made little headway for a number of years. By 1923 Charles Francis Jenkins in the United States and James Logie Baird in England led in transmitting shadows via wireless as a laboratory phenomenon. One writer pointed out: "Rarely in scientific history had success, from known principles, come so slowly and painfully as in television."[5]

The system of television first developed by Jenkins, Baird and others used the principles of the Nipkow scanning disc, a *mechanical* device. There were limits to the degree of refinement of the whirling disc method, and other scientists and electronic engineers were working along lines established by the Russian experimenter, Boris Rosing, who worked out a television system in 1907 that used the electronic principles of the cathode ray tube.[6] American experimenters such as Vladimir K. Zworykin and Philo T. Farnsworth worked to scan the picture with an electronic beam. The arguments between the proponents of the mechanical and electronic systems went on during the 1920s. Although those who favored the mechanical system had certain initial successes, such as the transatlantic broadcasting of moving pictures in 1928 and successful color transmission in the United States and Britain in the same year, the decade of the 1930s witnessed electronic television's triumph.[7] As early as November, 1936 the British Broadcasting Corporation inaugurated a regular television service.[8]

Television in the United States was still in the first, or laboratory, stage in the years immediately preceding the outbreak of the second World War in September, 1939. The second stage of development, that of experimental operation in which the program interests of the public might be explored, was just beginning, and the third stage, that of full operation on a national scale, was still some years ahead. Part of this slow but relatively orderly development stemmed from a position maintained by the Federal Communications Commission. This agency's predecessor, the Federal Radio Commission, which was established in 1927 to bring order out of chaos in radio broadcasting, had been interested quite early in the progress of experimentation in visual broadcasting. When federal regulation of wire and radio communication was permanently established and the Federal Communications Commission was created by the Communications Act of 1934, the FCC continued to encourage television experimentation. However, the FCC consistently refused to adopt standards of transmission and reception for fear that equipment manufacturers would cease their experimentation with the result that, in the long run, the public might suffer from a frozen but inferior service.[9] But the second stage of development—experimental development of program patterns—could not take place until the purchaser of a receiver could be reasonably sure that the set would pick up the signals from *all* nearby transmitting stations, and this required some agreement on technological standards. At FCC urging, members of the Radio Manufacturers Association cooperated with each other in establishing a National Television System Committee to work out technical standards. The objectives were to ensure that all receivers could pick up programs from any stations within range and that subsequent technological improvements would not make receivers purchased earlier worthless.[10]

In spite of the lack of standards, a number of stations were broadcasting experimentally. In the middle of 1938, 19 stations had been authorized by the FCC, but only a few were broadcasting programs regularly and only a few receivers were available for public purchase.[11] Nevertheless, television was on the eve of dramatic developments. As *Fortune* magazine summarized it: "Radio sired it, science nursed it, Wall Street and Hollywood have dandled it—and at last the public is to get it."[12] And the public did get it—when the National Broadcasting Company's experimental television station broadcast President Franklin Delano Roosevelt's speech at the opening of the New York World's Fair, April 30, 1939. As a result, would-be television station operators began to clamor for permission to operate commercially with a regular service to the public, and programing during the next few months included telecasts of a college football game, a six-day bicycle race in Madison Square Garden, a heavyweight boxing match, a visit of Great Britain's King George VI and Queen Elizabeth to the World's Fair, and a major league baseball game.[13]

In the year following the telecasting of the World's Fair opening, interest in television among manufacturers and broadcasters increased greatly. By June 30, 1940, 26 experimental stations were on the air and the FCC had received 59 applications for new stations. Research and experimentation were going on in the development of coaxial cable and microwave relay systems as methods of network distribution of television programs. The National Broadcasting Company, a subsidiary of the Radio Corporation of America, broadcast portions of the Republican national convention in July, 1940, transmitting the programs via coaxial cable from Philadelphia to WNBT in New York. Manufacturers were working on portable equipment to permit outside or "remote" broadcasts. Color television attracted serious attention from RCA and the Columbia Broadcasting System. RCA and CBS demonstrated their color systems—which reverted to a mechanical method of spinning discs employing color filters instead of a wholly electronic system—during 1940 to the FCC and the press; early in 1941 the National Broadcasting Company began public colorcasting.[14]

The Emergence of Telecasting to the Public

All outgo and no income was unattractive to pioneer experimental telecasters, and the Federal Communications Commission was under heavy pressure to permit the new medium to be used—as radio broadcasting had been from the 1920s onward—as an advertising vehicle from which a profit could be made. Thus, at the end of 1939, the Commission granted limited commercial exploitation but, before any commercials were aired, rescinded the permission when it found that one manufacturer was promoting the sale of television receivers in spite of the fact that no standards had been set. The FCC did not want public investment which might subsequently be lost.[15] A year later, however, the National Television System Committee agreed on an interlacing method of scanning, employing a "frame" of 525 lines.[16] The FCC quickly adopted the NTSC recommendations and commercial television began on July 1, 1941.[17]

WNBT, NBC's New York station, had among its early advertisers and program sponsors Ivory Soap, which offered a television version of the popular radio program of the day, *Truth or Consequences*. Botany Worsted, Adam Hats, Bulova Watch and a few other companies made up the sponsor list. WNBT's rate card called for a charge of $120 per hour at night, with lower daytime rates. In addition to the time charge, the advertiser had to pay for the use of the studios, program talent, announcers and other production costs.[18] Even these costs—modest by later standards—were high when the advertiser could reach a maximum of perhaps 5,000 receivers.[19]

The active involvement of the United States in World War II halted expansion of commercial public television between 1941 and 1945. No new stations were authorized and no television receivers were manufactured for civilian use.[20] Nevertheless, during the war six commercial and three experimental stations operated limited schedules of from six to ten hours of programing each week—much of it film.[21] In addition, there was a great deal of anticipation among those who were eager to build and operate commercial television stations when wartime restrictions were removed. On December 31, 1943, midway of the war, 14 applications had been submitted to the FCC; a year later the number had risen to nearly 100. In January, 1943, station operators and other interested groups formed the Television Broadcasters Association, and the FCC reported that there would be television service in "dozens of cities" when equipment restrictions were removed.[22]

The Commission lifted its wartime "freeze" on new stations in October, 1945 and by the end of the year 150 applications for new stations had been filed. Yet many applicants began to have second thoughts and a number of them soon withdrew their requests. Television was a costly business, there were few sets in the hands of the public (for example, there were scarcely a dozen sets in all of Washington, D.C. on the eve of commercial telecasting in the capital), station operators were uncertain whether color television would make the black-and-white variety obsolete, and there were yet no facilities for connecting stations into networks.[23] In addition, standard (AM) radio broadcasting and the newer FM service were growing as spectacularly as television; radio seemed to offer an opportunity for a more profitable operation with fewer problems than did television. (For growth in AM, FM and TV, see Table 1.)

The lull in television interest lasted only from the middle of 1946 to March, 1947. The Columbia Broadcasting System sought permission to operate its own version of color television, but the FCC denied the request because color was not sufficiently perfected. In addition, approval would have resulted in a change so drastic as to make obsolete all receivers in the hands of the public. The FCC's decision, reassuring to those counting on the future of black-and-white television, opened the gates to a flood of applications. By June 30, 1947 there were in use approximately 50,000 receivers serving audiences estimated at 300,000; by mid-1948 50,000 new receivers were being added each month. Television networks linked by coaxial cable were slowly coming into being, joining 24 cities in the fall of 1949 and culminating in a transcontinental broadcast of President Harry S Truman's participation in the Japanese peace negotiations in San Francisco on September 4, 1951. Full transcontinental commercial operation began a few days later. RCA and DuMont Laboratories perfected a method of photographing television programs directly from the face of the receiver tube—a process labelled kinescoping—as a means of making popular programs produced in New York, Chicago or Hollywood available to outlying stations.[24]

The upsurge in applications—by June, 1948 the FCC had authorized 109 stations and was faced with another 294 requests—pointed up a serious problem. There were only 12 channels set aside for television.[25] With this limited number of channels only the 140 most populous metropolitan areas in the United States could expect to have stations and the FCC soon realized that demand for channel assignments was quickly outrunning the supply.[26]

On September 30, 1948 the Commission stopped processing television applications and in effect "froze" the status of television until it could decide how to provide more channels. The existing 12 channels were located in the very high frequency (VHF) portion of the electromagnetic spectrum. At the

TABLE 1
THIRTY-FIVE-YEAR DEVELOPMENT OF BROADCASTING REFLECTED
IN NUMBER OF STATIONS AUTHORIZED OR ON THE AIR

Source, 1943–1974: Federal Communications Commission, *15th Annual Report* (1949), p. 30; *28th Annual Report* (1962), pp. 74–75; *38th Annual Report* (1972), p. 18; *40th Annual Report* (1974), p. 108.

AS OF JUNE 30	AM	COMM FM	EDUC FM	COMM TV	EDUC TV
1943[a]	912	48[b]	—	6[b]	—
1944[a]	924	52[b]	—	9[b]	—
1945[a]	955	53[b]	—	25[b]	—
1946[a]	1,215	456[b]	—	30[b]	—
1947[a]	1,795	918[b]	—	66[b]	—
1948[a]	2,034	1,020[b]	—	109[b]	—
1949[c]	2,006[c]	737[c]	34[c]	69[c]	—
1950	2,144	691	62	104	—
1951	2,281	649	83	107	—
1952	2,355	629	92	108	0
1953	2,458	580	106	198	1
1954	2,583	553	117	402	6
1955	2,732	540	124	458	11
1956	2,896	530	126	496	20
1957	3,079	530	135	519	26
1958	3,253	548	147	556	32
1959	3,377	622	154	566	43
1960	3,483	741	165	579	47
1961	3,602	889	186	543	54
1962	3,745	1,012	201	571	59
1963	3,860	1,120	221	581	70
1964	3,976	1,181	243	582	79
1965	4,025	1,343	262	589	92
1966	4,075	1,515	291	613	108
1967	4,135	1,708	318	626	127
1968	4,203	1,850	348	655	156
1969	4,254	2,018	375	680	177
1970	4,288	2,126	416	691	190
1971	4,343	2,250	461	695	199
1972	4,367	2,352	521	701	214
1973	4,434	2,560	680	765	237
1974	4,467	2,713	764	759	246

Source, 1975–1977: FCC Public Notices on broadcast station totals; these do not include outstanding construction permits, only licensed stations on the air, thus accounting for a seeming drop in totals from 1974 to 1975.

1975	4,448	2,698	757	706	243
1976	4,479	2,820	845	708	253
1977	4,502	2,937	903	725	258

[a]Stations authorized (licenses and construction permits); no figures available for number of stations on the air. [b]No separation available into commercial and educational stations in FCC's figures. [c]Beginning with 1949, figures represent those stations actually on the air under authority of license or construction permit.

time of the freeze the FCC pointed out that any expansion would have to take place in the ultra high frequency (UHF) spectrum area.[27]

For three-and-a-half years the freeze on new stations remained in effect while the Commission compiled data, evidence and opinions on solutions. Finally, on April 11, 1952 the licensing process began once more to function. Now, however, the television service consisted of 82 channels: channels 2–13 were the old ones, the so-called VHF channels; channels 14–83 were 70 new ones in the higher UHF range. As a result, it was theoretically possible for almost 1,300 communities to have more than 2,000 stations. Nearly one-eighth of the assignments were reserved for educational, noncommercial television.[28]

In the year following the lifting of the freeze nearly 400 new stations were authorized[29]—though most of these did not go on the air until another year had passed. Thus, as Table 1 indicates, between the middle of 1953 and the middle of 1955 television experienced its greatest period of expansion in the number of stations providing service to the public.

The public responded to this increase in stations by buying receivers by the millions. Even during the freeze the increase was great. From an estimated 1,750,000 sets in the hands of the public at the start of the freeze, the number increased to 12,500,000 in 1951 and, in spite of shortages of materials caused by the Korean conflict (1950–1953), doubled by the end of the year after the freeze was lifted.[30] The number of homes equipped with at least one television receiver has increased steadily until, in 1977, it was over 71.5 million homes in the United States.[31]

The UHF–VHF Problem

Before 1952 and the end of the freeze on new station licenses all receivers could pick up only channels 2–13; after the lifting of the freeze the growth in the number of all channels (2–83) receivers was very slow, reaching only about 8% in 1962.[32] This was a major factor, though not the only one, which spelled trouble for commercial television station operators on channels 14–83. As early as 1954 there were indications of UHF difficulties when in one year 69 authorizations to construct and operate such stations were returned to the FCC.[33]

To counteract the downward spiral of few receivers-small audiences-few advertisers-little revenue-poorer programs, plus the smaller coverage characteristic of UHF stations, the FCC experimented with and advanced a number of solutions. The principal successful effort was focused on persuading the Congress to pass "all channel receiving set" legislation requiring all receivers shipped in interstate commerce to be capable of receiving all 82 television channels. The Act became fully effective on April 30, 1964. By November, 1970 more than three-quarters of all TV receivers had the all-channel capability.[34] However, viewers found that tuning UHF stations on all-channel receivers was not satisfactory or easy and the FCC adopted a rule requiring all manufacturers to provide comparable UHF-VHF tuning through some sort of "push-button" or detent tuning device.[35] The hope is that detent tuning, an automatic process of channel positioning as far as the viewer is concerned, will eliminate much of the "stepchild" status of UHF television.

Color Television: Controversy and Development

Although the Federal Communications Commission had in effect decreed that the United States would develop a black-and-white system when it turned down the CBS color television proposals in 1947, the Commission soon discovered that CBS was not to be put off so easily. Following more experimentation and investigation, CBS demanded and received a new hearing in September, 1949, a hearing that resulted in nearly 10,000 pages of testimony and 300 exhibits. A year later the Commission decided that the CBS method was the best of the three systems then being developed experimentally and ordered that commercial television, using the CBS system, could begin in November, 1950.[36]

A major drawback of the CBS color system was its "incompatibility" with the technical standards in effect for black-and-white or monochrome telecasting. A standard receiver could not pick up a CBS color program at all—not even in black-and-white—and a CBS color receiver could not pick up programs from regular television stations. Thus a CBS receiver was useless when no color program was on the air, and viewers who wanted both black-and-white and color programs would have had to purchase a monochrome as well as a CBS color receiver. It must be remembered that all the popular programs of the day were in black-and-white, and color programs were still experimental. Another inherent weakness in the CBS system was the use of a mechanical whirling disc with the same intrinsic lack of refinement that had defeated the adoption of the whirling disc mechanical method in the 1920s. For these and other reasons a group of manufacturers who opposed CBS appealed to the courts, challenging the FCC's decision.[37]

The court test, though eventually unsuccessful, delayed the start of commercial colorcasting until June, 1951. Even then commercial color television did not begin in any significant way; in November the National Production Authority forbade color receiver manufacturing because the United States' effort in the Korean conflict was draining the supply of critical materials.[38]

As a result of these delays and obstacles there was no color television programming and no color receiver production for most of the next two years. During the entire period the National Television System Committee (NTSC) continued to work on a compatible, all-electronic system that would permit the growth of color television simultaneously and harmoniously with the older and well-established monochrome method. After re-examining the question, the FCC in December, 1953 reversed itself and gave the NTSC color system its blessing.[39] The FCC decision did not result in any dramatic upsurge in color television receiver purchases or programing. In spite of more than $70 million spent by RCA alone in color development by early 1956, the FCC noted that only about 160,000 sets were estimated to be in use by the middle of 1957.[40] The National Broadcasting Company was the only network to program in color to any significant degree in the 1950s and early 1960s. Each year, brave predictions that "this is the year for color" were met with public apathy. Reasons for refusal to buy color sets included the high cost of the sets compared to the monochrome ones, the belief that color was not yet perfected and the feeling that maintenance of color sets was both difficult and expensive.[41]

But then, for reasons that are not apparent, color set sales began to increase dramatically. By January 1, 1965 more than 2.8 million color receivers were in use. That figure reached 9.7 million two years later, and then began the really dramatic increases. From 14.6 million receivers at the beginning of 1968, the number nearly doubled in 1970. The American Research Bureau estimated that 54.3 million homes, representing 76 per cent of all television households, were equipped to receive color.[42] Few programs except old movies were telecast in monochrome in the 1970s. Color had become the way of life for a majority of television viewers.

Television's Economic Growth: From Rags to Riches

The economic status of broadcasting has always been an important concern of the Federal Communications Commission, and the Commission has kept close watch on television's financial condition through annual reports required of all commercial stations and networks.

At the beginning of commercial television in the post World War II years, revenue from the sale of time to advertisers did not begin to offset the costs of operation. In 1948 all four television networks and all 50 stations on the air reported losses amounting to nearly $15 million.[43] Though revenues increased almost 300% in the next year, expenses increased also, and losses rose to more than $25 million.[44] Television's revenues increased spectacularly between 1950 and 1960, rising from about $106 million in 1950 to over $1.25 billion in 1960. Expenses also rose, but not so rapidly as revenues; hence what had been net losses in 1950 and earlier now became increasingly impressive profits. In 1960, the net income before federal income tax was $244.1 million.[45]

In the years from 1962 to 1976, revenues continued to climb steadily (except for 1971), reaching nearly $5.2 billion in 1976. The net income before taxes has been less consistent. The peak was achieved in 1976 with income of $1.25 billion; but 1969's income was greater than that of the next three years. Table 2 provides details of revenues, expenses, and income for the 15-year period. The net income before Federal income tax in 1969 was 19.8%; in 1976 the comparable figure was 24.04%. It is obvious that, viewed nationally, television broadcasting has been a profitable venture.

National figures that put all markets and all stations together are somewhat misleading. Small market stations are less successful than those in large markets; stations affiliated with one of the three major networks generally provide their licensees with greater financial return than stations with no network affiliation; and UHF stations are much less likely to be profitable than are VHF stations regardless of the size of market or relation to networks. Not all VHF stations have been profitable and not all UHF stations lost money. The FCC noted that 9.1% of all VHF stations reporting for 1976 lost money while 66.9% of all

TABLE 2
BROADCAST REVENUES, EXPENSES, AND INCOME,
1962-1976
(in millions of dollars)

Source: Federal Communications Commission Public
Notices—"TV Broadcast Financial Data," August 22,
1973; "TV Broadcast Financial Data—1973," August
19, 1974; "TV Broadcast Financial Data—1975," August 2, 1976; "TV Broadcast Financial Data—1976,"
August 29, 1977.

YEAR	REVENUES[a]	EXPENSES	INCOME[b]
1976	$5,198.5	$3,948.3	$1,250.2
1975	4,094.1	3,313.8	780.3
1974	3,781.5	3,043.2	738.3
1973	3,460.0	2,800.0	653.0
1972	3,179.4	2,627.3	552.2
1971	2,750.3	2,361.2	389.2
1970	2,808.2	2,354.4	453.8
1969	2,796.2	2,242.6	553.6
1968	2,520.9	2,026.1	494.8
1967	2,275.4	1,860.8	414.6
1966	2,203.0	1,710.1	492.9
1965	1,964.8	1,516.9	447.9
1964	1,793.3	1,377.7	415.6
1963	1,597.2	1,254.0	343.2
1962	1,486.2	1,174.6	311.6

[a]Represents gross advertising revenues plus all
other broadcast revenues less commissions. [b]Before
Federal income tax.

UHF stations reporting showed a profit. Nevertheless, of the 418 (90.86%)
VHF stations that were profitable in 1976, 213 had profits (before federal tax)
of more than $1 million and 53 of those stations had profits in excess of $5
million. Of the 59 (33.14%) UHF stations that lost money in 1976, 26 lost
$100,000 or more and 4 of these lost more than $400,000.[46]

Since television's total profits were both public and impressive, it is not
surprising that those versed in financial affairs considered some television stations in some markets to be valuable properties. Two 1971 sales illustrate the
point. Chris-Craft Industries, Inc., licensees of WTCN, Minneapolis, sold the
station (with FCC approval) to Metromedia, Inc., for $18 million. The FCC
also approved the sale of four Time-Life stations to McGraw-Hill Company for
just short of $51 million. WBAP-TV in Forth Worth, Texas, was sold for $35
million.[47]

Pay-TV

The pattern of American broadcasting, radio and then television, has been
one of programs traditionally available without charge to anyone who owned a

receiving set and was within range of a transmitter. For nearly a quarter of a century, however, that concept of "free" television has been under attack by those who have advocated a competitive system of subscription television, sometimes called pay-as-you-see-TV, pay-TV, or simply STV.

On January 1, 1951 the Zenith Radio Corporation, with FCC permission, began a 90-day pay-TV broadcast test of its "Phonevision" system, transmitting programs to approximately 300 homes. The programming fare consisted of three first-run motion pictures each day. The picture on the television tube was "scrambled" and thus unintelligible; however, the customer wishing to see the film called the telephone company, which made a connection that returned the picture to normal and added a dollar to the viewer's telephone bill.[48] Zenith's experiment was only the first of several indications of pay-TV interest in the early 1950s and it soon became apparent that this was a matter which posed several thorny public questions.[49] Was the principle of pay-TV really in the public interest? Was pay-TV, which in the 1950s and early 1960s was envisaged as an over-the-air transmission, really *broadcasting* as the Communications Act of 1934 defined it? Or was it "common carrier"? What was the FCC's role in regulation of pay-TV? What effects would pay-TV, if developed, have on the established method of free broadcasting?

Since 1951 these and other questions have been argued at length, frequently in heated exchanges between the opposing sides. The 1950s were occupied with FCC solicitation of public comment on the issues, with the Commission's decision that it did, indeed, have the authority to control pay-TV and develop rules for experimentation to determine the degree of pay-TV feasibility.[50] In the 1960s the principal experiment was that of RKO General Phonevision Co., which began to operate WHCT (TV), Hartford, as a part-time pay-TV station in midyear of 1962. The pay-TV experiment ended in early 1969 and RKO General operated the station conventionally until it presented the station as a gift (with FCC approval) to a religious group.[51] In the middle of the experimental period RKO General reported that it had about 6,200 subscribers and was programing 36 hours weekly of pay-TV material, including feature films which conventional stations had no access to. The films constituted about 85% of the programing hours and the remaining 15% was divided among live sports, plays, operas, recitals and educational programs.[52]

In December, 1968 the Federal Communications Commission authorized over-the-air pay-TV, but provided a six-months' additional delay to permit the Congress and the courts to react.[53] The rules set up by the Commission, as later modified, included:

1) The pay-TV service had to be supplemental and not a replacement for an existing service.

2) Only one station per community could become a pay-TV station and only communities receiving five grade-A signals could be utilized for pay-TV.

3) There could be no broadcasting of films more than two years old except if these films were not available to conventional television.

4) A limit was placed on the number of films more than 10 years old that could be broadcast via pay-TV.

5) There could be no "series" type programs—programs with a connected plot and basically the same cast.

6) Sports events telecast in a community within the past five years were not available to pay-TV.

7) Every pay-TV station had also to broadcast conventional (non-pay) programs for at least the minimum number of hours which was required of every TV licensee.

8) Commercialization—sale of time to advertisers—was not allowed.

9) Sports and feature films could make up no more than 90% of the total pay-TV program fare.

10) The rules and policies regarding discussion of controversial issues and political candidates applied as much to pay-TV stations as to conventional television broadcasters.[54]

The status of over-the-air pay-TV has been clouded by the rapid growth of cable television and, more recently, the development of the multi-point distribution system (MDS). The Commission has been slow to approve the technical standards for unscrambling devices, but has done so in several cases: broadcast pay-TV stations are authorized for Milwaukee, Newark, Boston, Los Angeles, and Corona, California.[55] Whether over-the-air pay-TV will become a major activity is highly speculative. Anything that is written about the current pay-TV situation is out of date before it gets into print.

Cable TV

While many telecasters fear pay-TV, they fear it not so much from the over-the-air form as from the "cable-TV" version. What began in 1949–1950 as a small service to would-be television viewers in rural areas of mountainous or hilly terrain has mushroomed to become a potentially strong competitor to broadcast stations.

The community antenna television system (also called CATV and cable TV) began in areas where rugged terrain blocked line-of-sight signals from transmitters in one valley city to receivers in neighboring valley cities, thus making adequate reception either impossible or unsatisfactory. Enterprising people, singly, in partnerships or in small corporations, set up master antennas on tops of hills, piping the incoming signals from the transmitter down into the valley (by microwave relay or coaxial cable) where the received signals were then distributed by wire to subscribing households. The next step was the introduction of cable systems into urban areas already served by one or perhaps two signals from local stations but where the choice of programming was not extensive. The principal complaint about cable TV operations thus came from broadcasters who had had audiences to themselves until programs from some distant station or stations were brought via cable TV and thus became competition. This was considered particularly serious when the piped-in stations supplied network programs; the local telecaster suffered a loss of audience, especially if the station was not affiliated with a network, and a loss of audience meant a loss of revenue when advertisers reduced their use of the station. When an identical network program from a distant station was piped in and competed with the local station's carriage of the same network, the local broadcaster complained that the audience had no identity with the local station; and although the audience viewed the same program, the local advertiser could not be sure how much of that audience was exposed to the local commercials. Some broadcasters were concerned that programs, which *someone* had paid for, were used by the cable TV operators without payment for them and on which they made a profit.

What was originally a small enterprise conducted either as a cooperative effort or by an operator willing to risk capital for a modest return, has been modified by the appearance of large firms which buy, sell, build and operate many cable TV properties. Although the ownership situation changes daily, a few of the major multiple system owners (MSOs) include American Television & Communications Corp (ATC), which has holdings in California, Florida, Illinois, Iowa, Michigan, Minnesota, Missouri, North Carolina and other states; Storer Cable TV Inc., which has systems operating in California and elsewhere; Cablecom-General Inc., with systems in Arizona, Colorado, Oklahoma, Texas and other places. The largest MSO in the 1970s was Teleprompter Corp., with many systems in all parts of the nation and over one million subscribers.[56] *Cable Sourcebook 1977* reported that there were 3,500 operating systems in the United States serving some 11 million subscribers in 7,800 communities and available to more than 15% of the population. Monthly fees paid by subscribers to have their television receivers connected to a cable TV system range from $6–$9 and upwards; the installation fees averaged approximately $15. Altogether, cable TV operators received in excess of $770 million in 1976.[57]

• Although signal interference was an early concern of broadcasters regarding cable TV operations—when microwave relays were used to transmit signals from the mountain-top receiving sites to the valley—recent broadcaster concern has centered on the area of economic injury. The broadcasters have sought federal regulation of cable TV as a protective device against competition. The FCC was at first reluctant to regulate in any cable TV matters except where electromagnetic signals (i.e., microwave relay) were involved. However, the Commission gradually determined that it did indeed have full jurisdiction over cable TV, and the U.S. Supreme Court in 1968 upheld that contention.[58] Since that time the Commission has been struggling to construct various rules with the object of giving the audience a variety of program sources and at the same time providing some order and stability.

In its *Second Report and Order,* adopted in February, 1972, the Commission spelled out which signals each cable TV system must relay, what channels must be available for public access, educational access, and local government access, the technical standards that must be adhered to and the federal-state/local relationships.[59] Some of these rules, particularly in relation to access channels, were modified in 1976 and 1977, including the deregulation of systems under 500 subscribers. Early on the FCC attempted to restrict what has been called "siphoning" of free TV programing into cable pay-TV. When cable TV originated programs, either as a part of the service for all its subscribers or for cable-pay-TV, the cable system was bound by the same restrictions that the Commission had placed on over-the-air pay-TV. The Commission prohibited "presentation of sports events on STV or on a CATV-originated program if it had been presented on free TV in the community involved within the last five years."[60] In 1977 the U.S. Court of Appeals overturned the FCC's pay-cable anti-siphoning rules.

The Commission was reflecting broadcasters' fears of cable-pay-TV as well as over-the-air pay-TV. Although pay-cable companies were not prompt to begin telecasting programs for pay, some began by making for-pay programs available in hotel rooms in Newark, Atlanta and New York.[61] The cable TV people were themselves suggesting openly that cable could not exist without pay-TV.[62] In 1976 more than 600,000 subscribers were connected to about 225 pay systems in 35 states. *Cable Source Book 1977* reported that pay cable operators had reached about 25% of their potential audience count. Home Box Office, Inc., began the first national pay-cable network on September 30, 1975, using a domestic commercial satellite. Pay cable was being characterized as "the potential pot of gold at the end of the rainbow" which would shift the emphasis from regular cable to the pay variety.[63] Although the future of either pay-TV or cable TV was far from clear, it seemed that each needed the other, and both were seen by commercial broadcasters as economic threats to conventional broadcasting.

That in the late 1970s the regulatory future of CATV had not yet been decided was emphasized by the fact that in 1977 several FCC rulings regarding cable had been or were in the process of being decided by the courts, and others were related to Congressional action. The FCC petitioned the Supreme Court to review a U.S. Court of Appeals overturn of the Commission's 1975 and 1976 modifications of its pay TV and pay cable rules. The major networks, the National Association of Broadcasters and some stations were appealing a U.S. Court of Appeals affirmation of an FCC order substituting 35- and 55-mile zones for signal contours as the basis for protecting television stations. The FCC was examining its exclusivity rules in relation to the 1976 passage of a new copyright law. Several petitions before the U.S. Court of Appeals appealed the FCC television-cable cross-ownership divestiture rule (co-ownership where the commercial station is the only one with a city-grade signal over the cable community). Congress was considering a pole-attachment bill to resolve the problem between cable and utility companies, over which the FCC had claimed jurisdiction. In 1977 the FCC relaxed its rebuilding requirements for cable systems and extended to 1978 its deadline for refranchising of systems.

Noncommercial (Public) Television

Not all television in the United States is either primarily concerned with entertaining or diverting the public or is supported by money derived from advertising. A substantial and increasing portion of telecasting has as its objective enlightenment, instruction and enrichment of many kinds of audiences and derives support from local, state and federal government agencies, from private donors and public foundations, and even from gifts of various kinds from commercial broadcasters themselves. It is a form of broadcasting called, variously, noncommercial TV, educational TV (ETV), instructional TV (ITV)—when the objective is some sort of formal instruction—and public TV (PTV). The last term is one that has increasingly found favor as a way of separating noncommercial broadcasting into the primarily instructional and the culturally enriching—with "public" broadcasting representing the latter idea.[64]

Educational broadcasting was part of the beginning of radio broadcasting.[65] For a variety of reasons, educational radio broadcasting was less than the exciting success its proponents hoped that it would be.[66] When television emerged after World War II as a potentially great commercial medium, however, educators who had been interested in educational radio or who had had experience operating AM or FM stations on campuses of educational institutions began to exhibit interest in the new medium and its potential for the educational world.[67]

During the "freeze" on new television authorizations imposed by the Federal Communication Commission in the period 1948-1952, a number of educators and educational groups combined efforts to plead with the Commission to set aside channels for educational, non-profit noncommercial use. In spite of bickering and dissent among educators, opposition by some commercial broadcasters, and initial apathy and outright reluctance on the part of a majority of the Commission—changed to interest and support by the weight of the educators' testimony and the insistence of Commissioner Frieda B. Hennock—the Commission created a new category of stations—the educational noncommercial stations—and provided for 242 channels (80 VHF and 162 UHF) for educational use when it issued its allocation plan in 1952, marking—as one writer put it—"the beginning of a new era in American education."[68]

The first station to commence broadcasting under the new plan was KUHT, Houston, which began in 1953. It was followed by many others, so that by July 1, 1977, the number of stations on the air had grown to 258.[69] These stations were owned and operated by a wide variety of organizations, including universities and other institutions of higher learning, state systems and offices, local school boards and districts, community cooperatives formed into non-profit corporations, and private organizations.[70] The reach of these stations is potentially very great. The programs from the "public" stations and instructional material from the ITV stations have been within receiving range of more than 85% of the population of the United States. All but two of the 50 states have had stations in operation, and 29 states and four territories have had some form of ETV networks operating. A national interconnection service operated by the Bell Telephone System has provided 110 connections to public noncommercial (or ETV) stations.[71]

Since 1962 the picture of educational broadcasting has changed markedly. A very real commitment to educational broadcasting was made by the federal government in mid-1962 with the passage of the Educational Television Facilities Act of 1962, which provided matching funds to establish and increase the facilities of educational stations.[72] But problems of operating money still plagued noncommercial broadcasting. In an effort to develop greater national awareness of what it felt were needs of an alternative broadcasting service, a Carnegie Commission on Educational Television proposed active development by the federal government of a "public" corporation to give special attention to noncommercial broadcasting. The Carnegie Commission advocated substantial federal funding, an emphasis upon "public" programing as distinguished from "instructional" programing, and independence of the "public corporation" from the day-to-day political control of the federal government.[73] In 1967 the Congress passed and President Lyndon B. Johnson signed a bill creating the non-profit and non-political Corporation for Public Broadcasting, which was directed to: (1) improve noncommercial broadcasting in every way possible, including facilitating the production of quality programs; (2) develop arrangements for interconnection of stations into networks to improve distribution of programs; and (3) assist in organizing systems of stations to insure that quality programs were indeed produced and nationally distributed.[74]

From its beginnings, the Corporation for Public Broadcasting has been embroiled in controversy. Questions of funding, of policy control over the production of programs and the creation of networks, and of the philosophy of noncommercial broadcasting have been raised. Nevertheless, the fact that 258 PTV transmitters were on the air and the fact that the Public Broadcasting Service, an organization funded directly and indirectly by CPB but managed by its member stations, provided a network service which arranged for the production and distribution of a number of quality broadcasts, attested to the liveliness of the noncommercial broadcasting service in the United States.[75]

Liveliness has characterized both funding and audiences of so-called "public" television. Funding of noncommercial television services probably will never reach a level that satisfies everyone involved in the field. Nevertheless, in 1975 public television received more than $248 million from all sources, an increase of 148% over 1970. In six of nine categories of funding in the 1970–1975 period there were increases of more than 100%. In terms of audiences, a Nielsen survey reported by the Corporation for Public Broadcasting showed that more than 38 million households had seen one or more programs of public television in March, 1976.[76]

In 1977 public broadcasting was cited by the House Subcommittee on Communications for its lack of enforcement of equal opportunity and antidiscrimination laws, and the Carnegie Commission announced a new study to examine the future course of public broadcasting in light of continuing unclear purposes, national vs. local jurisdictional problems, inadequate funding, and new technologies, including satellites and non-broadcast services. In late 1977 President Carter sent to Congress proposals for new organizational and funding patterns for public broadcasting.

ORGANIZATION OF TELEVISION BROADCASTING

Television viewers are unlikely to be aware of the complexity of television broadcasting unless they have studied it or worked in it or in a related area such as a station representative firm or an advertising agency. To most viewers the anchor person on the early evening news or the master of ceremonies on a daily game show is the "talent" of broadcasting. However, telecasting is a business in which "show" business is only a part.

The Station and Its Organization

While every station management organizes its own staff to suit the particular circumstances, there are basic divisions of labor in television which apply no matter how large or how small the staff may be. In commercial television four categories of activities are always present: administration, engineering, programming and selling. In noncommercial television only the selling function (sale of time to advertisers) is absent. No one function is superior to the others; no station can operate if one of the categories of activities is absent. The larger the station the more formal and detailed the division of labor; the smaller stations (in terms of market and size of total staff) tend to merge functions into each other with each person on the staff assuming more than one set of responsibilities. The station organization diagrams on pages 22–25 illustrate approaches which these particular broadcasting organizations have taken in staff arrangement, lines of authority and responsibility, and the grouping of functions.[77]

Jefferson Pilot Broadcasting Company's Charlotte television station, WBTV, operates from the same building as its sister AM and FM radio stations, WBT and WBT-FM, and shares the building with Jefferson Productions, a facility that is capable of a wide variety of production services in both video and audio forms. Yet the station staffs are largely separate at the operational level. The corporate headquarters, of course, serves not only the Charlotte stations but those licensed to Jefferson Pilot and located in Richmond, Atlanta and Denver. It appears that WQED, operated by and licensed to Metropolitan Pittsburgh Public Broadcasting Inc. is less complex in its organization and has fewer employees than does WBTV, a fact reflecting the commercial nature of WBTV and the greater financial resources available to the Charlotte station.

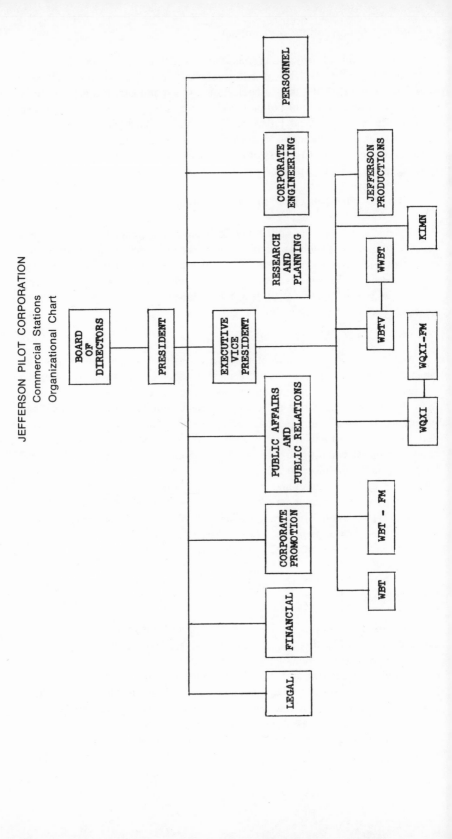

JEFFERSON PILOT CORPORATION
Commercial Stations
Organizational Chart

Noncommercial Station   Organizational Chart

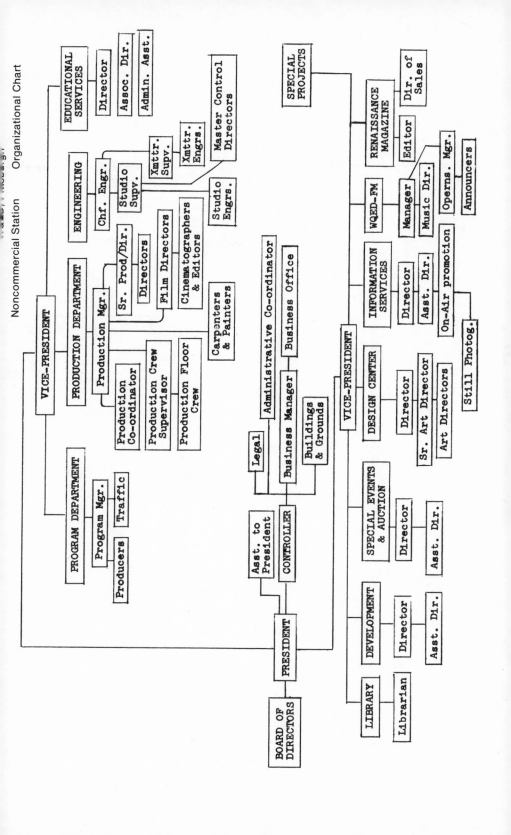

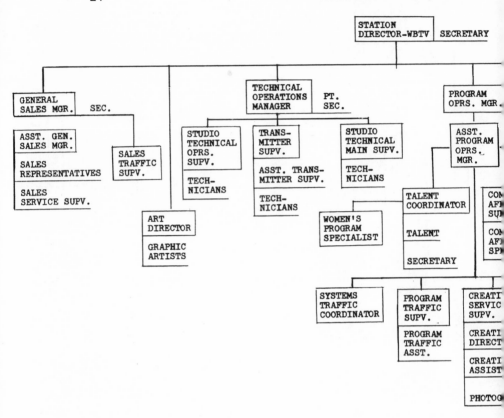

Television Networks

Few television stations would choose to operate day after day without the advantages of a network affiliation. From a network a station receives programs which are commercial, paid for by one or more advertisers, programs which are designed to permit the insertion of commercial announcements, and some programs which are non-commercial, usually public service. Each program supplied by a network reduces the amount of time which must be programmed by the individual station. The reduction in locally-programmed time permits either a reduction in the size of the station staff or a more effective utilization of the staff in other activities. In addition, the network presentations usually add prestige to the station because the artists (''talent'') have national stature and the programs usually meet higher standards of quality in production. Networks are also the best and sometimes the only source of coverage of national activities

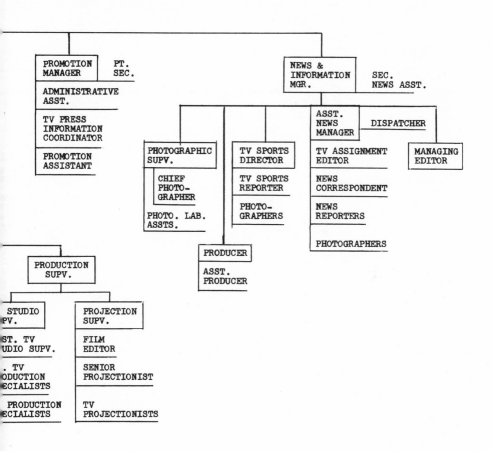

such as political conventions and elections, presidential inaugurations and major sporting events. Networks are also one of the sources of revenue for their affiliated stations, paying these stations a portion of the money which advertisers pay the networks for originating commercial programs.

The three major national commercial television networks are: ABC Television, owned by American Broadcasting Companies, Inc.; CBS Television Network, a division of CBS Broadcast Group which in turn is owned by Columbia Broadcasting System, Inc.; and NBC Television Network, owned by the National Broadcasting Co., a subsidiary of the Radio Corporation of America. Unlike radio broadcasting, there are no large separate regional television networks. There are some special networks put together specifically to produce and distribute to contracting stations programs of sports or special events of various kinds. Hughes Television Network not only produces live telecasts of sports but also offers entertainment specials and other special events.[78] Some group-owned stations, such as Westinghouse Broadcasting Co., Inc., operate to an extent as networks. Noncommercial broadcasting is characterized by a host of state ETV networks but has only one network with national dimensions, Public Broadcasting Service (PBS).[79]

Each national commercial network has several thousands of employees whose activities are broadly grouped into administration, programming, selling and engineering.[80] Since the network organizations are fundamentally program service agencies rather than actual broadcasters, the proportion of programming personnel to sales personnel is greater than in the individual television station. Because their staffs are large and exhibit a marked division of labor, networks also require large numbers of executive and supervisory personnel. A partial list for one network illustrates the complexity and degree of specialization required in the area of programming: a vice president in charge of prime-time TV; a vice president for prime-time program development and production; a vice president for variety programs; a vice president for dramatic programs; a director of comedy programs; a vice president for "Movies of the Week"; a vice president for prime-time programs, New York; a vice president for prime-time creative services, New York; a director and general program executive; a vice president as national program director; a vice president for daytime and childrens' programs. The other networks have similar program organizations.[81]

Since networks seem to represent a pinnacle of "status" in broadcasting, it is not surprising that competition for places on the network staffs is keen. Most commonly, the inexperienced aspirant is employed by the networks only as a studio guide or page, working up slowly from there. Even though he or she may possess experience and talent, an individual seeking network employment opportunities needs a degree of good fortune to become established in this rarefied broadcasting atmosphere.

Television and Labor Unions

While no television station or network executive would assign a "box" in the organizational chart to a labor union, the business of broadcasting is influenced by the existence of a number of national labor unions representing a variety of skills and professional areas; and the ways in which station and networks function are in part influenced by the presence or absence of unionized employees.

Following demands by Chicago musicians for special payments from radio station owners in 1924, labor unions have been organized for many different sorts of broadcast employees. In the years following the passage of the National Labor Relations Act of 1935 (the Wagner Act), unionization in broadcasting increased rapidly, with special impact upon musicians, technicians, announcers and actors. What many have called excessive and unreasonable demands by James Caesar Petrillo, then president of the American Federation of Musicians (AFM), were at least partly responsible for the passage of the Taft-Hartley Act in 1947 which shifted the balance of power in labor-employer disputes somewhat back toward the interests of the employers. Broadcasting, however, has been characterized by generally calm and restrained collective bargaining, and broadcast labor-management relations have only occasionally been marred by strikes, lockouts or other labor turmoil. Today organized labor is recognized as a part of the machinery through which broadcasting takes place. Organization of employees is particularly noticeable in the larger metropolitan areas and at the network levels; smaller stations and those in the South are less likely to have collective bargaining agreements with unions.[82]

In television, as in radio, the principal unions are: the American Federation of Television and Radio Artists (AFTRA), which represents most of those who perform before the camera and at the microphone; the American Federation of Musicians (AFM), to which belong most of those who play musical instruments behind the camera as well as in front of it; and two competing unions concentrating principally upon the technicians—the International Brotherhood of Electrical Workers (IBEW) and the National Association of Broadcast Employees and Technicians (NABET). All except NABET, which is independent, are affiliated with the American Federation of Labor-Congress of Industrial Organizations (AFL-CIO).

Television personnel belong, as well, to organizations originally set up in the motion picture and Broadway theatre worlds. Among these are Actors Equity Association (Equity) and Screen Actors Guild (SAG), which differ from AFTRA, and a large number of separate unions joined together in a major group, the International Alliance of Theatrical Stage Employees and Moving Picture Operators (IATSE). Among those unions affiliated with IATSE are make-up artists and hair stylists, stage hands, script writers, set designers and model makers, story analysts, publicists, and scenic and title artists. Independent organizations include the Directors Guild of America, the Writers Guild of America (divided into East and West groups), and the Composers and Lyricists Guild of America. Altogether, television employees across the nation, at both station and network levels, are represented in collective bargaining with employers by more than 50 labor organizations.[83]

The Station's Sources of Programs

Non-network stations obtain their programs from two sources: non-network program suppliers ("syndicators") and their own local studios. A network affiliate has, of course, a third major source, the network program. Local programs at individual stations may be as varied as the physical equipment and desire dictate. The programming may be "live" (broadcast simultaneously with the creation of the program either in the studio or from an outside remote point), videotaped or filmed, depending upon the station's equipment, the availability of personnel, the demands of the production schedule, and the management's policies and attitudes.

Syndicated programs are supplied on film or videotape and are usually of two types: films made originally for motion picture theatre exhibition and programs made especially for television. The feature films, scheduled in such programs as "Movie Matinee" or "The Late Show," usually are older motion pictures that no longer can be exhibited profitably in movie houses. More recent movies may be scheduled by stations in prime time periods. Films are customarily leased by the television station for two or more broadcasts within a definite period of time and are used primarily as programs in which commercial announcements from a variety of advertisers may be inserted. On the other hand, syndicated programs produced especially for television generally are series of programs of 12, 24, 36 or more episodes, each of which is one-half or a full hour in length. Many such programs in syndication were originally network prime-time shows which gain additional exposure and profit for the producers as "off-network" programs leased to individual stations. These syndicated programs provide opportunity for a variety of commercial inserts.

Another form of syndicated program is the industrial or commercial film produced by its sponsoring company as a public information or public relations gesture. Such programs are supplied free of charge to both commercial and noncommercial stations. The station benefits from receiving a program at no cost; the supplying company gains whatever public relations values may accrue from such broadcast exposure.

Network programs are in fact one form of syndication, but differ generally by the fact that each program is broadcast over a number of stations at the same time and each program is distributed from a central point (e.g., New York or Hollywood) to affiliated stations by coaxial cable or microwave relay circuits. Network programs also differ from other forms of syndication because the networks can and do produce and distribute some programs with greater timeliness than the usual syndicated program. Networks have demonstrated their superiority in this field with many documentary programs on social, political and economic problems; such programs tend to convey a sense of immediacy and urgency.

Television Stations: Their Sources of Revenue

Television stations are costly to operate, as illustrated by Table 3, "Revenues and Expenses of Typical Television Station, Nationwide, 1976."

To obtain revenue to pay the expenses of more than $3.125 million for this "typical" station and return a profit to those who invested their capital in a financially risky enterprise, the station must persuade many advertisers to spend considerable sums.

Almost all of a television station's revenues come from the sale of time to various categories of advertisers. About 44.4% of the revenue in 1976 came from advertisers who pay for network programs, a decline of about 6.5% from 1966.[84] A major portion in 1977 came from advertisers seeking to promote brand named products and services and there has been a slight decline in this category since 1966.[85] The impressive change has come in the area of local ad-

TABLE 3
REVENUES AND EXPENSES OF TYPICAL TELEVISION STATION, NATIONWIDE, 1976

Derived from: Federal Communications Commission Public Notice—"TV Broadcast Financial Data—1976," August 29, 1977. Total number of stations reporting: 680

I. BROADCAST REVENUES		
A. Revenues from Sale of Station Time		
(1) Sale of station time to networks	$ 396,876	
(2) Sale of station time to national		
and regional advertisers	2,817,539	
(3) Sale of time to local advertisers	2,043,561	
Total Sale of Station Time		$5,257,976
B. Broadcast Revenues *Other* Than from Sale		
of Station Time		
(1) Revenues from separate charges to		
advertisers (production costs,		
studio fees, etc.)	$ 72,007	
(2) Other broadcast revenues	68,182	
Total, Other Broadcast Revenues		$ 140,189
C. TOTAL BROADCAST REVENUES		$5,398,165
(1) Less commissions to agencies and cash		
discounts		867,417
D. *NET* BROADCAST REVENUES		$4,530,748
II: BROADCAST EXPENSES		
A. Technical Expenses	$ 382,444	
B. Program Expenses	1,348,376	
C. Selling Expenses	419,982	
D. General and Administrative Expenses	975,588	
Total Broadcast Expenses		$3,126,390
III: BROADCAST OPERATING INCOME (Net Broadcast		
Revenues less Total Broadcast Expenses)		$1,404,358

NOTE: Total *payroll* expenses (salaries, wages, bonuses, and commissions) of the typical television station are $1,124,569.

vertisers who are called upon by the station's own sales staff. The proportion of local advertising in 1977 increased more than 60% since 1966.

Although trade-outs and barter advertising are only a minor source of revenue, the station may benefit in reduced cost of certain equipment or programs or administrative expense. A "trade-out" is in effect a swap of station advertising time directly to a company that, for example, provides the station with its fleet of automobiles at a greatly reduced cost, taking the difference between the regular cost of the vehicles and the reduced price in the form of television advertising. "Barter" advertising usually means the supplying of a program by an advertiser to the station at no cost for the program and no charge for the advertiser's commercial message. For example, a 30-minute program might be designed to contain six commercial minutes. The station would receive the program itself free of charge and have the privilege of selling three commercial minute inserts. The advertiser who supplied the program would have the other three commercial minutes for use in promoting some product of its own.[86]

Advertising Agencies and Station Representatives

Most advertisers whose businesses are larger than a single retail establishment do not look after the details of their own advertising but entrust much of the development of ideas and the execution of advertising plans to advertising agencies. Modern advertising agencies employ specialists in the preparation of persuasive visual, verbal and aural messages in all of the media of mass communication. In addition, many advertising agencies have elaborate market and media research departments which seek constantly to ensure the most effective use of their clients' advertising money.

Of the two principal roles played by the agencies—the development of the advertising campaign and the execution of the campaign once the client has approved it—the campaign development role is more important to the television broadcaster. It is during this stage that decisions are made to advertise in Market A instead of Market B, to use television instead of or in addition to other media, to choose Station X over Station Y, and to allocate the advertising budgets to implement the preceding decisions. All of these decisions affect the television station's revenue.

Although many advertisers pay their advertising agencies directly for such services as special large-scale research, the preparation of brochures and catalogues, and the agencies' out-of-pocket costs for completed artwork or photoengraving, the advertising agencies derive most of their revenue in the form of commissions paid to the agency by the medium which broadcasts or publishes the advertising. For example, if Advertising Agency A on behalf of Client C contracts with Television Station X for a one-minute spot announcement in a choice time at night between two outstanding programs at a cost of $1,000 for a single broadcast, the agency would receive from Station X a commission usually amounting to 15% of the time, or $150. Since all newspapers, radio and television stations and other media of advertising customarily pay these commissions, the agency has no cause to favor one over the other. The recognized ethics of advertising generally prevent the client's going directly to the advertising medium to save the cost of the commission; even without the involvement of the advertising agency, Station X would still charge Client C $1,000 for the single spot announcement.[87] In return for its commission, the agency prepares the advertising message on film or tape and sends it to the station with all necessary scheduling and handling instructions; the station is thus relieved of the burden of production. In addition, the agency ensures that payment for the announcement is made to the station.[88]

Since most large advertising agencies and their clients are located in cities at some distance from most of the television stations which seek their business, it is not practical to have station salespersons call directly on advertising agencies. To sell time to these distant agencies, broadcasting has evolved organizations called station representatives. The station's "rep," as it is frequently called, is a firm of broadcast sales, accounting and research personnel with offices situated in the metropolitan centers where large numbers of advertising agencies are located. A firm of station representatives usually contracts with a number of broadcasting stations separated widely enough so that the stations are not in direct competition with each other. The salesperson from the station "rep" who calls on an advertising agency time buyer extols the merits of each of the stations he or she represents. One call thus serves to state the case for a number of stations.

Although there are various methods of payment for the services of station representatives, a widespread practice is the payment of commissions by the station to the firm of representatives on all sales of station time made in the representative's territory, which may include all sales to clients outside the home state of the station. Frequently the commission is fixed at 15% of the amount paid by the advertiser after the advertising agency commission has been deducted. To continue the earlier example, the station rep would receive 15% of $850 ($1,000 minus $150 agency commission), or $127.50. Thus, on much of the national non-network business the television station receives 72.25% of the amount the advertiser actually pays to have a commercial broadcast. It should be stressed that the advertising agency-station representative-station relations just discussed do not apply to network programs or network selling practices.

Federal Regulation of Broadcasting

Because broadcasting signals cross state lines it has been understood almost from its beginning that most regulation of broadcasting is the responsibility of the federal government. The Communications Act of 1934, with its many subsequent amendments, is the fundamental law governing broadcasting.[89] The Act established the principle that broadcasting was not a right of the broadcaster but a privilege to be enjoyed by those who were selected. The grant of privilege took the form of a federal license of limited duration to be issued only if there was a positive finding that the broadcaster who received the license would operate in the public interest, convenience and necessity.[90]

To administer the Act, to turn its principles into practical regulations and to judge whether broadcasters are indeed operating in the public interest, the Act created the Federal Communications Commission, an independent administrative, quasi-judicial and quasi-legislative agency composed of seven members, each appointed by the President of the United States to serve seven years.[91] To assist the commissioners in the highly technical and complicated regulatory process, hundreds of attorneys, accountants and engineers are employed to carry out the studies, investigations and preliminary work that go on in great volume day after day.

The license to broadcast is the controlling lever. Every broadcaster is conscious of the FCC's power to grant, to withhold or to take away a license. The authority of the FCC is clear, comprehensive and well established in the technical and engineering areas of broadcasting. There is little dispute that the FCC has the power to determine the suitability of the applicant's character and financial qualifications. It is in the programming realm, however, that station owners and the Commission disagree on the nature and degree of federal authority. The core of the dispute lies in the provision of the Act which forbids the FCC to censor any program; there is great difference of opinion on what constitutes censorship.[92] The federal courts have held that the FCC is not merely an agency to police the technical aspects of broadcasting but that it must also concern itself with the content of broadcasting.[93]

The broadcaster is concerned with FCC judgment of the station's entire program schedule, including the amounts of time devoted to news, education, religion and discussion of community issues as compared to the time spent in broadcasting entertainment features. The broadcaster may worry particularly about FCC displeasure with the amount of time devoted to advertising messages. Political broadcasting is a major concern as well. Basically, if a station broadcasts messages by one political candidate, it must make equal time and facilities available to the candidate's opponents. If the station editorializes for or against an issue, it must be prepared not only to broadcast opposing viewpoints but on some occasions even to seek out those who oppose the station's stance in order to maintain balance and fairness in the schedule. The Fairness Doctrine is also a subject of great concern to the broadcaster. If a station broadcasts a program presenting only one side of an issue determined to be a subject of controversy in the community, the station may be required to provide comparable time for the opposing or differing views on that subject.

As mandated by the FCC in 1971, the broadcaster is involved in a continuous process of ascertaining the needs of the public residing in the station's coverage area. The process of ascertainment requires that the broadcaster be in touch with community leaders on a systematic basis and compile a list of subjects of public importance in the community. The broadcaster is then required to show the kinds of programming created each year to meet the revealed needs. In addition, the FCC requires each applicant for a new station to present an affirmative action plan for equal employment opportunities for minorities and women, and for each renewal applicant to meet certain percentage standards for minorities and women in stations with over five employees.

While there is no single document which spells out precisely what constitutes the public interest, convenience and necessity in broadcasting, the broadcaster can turn to the law, the FCC rules and regulations, the various public policy announcements made by the Commission and the decisions by federal courts as guides. In addition, the licensee can rely on the codes of good practice developed by the National Association of Broadcasters, the principal spokesperson for commercial radio and television broadcasters in the United States. A conscientious broadcaster who truly desires to operate in the public interest has little difficulty in determining the proper course of action, and rarely will be in difficulty with the Commission.

The status of the public involvement in the regulatory scene changed drastically in 1966 when the U.S. Court of Appeals reversed the FCC and ruled that citizen groups could intervene in broadcast licensing, when it granted standing to a Jackson, Mississippi, citizen's organization in the renewal of the license of station WLBT-TV. Since that time the public has participated in the licensing process, particularly renewals, and a number of public interest broadcasting organizations developed, relating to the FCC through petitions, challenges, comments and other legal means. Some of the organizations that have been particularly active have been the United Church of Christ, the National Citizens Committee for Broadcasting, the Citizens Communication Center, the Black Media Coalition, Action for Children's Television, the National Association for Better Broadcasting, the National Organization for Women and numerous regional, state and local groups. In addition, through the opportunity to challenge license renewals, a number of minority and women's organizations have forced stations to agree to employment, training and programming more fully meeting the needs of these groups.

In late 1977 the House Subcommittee on Communications was in the final stages of a rewrite of the Communications Act.

TELEVISION'S IMPACT ON SOCIETY

Americans watch television—there is little doubt about *that*—but pertinent data acceptable to most serious students to describe how much, what kind and with what effects are difficult to obtain.[94] Nevertheless, research by responsible investigators is making clearer some of the unknowns.[95]

The Dimensions of Television

The A. C. Nielsen Company, a major mass media and market research firm, has studied national viewing habits for a number of years. It reports a long term annual increase in the average hours of household use of TV each day. In the mid-1970s the average television home viewed television more than 6 hours daily, about an hour more per day than was the case in the early 1960s.[96] As might be expected, the most viewing was in the 8–10 p.m. period, and the least viewing in the early morning hours. In the peak periods, more than 60% of all the TV households in America have their sets turned on.[97] In general, the more members of the household, the more the television set is used; those households with more than $15,000 in income tend to view television less—but not much less—than homes with smaller incomes; and women view television more than do men by a significant amount—over 5 hours per week more than men.[98]

There appears to be little except size that is significant in audience dimensions. The television viewer on the average is quite like a cross-section of the total population in economic, social, and educational status. Almost every one in a television home watches, and many watch a great deal.

The hours of viewing would not be significant if the number of television homes was small, but this is not the case. Earlier in this chapter it was pointed out that nearly every home has one or more television sets. The TV audience in the late 1970s consisted of inhabitants of more than 71 million homes whose total weekly viewing per home added up to more than 40 hours.[99]

The Controversy—Television's Alleged Effects

So much exposure to the television picture must result in affecting the viewer and his or her society in several ways—at least so both critics and defenders of television agree. The agreement stops at that point, however.

The critics on the one hand suggest that television is responsible for many of the ills of society—a rise in juvenile delinquency, a decay of ethical and moral standards, a weakening of critical abilities to distinguish the good in artistic and aesthetic standards from the mediocre, the encouragement of conformity, the inhibition of social change, the subjection of the public to economic and political exploitation, and the like. The appealing to the baser elements of human behavior through a superabundance of violence, the manipulation of humans as if they were puppets—all these and more are presumed ill effects that come from absorbing the daily fare of the television schedule.[100]

On the other hand, defenders of television hasten to claim that the medium is responsible for an "acceleration in cultural activities," resulting in more and more visitors to museums and increased patronage of libraries.[101] Some viewers believe that television promotes social interchange:

> I used to spend most of my time in the movies and generally had to go alone. Now I find my husband and I love to stay home and watch TV. We enjoy TV together. I think it is the best thing the American people get to enjoy together.[102]

Others believe that television has special benefits for young people:

> TV is entertaining for children, like the Walt Disney shows; and through TV they learn that adults are not all as they appear to be, making the kids less gullible. I approve of television by far over movies and the theatre.[103]

A different group, mostly social scientists and representatives of public interest groups, are much more cautious and ambivalent about the nature and extent of television's effects upon the political, social, cultural and economic climate in America. Some of these researchers argue that television and other mass media tend generally to reinforce existing patterns rather than to change them and are only one factor among many affecting the creation of tastes, values and behavioral patterns.[104] The impact of television upon children has become a subject of study by national public and private groups and has led to the establishment of a number of organizations that have made strong efforts to modify television programming to avoid what they consider harmful effects. The question of violence on television motivating or enhancing violent behavior on the part of children has been one of the principal areas of concern. The effect of television advertising on children has been another. So powerful is television considered, that its role in creating and/or reinforcing stereotypes of racial, religious, ethnic and sex attitudes has also been the subject of much discussion and action.

There is still another dimension to the argument. Robert T. Bower studied the American viewing public in considerable detail in order to compare findings with a similar study done a decade earlier by Gary A. Steiner. Bower found that, in comparison with magazines, newspapers and radio, television was thought by viewers to be superior in entertainment, in intelligent presentation of its subject matter, in its educational dimensions, in doing "the most for the public" and in creating "the most interest in new things going on." Bower found the viewers continued to place the entertainment role of television ahead of other functions, but with increasing emphasis on informational and educational elements. However, there has been a downward trend in the degree of favorable generalized attitudes toward television—as Bower put it, fewer "superfans" than before.[105]

Some Areas of Social Impact

When all the studies are assessed and all of the areas of the unknown in television's social impact are listed, it is proper to echo the regret of one television professional who wrote that "the large basic problems of how our medium and other media work remain a challenge."[106] Yet, that does not really provide the complete framework for thinking about television's impact. If substantial numbers of both average and influential people believe that television has certain attributes or creates certain effects, the belief has its own validity and the public acts upon its beliefs—mistaken through the public may be. On the basis of reputable study and on the basis of those beliefs, television does touch society in a number of ways, only a few of which we can note here.

Wilbur Schramm suggests two generalized effects of television in particular and of all mass media in general: 1) we have to some degree rearranged our patterns of living to accommodate the presence of television; and 2) we have gained large amounts of knowledge from viewing it.[107] We have fitted television into a busy life, each waking minute occupied by something. Television has thus *displaced* one or more activities to some degree. As for knowledge, much of what we know—whether poorly or well—about the world around us comes to us from television and other mass media. In the 1970s a number of studies showed that the largest percentage of the American public received their principal news information from television and that they believed television was the most accurate and trustworthy of all news sources.

Television appears to have annexed to itself the dominance of the area of mass entertainment. When it has come into competition with other entertainment or diversionary activity—movies, magazines, radio broadcasting— television seems to have pushed the older competitors into seeking new techniques or new roles to play. The other media have seemingly reacted to television rather than to possible changes in the audiences themselves.

In the political world, too, television is rightly or wrongly credited or charged with responsibility for certain changes. There is little doubt that television has in the past brought to the forefront new personalities, turning them into national figures, and at the same time exposing the feet of clay belonging to other national personalities. National and state candidates for public office use television in the belief that the medium may be decisive in the electoral process. Whether television appearances change voting behavior is a matter that requires more study; but television has been instrumental in streamlining political conventions to suit the technology of the medium and the presumed demands of the viewers. Television has taken the audiences behind the scenes in various governmental activities: city council meetings, state legislative proceedings and, occasionally, into the courts and congressional halls.

In the commercial world of advertising and marketing, television has repeatedly demonstrated its ability to introduce new brands of familiar categories of goods, to increase distribution of established brands and to make new products which serve old needs familiar household objects.

When all is said, however, the principal social aspect of television—both commercial and noncommercial—is the supreme place it presently occupies as the main and most sought-for source of entertainment for more people for more hours per week than any other medium or leisure time activity. ▬

NOTES

[1] Although educational broadcasting, both radio and television, is generally noncommercial in nature, obtaining its operating funds from a variety of sources, the preponderance of stations and hours of programing are commercial. This may not be true in the future.

[2] From the beginning, transmission of radio waves was understood to involve crossing political boundaries; hence, radio emissions (and later broadcasting) were clearly in the realm of interstate commerce. The advent of large scale community antenna television ("cable-TV" or CATV) in recent years has complicated the local-state-federal jurisdictional problems.

[3] It is this concept of *free* entertainment, whether held by the public or promoted by the broadcaster, that has been an important factor in the long birthing of subscription (or "pay") television.

[4] The Communications Act of 1934 defines broadcasting as meaning "the dissemination of radio communications intended to be received by the public, directly or by the intermediary of relay stations." R. Franklin Smith, in his article, " 'Oldest Station in the Nation'?" *Journal of Broadcasting,* IV (Winter, 1959-1960), 44, lists five elements required to class any station as a broadcasting station: "(1) utilizes radio waves (2) to send non-coded sounds by speech or music (3) in the form of a continuous patterned program service, (4) intended to be received by the public and (5) is licensed by the government."

[5] John Swift, *Adventures in Vision: The First Twenty-Five Years of Television* (London: John Lehmann, 1950), pp. 20–22.

[6] Asa Briggs, *The History of Broadcasting in the United Kingdom,* Vol. II, *The Golden Age of Wireless* (London: Oxford University Press, 1965), p. 521.

[7] Orrin E. Dunlap, Jr., *The Future of Television* (New York and London: Harper &

Brothers, 1942), pp. 162–164; Swift, *Adventures in Vision*, pp. v, 19, 24, 35–36, 39–40, 61–62. The work of Farnsworth and Zworykin was described in separate articles in the first number of *Television News*, I (March–April, 1931), 48, 58.

[8] Briggs, *History of Broadcasting in the United Kingdom*, II, 594. In 1934, members of an investigating committee in Britain reported that technical development in the United States was " 'at least as advanced' " as the British although there was no service broadcast to the public. Briggs, II, p. 583.

[9] Federal Communications Commission (FCC), *5th Annual Report* (1939), pp. 5, 45.

[10] National Television System Committee, *Television Standards and Practice: Selected Papers from the Proceedings of the National Television System Committee and Its Panels* (Donald G. Fink, ed., New York and London: McGraw-Hill Book Company, Inc., 1943), pp. ix, 4; Dunlap, *The Future of Television*, pp. 1, 22.

[11] FCC, *4th Annual Report* (1938), pp. 65, 176.

[12] "Television I: A $13,000,000 'If'," *Fortune*, XIX (April, 1939), 53.

[13] FCC, *5th Annual Report* (1939), p. 45; Dunlap, *The Future of Television*, pp. 1, 183–184.

[14] FCC, *6th Annual Report* (1940), pp. 39, 70–72; Swift, *Adventures in Vision*, pp. 108–109.

[15] FCC, *6th Annual Report* (1940), pp. 70–72.

[16] National Television System Committee, *Television Standards and Practice*, p. 17. A TV "frame" is a complete cycle of individual "lines" of the object sequentially scanned and is the equivalent of a single photograph or "frame" in a motion picture film. The interlacing involves scanning lines 1, 3, 5, 7, etc., in $1/60$th of a second and then scanning lines 2, 4, 6, etc., in $1/60$th of a second. The result is that in $1/30$th of a second the entire "frame" has been "half-scanned" twice, providing for the observing eye the illusion of continuity of motion (frame frequency) and continuity of illumination (field frequency). Thus American television standards are 30 complete frames of 525 lines each per second, half-scanned twice to provide a field frequency of 60 per second. Flicker and jerkiness are thus eliminated. Other nations' standards are different: England uses (but is phasing out) 405 lines for black and white but 625 lines (the European "standard") for color, while France uses 819 lines per frame. An American receiver will not pick up a French, British or other European TV program—an illustration of the desirability of uniform standards. In general, the more lines per frame, the better the picture definition and the finer the shades of contrast. However, a greater number of lines per frame occupies more spectrum space (a wider "channel") resulting in a reduced number of stations that can be authorized within a given band of frequencies. The 525-line frame is thus a compromise between a high quality picture and the maximum number of stations. A channel 6 mHz wide is required to accommodate the amount of signal or information transmitted in a 525-line frame. Because of this channel width, the FCC initially could find spectrum space for only 13 channels.

[17] FCC, *7th Annual Report* (1941), pp. 32–33.

[18] Dunlap, *The Future of Television*, pp. 33–34. In contrast, in 1977 NBC-TV's key New York station, WNBC-TV, charged $10,000 for one 30-second commercial announcement in prime time. See *Spot Television Rates and Data* (Feb. 15, 1977), p. 335. It should be noted that on the 1977 "Super-Bowl" football broadcast a *national* 30-second spot cost $130,000.

[19]FCC, *13th Annual Report* (1947), p. 23. At the outbreak of World War II, there were an estimated 10,000 receivers in the hands of the public, half of them in the New York area.

[20]"Memorandum Opinion of February 23, 1942," in *Federal Communications Commission Reports*, IX (August 1, 1941–April 1, 1943), 353–355; FCC, *13th Annual Report* (1947), p. 23.

[21]FCC, *11th Annual Report* (1945), p. 21; *Television*, II (May, 1945), 28–29.

[22]*Television*, II (January, 1945), 24; FCC, *11th Annual Report* (1945), p. 21.

[23]FCC, *11th Annual Report* (1945), p. viii; *Television*, II (September, 1945), 10; III (April, 1946), 37.

[24]FCC, *13th Annual Report* (1947), pp. 23, 26; *14th Annual Report* (1948), pp. 2, 30, 37–38, 39; *15th Annual Report* (1949), p. 6; *17th Annual Report* (1951), p. 13; *Television* II (October, 1945), 32.

[25]The FCC deleted channel 1 on June 14, 1948, because other radio services adjacent to channel 1 (44–50 mHz.) caused objectionable interference to television. See FCC, *14th Annual Report* (1948), pp. 39–40.

[26]FCC, *14th Annual Report* (1948), pp. 6, 39–40; *15th Annual Report* (1949), pp. 42–43.

[27]FCC, *15th Annual Report* (1949), pp. 42–43. Channels 2–13 were located between 54 mHz. and 216 mHz. The Commission proposed the expansion of television in the frequency range 470–890 mHz.

[28]FCC, *18th Annual Report* (1952), pp. 107–111. The report gives a chronological account of the development of the television issue. The 2,053 assignments in 1,291 communities contrasted with only 400 assignments in 140 metropolitan areas under the old system.

[29]FCC, *19th Annual Report* (1953), p. 93.

[30]FCC, *15th Annual Report* (1949), p. 41; *17th Annual Report* (1951), p. 113; *19th Annual Report* (1953), p. 113.

[31]American Research Bureau, *Television U.S.A.* An Arbitron Report, February/March, 1973. (New York: American Research Bureau, 1973), p. 7; A. C. Nielsen Company, *Nielsen Television '73* (Chicago: A. C. Nielsen Company, 1973), p. 5; A. C. Nielsen, *Nielsen Newscast* (No. 4, 1976), p. 2; *Broadcasting Yearbook*, 1977, p. A-2.

[32]*Broadcasting*, March 25, 1963, p. 136.

[33]FCC, *20th Annual Report* (1954), p. 91. Other CP holders never completed station construction; some built stations but lost so much money that they eventually suspended operations, either surrendering their CPs to the FCC or holding on to them, hoping for better times.

[34]FCC, *37th Annual Report* (1970), p. 37. The separate reference to UHF set penetration was not reported in later FCC Annual Reports.

[35]FCC, Docket No. 19268, Memorandum Opinion and Order, September 7, 1972; letter, Commissioner Robert E. Lee to author, Washington, D.C., Aug. 10, 1973.

[36]FCC, *16th Annual Report* (1950), pp. 6, 10–11, 103, 105.

[37]FCC, *16th Annual Report* (1950), p. 11.

[38]*Radio Corporation of America, et. al. v. United States*, 341 U.S. 412, 71 Sup. Ct. 806 (1951); FCC, *17th Annual Report* (1951), pp. 13, 113; *Broadcasting-Telecasting*, June 4, 1951, pp. 23, 62, 70, 76–78.

[39]FCC, *19th Annual Report* (1953), pp. 96–97; *20th Annual Report* (1954), pp. 90–91.

[40]*Television Digest*, August 25, 1956, p. 14; FCC, *23rd Annual Report* (1957), p. 105. In comparison with the number of color receivers, an estimated 44,500,000 monochrome sets were in use.

[41]*Broadcasting*, August 26, 1963, p. 65. Only RCA manufactured color sets to any significant degree for several years, and its least expensive model was priced at $495.

[42]*1971 Dimensions of Television* (Washington, D.C.: National Association of Broadcasters, 1971), p. 11; American Research Bureau, *Arbitron Television Census, Fall, 1976* (New York: American Research Bureau, 1976), no pagination.

[43] FCC, *15th Annual Report* (1949), pp. 3, 54. The four networks were ABC, CBS, DuMont, and NBC. DuMont ceased operating September 15, 1955. See FCC, *22nd Annual Report* (1956), p. 22n.

[44] FCC, *16th Annual Report* (1950), p. 118.

[45] These yearly changes can be followed in the annual reports by the Federal Communications Commission.

[46] FCC, Public Notice, "TV Broadcast Financial Data—1976," August 29, 1977, Table 7.

[47] FCC, *38th Annual Report* (1972), pp. 5, 163. The 4 Time-Life stations were WFBM-TV, Indianapolis, KLZ-TV, Denver, KOGO-TV, San Diego, California, and KERO-TV, Bakersfield, Cal. WBAP-TV has changed its call letters to KXAS-TV. *Broadcasting Yearbook 1975*, Broadcasting Publications Inc. (Washington, D.C., 1975), p. B-174.

[48]*Broadcasting-Telecasting*, Jan. 1, 1951, p. 60; FCC, *16th Annual Report* (1950), pp. 11, 103–104. Other systems use other methods for denying the program to the non-paying public.

[49]*Broadcasting-Telecasting*, March 26, 1961, p. 63; FCC, *19th Annual Report* (1953), p. 98.

[50] FCC, *21st Annual Report* (1955), pp. 98–99; *23rd Annual Report* (1957), pp. 111–112; *25th Annual Report* (1959), pp. 63–64.

[51] FCC, *32nd Annual Report* (1966), p. 106; *38th Annual Report* (1972), p. 63.

[52] FCC, *32nd Annual Report* (1966), p. 106.

[53] FCC, *35th Annual Report* (1969), p. 40.

[54] FCC, *35th Annual Report* (1969), p. 40; *36th Annual Report* (1970), p. 40; *38th Annual Report* (1972), p. 49. Sports caused the most furor and resulted in the most detailed of the FCC's rules concerning pay-TV.

[55]*Broadcasting Yearbook 1977*, p. B-145.

[56] Broadcasting Publications, Inc., *Cable Sourcebook, 1974* (Washington, D.C., 1973), pp. 6–25; and Television Digest, Inc., *CATV Atlas* (Washington, D.C., 1976), p. 6a.

[57] Broadcasting Publications, Inc., *Cable Sourcebook, 1977* (Washington, D.C., 1976), p. 5.

[58]*U.S. et al.* v. *Southwestern Cable Co. et al.* (1968), reproduced in Frank J. Kahn, ed., *Documents of American Broadcasting* (2nd ed., New York: Appleton-Century-Crofts, 1973), pp. 571–572, 579.

[59] 36 FCC 2d 143–260 (1972).

[60] FCC, *36th Annual Report* (1970); 36 FCC 2d 239–240 (1972).

[61] Paul F. Kagan, "Clearing the Channels; Pay-Television Is an Idea Whose Time Has Come," *Barron's National Business and Financial Weekly*, Nov. 13, 1972, pp. 11, 25, 27–28.

[62]*Broadcasting*, July 31, 1972, p. 46.

[63]*Cable Sourcebook, 1977*, p. 5; *Broadcasting*, October 6, 1975, p. 26; *Cable Sourcebook, 1974*, pp. 4–5.

[64] The term became the vogue after the passage of the Public Broadcasting Act of 1967. There is no single term that satisfactorily describes the nature of noncommercial broadcasting. It is hoped that the terms used will be understood from the

context. The FCC Rules and Regulations continued to use the term "non-commercial educational" and did not adopt the term "public."

[65] Claims of WHA, the University of Wisconsin station, to the title of the nation's oldest broadcasting station are discussed briefly in Smith, " 'Oldest Station in the Nation'?" *Journal of Broadcasting,* IV (Winter, 1959–1960), 54–55. An analysis of station ownership made in early 1923 by the American Telephone and Telegraph Company revealed that of 583 stations in existence on January 1, 1923, 72 were operated by educational institutions. See *Radio Broadcast,* II (April, 1923), 522, 524, 526.

[66] Harry J. Skornia, "Educational Radio: Its Past and Its Future," in *Educational Television: The Next Ten Years* (Stanford: The Institute for Communications Research, 1962), pp. 354–360.

[67] Richard B. Hull, "A Note on the History Behind ETV," in *Educational Broadcasting: The Next Ten Years,* pp. 334–335.

[68] *Ibid.;* Leo A. Martin, "The Educational Television Stations," in *Television's Impact on American Culture* (William Y. Elliott, ed., East Lansing: Michigan State University Press, 1956), pp. 197–198.

[69] FCC Public Notice, "Broadcast Station Totals," July 14, 1977.

[70] Robert L. Hilliard, "The Organization and Control of Educational Television," *Peabody Journal of Education,* XL (November, 1962), 170–181.

[71] FCC, *38th Annual Report* (1972), pp. 54, 56; National Association of Educational Broadcasters, *1975 NAEB Directory of Public Telecommunications,* pp. 106–120.

[72] The Act is reproduced in Kahn, ed., *Documents of American Broadcasting,* 2nd ed., pp. 565–569.

[73] The report was published as *Public Television: A Program for Action* (New York: Harper & Row, 1967).

[74] The Public Broadcasting Act of 1967 (P.L. 90–129, 90th Congress), November 7, 1967, reproduced in Kahn, ed., *Documents of American Broadcasting,* 2nd ed., pp. 585–596. The Act extended the 1962 Facilities Act and amended the Communications Act of 1934 so as to incorporate the noncommercial broadcasting provisions within the broader context of the Communications Act of 1934, the basic law of broadcasting.

[75] The internal controversies of public broadcasting are dealt with in "Public Broadcasting Service: Background Paper," Section B., "History," a mimeograph document prepared by Michael E. Hobbs (and others) for PSB affiliate station information, December, 1973.

[76] Corporation for Public Broadcasting, *Annual Report 1976,* p. 3.

[77] These stations are not selected as "typical" of commercial or noncommercial organizational arrangements; there is no such typicality in broadcasting. Appreciation is hereby expressed to the managements of Jefferson Pilot Broadcasting Company and Metropolitan Pittsburgh Public Broadcasting, Inc. for their cooperation in supplying the organizational charts and for permission to publish them.

[78] *Broadcasting Yearbook 1974,* pp. E10–E17.

[79] FCC, *38th Annual Report* (1972), p. 56, noted that 23 states and 3 territories had ETV networks of some kind.

[80] FCC, Public Notice, "TV Broadcast Financial Data," August 29, 1977, Table 14, shows that the three national networks employed 13,802 people at the end of 1976. Total employment, full- and part-time, for networks and all TV stations was 64,833.

[81] *Broadcasting Yearbook 1974*, pp. E10, E13, E16. The list is from the ABC Entertainment section of ABC Television Network.

[82] An excellent study of a portion of the story of union-management relations in broadcasting is that by Grover Cleveland Wilhoit, Jr., "Labor Union Organization in Radio Broadcasting: The Wagner Act to the Taft-Hartley Law" (unpublished M.A. in Communication thesis, University of North Carolina at Chapel Hill, 1963). A more recent and very helpful source is that of Allen E. Koenig, ed., *Broadcasting and Bargaining: Labor Relations in Radio and Television* (Madison: The University of Wisconsin Press, 1970).

[83] See *Broadcasting Yearbook 1976*, pp. F39-F40, for a list of union organizations which are active in broadcasting. Gregory Schubert and James E. Lynch, "Broadcasting Unions: Structure and Impact," in Koenig, ed., *Broadcasting and Bargaining*, pp. 41–66, have a useful discussion of the major unions.

[84] FCC Public Notice, "TV Financial Data—1976," August 29, 1977, Table 1.

[85] *Ibid*. National advertising is also called "national spot" advertising because the advertiser "spots" advertising in markets of choice, on stations of choice, and (within limits) at times and frequencies of choice.

[86] There are many variations of the "barter" arrangements and that sketched here is only one—and a very simplified one—of this category.

[87] Rates for advertisers vary greatly from station to station and market to market, each station having complete authority to set its own. Ethically, and by FCC rule, a station should not deviate from its published rates to favor one advertiser over another. "Rate cutting" is unfortunately a common practice among some radio and television broadcasters. The business and advertising elements of broadcasting suffer from a number of unethical and even fraudulent practices on the part of a minority of station owners and operators.

[88] In all descriptions of agency-station relationships, the theoretical ideal has been set forth. In actual practice, there are many deviations from the ideal. The degree of quality and reliability varies among agencies just as it does among broadcasters.

[89] *Public Law No. 416*. U.S., *Statutes at Large*, XLVIII, Part I, 1064–1105. The Act also covers interstate telephone and telegraph communications as well as all other non-broadcasting emissions.

[90] At the time of writing, the license period cannot be longer than three years in the case of broadcasting or more than five years in all other forms of radio transmission. In the late 1970s there were bills before both houses of Congress to extend the license period for broadcasters.

[91] The U.S. Senate must confirm the appointments. No more than four commissioners may belong to the same political party. The chairman of the FCC, one of the seven commissioners, is by custom a member of the same political party as the President.

[92] Section 326, Communications Act of 1934.

[93] For example, see *National Broadcasting Company, Inc.* v. *United States*, 319 U.S. 190 (1943).

[94] Joseph T. Klapper, *The Effects of Mass Communications* (Glencoe, Ill.: The Free Press, 1960), p. 54, points out that this is true for the whole area of mass communication. He writes: "Many of the data commonly presented are, in fact, of questionable pertinency."

[95] Particularly useful is the work by Wilbur Schramm, *Men, Messages, and Media: A Look at Human Communication*

(New York: Harper & Row, Publishers, 1973), pp. 189–290, which discusses media effects and the work of researchers who have studied mass communication most closely in the past few decades. For the serious student, the *Handbook of Communication* (Ithiel de Sola Pool, Wilbur Schramm, eds. (Chicago: Rand McNally College Publishing Company, 1973), is indispensable.

[96] *Nielsen Television '73* (Chicago: A. C. Nielsen Company, 1973), p. 8; and *Broadcasting Yearbook 1977* (Washington, D.C.: Broadcasting Publications Inc.), p. A-2.

[97] *Ibid.*, p. 7.

[98] *Ibid.*, pp. 9, 10.

[99] *Ibid.*, pp. 5, 8; *Nielsen Newscast* (Chicago: A. C. Nielsen Company, 1976), p. 2.

[100] Schramm, *Men, Messages, and Media*, pp. 234–235; Paul F. Lazarsfeld and Robert K. Merton, "Mass Communication, Popular Taste, and Organized Social Action," reprinted in Schramm and Donald F. Roberts, eds., *The Process and Effects of Mass Communication* rev. ed. (Urbana: University of Illinois Press, 1971), pp. 554–578.

[101] Frank Stantion, *Mass Media and Mass Culture: Great Issues Lecture, at the Hopkins Center, Dartmouth College,* November 26, 1962, pp. 7ff.

[102] Quoted in Gary A. Steiner, *The People Look At Television: A Study of Audience Attitudes* (New York: Alfred A. Knopf, 1963), p. 79.

[103] Robert T. Bower, *Television and the Public,* (New York: Holt, Rinehart and Winston, Inc., 1973), p. 159.

[104] Schramm, *Men, Messages, and Media,* pp. 234–290; Kurt Lang and Gladys Engel Lang, *Politics and Television* (Chicago: Quadrangle Books, 1968), pp. 15–16; Klapper, *The Effects of Mass Communication,* pp. 5, 249–257.

[105] Bower, *Television and the Public,* pp. 14, 24, 184–187. The earlier study was that of Steiner, *The People Look at Television.*

[106] Norman E. Cash, president of the Television Bureau of Advertising, in a front note, in Leon Arons and Mark A. May, eds., *Television and Human Behavior: Tomorrow's Research in Mass Communication* (New York: Appleton-Century-Crofts, 1963).

[107] Schramm, *Men, Messages, and Media,* pp. 246–261.

BIBLIOGRAPHY

Documents

There are not many compilations of documents relating to broadcasting. Two such publications deserve inclusion, however. Both are the product of the same editor and they are useful for the serious student who wants to go to the sources for authenticating and enriching detail.

Kahn, Frank J. *Documents of American Broadcasting* (with the Red Lion Case Addendum). Rev. ed. New York: Appleton-Century-Crofts, Educational Division, Meredith Corporation, 1972.

Kahn, Frank J. *Documents of American Broadcasting.* 2nd. ed. New York: Appleton-Century-Crofts, Educational Division, Meredith Corporation, 1973. The first is a reprint of the 1968 edition with merely the addition of "Red Lion." The 1972 publication is therefore only slightly revised. Both the 1972 and 1973 editions cover the devel-

opment of broadcast regulation, freedom of expression (regulation of programing and broadcast journalism), and
regulation of competition. In the 1972
version, documents of educational
broadcasting have been included but
omitted in the 1973 edition. The second
edition contains a section of nearly 50
pages on two cases: the WLBT (Jackson, Miss.) case and the Citizens Communication Center case. Because of the
differences between the 1972 and 1973
editions, only briefly noted here, both
editions should be at hand.

History and General

Of the many works available, only a very few of the more recent ones can be noted:

Barnouw, Erik. *A History of Broadcasting
in the United States.* 3 vols. New York:
Oxford University Press, 1966, 1968,
1970. The three volumes are the most
comprehensive historical study of U.S.
broadcasting so far produced. Barnouw
divided the work into: Vol. I, *A Tower
in Babel* (to 1933); Vol. II, *The Golden
Web* (1933–1953); and Vol. III, *The
Image Empire* (from 1953). The scope
of Barnouw's research is impressive.

Brown, Lester L. *Television: The Business
Behind the Box.* New York: Harcourt
Brace Jovanovich, Inc., 1971. Les
Brown is the editor of the radio-TV section of *The New York Times* and he has
a real "feel" for the significant detail.
With both wry humor and (sometimes)
biting irony, he looks at the way TV in
America really works. He penetrates the
fog of ratings, reveals how program
planning and placement for a new season is accomplished, and he does his
looking in terms of people—who decides—who benefits. His looking is
mainly at the national scene and is written especially in terms of the major networks. Agree with him or not, the student will always be challenged.

Head, Sydney W. *Broadcasting in America.* 3rd. ed. Boston: Houghton Mifflin
Co., 1976. Not only is this still the best
single volume on broadcasting in
America (in the widest sense), but it is
even better than the earlier editions.
The author packs thought-provoking
conclusions into a closely argued book
based on sound and thorough scholarship. Dealing with the physical bases of
broadcasting, the origins and growth of
broadcasting, the economics and social
control, Head concludes with an assess-
ment of the influence of broadcasting
and a look at the next fifty years.

Koenig, Allen E., ed. *Broadcasting and
Bargaining: Labor Relations in Radio
and Television.* Madison, Milwaukee,
and London: The University of Wisconsin Press, 1970. There is nothing else
like this book easily available to the
scholar and student. The editor has
sought and found a variety of points of
view on many topics, including the
clash of unions and free enterprise, the
structure of broadcasting unions and
their impact, both theoretical and practical. Sections on federal action and ar-
bitration, special problems (e.g., the
creative artist, the technical union, special ETV considerations—both from
management and the teachers' point of
view—and blacks in broadcasting). A
very useful source for student or teacher
of information in an area hard to research.

Lichty, Lawrence W. and Malachi C.
Topping. *American Broadcasting: A
Source Book on the History of Radio
and Television.* New York: Hastings
House, Publishers, 1975. An anthology
of 93 selections by broadcasters, journalists, educators and others describing
and analyzing various facets of broadcasting, including technical, stations,

networks, economics, employment, programming, audiences and regulation. Includes detailed tables.

Mayer, Martin. *About Television*. New York [etc.]: Harper & Row, Publishers, 1972. Somewhat similar to Les Brown's work noted above but containing different and equally readable material. Mayer discusses prime time, daytime, and children's programing, sports, political and "public" broadcasting. He includes good discussions on local TV and on cable. A useful summary of television in the early 1970's.

Rivers, William L., and Wilbur Schramm. *Responsibility in Mass Communication.*

Rev. ed. New York, Evanston, and London: Harper & Row, Publishers, 1969. This edition has been so revised from the early one that it is, in effect, a new book, covering the impact of mass communications, freedom and government, freedom and society, truth and fairness, and the responsibilities of government, media and the public to each other. The appendices include the various codes of journalism, broadcasting and movies (the last now all but defunct), and even the brief code of public relations practitioners. Plenty of thought-provoking material here and in the earlier edition.

Government Regulation

Although there is substantial literature on government regulation, much of it is old. The National Association of Broadcasters publishes a good bit of material and distributes it to member institutions of the Broadcasting Education Association. Five contrasting publications are of principal importance.

Federal Communications Commission. *Annual Reports*. Washington: United States Government Printing Office, 1935—. Though including much more than television, the annual reports summarize governmental actions relating to television, industry, statistics, technological development and controversial issues.

Cherington, Paul W., Leon V. Hirsch, and Robert Brandwein, eds. *Television Station Ownership: A Case Study of Federal Agency Regulation*. Communication Arts Books. New York: Hastings House, Publishers, 1971. The way in which the FCC functions in the process of station licensing is the focus of this book.

Coons, John E., ed. *Freedom and Responsibility in Broadcasting*. Evanston, Ill.: Northwestern University Press, 1961. Though old, it is still useful. The comments by 20 leaders from government, broadcasting, law, education and journalism at a conference at the Northwestern University School of Law deal

with timeless issues in broadcasting.

Emery, Walter B. *Broadcasting and Government: Responsibilities and Regulation*. Rev. and enl. ed. East Lansing: Michigan State University Press, 1971. The late Professor Emery brought his older work up to the beginning of the 1970s. He provided newer illustrations and expanded the text on a very central topic. During a long career, Emery had served with the FCC in various legal capacities and taught both law and regulation of broadcasting for many years. The book reflects his experience and knowledge.

Noll, Roger G., Merton J. Peck, and John J. McGowan. *Economic Aspects of Television Regulation*. Studies in the Regulation of Economic Activity. Washington, D.C.: The Brookings Institution, 1973. This is a study of economic, technical and institutional factors affecting broadcasting's programming and the FCC's efforts to promote local programming through regulation. An important study.

Research and Social Impact

The social impact of television is the most controversial of its many aspects. Judgments in this area must be founded on sound research—too often they are not—and some excellent work is being carried out. Much of the research does not deal with television alone but considers it as one of several mass media to be studied.

Bogart, Leo. *The Age of Television: A Study of Viewing Habits and the Impact of Television on American Life.* 3rd. ed. New York: Frederick Ungar Publishing Company, 1972. This edition includes the original text of the 1958 (2nd) edition with a new introduction and extensive notes that update the older work. About 150 pages of an appendix and notes are devoted to new material.

Bower, Robert T. *Television and the Public.* New York: Holt, Rinehart and Winston, Inc., 1973. Bower has done a study that compares the television audience of 1970 with the audience as studied in 1960 by Gary A. Steiner (*The People Look at Television,* New York, 1963). Bower's studies illuminate changes in audience attitudes toward a number of aspects of TV and describe audience behavior.

Feshbach, Seymour, and Robert D. Singer. *Television and Aggression.* San Francisco: Jossey-Bass, Publishers, 1971. The authors carried out elaborate experiments under realistic conditions and concluded that television may tend to purge violence from real life behavior. The findings are in contrast to those in the final report of the Surgeon General's Scientific Advisory Committee on Television and Social Behavior (listed below). The Feshback and Singer work is controversial and deals with a still unresolved issue.

Klapper, Joseph T. *The Effects of Mass Communication.* Glencoe, Illinois: The Free Press, 1960. Although old, it still is cited by more recent researchers as being very useful. Klapper analyzed the research available to him in 1960 and his tentative conclusions still provide the student and teacher with an ex-

cellent frame of reference for assessing television's place in society.

Lang, Kurt, and Gladys Engel Lang. *Politics and Television.* Chicago: Quadrangle Books, 1968. Work by these two sociologists is always thought-provoking. They have been researching the problems of television and politics since 1951—from the MacArthur Day Parade in Chicago through the 1964 Presidential election. Those who are interested in the political dimensions of television cannot afford to ignore the insights of the Langs.

Milgram, Stanley, and R. Lance Shotland. *Television and Antisocial Behavior: Field Experiments.* New York and London: Academic Press, 1973. This book is particularly valuable because it reports on a study in which Milgram and Shotland controlled the programing content to which the viewer was exposed—three variations of portrayed antisocial behavior. The study was designed to examine the imitative elements that might be involved when audiences view antisocial acts. Much of the book is taken up with a presentation of the research proposal and a full script of one of the program versions. But the important contribution is one of research findings in a field condition with as little laboratory contamination as possible.

Schramm, Wilbur. *Men, Messages, and Media: A Look at Human Communication.* New York: Harper & Row, Publishers, 1973. An excellent work that summarizes in very clear text the years of research and great knowledge of the author. Schramm has also had the benefit of the researches of his many able students. The book moves from the broad topic of communication—how it developed, what it does, the processes, the signs, the codes and the pathways—to the somewhat more specialized problems of mass communication. Schramm pays particular attention to the problems of effects of mass media and mass communication.

Schramm, Wilbur and Donald F. Roberts, eds. *The Process and Effects of Mass Communication*. Rev. ed. Urbana, Chicago, London: University of Illinois Press, 1971. This is an up-to-date (for the early 1970s) version of an important source book. Here, as in the 1954 edition, are the important articles by the big names in mass communication study. Only four of the articles in the 1954 edition have been retained in this one, however.

Stanley, Robert H. and Charles S. Steinberg. *The Media Environment: Mass Communications in American Society*. New York: Hastings House, Publishers, 1976. A survey examining the content,

structure and control of the communications media and their impact on American society. About one-third of the book deals with broadcasting and television.

U. S. Surgeon General's Scientific Advisory Committee on Television and Social Behavior. *Television and Growing Up: The Impact of Televised Violence; Reports to the Surgeon General*. Washington: United States Government Printing Office, 1972. This might well have been included under documents but it is an obvious choice for research. This summary of research and the unanimous findings of the committee repeatedly aroused a large amount of controversial discussion. It found some relationships between televised violence and antisocial behavior although the summary is couched in carefully qualified terms. Backed by accompanying technical volumes of the research reports, the committee's work is an important contribution to the study of television and society.

Periodicals

The field of television is changing so rapidly that books about it are frequently outdated when they are published. Only through the regular use of a few of the more significant periodicals can the student, the teacher and the broadcaster hope to stay abreast of the field.

access. Washington, D.C.: The National Citizens Committee for Broadcasting. An "alternative" periodical, representing the public interest point of view against that of the broadcasting industry and frequently critical of what it considers government inaction. Contains commentary by NCCB chairperson and *access* publisher Nicholas Johnson, former FCC commissioner.

Broadcasting: The Businessweekly of Television and Radio. Washington, D.C.: Broadcasting Publications, Inc. Weekly. A news magazine of broadcasting emphasizing the commercial

and governmental aspects. One of the few "musts" in broadcasting although the student and teacher must always keep in mind the particular editorial orientation of the magazine—*against* government intervention and *for* commercial broadcasting, right or wrong.

Broadcasting: Yearbook Issue. Washington, D.C.: Broadcasting Publications, Inc. Annual. It is a compendium of station listings in radio and television and a wealth of other indispensible reference material.

Journal of Broadcasting. Athens, Ga.: School of Journalism, University of

Georgia. Quarterly. Wide-ranging articles of scholarly and semi-scholarly nature; it includes both national and international topics. Its objective is to bridge the gap between institutions engaged in teaching prospective broadcasters and commercial broadcasting.

PTR: Public Telecommunications Review. Washington, D.C.: National Association of Educational Broadcasters. Bimonthly. Formerly the *NAEB Journal,* the *Review* focuses on educational or "public" radio and television with short articles and comments.

Television Factbook. Washington, D.C.: Television Digest, Inc. Annual. Compilation of detailed information about television stations, including coverage maps. Key personnel are listed and other reference material is of considerable value.

Television Quarterly. Boston: The National Academy of Television Arts and Sciences in cooperation with the School of Public Communication, Boston University. Quarterly. More serious features and articles than in the "pulps," but not scholarly in the usual academic sense. A very useful publication for the creative departments.

TeleVISIONS Magazine. Washington, D.C.: Washington Community Video Center, Inc. Articles on all aspects of television communication oriented toward the needs of public interest groups and organizations seeking access to the visual media.

Television/Radio Age. New York. Weekly. A news magazine emphasizing commercial aspects of both media. Includes a separate section on developments in the FCC.

EARLY D. MONROE, JR.

Senior Engineer, Cable Television Bureau
Federal Communications Commission

●Early D. Monroe, Jr. is Senior Engineer for the Cable Television Bureau of the Federal Communications Commission, responsible for technical matters in the Policy Review and Development Division. His special areas of work at the FCC have included radio broadcast, television broadcast, cable television, satellites and microwaves. He is an adjunct professor at Howard University's School of Communication, teaching New Communication Technology, and Cable Television and Urban Communication. He is also Executive Director and a Board Member of Afro-American Datanamics, a non-profit computer corporation he helped develop to concentrate on research, computer assistance for small minority businesses and teaching through computer terminals.

He is a board member of Howard University Cybernetics' Laboratory (teaching via data terminals); member, Institute of Electrical and Electronics Engineers (IEEE) and former vice president of its Washington, D.C. Chapter; Board Member, National Urban League Law and Consumer Affairs Division (Telecommunication Advisor); Chairman, Howard University Department of Applied Communications Curriculum Committee; Member, Cable Television Advisory Committee (C-TAC); Member, Society of Broadcast Engineers; Co-Chairman, National Conference of Black Lawyers Communication Task Force; Chairman of Mt. Olive Baptist Church Communication Network Committee.

Mr. Monroe is a graduate of Southern University School of Engineering. He has done graduate work at Howard University and George Washington University Schools of Engineering. Mr. Monroe has published a number of technical and non-technical policy, educational and instructional papers in professional journals covering broadcast licensing, Instructional Television Fixed Service, Multipoint Distribution Service, domestic satellites, the electromagnetic spectrum and television networks. He is a frequent speaker on telecommunications, guest lecturer at various universities and chairperson and/or participant in regional and national communications conventions and conferences. He is listed in the 1977 *Who's Who in Black America* and in *Black Journal's* "100 Most Influential Black Americans."

*Mr. Monroe has written this chapter in his private capacity. No official support or endorsement by the Federal Communications Commission is intended or should be inferred.

2

STUDIO AND

CONTROL EQUIPMENT:

TECHNICAL ASPECTS

BY EARLY D. MONROE, JR.

ELECTRONIC EQUIPMENT is used to carry the information or "intelligence" that is transmitted through television. Using electricity and electrical currents, television works in much the same way as does radio. In radio, sound is changed into electromagnetic (invisible light) waves which are sent through the air. In television, both sound and light are changed into electromagnetic waves.

There are numerous conduits through which the signal leaving the station must pass besides the cameras and microphones and cables. Signals are superimposed over radio waves to the transmitter, the transmission line, the antenna, and then transported to the receivers. The TV camera picks up a scene, changes the scene into a pattern of light and converts the light pattern into electrical impulses and electromagnetic waves. The electrical impulses modulate, or tune the electromagnetic carrier waves and send them through the air to the television receiver where they are converted into a pattern of light that can be seen on the television viewing screen.

The carrier waves used to transmit broadcast television signals from a station to a receiver are either very high frequency (VHF) or ultrahigh frequency (UHF). Receivers have three distinct reception bands: VHF channels 2–6, VHF channels 7–13 and UHF channels 14–69.*

* See the end of this chapter for a more detailed explanation of the transmission process.

Visual signals are transmitted by a scanning process. The series of lines which we perceive to be a solid image are sent one line at a time by an electronic beam that reads across two lines from left to right and then returns and repeats until it reaches the bottom. This process of scanning is similar to scanning the lines of a book when reading. However, the television receiver must by synchronized to scan the picture screen on the corresponding line of the studio camera.

Another important concept, persistence of vision, applies in television as it does in film. The brain retains an image for a fraction of a second longer than it actually appears in view. As a series of pictures are projected before us, we get the sensation of motion of a continuing solid image, when actually the eye is seeing a series of still pictures. In film, the images pass through the projector at a rate of 24 frames per second (fps) and in television at a rate of 30 fps. In television, one may detect "flickering" if the brightness control dial has been set at its maximum brightness.

The television studio revolves around three basic facets: video, audio and lighting. Combining and coordinating many different kinds and uses of equipment is necessary to make a single product. It is important, therefore, that the directors and technicians have equipment that is flexible enough to meet different particular needs.

THE STUDIO

The size and shape of a television studio should be designed to accommodate the equipment, props and movement of cameras and performers. Some studios can be as large as 5,000 square feet. However, a studio 40 by 60 feet is considered a more common size when compared to a studio measuring 40 by 40 feet, which is considered small. A studio should be designed to allow for expansion and should permit a set to be left permanently, if necessary. The studio should be located on the ground floor or near a service area, so as to allow for equipment to be brought in from the outside. There should be only one entrance, to prevent people from walking on the set during a taping or at a performance of a live telecast. A viewing room should be near, for visitors to watch the show and sometimes for talent to wait before going on-the-air.

The studio should have a smooth hard floor for easy camera movement. The level should not deviate more than $1/32$ inch in a 5-foot square. Most floors are concrete and reinforced with "cut joints" to prevent cracking. Some designers prefer to keep the floor covered, making it more durable and less likely to be ruined by spots and spills. A tiled floor is less abrasive to camera cables. Because there can be no columns, large steel trusses must be used to support the ceilings. Ceilings should be between 15 and 20 feet—two stories—high. High ceilings are needed not only to keep lighting equipment out of view of the camera, but to permit the heat generated by lights to rise as high as possible, keeping it away from the crew. With a high ceiling, flats and other props can be "flown" and stored until needed. No matter how high the ceiling, however, a good air conditioning system is necessary to keep the studio cool under the hot lights.

The walls of a studio should be sound-deadened. "A room dominating in high frequencies is called a brilliant room. Too much absorbent material can create a dead room." [1] This is a prevalent problem in large studios that use boom microphones. Always check a studio for noises that can not be heard by the human ear, but are easily picked up by the sensitive microphones. One method is to take a tape recorder and place it in various areas.

CAMERAS

Although monochrome (black-and-white) cameras are still manufactured, virtually the entire U.S. television broadcasting industry converted to color by 1970. Recent technological advances, therefore, have been principally concentrated in color cameras.

Color cameras are available in a variety of sizes. Today's studio cameras have become smaller and more efficient. A regular full-size studio camera weighs approximately 100 pounds as compared with the older cameras of 250 pounds. The portable MINI-CAMS weigh as little as 8 pounds. The individual transistors which relayed information from the photoconductive tubes have been replaced by integrated circuits which are cheaper, work faster and take up less space. Because of the use of integrated circuits, maintenance of the newer cameras is more convenient. Rather than searching through and testing hundreds of inaccessible transistors, printed circuit cards containing thousands of miniature transistors may be recovered, tested and replaced with new circuit cards if necessary, all with a minimum of effort. Color cameras are basically three cameras in one, each having lenses, a viewfinder, photosensitive pick-up tubes and camera control units (CCU's). These cameras work on the principle of incorporating dichroic prisms which split incoming light entering the lens into spectral colors of red, blue and green. The operator views the picture in black and white. Color viewing tubes are available in plumbicon cameras.

An innovation of the 1970s is a small electronic or video camera, consisting of just a body and lens. Because of this structure, the picture produced by the video camera needs to be displayed on a separate monitor or television set, making it difficult to aim and focus the camera. As a result, most portable and studio cameras have a viewfinder which serves as a monitor. Because the quality of an electronic picture is completely determined by the video camera, proper camera adjustment is essential. The video camera is similar to any other camera in that light reflected from an image is focused by a lens onto a plane inside the camera. Unlike the conventional camera, the video camera holds no film or videotape, but instead contains a camera tube. The camera tube and associated amplifiers and electronics largely determine the light sensitivity of any particular video camera. The sensitivity rating of most video cameras is between 20- to 10,000-foot candles.

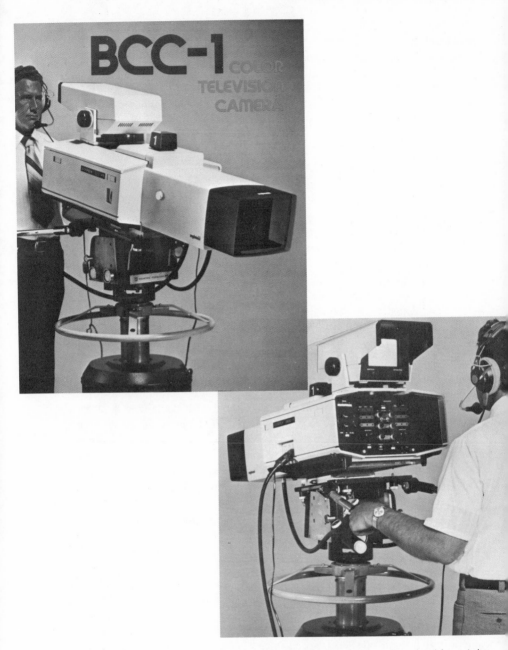

Fig. 1. Ampex BCC-1, a standard studio color camera. Uses the plumbicon tube. *Ampex Corporation, 401 Broadway, Redwood City, California 94063.*

TUBES

Image Orthicon

The image orthicon tube was the workhouse of black-and-white television and was later used in a three-tube configuration in the earliest color cameras. It is a relatively large tube, 3 inches in diameter by 15 inches long. Housing the three tubes (with heat deflectors and color splitters) in a color camera head created a large and cumbersome piece of equipment.

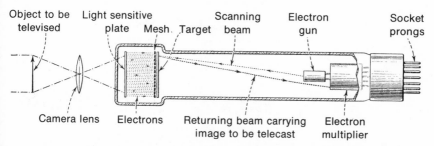

Object to be   Light sensitive   Scanning   Electron   Socket
televised   plate   Mesh Target   beam   gun   prongs

Camera lens   Electrons   Returning beam carrying   Electron
                                     image to be telecast   multiplier

Fig. 2. Sectional view of the image orthicon camera tube showing how light from an object is converted into electrons and then into electrical signals by the action of an electron gun. *From: Dunlap, Orrin E., Jr., UNDERSTANDING TELEVISION. New York: Greenberg, 1948, p. 31.*

Another problem confronting the image orthicon was that as the tube got older, it had a tendency to "burn-in," which causes the tube to retain or hold an image a few seconds after the camera is moved to another image, creating a ghosting effect.

Vidicon

In 1950 RCA introduced the photoconductive vidicon tube which rapidly became significant in image transmission, first for monochrome and later for color. It is a smaller tube, usually 1 inch in diameter and 6 inches long.

The operating principle is somewhat similar to the image orthicon, but the design is considerably simplified. The tube is durable and very long-lived with an average life often exceeding 2,000 hours, nearly twice that of an image orthicon. The vidicon tube costs about $250. The longer life and lower purchase price recommends the tube for cameras used in individual situations and in educational television, where costs are a vital concern. The principal disadvantage of the vidicon is its sensitivity. In studios using the vidicon tubes, light levels must be three times higher than those using the image orthicon. There is usually, however, sufficient light available from projection devices so that the vidicon can operate in its optimum range.

Vidicon cameras are smaller and lighter than image-orthicon cameras, and although, as a rule, the larger the vidicon tube, the sharper and brighter the pic-

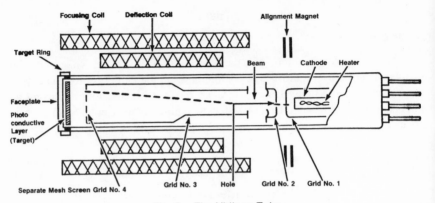

Fig. 3.   The Vidicon Tube

ture, great effort has been made to produce small-sized, high quality vidicon tubes.

The vidicon tube employed by the Sony AVC-3400 video camera is comparatively small, measuring $^{11}/_{16}$ inch in diameter at the target ring and 3-$^{15}/_{16}$ inches in length. Yet, it is a standard, commonly used tube and is referred to as a ⅔-inch vidicon tube.

Plumbicon

Today, the most widely used tube among broadcasters is the plumbicon, developed by the Philips Corporation. Plumbicon is a tube that is basically a vidicon tube with a different photoconductivity surface. A very expensive tube, it is a variation of the lead-oxide coated pick-up tube, and offers sensitivity comparable to that of the image orthicon without the burn-in effect. When first introduced in 1963, the plumbicon was 1-½ inches in diameter and by 1974 the size had been reduced to ⅔. It is usually employed in high quality color television cameras, but there are some manufacturers who produce plumbicon monochrome cameras. Several years ago, the most popular plumbicon cameras were the Norelco PM-40 and the Sarkes Tarzian 2700-L. In the late 1970s, the plumbicon still had the position of being the world's primary color camera tube in both the large studio cameras and the compact portable color cameras.

Tivicon

The tivicon is a specialized tube, highly sensitive in situations having very low light levels. The tivicon tube (silicon diode) can produce a good black-and-white picture in total darkness with only infrared illumination. Tivicon tubes can be fitted to most low-cost cameras, thereby making possible good pictures, even under low light situations, such as street lights, dusk, bars and night clubs.

Chalnicon

In the late 1970s a new kind of vidicon type camera tube called the chalnicon was introduced. It successfully used a cadenium selenide (CdSe) photoconductor as a target material. Its photosensitivity is as high as 10 to 20 times that of ordinary Sb2S3 vidicons, and its spectral response covers the entire visible spectrum. The chalnicon and the ⅔-inch saticon, introduced in 1975, are cheaper than the plumbicon, but at the end of the 1970s were still relatively new and had not experienced wide use within the industry and their performance levels still remained to be tested and given critical evaluation.

CAMERA MOUNTING EQUIPMENT

Television cameras are mounted on panning and tilting devices which permit the flexibility of control needed by camera operators. These devices are called friction heads or cradles. The cradle is the later design and approximates the old rocking chair idea. No matter how the camera is tilted it remains in balance. The camera pan and tilt head are in turn mounted on pedestals or dollies, of which there is considerable variety. The simplest is a tripod, which may be of metal or wood and which is usually mounted on a three-wheeled dolly. The principal disadvantage of this type is the lack of vertical movement except by manual adjustment of the tripod itself. More sophisticated pedestals incorporate mechanisms for readily raising or lowering the camera. Some use a hand wheel. Others are so carefully balanced by weights that the pressure of a finger on a large ring is enough to move the heavy camera up and down. Others are activated by electronic motors which operate very quietly. Still others are operated by compressed air.

In larger studios, the use of power-operated dollies is common. These electrically controlled devices enable the camera operator to maintain complete control of the camera while a second person mechanically moves the dolly. As a result, many obstacles are avoided. Camera cranes, similar to those used in motion picture production, are also found in large studios. The camera operator rides the crane in a fairly comfortable seat and operates the camera conventionally. Gross movements are controlled by dolly manipulators who move the camera boom in any desired direction. Such cranes easily elevate the camera to 10 feet or more and can lower it almost to the floor of the studio.

"Not only economics but studio space will determine how elaborate a mounting can be usefully employed under average production conditions."[2] Usually, the more complicated or cramped the settings or studio, the less opportunity for using cranes. For field work at sporting events and similar remote pick-ups, tripods with or without dollies are generally used, since actual movement of the camera from one position to another is rare.

Fig. 4.   A sophisticated "crane." The RCA TV-26 mobile unit consists of a gooseneck trailer connected to a flat-bed truck. On site, the truck can be unhitched to serve as a roving camera mount, as in this illustration. *Courtesy RCA.*

Portable Equipment

The growth and increasing acceptance of electronic news gathering, often referred to as ENG or EJ (electronic journalism), has spawned a burst of activity in the development of increasingly smaller and lighter cameras and equipment. ENG or portable video fits neatly into a studio's budget. The average cost of an ENG system using a ¾-inch portable Video Tape Recorder (VTR), ENG camera and a Time Base Corrector was, in 1977, about $50,000, which is the cost of a very ordinary quadruplex VTR. Some stripped-down ENG Systems cost as little as $20,000.

Where local coverage used to be done with film equipment, the dependence on 16mm film has been reduced by ENG, which permits high quality and near instantaneous broadcast of live news. An ENG crew can be sent out in a microwave-equipped van. The camera signal is relayed to the station's transmitter for immediate record and broadcast. If the ENG unit is sent to an area where dragging a camera cable attached to the van is not feasible, an individual can carry the lightweight ENG camera, a power source and a portable VTR into the area and cover the story. The video-tape can be edited on the way back to the studio with a tabletop digital editor, and the tape will be ready for broadcast by the time the van arrives at the station.

Without a digital time base corrector, little of this would be possible since the portable units use the narrower video tapes which put out poor quality pictures, unacceptable by FCC standards. The time base corrector stabilizes and improves the signal, allowing a high quality picture to be broadcast from the narrow tape. The development of time base correctors and MINI-CAMS, ¾-inch videotape recorders, have revolutionized the broadcast industry, making portable equipment an integral part of any television studio.[3]

Fig. 5. Ampex BCC-2 portable color television camera and power pack. *Ampex Corporation, 401 Broadway, Redwood City, California 94063.*

MINI-CAMS

MINI-CAMS, first introduced in 1965, are cameras weighing about 20 pounds easily carried on the shoulder and capable of recording color video of the highest magnitude on relatively compact videotape machines.

Most of these MINI-CAMS have built-in microphones and can be powered with the 6-to-8 pound battery belts available. The 20-pound RCA MINI-CAM (TK-76) and the 22-pound Ampex MINI-CAM (BCC-4) both have self-contained camera control units, thereby eliminating the CCU back-pack, and can operate on +12 volts DC. This makes it possible to use a rechargeable battery belt to operate the cameras for 90 minutes, or even a car cigarette lighter outlet or a vehicle battery terminal post to power the cameras.

Most of these MINI-CAMS use ⅔-inch vidicon tubes. The higher quality MINI-CAMS use a three-tube color system which provides improved color and resolution compared to the one- and two-tube systems employed by manufacturers such as JVC or Akai. Of all the three-tube cameras on the market, the most popular color portable in the late 1970s was the Microcam, developed by Thompson-CSF Laboratories in cooperation with CBS. The camera head, which contains tubes, zoom lens and electronic viewfinder, weighs only eight pounds, about two-thirds the weight of its nearest competitor.[4] The small electronic pack, designed to be worn over the shoulder, weighs about three pounds. The power consumption of the camera is reduced to just 20 watts, thereby conserving the charge in a small power source and enabling the camera to operate on standard flashlight batteries in an emergency.[5] Laboratories are developing a smaller microcam, the Microcam II, which is expected to be ready for broadcast use by 1981. Another color camera designed exclusively for ENG use, in 1976, is the Ikeyami HL-351 MINI-CAM. It features higher picture quality and enables the head to be controlled at the back-pack. Lightweight and easy to handle, the Ikeyami uses a one-inch plumbicon tube.

"As the invention of the transistor ushered in a new era in electronic communications, the electronic circuit is ushering in another era . . . Integrated circuits are now being manufactured containing hundreds of transistors at costs of less than a penny a transistor."[6]

Accessories to the MINI-CAM

Power Belts. A useful accessory to the miniaturized video tape recorder and MINI-CAMS is the miniaturized power source. Obviating the dragging along of a cable attached to a power generator, the lightweight (6–8 pound) power belts give the camera operator independence of movement previously not possible. Depending on the power consumption of the mini-VTR's and the MINI-CAMS, the power supply of the battery belts can last from 30 minutes up to seven hours. These battery belts are rechargeable and come in regular and fast-changing models.

Steadicam. TeleVisions magazine reported that "A man around the [1976

Fig. 6.   Ampex MINI-CAM BCC-4. *Photo courtesy of Ampex Corporation.*

NAB Convention] exhibit floor with a Rube Goldberg type device strapped to his torso: a gyroscopic camera brace that looked like the mechanical arms to a giant dentist's drill. On this brace was mounted a cumbersome RCA portable color camera with a large monitor on top. The demonstration proved a man could bounce all over the place and the camera movement would still remain completely smooth.''[7]

Although somewhat skeptically, the article pointed out that this new device may help improve the picture quality of a hand-held camera. The operator supports the whole camera structure by means of a body brace which is a padded, close-fitting, harness-like jacket, designed to sustain the total weight of the system mainly on the operator's hip. Attached to the breast plate of the jacket is an articulated support arm which can be moved in any direction in which the operator's own arm can be moved. The total weight of the camera system is supported by the body brace, and the operator can easily control and guide the "suspended" camera in any direction he or she wishes with a gentle movement of the hand.[8] It produces jitter-free shots of studio-quality smoothness even while the operator runs up and down stairs. The Steadicam weighs 13½ pounds and contains a power unit for the device and camera. The 1977 $35,000 price tag, however, was somewhat prohibitive for all but the larger stations.

Video Tape Recorders

At one time film was the standard medium for recording sound and visual images. But in 1956 Ampex introduced the first major video tape recorder (VTR), which marked the beginning of the video tape revolution. A portable, record-only VTR back-pack was introduced in 1967, preparing the way for electronic newsgathering techniques. Recognizing that the equipment used for the first generation of ENG operations was designed originally for industrial or institutional use, a number of manufacturers developed videotape recorders for use in the field and for editing news stories, all designed and built for professional use.[9]

The video information is picked up by television cameras and relayed to the VTR through cables or by microwave transmissions. The VTR also records sound information at the same time it is recording video signals. Television stations use combination recording-playback units. There are two types of VTRs, those using transverse scanning techniques (quadruplex VTRs) and those using helical scanning techniques.

Quadruplex

The Ampex machine utilized a quadruplex system, that is, using 4 heads to scan the information placed transversely on a 2-inch tape. This means that instead of recording the information on audio style longitudinal tracks (-------), the Ampex VTR recorded the video information on a single track laid down transversely, or across the width of the track (////////////////). Through this method, less tape could contain more information. Slowing down the speed of the tape made the quadruplex recorder an even more viable piece of equipment.[10] The 2-inch wide tapes produce a high quality picture.

One of the most widely used VTRs in the late 1970s is the RCA Quadruplex TR-600 automatic. Designed as a unified, integrated system, it incorporates numerous automatic subsystems for easier operation. For versatility, it records in highband and plays in lowband. It is capable of operating at both 15 and 7.5 ips (inches per second) tape speeds and includes fast lock-up and rewind devices which enables it to rewind a 4800-foot tape reel in 2½ minutes. Demonstrations of this machine have revealed that it is capable of locking up stabilized, high quality pictures in 1.5 seconds. This is possible due to its advanced circuitry and built in subsystems.[11]

Helical Scan

Helical scanning systems were developed in 1960. Originally, the helical configuration was used on 2-inch tapes, but gradually was placed on 1-inch, ¾-inch and ½-inch tapes. Due to the decreased size of the video-tapes, the equipment using helical scan tapes could be made smaller and lighter. However, helical scan produces a picture of lower quality than the quadruplex and is used primarily in portable and cassette VTRs.

Fig. 7. RCA TR-600 Video
Tape Recorder. *RCA Corp.*

VTR Operation

Magnetic tape recording is not a new concept. Its operating principle is that:

. . . the images are converted in intensity corresponding to the level and extensity of the sounds and light being recorded. This varying electric current is then fed into an electromagnet. Tiny metallic particles (bounded to backing) pass an electromagnet which varies in strength according to the variations of the electronic current. This forces the metallic particles on the tape to shift position to an extent determined by the varying levels of the magnetic field.[12]

The videotape recorder is characterized by the width or format, as noted earlier: 2-inch, 1-inch, ¾-inch, ½-inch and ¼-inch. Two-inch tape is normally considered broadcast quality. Most in-house (industrial) productions are on 1-inch tape and later duplicated on the less expensive ½-inch or ¾-inch tape and distributed. This is because the 1-inch produces a higher quality picture than the smaller formats.

An instrument called a wave form monitor shows the strength of the voltage of any signal at any point. This allows the television system technician to monitor video signals and determine when adjustments are needed. The wave form monitor also shows the various shades of color and black-and-white and tells whether the shades are evenly spaced. It allows the technician to balance cameras so that they will generate pictures of similar brightness and color.

When recording, the recorder operates at various speeds signified as inches per second (ips). The standard speeds are: $^{15}/_{16}$, 1⅞, 3¾, 7½ and 15 ips. The speeds 7½ and 15 ips are recommended because they pick up the widest ranges of frequencies.

Problems such as poor audio quality can sometimes be traced to the VTRs. This is only one aspect to consider, the others being the original source material, transmission and the home receiver. In order to give satisfactory sound quality, the VTR should have a band width of 50 Hz to 12 kHz and a signal to noise ratio between 47 and 50 dB. Poor sound quality can also be related to tape sizes. "There are some difficulties caused by the different gauges used in VTR's, from quarter-inch to two-inch gauges. Once you move from the quarter-inch (which is also the size of standard audio tape), audio heads can become a nuisance, because there are no universal standards for low gauge VTR's. Therefore, you have several manufacturers producing machines with different characteristics that are not necessarily compatible with each other."[13] In older tapes, the iron particles on the tape caused a background hiss. The size of the particles was reduced, also reducing the level of hiss.

Some of the other causes for noise are: the amount of electronic equipment used; microphone placement; lack of balance between the amplifier, audio controls and tape recorder; the automatic gain control on recorders. Some manufacturers of VTRs do not emphasize good audio quality. For example, the 2-inch Ampex VTR has only a single track for audio and does not allow for much diversity. The 1-inch and ½-inch helical tapes lack good audio quality.

Time Base Correctors

Servos are the motor-driven rotating heads which drive the tape at a constant speed and sense the information laid on the video tape. When the machine is running correctly, the servos will space the signal information evenly, thus producing a high quality picture.[14] But due to certain technical imperfections, the tape speed cannot always be driven at a constant speed and minor timing errors are created. In 1960 a device was introduced to correct the timing errors of quadruplex VTR's and soon these Time Base Correctors (TBCs) became a standard refinement for the increasingly popular machines.

These early analog TBC's were completely unable to handle the larger errors of helical scan VTRs. As long as the time base errors of helical scan equipment could not be compensated (or as the professionals say, the correction "window" was too narrow) there was no way that studio engineers could take advantage of the inherent tape economy of helical systems for broadcast purposes.

Although available for many years previously, it was not until 1973 that ¾-inch and 1-inch tape were brought up to FCC broadcast quality standards by the digital Time Base Corrector. The importance of the TBC in making the 1-

Fig. 8A. Ampex VPR-10, Portable Video Recorder. *Ampex Corporation.*

Fig. 8B.   Ampex TBC-1, digital time base corrector. *Ampex Corporation.*

inch and ¾-inch tapes viable for broadcast use cannot be emphasized enough, for without a device to correct the distortions of the narrower tapes, the usefulness of the 1-inch and ¾-inch tapes would be severly limited. In the helical scan format, the head traces a nearly longitudinal path. The tape speed variations caused by the scanning device skipped entire lines of information or picked up only portions of an information signal. The Digital Time Base corrector solved this problem by converting the analog signals from the original tapes into computer-type digital pulses where the pulses can be manipulated electronically to compensate for extreme stability errors.[15] TBCs also correct time base errors which result from the hooks and tears in the picture caused by a lack of synchronization.[16] TBCs will not correct major flaws, but they can fill in space made by missing tape oxide (drop-out compensators) or stretched tape caused by humidity. Some VTRs, particularly 2-inch, have TBCs built into them. TBCs can be analog, digital or a combination of both. In the analog process, the entire signal is held up or moved ahead in relation to the timing difference. In the digital process the signal is broken down electronically and rebuilt to meet broadcast standards. Quad tape machines can use either process. Helical tape machines use the digital process.

It is safe to say that the development of TBCs has been as responsible for the fruition of the ENG concept as the color MINI-CAMS. By purchasing a TBC and a low-cost color portable camera and VTR, local stations can turn their news crews loose with the portable video equipment, confident that the tapes made in the field can be rebroadcast.

Future Tape Size

As with cameras, VTRs have become smaller and have more convenience features. They are more efficient, particularly because of the precision machining of movable parts and the replacement of individual transistors with integrated circuitry. Because tape is made from petroleum products, shortages of fuel will most certainly affect the cost of video tape. It can be expected that the present standard 2-inch quadruplex videotape will be replaced by a narrower tape size, cheaper than the 2-inch tape. With the improvement of helical scanning equipment and the benefits to industry users and manufacturers that standardization offers, it is likely that ¾-inch tape will become the new industry standard.[17] In 1976 three manufacturers introduced 1-inch helical scan VTR's with state-of-the-art features, but most manufacturers have concentrated their energies on the ¾-inch market. One-half-inch tape has more or less been abandoned as a viable medium to work with, due to the extreme instabilities inherent in its signal.[18]

Video Cartridge Machines

Prior to the development of the cassette or cartridge machines, short program segments, such as advertisements and public service announcements, had to be copied onto a master tape which was then edited onto the video tape pro-

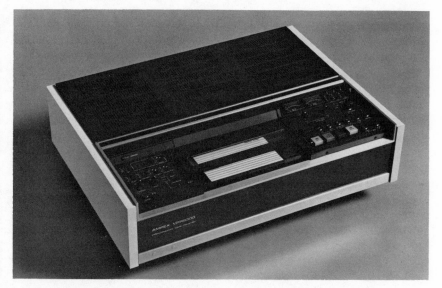

Fig. 9.   Ampex videocassette tape recorder VPR8300. *Ampex Corporation.*

gram material. This caused extra wear on the recorder heads, tied up VTR's
and lowered the signal quality of the copied and re-copied short segment. It
was in response to these problems that the major manufacturers developed the
quadruplex cassette video recorders. These recorders were especially designed
to record and play back the short program segments on short lengths of tape
housed in plug-in cartridges. Despite the relatively high cost of these machines,
they were quickly accepted by stations throughout the United States to assist in
handling the fast sequences of commercials and other announcements provided
in network continuity.

The recorders contain a movable store of bins which carry the cassettes.
When a particular cassette is desired, the recorder bins carry the desired cassette to a "port" where the cassette may be extracted. The tape is automatically
rewound, unthreaded and returned to the storage bin. This process is analogous
to the 45 rpm selection, transport, play and return of an ordinary jukebox.
There are two cassette transports so that another cassette may be positioned for
play while the preceding cassette is still playing. The RCA model holds 22 cassettes, the Ampex model holds 24.[19] Both models may be interfaced with a
computer, enabling station engineers to pre-program desired tape cassettes and
to get printed read-outs of previously played cassettes, the latter a great assistance in determining billing.

Videodiscs

In late 1977, although many companies were working on the development
of videodiscs, Philips-MCA and RCA had taken the lead in production and dis-

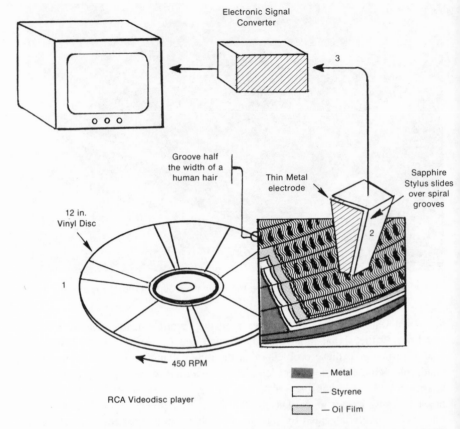

Fig. 10A. The picture and sound code on a spinning disc (1) is picked up by a stylus (2) that transfers signals to a converter (3). The converter processes the signals into electronic form accepted by a TV set.

tribution. The videodisc is a phonograph-type system capable of playing color video programs. All of the systems, in use and in development, have a 30-minute program capacity per side. The videodisc looks like an ordinary phonograph record made out of transluscent plastic. The principal difference between the RCA and Philips systems is that the former uses a tracking stylus and the latter uses laser optics for converting the disc intelligence into video signals.

The RCA plastic disc is layered with copper and has pre-cut grooves, used for tracking purposes only. During recording, as the disc spins at 450 rpm, the copper layer is bombarded by a thinly focused electronic beam being modulated by the intelligence. This beam places a sequence of slots 0.1 to 0.2 microns wide on the disc. Copies of the master are made by pressing, reducing the cost per disc to less than a dollar. During playback, a sapphire stylus tracks the disc, similar to the process for playing a phonograph record. But instead of vibrating in order to pick up the intelligence, the stylus has a metal layer on it which senses the capacitance of the copper layer. Through transduction, this capacitance is converted to frequency changes which in turn generate the two signals required for playback on a television set.

The Philips-MCA player uses laser optics for both recording and playback. "A laser beam modulated with the combined video and audio signal is focused on a tiny area of the master disk . . . impact of the beam burns a tiny pit into the disk, and the depth of the pit varies in accordance with the video audio signal. . . . The disk itself spins at 1800 RPM and as the laser travels . . . the width of the disk, it burns in a fine spiral of 13,000 grooves per inch. The pits in this groove represent the program."[20] After the master disc is cut, pressings are made and coated with plastic to prevent scratches of the information surface. The laser scans the grooves and responds only to the intelligence and not to scratches, fingerprints or other marks. As it scans the disc, the laser beam is reflected through a system of prisms and mirrors that connect to a light-sensitive diode that converts light energy into electrical impulses which are fed into a TV receiver. The Philips player has freeze-frame capability, good protection

Philips-MCA Videodisc Player

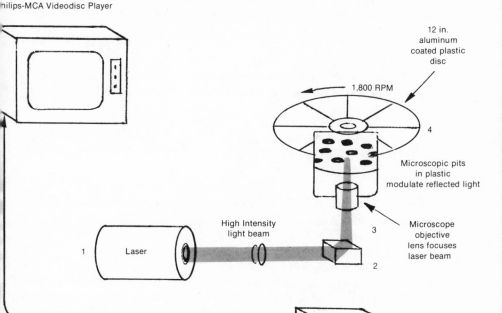

Fig. 10B. A laser (1) generates a light beam aimed by a prism (2) and focused by a lens (3) on a disk (4) coded for picture and sound. Reflected light strikes a photodetector (5) that converts it to signals that are processed and fed to a TV set.

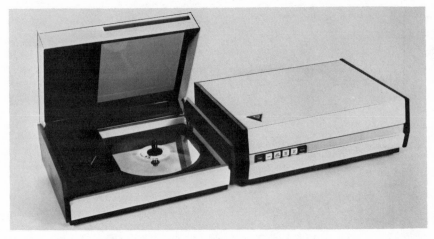

Fig. 10C.   The MCA Disco-Vision Industrial Player (1977 prototype).

of the disc from damage and no parts that require periodic replacement. Both RCA and Philips systems are comparably priced and when available for the home market in late 1977 or early 1978 are expected to cost about $500 for the playback unit.

Equipment Sources

Video cassette, videodisc and super 8mm film are the three basic recording systems. Some widely-used manufacturers of these systems are:
1) Magnetic tape
   a. Video cassette (Sony)
   b. Panasonic (Matsushita Electric)
   c. JVC Video Cassette (JVC Industries)
   d. VCR (Philips)
2) Disc
   a. TeD (Teldec: AEG-Telefunken)
   b. Philips/MCA Video Disc
   c. RCA Selecta Vision
3) Super 8mm film
   a. Eastman Kodak VP-1
   Video cassette was developed and marketed by the Sony Corporation of Tokyo. It is composed of ¾-inch tape and the size of the recorder is 221 x 140 x 32 mm; the tape is held on coplanar spools—standard cassette playing spools. Standard cassette playing time is 63 minutes. This system uses a 525-line field, U.S. standard TV signal, and it has an extra recording unit which allows for direct recording of TV broadcast programs. Panasonic, formerly Matsushita Electric of Japan, makes ½-inch EIA-J cassette systems and ¾-inch magnetic tape systems compatible with the Sony System where there is 60-minute re-

cording time in ¾-inch format and 30-minute recording time in ½-inch format. JVC video cassette systems made by Victor Company of Japan allows off-the-air recording automatically and can also play one program and record another on a different channel simultaneously. VCR, produced by Philips of Eindoven, Netherlands, is based on ½-inch magnetic tape with a cassette size of 126 x 146 x 41mm. The unit playing time is 60 minutes. Chromium-dioxide tape is used and the system operates on a 625-line, 50-field video signal and Pal color system which is not compatible with the U.S. color system.

TeD is made by Teldec of Berlin and London and was marketed in Europe in 1975. The playing time of a 12-inch disc is 12 minutes, and information is recorded at frequency modulation (FM). The signal is reproduced by a diamond stylus with pressure sensitive ceramic pick-up. The special groove has a fine pitch with 130 groovers per minute. A videodisc recording has a lifetime of 1000 playings. The Philips-MCA videodisc, manufactured by Philips, will play back on the standard TV receiver. This player picks up video information by a low-powered laser beam. Its playing time is 60-minutes per disc. The RCA videodisc allows recording on both sides for 60 minutes. The player uses a sapphire-tipped stylus and pick-up arm.

The Eastman Kodak VP-1 film cartridge is used interchangeably on optical sound super-8mm projectors or on video players. A 22-minute length can run at 18 or 24 fps. with still frame or single advance.

Editing Videotape

Editing film is relatively convenient because a series of still pictures can be examined and cuts and splices made with some precision. With videotape, the visual information cannot be seen. This was the major reason for the early reluctance to utilize videotape; edits were difficult and imprecise. When editing videotape, the magnetic tracks were made visible by applying a fast drying solution of iron dust which settled on the magnetized areas of the tape. The tape could then be cut and spliced to another tape which had undergone the same procedure. The problem with mechanically splicing the tapes, other than being slow, was that the extra thickness created excessive wear on the recorder heads, and the spliced tape could not be used again.

The first electronic system of editing was developed in 1961. This system employed a "pulse" laid down on the track, approximately at the point the edit was to take place. The tape was then replayed with an erasure at a designated number of frames after the point. The pulse was read by the scanning head and the recorded information fed into a master recorder. At the end of the segment, the master recorder was re-cued to begin recording at the point the previous segment ended. Pulse editing is faster than the mechanical splicing method, but it is extremely difficult to correct any errors since the erasure occurs on the original tape. The current method of editing tapes was developed in 1971 for quadruplex systems. In this system each frame (30 per second) is given an "address" or a time reference number which is then laid on one of the tape recording tracks. The address can be identified on a counting device while the video portion of the tape is being monitored. For a time code edit, selected addresses are identified, programmed into a memory bank, and the tape is replayed into a master recorder interfaced with the computer memory bank. The editing is done automatically, controlled by the edit instructions programmed into the computer.[21] The method of time code editing using helical scan equipment was made available in 1975. Digital time codes, i.e. time codes using binary numbering systems (0, 1, 10, 11, 100, etc.), are becoming the standard method of editing. This is primarily because digital editing, as it is referred to, is faster and more accurate. By assigning digital addresses, computers based on digital logic systems may be successfully interfaced with editing terminals to create fully automatic edits.

Typical of usually used editing equipment is the Ampex EDM-1 video tape editing system, a computer-controlled switcher with special effects. The floppy-disc memory can store up to 3,200 edited scenes. The EDM-1 can interface up to eight on-line video, audio or disc recorders. Its computer filing permits individual scenes to be identified by time code and real language. The basic unit consists of an operations control center with audio and video monitoring and advanced switcher with special effects, video display monitor and a typewriter style keyboard. The Edimatic-100 editing system performs frame accurate edits without SMPTE code by counting control track pulses. It has up to ten memorized edit points which can be selected by push buttons. The unit can edit tapes on quad and helical video tape recorders. Moreover, it can perform on-line and off-line edits from camera to VTR. The RCA AE-600 editing system features microprocessors, large scale integrated circuitry and locally controlled or remote controlled editing. This system permits split audio and video editing only.

Automatic Cartridge System for 16mm TV Film

The cartridge permits rapid and convenient handling of film and tape media. Cartridge film for pictures and cartridge tape for sound have been widely used for some time in the business and consumer fields as has cartridge audio tape for broadcast use. In the mid-1970s the cartridge concept for video recording began to gain wide acceptance in the television industry. RCA produced a cartridge system for film, the TCP-1624, which includes a cartridge projector and all automated equipment to effectively project film. It works this way:

Film cartridges are loaded in a circular magazine which has a capacity of 24 cartridges. The magazine is removable from the projector, making it easy to load. The TCP-1624 automatic projector is designed to occupy the same position in a telecine island (see page 81) as a standard TV reel-to-reel projector. After being loaded, the cartridge is transferred from the magazine to a sensor path. During this process the sensor detects the presence of the leader when it enters a slack bin and causes the film drive at the cartridge to stop. The sensor

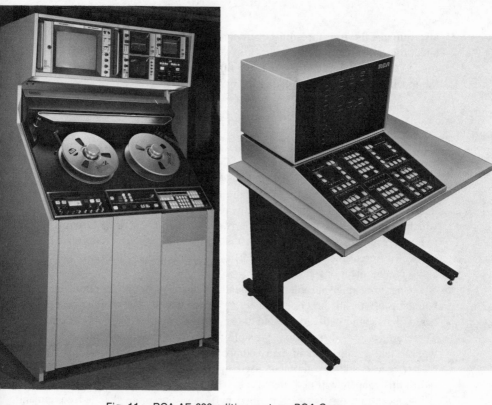

Fig. 11.   RCA AE-600 editing system. *RCA Corp.*

Fig. 12.   RCA TCP-1624, automatic
film cartridge projector. *RCA Corp.*

also initiates the film threading cycle which starts at the lower sound sprocket and progressively establishes the film's running paths, back toward the cartridge. After this is accomplished, the film runs to a cue mark and is played by the touch of a button when called for by the technical director.

AUDIO

"Sound reproduction . . . is an art as well as a science with considerable scope for individuality of approach.[22]

Television has approached, but has yet to meet, the challenge of the state-of-the-art audio transmission. The audio component of television is radio transmission, that process whereby sound waves are converted into electrical signals which can be made to modify a carrier wave and are transported through the air to home receivers. Radio transmission is achieved through the interrelated functions of different pieces of equipment, with each piece an electronic link in the audio communications chain.

There are many problems in sound production. Sound is often reflected, bouncing off in all directions. In trying to receive sound, it must be remembered that sound will go around those objects smaller than its wavelength. Therefore, ". . . it is seldom possible to assess what a microphone will hear without taking into account many complex factors."[23]

(Because audio equipment used in television is similar to that used in radio, this chapter will not attempt an exhaustive description of equipment, but will concentrate on its use for video purposes. For more detailed equipment analysis, see Chapter 2, Studio and Operating Facilities, *Radio Broadcasting*, Hastings House, 1976 revised edition, the companion work to this one.)

Microphones

The microphone is the principal tool for sound pick-up. It is the first electronic link in the communications chain between source and receiver. Basically, what the microphone does is to convert sound waves to electrical current. There are two major ways of doing this: the pressure mike converts changes in air pressure to electrical signals; the pressure-gradient mike responds to differing relationships between the air pressure at the front and back.

The pressure microphone consists essentially of a diaphragm enclosing a cavity that is sealed off from the air. It is considered omni-directional, i.e. able to pick up sounds from all directions. The diaphragms in pressure-gradient microphones are exposed to air on both sides. Because they pick up sound from two sides, they are considered bi-directional. Some mikes are uni-directional, that is, they can pick up sound from one direction only.

The most important mikes in use in television are the (electrostatic) condenser mike and the ribbon mike. With the *electrostatic (condenser) microphone,* a pressure mike, the vibration of the diaphragm between two close-positioned metal plates (known as condensers or capacitors) creates an electrical field. The vibrating diaphragm causes voltage variations in this electric field. Once induced, those voltages must then pass through channels to a head amplifier that increases the signal's intensity before it leaves the mike by way of the microphone cable—the second component in the electronic chain.

There is also a *uni-directional electrostatic microphone* which allows for only a portion of the sound waves to reach the back through an acoustic delay path. This delay is created by using a porous backplate or by drilling a solid plate with a complete pattern of holes. A similar microphone called the *electret* has the advantage of maintaining a permanent electrostatic charge due to the special plastic material the diaphragm is made from. These microphones have excellent quality.

The *ribbon microphone* is a pressure-gradient. It features a narrow strip of corrugated metal stretched between the poles of a powerful magnet. As with other mikes, the movement of the ribbon between these two poles creates an electromagnetic field. As the electrical current passes through a step-up transformer, the microphone output is created. The ribbon microphone can become uni-directional by making the microphone asymmetrical, partially restricting access to the back or by causing the sound to take longer getting to the back. What this does is to decrease the back sensitivity and to increase the front sensitivity, creating a uni-directional response. The two types of uni-directional ribbon mikes are known as *cardioid* and *hypercardioid*.

Mikes with *double elements,* i.e. one pressure and one pressure-gradient, have variable directional characteristics. Variable directivity is produced by varying the proportion of one output to another. The cardioid mike is an example of this type of hybrid.

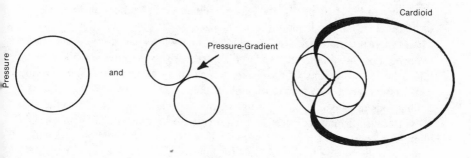

Fig. 13.

Another double element microphone is the *back-to-back electrostatic.* The two pressure elements share the same backplate and vary polarity with respect to one another. Because the electrostatic is an omni-directional mike, two of them back-to-back would form a bi-directional pattern. By restricting the back pick-up, it can be made uni-directional. Thus, the double element electrostatic has all three directional capabilities. All these microphones are used in close proximity to the sound source. The need to have unseen microphones prompted the development of the super-directional microphones. The best overall pick-up discrimination between incident (origination signal) and ambient (unwanted noise) sound is 4:1. Having to move the microphone further away calls for greater selectivity to maintain the desired incident-to-ambient ratio. The *reflector microphone* draws the signal input to the microphone by placing the microphone at the focal point of a parabolic dish. The concept works best with a cardioid microphone facing the reflector, the back of the uni-directional mike being toward the unwanted sound. The reflector mike is only effective for sounds smaller in wavelength than the diameter of the reflector, but is efficient for narrow angle acceptance. The *rifle microphone* picks up sound only in the direction it is aimed. This long, slim, cylindrical-tubed mike features a series of holes or a split on one side through which unwanted sounds are made to filter in, out of phase, and insures good uni-directional pick-up of the intended source.

Mike Selection for Program Type

Talk shows have traditionally used uni-directional mikes on floor or table stands. They get the job done efficiently, but are part of the picture. The demand for out-of-shot microphones has in most instances replaced hand-held mikes by more inconspicuous types, such as the *tie-tack* and *lavalier* microphones. Lavalier microphones are suspended around the neck by a lightweight cable. Tie-tack microphones are literally that. These electronic miniatures can be worn on or be completely concealed in a person's clothing. Electro-Voice makes a microphone so tiny that it can be the size of a pencil eraser. SONY's lavalier is one-half the size of a pen-light battery. The convenience and efficiency of these small, lightweight microphones make them an integral part of daily television production.

Drama programs require microphones that will enhance the "real" look, showing nothing that might suggest a studio. This requires mobile use of microphones on mounts that will not be caught by the camera. The "fishing rod" mount has a microphone on a short pole. Used to cover awkward areas, fishing rods are advantageous for use below the line of shot or just to the side of it. Because fishing rods are hand-held, operators appreciate their lightweight aluminum or bamboo poles combined with a line (or rifle) microphone with a pistol grip that, aside from being lightweight, gets good directional control.[24]

A sound boom microphone is, in effect, a fishing rod mounted to a storeroom truck. The machinery it is mounted upon is known as a "pram"—a raised platform, often with a seat for the operator, mounted on wheels. The microphone may be maneuvered by both the racking handle and the electronic switch. The boom may be "racked" in and out, or swiveled on horizontal and vertical planes. A *boom microphone* is usually used for groups—in variety and drama programs. The boom is a flexible extendable arm which can place the microphone over the action and close enough to provide acceptable pick-up.

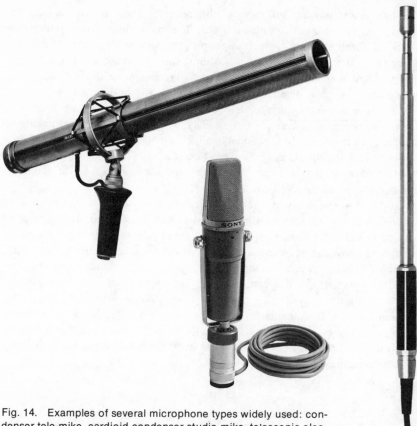

Fig. 14.   Examples of several microphone types widely used: condenser tele-mike, cardioid condenser studio mike, telescopic electret condenser mike. *Courtesy SONY Corporation.*

The mike used must have a great capacity to discriminate between wanted and
unwanted sound so that it will not cramp camera headroom by being placed too
close to or inside the picture range. Some of the more popular mikes used on
booms are made by Electro-Voice, Sennheiser and RCA. Boom microphones
must be robust and durable enough to withstand the shaking caused by physical
manipulation while suspended in the air. All boom mikes are shock-mounted.
The most useful type of boom microphone is the cardioid because it is narrow
enough to discriminate between incident and ambient sound, but is open
enough to pick up more than one source.

The most useful boom mikes are unidirectional because they provide sufficient discrimination and good sound quality at a reasonable working distance
from the artist and can pick up dialogue from several performers who may be
separated by several feet. For best audio quality, the dead areas on the mike
must be evenly "dead" over the full frequency spectrum. To obtain this, it is
best to use a good quality condenser mike for the boom, provided there is suit-

able shock mounting and sufficient windshielding.[25] There are several considerations in effective operation of the boom. The boom must avoid cumbersome positioning of the "pram" which might prevent flexible movement of the camera or mike. It is necessary to avoid casting a shadow on the set. These difficulties, coupled with advances in tie-tack and lavalier mike quality and convenience, have begun to restrict boom mikes principally to dramatic programs.

Slung microphones are used to cover static sources and are suspended downward from the juncture of three cables. They are not good for picking up moving sound sources. If directional qualities are not needed, the personal condenser mike hung upside down is a good choice. They should be suspended by elastic interposed between the microphone and the sling cables to avoid the transmission of sound along the sling lines.

When a scene requires a long-shot, cables can present a visual problem. Microphones with miniature radio transmitters alleviate this problem. The components of the radio transmitter system are small personal mikes of either type mentioned above, the FM transmitter linked to the mike by lightweight wire, and the receiving antenna in the control room. The transmitter may be concealed in a pocket or underneath clothing. The microphone and the transmitter may be combined into a single object, such as a baton, concealing both. One transmitter, made by Sennheiser, is so small that it can be concealed inside the human ear. The major drawback in using the radio transmitter is that the site at which it is to be used must be surveyed in advance for reception quality and possible acoustical interference.

LIGHTING

"No matter how long the night, the day is sure to come." This African proverb from the Congo expresses the ancient affinity for light. In the television studio, the preference for adequate light is more than an affinity—it is vital to the successful operation of the station.

Chapter 6, Staging, covers the functions, types and instruments of studio lighting. We would re-emphasize here the integral relationship between lighting and the other production elements: the need for the camera to produce a picture of transmission quality; the avoidance of shadows by sound equipment; the distortion sometimes suffered by microphones in the direct heat of strong lamps; and the high-pitched sounds radiated when electric dimmers create movement of the lamp filaments. It is important always to keep in mind that television and sound operations and lighting are interrelated and require mutual understanding.[26]

A relatively recent introduction in lighting equipment is the tungsten-halogen or quartz lamp, which is smaller and lighter in weight than previous lamps using comparable wattage. Inasmuch as the light requirement for color, as opposed to monochrome pictures, is nearly double, the increased efficiency of the quartz lamp is highly significant.[27] In addition, the tungsten-halogen or quartz light has a longer life. Because it also maintains a constant color temperature or light intensity for the life of the lamp, there are no light-intensity color changes on the recorded program, a particular concern when editing tapes.[28]

Another relatively recent innovation is the high intensity HMI lamp. HMI lamps are filled with mercury, argon and various rare earth elements to provide a quality approaching natural daylight. HMI lamps produce several times as much light as the tungsten filament lamps of the same wattage.[29]

With the advent of electronic news gathering (ENG), the need for portable lighting systems became necessary because shooting does not always occur under satisfactory light conditions. Lightweight—as little as 28 ounces—models are designed to be handheld and to operate on battery belts for a power source. Some are equipped with a tungsten-halogen source.

THE CONTROL ROOM

The control room is the brain cell of television, responsible for directing all studio life. Through memory—including computer memory—creativity and foresight, this controlling entity pools the assets of its internal studio workings, adjusts them and sends them out through the head of its electronic nervous system, the transmitter.

The control room facilities exist to effectively coordinate the numerous video and audio elements that combine to produce a television program. Studio or remote camera shots must be monitored continuously and the desired camera shots switched to the on-air channel. Most switchers not only control which cameras appear on the air, but also control over 50 electronic special effects. Control apparatus must also be provided for the quality and amplitude of the various audio sources. The projection apparatus for film and slides are controlled in the control room. An essential element of all of these control functions is the intercommunications system that will allow all personnel to efficiently coordinate their efforts.

All the equipment in the control room performs some overseeing function, allowing the directors of different areas to supervise their respective operations and to determine the variable characteristics of studio output. Among the basic equipment are: monitors—for previewing and critiquing of either video or audio transmissions; switchers—for the selection of equipment to be placed on on-the-air channels; and special effects—for video and audio. Other production-oriented equipment, such as the cartridge (cart) machines and recorders, are also in the main or subsidiary control room.

The control room is usually located adjacent to the studio, on a higher level and with a large glass window looking into the studio. In some stations the control room is located in another part of the building; the only connections between the two are the camera monitors, the audio and the intercom. "Flying-

Fig. 15.   RCA control console, showing video, audio and director positions. *RCA Corp.*

blind" has its drawbacks; in the event something goes wrong, the persons in the control room sometimes don't know what has malfunctioned. With the glass window adjacent to the studio, the problem sometimes can be more easily identified.

The control room is divided into three basic areas: video, audio and program. Each function should have enough operating space. The director must be aware of everything going on related to the program. He or she must see all the shots of the cameras and must be able to hear what is being said on the mike. Most importantly, the director must be in contact with the camera operators to give instructions for shots. The program control board consists of a monitor for all cameras, a preview monitor and a program outmonitor. There is also a speaker that is connected to the on-air mikes (by way of audio control). There are intercoms to all cameras and a monitor for the film chain/video tape. Seated next to the director is the technical director (TD).

The basic tool of the TD is the switcher. The switcher is used to punch-up any camera on the program out-monitor. The simplest switcher consists of a row (bank) of buttons, one for each camera chain, which punch up the following: black, colorbars and video-tape. With the use of other banks and program levers, the TD can do dissolves, super-impositions, fade-ins, fade-outs and other special effects such as wipes, split screens, one-corner insertions, among others. Not only does the TD punch-up the shots, but also is the crew chief. On occasion, the TD or switcher relays the commands of the director to the studio personnel. (See Chapter 5, Directing, for operational specifics.)

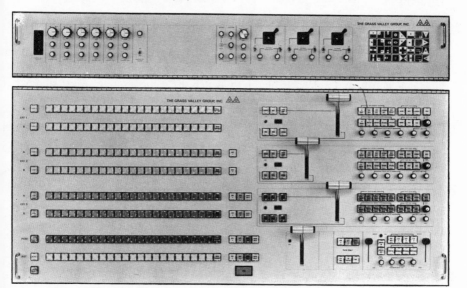

Fig. 16.   GVG Production Switcher, model 1600-7J. *The Grass Valley Group, Inc.*

CONTROL EQUIPMENT: VIDEO

Monitors

Each studio camera, film pick-up chain and remote camera is represented on a control room picture monitor which looks like a home television receiver without control knobs. There are also preview or pre-set monitors and on-air or program monitors. The preview monitors allow control room directors to preview and perfect a camera shot before it goes on-air on the program monitor. Because of the great number of monitors needed for all the video sources, monitors are only about 12 inches wide. Usually, only the preview and program monitors are color, because color is more expensive and it is easier to determine picture quality in black-and-white.

Many studios have additional, separate monitors for engineering control, with one monitor for each camera. These monitors determine that the color, scanning, light and voltage levels are correct. One person is able to operate the control units for about four cameras, and in some stations with small staffs, there may be no single individual assigned to work the monitors. These monitors permit production and engineering personnel to carry on their functions without disturbing each other, which might happen if they shared the same monitors.

Switchers

The switcher is a flexible device which allows the technical director to choose any of the individual cameras for the on-air channel and to produce special effects from camera shots. The simplest switchers utilize one mix/effects system consisting of a row of buttons, one for each camera chain, and a handle to control fading in and out of whatever picture button is depressed. (See Chapter 5.) Usually there is a release button to switch a camera off-the-air instantaneously and a depress button to switch the camera on-air. Most studios utilize complex switchers, some of which are custom-built to their specifications. Some permit inputs from over 20 video sources. These inputs are used to feed the eight output buses which include six buses to feed the three mix/effects systems, a pre-set, and a program bus. Each mix/effects system is complete in that it contains its own special effects generator. (A bus is an output which connects with another piece of equipment, such as from a switcher to a VTR.)

A quad split-generator allows four picture sources to be displayed simultaneously, while a downstream keyer unit provides the fade control of inserts as well as complete system fade-to-black control. Other switchers allow for the use of four levels simultaneously. Two levels are used for keying (cuts, dissolves, and wipes) to and from processed signals while levels three and four are used for background video signals with the ability to cut, dissolve, or wipe.[30]

Normal and bypass modes of operation are provided on some switchers. In the bypass mode, the preview/bypass bus functions as an independent switcher for video and audio sources. This is most useful in network operation where the network sources can be switched to bypass, thus freeing the primary switcher for production use. In normal operation the bypass bus serves as a preview/prelisten capability. Some control rooms also have a sub-switcher that is used for tape projections and film projections. This enables the technical director to do two programs at once. One program may be aired while the other is taped. Sub-switchers are also used for instant replay and slow-motion. Another type of switcher is the routing switcher which feeds and switches audio and video signals from any camera or switcher to those in other control rooms.

Special Effects Generators

As switchers became more complex and special effects were included through special generators, the term "special effects generator" began to be applied in many instances to the entire switcher unit.

There are a variety of special effects generators available, varying in size, price and complexity. All of them allow the operator to give variety to program format by changing picture coloration, mixing, wiping and fading signals from different electronic sources. This may involve creating a pattern of triangles from one camera image interlocked with triangles from another camera image, or a picture divided into quarters with an image from each of four different cameras in each quarter. One image may be manipulated to "grow" or wipe across the original image in an unusual pattern merely by pushing a button. In some switchers, special effects are selected by a rotary knob. Others use buttons to select each pattern with separate control levers for the independent control of the size of the various mix/effects systems.

Some switchers can create up to 54 different effects, including rotational and split-screen effects. Some of the more common types of special effects used are: corner insertions, split screens, circular iris effects, wipes to a new background behind a title, wipes from a title over one background to another title over another background, wipes over a chroma-key and a title over a chroma-key, wipes to a new background behind a chroma-key and a title, and wipes from a title keyed over a chroma-key over a third source to a fourth source.[31] The development of the chroma-key enhanced special effects possibilities. For example, it enables the operator to instruct a camera monitor to "ignore" a certain color, such as blue. Thus, if a subject on a blue background is shot by this camera, the background becomes a blank space which can be filled in with an image from another camera by superimposing the first image over the other. This is how the "Invisible Man" sequence is done. (See Chapter 5 for more specific application.)

Character Generators

The electronic character generator consists of a keyboard, with additional keys to the side of the keyboard that can shift the typeface style or size, depending on the level of sophistication of the machine. Before the electronic character generator was developed, written or graphic information (e.g. program titles and credits, sports scores, weather information) was printed on poster boards in the station art department. These cards were then placed in front of a camera for eventual telecast. With the electronic character generator the information is typed in the desired style and format. This information is then stored in the memory bank of the character generator. The memory can be instructed to change the character information—to "roll" the information vertically, to "crawl" the information across the screen and to operate at varying speeds.

If information is converted to digital form, the character generators may be interfaced with a larger, more complex computer. Complicated instructions may be programmed into this computer as well as large quantities of information. By connecting the computer to a VTR, the pre-programmed display information will be automatically recorded at pre-selected intervals or address points on the video tape. Automated control circuitry permits the special effects generator to be interfaced with a computer pre-programmed to carry out various switching functions. The digital computer provides electronically generated graphics. In the 1970s computer techniques were extended to generate cartoons and abstract artistic effects directly into the video format.

Telecine

The term telecine is derived from television and cinema. The telecine is controlled from the control room. Switchers select which film projector or slide machine will be used. The machines can be started or stopped and projection lights turned on or off in individual equipment. Some studios operate the telecine area by a computer that turns the machine on and off and changes slide drums automatically. In some cases multiplexer mirrors are also controlled by the switcher or technical director. These mirrors permit several projection devices to share a single television camera. Some color telecine systems use as many as three film sources plus live scenes. A fully integrated film/slide/live unit is capable of transferring super 8mm film, 16mm film and 35mm slides to a standard television format as well as picking up opaque displays, rear screen projections and limited action live scenes.[32]

Electronic Still Store

It is usual for television studios to keep thousands of slides and still photographs on file for background sets, graphics or reference use. Keeping so many scattered "stills" in some kind of system for easy retrieval has been a great inconvenience: providing space for storage, not being able to find desired slides or photos, and scratches and dust on the stills. In the late 1970s Ampex began marketing the Electronic Still Store which records, stores and plays back still pictures for television broadcast. The system uses digital techniques to store video images on a computer-disc memory and assigns an address to each still to facilitate rapid and accurate access. The system can store 1,500 still frames and the access to any one picture can be obtained in less than a tenth of a second. The system has two simultaneous and independent outputs, important when dissolves to another still or previews are required. Selections may be preprogrammed for sequential delivery.

CONTROL EQUIPMENT: AUDIO

Sound output often differs from sound input. It is, therefore, the responsibility of the audio control room to collect all inputs, and control, process and combine them into either single or multiple outputs for recording, reproduction or transmission.[33]

There are three major concerns of sound control: to keep within the dynamic range of the system—above intrusive noise and below overload distortion; to adjust the volume range to suit listening conditions and the environment; and to ensure that separately produced items match and are balanced in broadcasting. Of course, the only way to determine whether or not these goals have been achieved is to monitor what is being broadcast. Good quality loudspeakers are essential.

Audio Equipment and Functions

In some stations the control area is separate from, though adjacent to, the video area. Whether separated or in the same room, however, the audio control desk is a separate unit. The audio engineer can control audio coming from remote locations (two-way communication) and from the telecine, as well as from the studio. In addition to faders for volume control from each audio source, the audio console includes turntables, magnetic recorders, automatic tape cartridge equipment and patch panels for amplifier imputs.

Most audio sources come from tape cartridges (carts) and in many studios they have replaced reel-to-reel tapes. Carts are plastic containers enclosing continuous loops of magnetic audiotape. The time lengths may be as short as 15 seconds or as long as one-half hour. Commercials, station identification and other material frequently repeated are prerecorded and stored in easily accessible racks. Anyone at the station can simply place the cart in the playback cart machine and activate the machine. After playing, the tape runs until it returns to the starting point where it is then ready for the next play.

Volume control and switching are the primary functions of the sound control room, performed by four basic controls. The pre-set or balance attenuator provides the added precaution of pre-controlled volume in addition to the channel controls. Such a precaution is taken because of the vast range of levels possible in television sound. The other three controls—channel, group and main faders—restrict unwanted sound and balance each respective channel with other incoming sounds. Because the main fader deals with all channels, its levels are usually untouched, once set.

Volume control involves equipment with a wide range of capabilities. The regulation of sound levels requires a meter and adaptation to each type of material. The primary control facilities permit:

Pre-hear—Allows for audition of a channel before it is faded up.

Prompt Cut—Interrupts the dialogue mike output only, so that a performer may be given a cue without the audience hearing it.

Foldback—Playback, for the studio.

P.A.—Public address system by means of feeding some microphones to the audience's loudspeakers.

Echo—Artificial reverberation made available to each channel as a special effects feature.

Sound control is also concerned with *frequency response* regulation—through equipment such as the equalizer that can accentuate or diminish treble and base response; *automatic control*—by means of limiters and compressors that gauge the output levels and readjust them, if necessary, automatically; and *multi-way clean feed systems*—which allow for a number of outside sources to contribute to a hook-up with every other output, except their own. Each of these controls contributes to the master task of sound control and coordination with the video signal output.

Although television sound equipment and techniques have made noticeable strides forward, the state-of-the-art is not all it could be. There are two major hinderances to completely innovative television sound. One is that digital audio demands exceptionally good fidelity that is technologically difficult to achieve;

the second is that TV is principally a visual medium and sound has been a modestly maintained stepchild.

One important development in television sound, however, has been the thrust toward miniaturization through the use of digital techniques and integrated circuitry. Equipment has become increasingly more compact, making it more stable and easier to operate. Further innovations include slightly better fidelity in the output, better audio pick-up, solid-state engineering and extensive use of multi-track systems. Digital tape recorders, digital power amplifiers and digital pitch changers, used in record-oriented industries, can create perfect harmony from off-harmony input signals.

A most important recent innovation is the digital voice carrier system, known as pulse code modulated system (PCM), which allows for the more efficient transmission of voice signals by encoding samples of the signal. The most commonly used PCM system in this country has 24 voice circuits, allowing for a wide rate of information to be carried. Although not yet used in television in mid-1977, future incorporation of the PCM system could spark television's digital audio revolution. It is not unreasonable to expect an automated television broadcasting system to be used in the future; we presently have the automated audio system in radio stations.

Intercom

Circuits from the director and technical director to the camera operators and video control technicians—from audio control to the boom operators, engineering circuits that can be isolated so that the video control engineer can talk privately with a camera operator whose camera may be in trouble, circuits to telecine, to the lighting director, to the VTR and film chain operators, between the director and the floor manager who cues the action, and a public address system by which the director can speak to everyone in the studio at the same time—make up the studio/control intercommunication system.

AUTOMATED SYSTEMS

Modern studio control rooms are becoming computerized. The computer, or a series of computers, determines the program schedule, placement of commercials, and starts up carts, film, and tape machines. There are various computerized approaches. In one, teletype or IBM typewriter input is used with a simple computer language. Another includes a random spot locator. One tape containing up to 100 items is utilized and 50 pairs of switches allow for 50 items to be selected in any order. The primary use of this system is for spot commercials to be introduced into program material. After playback of each section, the next one is automatically set up. In another, cartridge carousels, holding up to 24 carts and allowing a sequence of 52 playbacks, are set manually and run by computer, permitting replay of spot commercials.[34] In another system, cartridges are inserted into a tape machine where a computer reads the machine to see what carts are present. This computer will tell another computer where a cart is loaded, and that computer finds and starts the cart. The computer starts various tapes rolling. It analyzes what is on-the-air and counts down to the last three seconds of the item and starts up the next item to go on-air. The monitor shows what items are coming up and the time left on the information already on-the-air.

Computers also note the time and transmission of information and print up station logs. Program logs are sometimes determined up to 30 days in advance. The computer-prepared log may include the time the item goes over the air, the duration, whether it is a video or audio source, the number of the film, a description of the item, and whether it is a commercial. The computer may later print up another log showing what actually went on the air. If items to be aired are changed at the last minute, they must be recalled from the computer and others inserted. When an item that is due to air is not found by the computer, the technical director must insert something else. The technical director can manually override the system at any time.

The computer used in an automatic broadcasting system is a specially developed real-time machine that can store large amounts of information inexpensively. Depending on the size of the memory, a few days, a week, or up to a month's worth of programming can be held in the computer at one time.[35] In addition, once a number of commercial slots have been programmed into the day's schedule, the computer can be asked for information on what spots are unfilled. This information can be requested from a distance using normal telephone circuits.

Digital Networks

Digital communications networks have been regarded as extremely efficient, compared with the current analog networks, for future use. The 1980s should see the use of digital techniques throughout the entire industry. Such a development would be contingent on the increasing standardization of digital equipment; it is expected that analog signals will be completely replaced with digital-pulse information. The change-over process is being hastened by researchers and manufacturers who are developing such techniques as equipment designed for "real time" rather than pre-designed standards of time; a video frame synchronizer to allow for direct video tape to broadcast lineage without passing through station synchronization; Long Lines systems to provide digital distribution of interstate television network transmission. These all point to a new level of technology, faster, more efficient and capable of performing highly complex functions.

As television moves from the 1970s to the 1980s, it is in a state of transition. Caught between complete analog and complete digital systems, the modern station must find the way to make the best of both worlds while preparing for the future. The transition process entails the utilization of a video service through an analog system—analog transmission lines and analog switching—or an analog/digital mixed system until such time as a nationwide digital network for video signals can be established. Switching systems should employ integrated circuitry. Though sound equipment may be analog, it should be miniaturized, easier to handle and capable of high fidelity output. The station—studio and control room—should have the look of a computerized telecommunications complex through which highly sensitized, highly effecient intelligence flows.

TRANSMISSION

The signal used for the transmission of black-and-white television is a very complex signal in which the overall intelligence is made up of various individual parts or components. Basically, the transmitted television signal consists of two separate carriers: one modulated with the sound, and the other with the visual, or video, portion. A television receiver receives both carriers simultaneously, builds up, or amplifies the level of both, and then separates the two for demodulation. The sound portion of the television signal is a standard FM wave.

FM is used rather than AM for the television sound because of its better immunity to noise and interferences, and it is more efficient as far as transmitter power requirements are concerned. In addition, FM signals generally have a much better signal-to-noise ratio than do comparable AM signals.

Although the sound portion of a television signal is frequency modulated, the video portion is amplitude modulated onto its separate carrier. AM is used for the video portion mainly because of the possibility of multipath reception of the transmitted signal. This occurs when the same signal, because of the reflections from buildings and other objects, reaches a receiving antenna from more than one path. Since the distance traveled by these multipath signals is usually different, different parts of the signal arrive at the antenna at the same time. For AM signals, this causes interference at the television receiver in the form of multiple images, or ghosts, on the screen. For FM signals, the interference would be much more bothersome since it would be in the form of continously shimmering bars on the screen.

The Video Signal

Essentially, the scene to be transmitted is scanned by electronic circuits which produce a voltage output that is proportional to the brightness or darkness of the particular area being scanned. The scanning breaks the scene into many horizontal lines, each of which varies in brightness along its length. Basically, the scene is broken into a series of sequential lines, and a continously varying voltage is produced whose amplitude is proportional to the instantaneous brightness of each point in the lines. This varying voltage is the modulating signal or intelligence used to amplitude-modulate an r-f (radio-frequency) carrier in a multiplex manner.

After transmission on one of the television broadcast channels, a varying

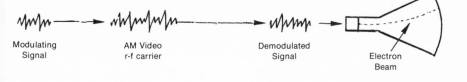

Modulating
Signal

AM Video
r-f carrier

Demodulated
Signal

Electron
Beam

The modulated signal
produced by the
scanning process

→

amplitude modulates
an r-f carrier in
the VHF or UHF
band for transmission.

→

Then, after transmission,
the original signal
is recovered

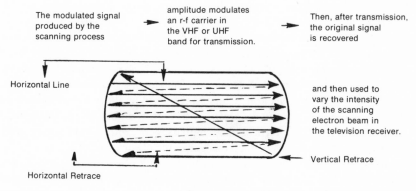

Horizontal Line

and then used to
vary the intensity
of the scanning
electron beam in
the television receiver.

Vertical Retrace

Horizontal Retrace

Fig. 17.

voltage that corresponds to the modulating signal is recovered from the modulated carrier by the demodulation process. This voltage then, according to its amplitude, regulates the intensity of a beam of electrons produced in the picture tube of the TV receiver. Visual reproduction of the original scene occurs as a result of a coating on the face of the picture tube. When this coating is struck by the electron beam it emits light, with the amount of light being proportional to the intensity of the beam. Therefore, when the electron beam has a high intensity, which corresponds to a point of extreme brightness in the original scene, a large amount of light is emitted from the point on the picture tube struck by the beam. Similarly, points of low brightness will emit little light. As you probably have observed from your own experience, even without a video signal a television screen is bright as long as it is turned on. This brightness is called the *raster* and is produced by the electron beam being scanned across the face of the tube by circuits inside of the television receiver. Without a video signal the beam has a constant intensity, so the screen brightness is uniform across the face of the tube.

The scanning of the original scene at the transmitting end and the reproduced scene at the receiving end must take place very rapidly so that the human eye only sees complete pictures on the TV screen rather than seeing the picture being produced line-by-line. In actual practice a scene is broken into 525 individual lines. The television video signal carries 30 complete still pictures each second, but because of the persistency of vision of the human eye the rapid sequence of these still pictures gives the impression of continuous action. Each picture is broken into two frames, each containing an alternate line of a picture. When they combine on the screen, the lines of one frame are interleaved with those of the other frame. This is called *interlacing*. Therefore, with two frames per picture and 30 complete pictures, 60 frames produce 30 complete pictures per second.

The scanning process that produces the pictures is not continuous. After each complete line there must be a time lapse before the next line begins to allow the scanning beam to return to its new starting position. Moreover, after the 525th line has been scanned, there must be a time lapse to allow the beam to return to its initial starting point. These time lapses between lines are called horizontal and vertical retrace times and represent periods when no picture information is being transmitted.

The electron beam of the receiver is cut off during retrace by portions of the video signal called *blanking pulses*. These pulses are high signal voltage levels that cut off the electron beam and therefore produce no brightness on the screen. There are *horizontal blanking* pulses for cutting off the beam during horizontal retrace, and vertical blanking pulses for cutting it off during vertical retrace. To assure that the circuits that scan the electron beam are synchronized with those that scan the original scene at the studio, sync pulses are also transmitted and they ride on top of the blanking pulses. The sync pulses occur during retrace, at which time no picture information is being received.

Color

In color, brightness components are transmitted in much the same manner as the black-and-white picture signal. However, color information must be transmitted by a color television signal. Color television signals are compatible with both black-and-white and color TV receivers. This means that a non-color receiver produces a black-and-white picture of the color signal and a color receiver produces a color picture. Color is the combination of those properties of light which control brightness, hue and saturation. Brightness is that characteristic of color which enables it to be placed on a scale ranging from black to white or from dark to light. Hue is the variable of a color described as red, yellow, blue or green. Saturation refers to the extent to which a color departs from white or the "neutral" condition. Pale colors, or pastels, are low in saturation, while strong or vivid colors are high in saturation. Brightness is the only attribute of a color signal that can be transmitted over a monochrome or black-and-white system.

To produce a color image, provision must be made for the transmission of additional information pertaining to all three of the variables of color. However, because the primary-color process can be employed, it is not necessary to transmit information in exactly the form expressed by the three variables. Virtually any color can be matched by the proper combination of no more than three primary colors. While other colors could have been used as primaries, red, green and blue were selected for color television.

NOTES

[1] John Quick, *Small Studio Video Tape Production*, (Reading, Mass.: Addison-Wesley Publishing Co., 1976), p. 24.

[2] Gerald Millerson, *The Technique of Television Production*, (New York: Hastings House, 9th Edition, 1972), p. 27.

[3] "101 Years of Television Technology," O'Brien and Monroe, *SMPTE Journal*, July, 1976, p. 478.

[4] "Goods on Display at NAB," *TeleVisions*, Summer, 1976, p. 12.

[5] "New Products and Developments," *SMPTE Journal*, February 1976, p. 124.

[6] "Goods on Display at NAB," *op. cit.*, p. 12.

[7] "Goods on Disply at NAB," *op. cit.*, p. 12.

[8] Ed DiGuilio, "Steadicam—A New and Revolutionary Concept in Camera Stabilization Systems," *Cinema Perspectives*, Fall, 1976, p. 13.

[9] Sol Libes, *Fundamentals and Applications of Digital Logic Circuits*, (Rochelle Park, N.J.: Hayden Book Company), 1975, pages 10–11.

[10] "101 Years of Television Technology," O'Brien and Monroe, *op. cit.*, p. 470.

[11] *RCA Broadcast News*, March, 1975, pp. 7–8.

[12] John Quick, *Small Studio Video Tape Production*, *op. cit.*, p. 38.

[13] Bob Skalnik, "Audio Production Problems," *Educational Broadcasting*, May/June 1976, p. 24.

[14] Harry Kybett, *Video Tape Recorders*, (New York: Bobbs-Merrill, 1974), p. 40.

[15] Parry Teasdale, "TBC's," *TeleVisions*, Summer 1976, p. 11.

[16] Carol Schmidt, "So You Want to Buy a TBC?," *Educational Broadcasting*, September/October 1976, p. 15.

[17] Parry Teasdale, "TBC's," *op. cit.*, p. 12.

[18] "VT on TV," *Tele Visions*, Summer, 1976, pp. 4–9.

[19] "Application of Quadruplex Cassette VTR's in Programming, Editing and Production," *SMPTE Journal*, October 1974, p. 835.

[20] Hans Fattel, "Battle for the Video Disk," *Science Digest*, December, 1975, p. 73.

[21] Gordon White, *Video Recording, Record and Replay Systems*, (New York: Crane, Russak and Company, 1972), pp. 118–122.

[22] Glyn Alkin, *TV Sound Operations*, (New York: Hastings House, 1975), p. 9.

[23] *Ibid*, p. 12.

[24] Glyn Alkin, *TV Sound Operations*, *op. cit.*, p. 30.

[25] *Ibid*, p. 38.

[26] *Ibid*, p. 44.

[27] Daniel L. Aron, "Motion Picture and Television Set Lighting Equipment," *SMPTE Journal*, July, 1976, p. 535.

[28] RCA Catalogue CA. 6101A, "Television Color Studio Lighting."

[29] Daniel L. Aron, *op. cit.*, p. 536.

[30] *BM/E*, May 1976, p. 78.

[31] *Ibid*.

[32] *Broadcasting*, August 8, 1975, p. 29.

[33] Glyn Alkin, *TV Sound Operations*, *op. cit.*, p. 60.

[34] Alec Nisbett, *The Technique of the Sound Studio*, (New York: Hastings House, 3rd Edition, 1974), p. 57.

[35] *Ibid*.

GLOSSARY

analog—pertains to transmission by amplitude or frequency modulation, or any form other than by digital techniques.

AM—see modulation.

binary system—a numerical system utilizing only two digits (0, 1) in combinations to represent any possible value.

broadcast quality—industry standards establishing the expected transmission quality for commercial broadcasts.

camera chain—the camera and its power source.

carrier—a wave used to carry signals from station to receivers.

channel—a passage through which a message (or signal) is conducted; a route.

digital—describes any equipment using a system of encoding a signal with binary pulses before it is transmitted; once it is broadcast, the receiver must be able to decode the signal.

fidelity—the faithful reproduction of sound.

FM—see modulation.

frequency response—pertains to the range of frequency capabilities of a given product; i.e. the height and depth of its parameters and the level at which its quality is best.

Hertz—the unit measure for frequency; number of cycles per second.

input—the original signal from a given source.

interface—the matching of one machine to another so that they may function as a team.

integrated circuit—a miniaturized electronic chip with more than one capability.

modulation—the act of superimposing a signal onto a carrier wave so that it may be transported from one place to another.

AM (*Amplitude Modulation*)—occurs when a signal modulates a carrier in such a way that the height, or amplitude, of carrier wave changes.
FM (*Frequency Modulation*)—occurs when a signal modulates a carrier wave by changing how frequently it repeats its wave form.
PM (*Pulse Modulation*)—uses only samples or sections of the signal—known as "pulses" to modulate the carrier; there are several types of pulse modulation; digital utilizes pulse code modulation (PCM).

noise—any unwanted sound.

PCM—a kind of pulse modulation that involves coding each pulse; see modulation.

signal—a wave carrying intelligence.

signal-to-noise ratio—a statement of the relationship of wanted sound output to unwanted noise.

BIBLIOGRAPHY

Alkin, Glyn, *TV Sound Operations.* New York: Hastings House, 1975.

Bermingham, Alan, ed., *The Small TV Studio.* New York: Hastings House, 1975.

Coleman, Howard W., ed., *Color Television.* New York: Hastings House, 1968.

Ennes, Harold, *Television Broadcasting—Tape and Disc Recording Systems.* New York: Bobbs-Merrill Co., 1973.

Hilliard, Robert L., ed., *Radio Broadcasting,* 2nd edition. New York: Hastings House, 1976.

Hunter, William. *Digital Logic Electronics Handbook.* Blue Ridge Summit, Penna.: TAB Books, 1975.

Jones, Peter, *The Technique of the Television Cameraman.* New York: Hastings House, 1965.

Kybett, Harry, *Video Tape Recorders.* New York: Bobbs-Merrill Co., 1974.

Libes, Sol. *Fundamentals and Applications of Digital Logic Circuits.* Rochelle Park, N.J.: Hayden Book Co., 1975.

Mileaf, Harry, ed., *Electronics One.* Rochelle Park, N.J.: Hayden Book Co., 1967.

Millerson, Gerald, *The Technique of Television Production,* 9th edition. New York: Hastings House, 1972.

————, *TV Camera Operation.* New York: Hastings House, 1973.

Motil, John M., *Digital Systems Fundamentals.* New York: McGraw-Hill, 1972.

Nisbett, Alec, *The Technique of the Sound Studio,* 3rd edition. New York: Hastings House, 1972.

Oringel, Robert S., *Audio Control Handbook,* 4th edition. New York: Hastings House, 1972.

Quick, John, *Small Studio Video Tape Production.* Reading, Mass.: Addison-Wesley Publishing Co., 1976.

Robinson, Joseph F., *Videotape Recording.* New York: Hastings House, 1975.

Ryan, Ray, *Basic Digital Electronics.* Blue Ridge Summit, Penna.: TAB Books, 1975.

White, Gordon, *Video Recording, Record and Playback Systems.* New York: Crane, Russak and Co., 1972.

Zettl, Herbert, *Television Production Handbook.* Belmont, Calif.; Wadsworth Publishing Co., 1976.

BERNARR COOPER

Chief
Bureau of Mass Communications
State Education Department
The University of the State of New York

● Dr. Cooper administers policy and coordinates all work in New York State for the educational uses of broadcast media including those of CATV, ETV stations, radio, satellites, the Instructional Television Fixed Service and closed circuit. He aids colleges, universities, teacher training institutions, elementary and secondary schools, both public and private, in their plans to use broadcast and other mass media.

He directs the preparation of grant proposals and administers those received from various sources, including more than $3.8 million for the first children's television series dealing with racial isolation and ethnic minority problems. The series, entitled *Vegetable Soup,* was the first television series for young people to be broadcast on both commercial and educational television stations during the same season.

Dr. Cooper's educational administration and communications experience includes broadcasting and utilization training of more than 165,000 teachers in three countries and in four languages. He has served as an advisor and consultant to the Broadcasting Corporation of Japan on the production of educational, informational and entertainment broadcasts, as an advisor to the United Nations Command on the building and staffing of 12 radio stations in the Korean and Chinese prisoner of war educational program, and as a consultant to the Australian Broadcasting Commission. He has been cited for his work with Military Intelligence and the United Nations Command. He was the general manager of KNME, one of the early ETV stations in the United States. His early broadcasting experience includes all three of the major networks, and he has produced more than 1,200 radio and television programs.

Dr. Cooper received the A.B. degree from Wabash College, where he was elected to Phi Beta Kappa, and earned the Ph.D. degree from Stanford University. He has taught at Stanford University, Florida State University and the University of New Mexico. In addition to more than 75 articles on communications and broadcast criticism and three monographs in Japanese, Chinese and Korean, he is the author of a text on radio production, written and published in the Japanese language. He was a recipient of one of the first grants to conduct a television utilization training course for teachers in the United States. Dr. Cooper is listed in more than 14 *Who's Who* compilations and directories of scholars. He is a Fellow of the Worldwide Academy of Scholars.

3

PRODUCING

BY BERNARR COOPER

ONE OF THE MOST anomalous terms in all of television is, perhaps, the word "production." The "producer"—who and what that person is—has been widely and variously described by television personnel. Depending on whether one is talking to the top echelon of administration in one of the networks, an advertising agency media representative, or a performer on a particular program, one may run a whole gamut of adjectives and expletives.

To the uninitiate, the producer is a person behind an invisible and impenetrable mask of function. Precisely what the producer does or how it is done is a kind of never-never, misty, not quite comprehensible matter of not inconsiderable importance. One reads on occasion in some syndicated television column of a change in producers on some program being planned or being produced for airing at a later date. The implication of such reportage seems to be that an important change for that particular program has taken place. Has it? What precisely does such a change mean? How will it affect the final viewer product that "hits" the air? Indeed, we come the full circle of the original question—the producer: who and what?

At the outset, let us make one thing clear. The position of a producer is not one in which the novice, the newly-entered-to-the medium, is likely to begin. The concept of production is based upon a whole continuum of experience, understanding and breadth of undertaking in the television medium. The college diploma may represent the completion of an experience in one kind of learning. It does not represent a passport to the inner recesses of all knowledge, information or ability. In some stations, where staff is short or funds for personnel are limited, the producer may even direct a rehearsal or an on-the-air presentation. At the local level the producer frequently may do voice-over-work and switching even while directing a rehearsal or an on-the-air presentation. At the local level the producer-to-be may even start as a copywriter, in traffic, in announcing or in graphics work. Eventually, the "future producer" at the local level may move to simple tasks of directing or switching. It is wise to move through the "sales" experience, to eventually have a total concept experience involving both client relationship and need and the actuality of exigencies of studio potential and application. It is when the individual has come to know the "tools" in an ongoing work-a-day situation and how these may or may not be used—when you have a concept of what the nuts and bolts of studio hardware can be relied upon to do—that you are ready to become the most difficult and tenuous of all of television's contributors, the "producer."

What, then, is a producer? At the highest level of performing function, the producer is three persons in one—a highly imaginative initiator of ideas, an interpreter of desired ends, and an efficient executive. The producer is an individual of high intellectual achievement, insight, understanding and capability.

In the golden days of radio, the term "producer," "production-man," "director," were used interchangeably to mean the same person. This sometimes occurs even today in a small television station. Generally, however, the producer has several types of directors working under his or her supervision. The producer is the final coordinator of the work done by such people as the musical director, the dance director, the dialogue director and the like. Frequently, an idea may start with the producer, but there are variations to this procedure, as we shall learn. The producer is called upon to see that one or a combination of the following occurs in every telecast: information, education, entertainment.

The producer, then, is the individual who has the over-all responsibility for a production of any kind, any size, any depth, any duration. The producer may originate an idea. The producer is always the one who plans and coordinates, sees to it that personnel and material are ordered, planned for, paid for and functioning under all conditions of preparation and final airing. The producer deals with "things" and "concepts." The producer is distinguished (where distinction is necessary because of organization lines) from a director because the latter deals with performers and the technical aspects of presentation in rehearsal and on the air (see Chapter 5). Thus, if we consider that the producer is the idea person and the coordinator of all aspects of the production, and the director is the interpreter and amplifier of the ideas and coordination, it is not too difficult to understand how both of these persons may be the same individual in a local station set-up.

The authority of the producer is wide, the responsibilities great, and are always limited by the exigencies of the budget. There is no ideal situation which adequately describes and pinpoints the functions, activities and responsibilities of the producer. All that can be provided is an overview with specific functions in special areas.

THE PRODUCER AS AN INDIVIDUAL

It is important to determine not only *what* the producer is, but *who* he or she is. The very use of the word "who" implies the characteristics and personality of the human being as related to the particular job.

Influence of Radio

It is generally agreed that much that has formed the pattern of presentation in the television medium has come from radio. This is natural and to be expected. Television began as an experimental offshoot of radio with video portions that accompanied the already known, understood and well-patterned approaches to sound. Indeed, in the early days of television the technique of radio (with some kind of visual accompaniment) was the general method of approach, and the early simulcasts in the two media are proof of this duality of thinking.

One of the most obvious characteristics of the radio medium was its lack of ability to control its audience. Whereas in theatre and movies the audience came to the place of presentation for the express purpose of seeing and hearing the production, this was not true in radio. In radio (as in "free" television) no fee was paid at the time of listening as was typical in movies and theatres. There was no special seat. The listener to the radio show could be, often was, and still is distracted by a host of extraneous factors—the newspaper, a book, a ringing of the telephone—any one or a combination of many attention-diverting occurrences. Whereas radio lacked the ability to control its audience, television, the psychological investigator informs us, has its own built-in control. The extent of the control, described below, in many instances depends upon the skill, the ability, the concepts of the producer and, ultimately, of the interpreter—the director.

TV Audience Control

The particular viewer-control influence that seems to be at work in television has been interestingly described with the phrase "the narcotizing dysfunction." This phrase, carefully delineated by Paul Lazarsfeld and Robert K. Merton, aptly describes the influence of television medium-watching upon the individual. (The full delineation of the narcotizing dysfunction is excellently expressed and defined in *Mass Culture, the Popular Arts in America*, edited by Bernard Rosenberg and David Manning White.)

Psychologically, it is known that the human being is incapable of retaining as many sound impressions as visual impressions. Yet the goal of the producer in television remains the same as that of the producer in radio. Both must conceive, plan and implement the purpose of moving an audience, emotionally, to some specific kind of action, to some new or added directions of thought or to a combination of these.

Leadership

It was indicated earlier that the producer is highly imaginative, an initiator of ideas, an interpreter, and an administrative executive. With a host of functions and materials, as well as persons whose work must be coordinated, the producer must obviously be an individual capable of leading others as well as working closely with them. As in all forms of good leadership and administrative and executive acumen, the producer must lead when appearing to be following, must request thinking and action when actually initiating such thought and action. If we were to stop with only this aspect, we would be opening the door for the creation of a truly authoritarian monster. Those who have recognized that the producer must have the ability to lead frequently misinterpret that ability for the *need* to lead. The implications involved in considering such a need open a Pandora's box of such psychological proportions that it would take (and frequently has taken) the consultation services of outstanding psychologists to bring about a revision and change in personality. It is necessary to give obvious direction to the phrase "ability to work with others." Too frequently this phrase has been misinterpreted and reinterpreted to mean "working others." The skillful authoritarian uses people rather than encouraging them to make the necessary contribution which must be made if a producer is to function as a superior director and leader of the team. The word "team" has been sorely abused in educational literature; yet it is precisely the original, deep and thorough meaning of "team action" that the producer must bring about to successfully fulfill not only his or her own function, but the function of the medium and, therefore, the eventual goals of educating, informing and entertaining. Having organized the team, having brought it to a point where it is making a contribution to the general thought and concept of the program to come, the producer's next necessary qualification is that of being able to delegate authority. Once members of the team have begun to think, to act and execute tasks with imagination and dispatch, the producer must "let go."

Self-Discipline

One of the prime requisites of the good producer is to be a self-disciplinarian. The producer must be capable of setting all kinds of self-discipline approaches in order to be capable of doing so for others. To be successful in the role of telling others what to do, the producer must be capable of being self-directive and highly organized in a work situation. To expect other directors' services outside of the station or the network, suppliers of various equipment, writers and the like to adhere to specific schedules in order to meet broadcasting needs, the director must adhere to a rather rigid schedule.

Preparations must be made and, in order that all of the contributing services and personnel may make their contributions at the proper time and in the proper amounts for the indicated needs, the all-over director of directors—for this is what the producer is—must be highly organized. The producer must anticipate needs, must be able to foresee likely pitfalls in the total process of pulling any broadcast together. In addition to working with highly artistic people, the producer also works with rigidly objective technicians. The engineers, sound-effects people, projection personnel, recorders, technical director—all of these people are highly skilled, highly organized, and must themselves adhere to the particular requirements of the particular job they do. In order to bring together and synthesize the work of everyone into a cohesive whole that finally makes for a desirable broadcast product, the producer must be an outstanding self-disciplinarian.

There are other related personal characteristics that must be developed and finely-honed in order that the producer may reach this goal. The producer must have an inborn sense of observation. Everything which occurs in life, and for as long as the producer can remember, will be grist for the mill of expertise. The sense of observation which the producer carries at all times facilitates retention of things which are seen in life. All of these form a basis for judgments, ideas, organizational entities, cost accounting and the visual and oral impact that the good producer must see in the mind's eye before even starting to plan a production.

Taste and Mixture

Tied closely to the sense of observation—and hearing and seeing well and remembering accurately for future needs—is the sense of good taste. It has frequently been called showmanship. Precisely what is meant by showmanship is hard to define. In one manner of speaking it is a sense of the dramatic—a sense of the interesting—a sense of that which is complete in accomplishing an all-over effect. Showmanship, like good taste, cannot be taught. It is an inborn thing. It develops with use, it matures with professional aging, but it defies explanation, definition or learning. It is the incredible potential of knowing what is precisely right at the right moment to accomplish the given need. It is for the producer what the selective use of seasoning and flavors is for the good cook.

When we speak of effect, we speak of another personal qualification necessary to the good producer: the ability to take all of the technical and personnel potential available and move smoothly to the point of in-studio preparation. Thus, a director is inevitably led to the one resulting effect that the producer had in mind when first beginning to assemble the necessary ingredients for the given program. The ability to assemble the proper material and personnel in the proper amount—depending upon the budget—is the one ingredient that the outstanding producer has which can be duplicated by no other member of the total production team.

Temperament

One intermediate conclusion from all of the above is that, with the tremendous amount of responsibility and need to coordinate the efforts of many, the producer has no time for temperament. Temperament, as used here, means those displays of excessive emotionalism and temper tantrums which frequently are the refuge of the frustrated, of those who cannot achieve under given conditions, who find anger and some kind of violence an outlet and replacement for the coordinated action and thought which should take place. The producer has no time to permit an indulgence in temperamental outburst on the part of any member of the team. Within the total production team, emotionally highly-keyed individuals sometimes are found, but one must not mistake the high-keyed individual for the nonsensically temperamental.

Time

Broadcasting proceeds with the inevitable forward movement of a clock. Time is the governing factor of all that is done in the radio and television media. Without a recognition of time as the master of the total direction in which a broadcast moves, one is deluding oneself. It may be argued that if time truly controls all accomplishment in the broadcast media we are indeed slaves to a clock and perhaps these are not the media for truly artistic output. No semantic quibbling can change reality. An examination of the products of the broadcast media will clearly suggest that artistry in almost pure form has existed many times during the history of the development of broadcasting.

Since the producer, like all the members of the team, works under the constant pressure of time, a myriad of detail and seeming confusion constitute the usual atmosphere in which the producer—and, subsequently, the director—must work. A careful analysis of what usually constitutes studio confusion will indicate that in the well-planned situation the confusion is only one of simultaneous and seeming unrelated actions. Such actions culminate in a total product, the all-over plan of which may be unknown to any given member of the team. But the all-over *place* in the plan for each member is a matter of well-constructed and agreed-upon organizational approach. Within this seeming confusion, the producer must work calmly, swiftly and efficiently. And while working at what seems to be breakneck speed against the moving hands of a clock, because of total pre-planning the producer is able to handle a multitude of details, seeing that each is completely executed and fitting into the all-over design of the entire broadcast product.

BACKGROUND AND EXPERIENCE

As we review the desirable personal and psychological characteristics of the good producer, it would seem that we have set an impossible level to be achieved by a single human being. We have said that the producer is an interpreter, an executive and an administrator. The producer has the ability to see many details and handle them in terms of the total broadcast product being sought. The producer must be able to delegate authority and yet be a rigid self-disciplinarian, fitting the working schedule to the time requirements of the broadcast schedule. The producer must know how to coordinate and inspire the best efforts of the team in order to achieve the best results. The producer has an inborn sense of observation and an inborn sense of good taste which contribute to a product that must meet the most rigid requirements of a combined scientific and art form. The producer, to achieve all of the above, needs to have had varied experiences.

Technical

Certainly, to handle and continue to understand a multiplicity of developments in the equipment field which will affect the total planning process, the producer must have some technical background. This is not to imply engineering qualifications. But he or she will want to know, at least in lay terms, the basic function of amplifiers, microphones, cameras, video and audio consoles, and visual and audio equipment. The producer must know the principles of operation, limitations and the normal uses of all equipment likely to be used on a regular basis and should know the relationship of one piece of equipment to another. Such general knowledge need not be pursued in depth and can usually be acquired through reading, inspection of the equipment, and by working closely with an engineer when questions arise.

Music

It is helpful to the producer to have a knowledge of the workings of unions such as the American Federation of Musicians, and of music-control groups such as the American Society of Composers, Authors and Publishers. Such knowledge is necessary to the producer in the process of budget-planning. Another aspect extraordinarily useful to the producer is a general knowledge of the *content* of music. The good producer should have some acquaintanceship with the standard classics in the field of symphony, opera and musical comedy and should be able to work confidently in suggesting theme, cue, background, and fill music. It should even be possible to suggest the kinds of musical instruments that need to be considered in planning specific musical programs or musical background effects. A producer who would specialize in producing all-musical programs should certainly have a thorough musical background, ability on several instruments, hopefully some conducting experience—in other words, ability to both comprehend and execute some of the requirements of the composer. A strong sense of routining, programming and knowledge of methods of investigation to measure the taste of the potential audience are also needed.

Theatre

There is ample evidence to indicate that a good producer will benefit from some experience in the field of theatre. The opportunities for broad professional theatre background are extremely limited. However, with the development of the off-Broadway theatre in recent years and with the burgeoning of community theatre activity throughout the United States, more and more opportunity for experience is presented to the individual who will eventually be a producer in television.

The broad areas of theatre exprerience that can benefit the TV producer are in directing, stage-managing and acting. The director in the theatre faces many of the same problems that plague the director in television. Relationships to management, to the producer of a commercial production or to the producing agency of a community theatre are similar to those of the television producer to the advertising agency, to the management of a station or to a network. Directing experience in the theatre provides insights for the television producer in determining the ways in which a director's mind is likely to develop a given program problem and product.

Stage managing offers an insight into some of the production problems which the television producer faces. Some directorial problems become clear as the stage manager in the theatre acts as a "leg-man" for the director's needs. The stage manager quickly learns, through practical applications, some of the immediate problems that are met in rehearsal and performance. Both the director and the actor, out of a continuing experience of appearing before or preparing for various audiences, learn what different audience reactions are likely to be. The urban audience is not the rural audience. The audience at a high socio-economic level—with college background—is not the audience that has had a terminal high school education. Although many times one must reach both audiences with the same products, one must know when to abandon the undesirable or unnecessary to achieve the total end-product. Most important, the theatre producer, director, stage manager or actor will have had the advantage of watching master artists work over a long period of time, under varying conditions and to various audiences. Learning from such people who are skilled and knowing provides knowledge that can be procured in no other way, except over a long, intensive time-period of experience.

A valuable complement to experience in practical theatre is a knowledge of the entire field of dramatic literature, which provides insights into the history, political developments, manners and morals of periods of time, persuasions of leaders of various cultural and ethnic groups, and the day-to-day problems of the common person of various ages. If one has a solid background of dramatic literature and the times in which outstanding works were written (the factors influencing the writers of those periods and the sociological implications of what those writers had to say), one may become a true student of the entire panorama of our evolvement from, and involvement in, both natural and human phenomena. Most important, a wide acquaintance with world dramatic literature will give to the producer a knowledge of the works in the field of drama and an understanding of writing techniques. Such knowledge gives to the producer a basis for judging the content of scripts submitted for consideration, with a view to the type of directorial treatment that will be called for. A producer taking a practical look at a script not only examines the flow of ideas, manner of concept, and the performance qualities required, but also projects the kind of and even the specific individual who might direct this particular presentation.

Culture and Living

There is no doubt that the good producer also needs a broad cultural background. Solidly based in sociological approaches to various art forms, this will open a whole world of imaginative potential when bringing to production planning a clarification of content for the viewers.

One cannot leave the discussion of the background and qualifications of the producer without making note of the necessity for a comprehensive working and living experience. Nothing can take the place of having planned and produced hundreds of productions with a view to making each presentation a finer product than the one before. We must also take into account that fullness of living and observing life that comes only to those who are aware that all such observations will, in the final analysis, be grist for the mill of thought, of outlook, of breadth which every broadcast shall demand as the full contribution of the producer to the work.

How may we sum up the desirable background for the future television producer? First, it should consist of a basic technical knowledge of the equipment with which he or she will work. Second, it should include knowledge of the field of music. Third, the producer should have a background in which theatre experience provides a knowledge of the masters of the drama. Fourth, a broad cultural background will contribute insights and goals of desirable production achievement not otherwise possible. Fifth, there should be a breadth of working and living experience not required of nor usually attained by any other member of the production team.

RELATIONSHIP TO NON-STATION AGENCIES

The Producer and the Advertising Agency

The function of the advertising agency in the actual production of television programs has varied over the years. At one point in the historical development of the medium it was considerable. It is now negligible insofar as the actual total programming and packaging concept is concerned, although advertising agencies work closely with production firms in creating particular types of programs desired. An agency now usually concentrates upon a carefully selected buying of available programs, and station or network time. The particular time of day during which a program is to be aired and the viewer for whom it is being aired will determine what the actual content will be. The producer of such a program may enter into the planning concepts early or after the idea has been firmed up. He or she may be given the job of creating everything necessary for the total production package or may be brought in at the point at which a script has been pulled together for a series or for a special program.

At whichever point of entry, it is the producer's job to consider, in the light of total agency and client needs, the abilities of personnel, the equipment and other services required in order to accomplish the task at hand. The final production team usually includes artists who create visuals and who design sets, photographers, carpenters, specialists in the creation of product displays and, frequently, the writer.

It must be borne in mind that when we speak of the relationship of the producer to the advertising agency, distinctions are made between the large advertising agency which services the network and the local advertising agency which specializes in rendering service to a smaller client. The large advertising agency is not usually a production agency. It may designate talent; it may designate the producer; it may designate many different areas of personnel that it wishes to employ to accomplish a particular task. For the most part, however, it will leave such matters in the hands of the production organization or the network.

The local advertising agency may perform one of a number of different services. It can, for example, provide not only the producer but the writer; it may provide "live" program scripting; it may provide the entire message in "canned" form, such as a film or video tape. In many instances the local advertising agency provides photography for slides and telops, films, jingles and animation; sometimes it jobs out these various functions to a local station or other organization with adequate facilities.

The Producer and the Station "Rep"

The function of station "reps" (sales representatives) is to get advertising placed on stations that they represent. There are over 200 such agencies throughout the country, and there is a National Station Representatives Association, located in New York City. Station reps handle promotional advertising and determine the stations and the markets in which programs and commercials are to be placed. It is the function of the station rep to have available all matters of information related to the market of the station or stations. Frequently, the producer called upon to do a new, unusual or different kind of production job overlooks the potential value of the station rep. Insights which the rep can supply into the market, its kinds of people, its size, its socio-economic level, its major interest, can have meaning for the producer and may frequently offer an approach that will make the difference between success or failure in marketing a given product or meeting a given client's needs, particularly where such needs are clearly sectional. This is in addition to the over 200 advertising agencies handling major radio and TV accounts.

Music and the Producer

Earlier in this chapter we mentioned that the producer is responsible for all of the elements which go into the total program. Not the least part of the program product is music. However, music presents special problems to the unwary. The producer with accumulated experience in other aspects of programming, in both television and radio, is particularly careful of music copyrights. Music to be used in programs must be carefully planned, accurately logged, and scrutinized for copyright control.

Where new and original music is to be composed for a program, it may be contracted for. The one-time use of such music presents no special difficulties, since a contract will adequately protect the composer as well as the conductor of the score. A composer who is a member of the American Society of Composers, Authors and Publishers (ASCAP) will be protected under the usual contractual arrangements with radio and television stations that are subscribers to the ASCAP list. The same is true for music controlled by Broadcast Music Incorporated (BMI). The contracts for the continued use for such music are standard and clearly spell out the conditions under which music is controlled, the amount that is to be paid, and the way in which payment is to be made. ASCAP, BMI and one other controlling agency—the Society of European Stage, Authors, and Composers (SESAC)—are the agencies with which most stations hold a music-use license.

The Copyright Law

On October 19, 1976 the United States Congress passed a general revision of the copyright law, Public Law 94-553 which includes such provisions as:

1. Exclusive rights to copyrighted works remain with the owner of the copyright for all literary, musical, dramatic and choreographic works that have pantomimes, motion pictures or similar forms. Such works may not be performed publicly without the specific permission of the copyright owner. In addition, the right to display such works, whether they are performed or not, are also the exclusive domain of the copyright holder.

2. There are some limitations on the exclusive rights. One of these is "fair use": for purposes of criticism, comment, news reporting, teaching, scholarship or research, use of a copyrighted work is not an infringement of copyright. However, this does not permit unrestricted use of a copyrighted work which has been broadcast nor does it permit the copying of a work as a whole, unless it is for the above described purposes and for a non-profit educational use which has no overtones of a commercial nature of any kind. Libraries may copy audiovisual works if the copies are to be added to the collection of a library, or a library may reproduce and distribute such a copy if the copy contains a notification that it is a copyrighted work, and if the number of times any such work is copied during a given year follows the requirements of the law.

Specific attention should be given to the limitations that are placed on exclusivity of rights, the need for a compulsory license for secondary transmission such as through a cable television system, the distribution procedures of copyrighted works, and the payment of copyright fees. As has been true in the past, in order to be appropriately copyrighted, works must be registered with the Copyright Office.

Fees in payment for the use of the copyrighted work under the conditions described in the law should be deposited with the Register of Copyrights. Any interest accrued is subsequently paid to the Copyright Royalty Tribunal. The role of the Tribunal is carefully defined in the Act and the four major objectives of the Tribunal are designed to see that a fair return for creative work is made to the copyright owner and to maximize the availability of creative work to the public.

One interesting provision of the Act is that every five years the Register of Copyrights must submit a report to the Congress which indicates how well the Act is meeting both the rights of creators of material and the needs of users of copyrighted material, based on consultation with representatives, authors, book and periodical publishers, other copyright owners and library users.

Unions

In most large cities most good stations are unionized, and there can be no question of unionization at the network level. But in many of the less-than-large areas, the union situation can be complicated. How do unions affect the work of the producer? The first concern is when the producer begins to draw up budget requirements for a particular program. The standards of salary and working conditions established by the union must be taken into account in all-over budgeting. Not only do unions define minimum salaries, but producers must also budget time around the number of rehearsal hours permitted any individual before overtime pay goes into effect.

In markets where unions, talent agencies, and basic minimum conditions of work, employment and salaries exist, sufficient information by the producer new to that area can be elicited either from the union representative, union headquarters or the lawyers of the particular station or network.

Producing the News Program

The position of news is unique in the entire scheme of television programming. The evening news, particularly, carries with it a prestige/rating-seeking approach to getting an audience.

In the area of television news programming, great competition exists among the three networks and, through them, the local stations around the United States. Network news programming has a decided impact upon both evening ratings and revenue.

Networks and Local Stations

The evening network news coverage usually is preceded by the local news coverage which leads directly into it. Thus, since prestige is being sought by the evening news broadcast, network news must be preceded by the type of local news with personalities who will attract and hold audiences for the evening network program. If a local news personality does not appeal to the viewer or is not capable of maintaining a believable journalistic approach to what is being broadcast, the viewer will turn to another station. Not infrequently the viewer will complain to the Federal Communications Commission about the inadequacy and lack of proper coverage at the local level. This can reflect upon the renewal of the license for a television station. If a weak or unlikely type of local news personality precedes the network coverage, this affects ratings of the news program and, therefore, the kinds of revenue that will accrue to the station from the commercial inserts. The local level personality must hold a local audience for the network news which is to follow. The network news which follows must be dominated by personalities who have both journalistic authority and sufficient personal charisma to attract and hold audiences that will continue to tune in to that particular station's nightly news broadcast. Because of this personality phenomenon, the kind of news scripting that develops must also be of acceptable professional quality and must command both respect and attention. The scripting or writing of the news to be presented is frequently managed by specific television news writers, or in some cases by television news "doctors." Every effort is made to make the news segment of the programming day one of noteworthiness, appeal and acceptability.

Breadth and scope of coverage is an aspect with which the news producer is concerned. The news producer at the local level has a relatively limited geographical construct to cover. True, people at the local level are intensely interested in what happens in their locality, but world-shaking events which occur any place in the world make for a news broadcast which is rarely superseded in terms of interest and "pulling" power. When network level news producers have the news of the entire world to "pull" upon, they can cull and select and make vital and dramatic every single second of air time which they fill.

At the local or regional level, news reportage is more or less standard in its approach. Local newscast talent tends to be fairly standard. However, the news gathering talent available in such areas as New York City, Los Angeles or Chicago is exceptional and tends to be of outstanding caliber. The kinds of talent in all fields of endeavor which are concentrated in large cities are quite different from the kinds of talent that you will find in most areas throughout the United States. The appeal of the large urban area, particularly of New York City, is that such areas are centers for the performing arts, for the best of talent in management and for broadcasting and news reporting. Stories of national and international significance usually take place in New York, Washington, sometimes in Los Angeles or Boston, but rarely in other parts of the United States. With this combination of concentrated talent and circumstance, and a concentration of behind-the-scenes ability in terms of news producers, vice-presidents-in-charge-of-news, camera operators, network level engineers and film producers of outstanding ability, there is a caliber of news reportage substantially superior to that usually found in the suburban, rural or regional areas.

Rating Pressures

In recent years more and more emphasis has been given to local-level news and news gathering. The total concept of the ENG (Electronic News Gathering) thrust has made a difference in the kind of coverage that can be expected and that is frequently demanded by the local viewer. Miniaturized camera circuitry has led to the development of the light camera, mounted on the shoulder, and the light-weight videotape recorder which makes for ease of portability. In this way, it is possible to have inexpensive field work which makes for instantaneous news gathering attractive to the viewer. If a minor change or even a sustained change takes place in the viewership for the news hour, the station and the network will make every effort once again to raise the viewership to the level expected. The scriptwriting news "doctor" may have to be brought in or the appropriate on-air personality change may need to be made. To back up such changes, other changes are made behind the scenes. Such changes might include program directors, or the vice president in charge of news at the network level. At the local level it might be the news director and, where necessary, even the station manager.

The phenomenon of declining audiences, at the local and regional levels, usually means a regular "turnabout," or personnel changes which are made almost every two to three years. If the person in charge of news has done a good job, usually he or she is elevated. If people have done a "so-so" job or have failed, they may be moved laterally or may be moved out entirely. When viewership declines, the news gathering team at the local level must be turned around, must seek some retreading approach to the work it has done, or must seek to do its work elsewhere. A new "head" in a news operation requires a new "body" and a complete staff change. A new "head" is faced with the question, "What can I do that wasn't done before, that is different, that will bring us better ratings and more audience and, therefore, give us the opportunity for attracting more revenue through more advertising?"

Changes that seem necessary in news writing and news production frequently bring about all kinds of innovative moves. Some of these have led to the emergence of the woman newscaster. Everything that can bring about an attractive rating is tried in order to bring forth an audience that will be more attentive, and that will be attracted by new approaches that are appealing.

The Journalist: Visual and Print

The producer of the news program should be a trained and experienced journalist.

News reporters for television should have been working reporters in the print medium and have had considerable experience before coming to television. The reporters' tools of perception, their approaches to reportage—all of these must be at the peak of development and must reflect both excellent training and experience by the time they arrive at the television medium.

But television reporting is not reporting for the print medium. It is heavily oriented toward the visual. It is, in fact, a mirror held up to the realities of life, and this mirror must give back reflections that translate into film and videotape and the editing of the two for a news story. Several distinctions must be made between the print reporter and the television reporter. Print reporters can go back to a geographical location after an event has taken place. They can question observers of the event, participants in the event, even the victims of whatever disaster has taken place that they are reporting upon; and as a result of their investigation, they can put together a vivid reportage in printed form that will recreate the entire circumstance for the reader as if the reader were there. Television reporters do not have this luxury. If the television reporters have missed a particular event or segment of events, this has then been missed in terms of the entire television viewing audience. The 95-yard end run which determined the outcome of the football game—if this is not on film or on videotape, if the camera operator for some reason was not there or was looking the other way, or if the camera was not loaded with adequate film, or if the video recorder was not operating properly—then the circumstance has been missed, the event is gone and perhaps the most important segment may never be seen.

Television reporting is not the same as reporting for the print medium. This was vividly portrayed on several occasions when the television industry was being struck by the television news reporters. In some instances, newspaper reporters were brought in to take over the chores of the regular television news staff. The very fact of their being print-oriented persons immediately had an impact on what they were *not* able to do in terms of the requirements of the television medium. The appeal of television journalism over that of any other medium—print or even radio—is that the viewer sees as well as hears on-the-spot reportage. The viewer is there to talk with the victims of an accident, to understand the difficulties of a political situation as it erupts in internal rioting and revolution. The television medium brings to the eyes of the viewer and, therefore, to the eyes of the world, a feeling of immediacy for an entire situation. Such a feeling is not available through radio because radio may only hear what is being said or may only hear the reporters as they interview people on the spot. When you can see what is taking place, when you become involved in the situation itself, then you have reportage of such an impact value that all else seems to fade in importance.

Multiple Local Station Role

There are probably fewer clear-cut divisions among the producer, director and talent on the news program than in almost any other program type. This is particularly true on the local level.

In the local station the producer, director and newscaster are frequently one and the same person. Top-level management at the local level will frequently exercise some of the prerogatives of the producer. Management may dictate to the newscaster the type of programming approach it wishes. Indeed, frequently it may dictate what the editorial policy of the station is. In the most desirable situation it will permit the newscaster a freedom in interpretation of the news that need not necessarily be the policy of the station. Since the producer is frequently the newscaster and, therefore, the one who determines the content of what shall be presented, we have an interesting dual role. Selection of news items, determination of which are important, which shall take precedence and which shall be "fill" are made not by one person and executed by another, as they frequently are at the network level, but are made by one individual, alone. The responsibility of the newscaster at the local level is a heavy one.

The newscaster-producer must be a well-read individual. Where a news summary is more than a five-minute precis of headlines, singular importance must be attached to the kind of individual who shall be responsible for this particular program. There must be a keen sense of rapport between the newscaster-producer and the director of the program. Having determined what the news item shall be and having begun the necessary writing before airing the news, the newscaster-producer must now work in close coordination with the director, particularly in terms of camera shots that shall be called for and for film, tape or still inserts at the proper moment.

Visuals

One of the most important determinants of a news item, apart from its news importance, is the available supporting video material. Without consideration of visual contributions and their impact upon the viewer in terms of news value, there would be no reason to use the television medium for news reporting. The director must ask such questions as: Is a video tape recording available on such-and-such particular news story? Is film being flown in from abroad? Do we go by direct wire or do we go by microwave to some distant point for a particular news pick-up? How many remote switches are involved? Are stills being used in the studio? Will slides be used? Will video be from the slide and film chain, or will it be from a rear screen projection (a large, translucent screen background to the set on which a still or motion picture is projected from the rear)? How many commercials must be inserted? Where do the appropriate places for these inserts come?

It is clear, then, that not only is understanding of news activity necessary, but the producer of the news program is closely tied to the skill and the precision of the supporting technical team responsible for the split-second timing of the video. If television news reporting were to be simply a voicing of the kind of verbalization that appears on the pages of a newspaper, then it would be less expensive, more expeditious, far less costly and far less time-consuming to prepare a news broadcast as if for radio rather than for television.

Some of the basics in news coverage of the international front have not changed very much from the early days in which these were first conceived. When stations in New York City were still experimental before World War II, the early international news broadcasts were largely supported by and dependent upon good maps. In June, 1942, to all intents and purposes, news broadcasting by television came to a halt. Skilled technical television personnel went to work for special projects in war research and it was not until the end of 1946 that television news broadcasting resumed its development. Put in the position of meeting a challenge for news coverage from abroad, it began to formulate a distinct method of approach and presentation peculiarly its own. During the Korean war, from 1950 to 1953, television provided a visual effect of what was being experienced, through films quickly flown to this country. This was not a period when television news reporting was held in particularly great repute. But because television had begun its first experiment with 15 minutes of news, five days a week in 1949, by the time of Korea it was ready to meet its obligation to the viewing public.

The true effectiveness of television news reporting depends to the greatest extent on the technical potential of the medium to meet the requirements of factual reporting that is no longer once-removed from participation by the viewer, as in newspaper reporting. To make a viewer a true participant through use, in the early days, of film and, later, of video tape was and still is the hallmark of the good news broadcast.

Planning and Personnel

What must the producer plan for? What personnel will be needed? What additional materials and sources must be taken into account? Let us separate the role of the producer from the role of newscaster and writer. When these are different persons in a large station or network situation, the television news producer must take into account an expanded list of needed personnel and extended functions of a production team. Not the least of the group will be the film and/or video camera operator. Sometimes it may be sound and motion, sometimes silent. The kinds of facilities available in a given news coverage situation will affect the kind of material the camera operator can obtain, and in turn affect the planning of the producer.

The producer's staff also includes a good librarian. The film and tape library is to the telecast what the "morgue" is to the news story. The camera operator's ingenuity determines not only what will be captured for the immediate telecast, but also for permanent acquisition by the library. The good library serves the same purposes as the rich resources of a print library. Nothing which is news happens in isolation. The story does not begin now and end in the next few minutes, nor did it begin yesterday, nor will it end tomorrow. There is a continuity of history that runs as a thread through all of newscasting. The library must be a repository of all which is likely to be meaningful.

In some stations, the film/tape crew—made up of camera, sound, and light specialists—may be large and well developed. In other stations, it may be a two-person operation—including the newscaster-producer. A most important job is that of outside "contact." This person decides what represents a news item, is completely responsible for content, decides on the over-all approach, and suggests the shots, but of course, in technical matters defers to the most skilled technician, the camera operator, who must judge lighting, distance, and the like. In addition to camera contact, and sound and light people, the producer must also have a film/tape editor. The editor must be provided with all necessary film and tape cutting and editing equipment. The producer must have an arts and graphics staff that will include all-purpose artists capable of quickly producing charts, graphs, captions, still photographs and other visuals. The production team also includes special engineers and technical personnel, camera operators who go out on location, projectionists in telecine, the audio and video control personnel. In large operations there may be numerous assistants to the producer. The director is a member of the staff. There are traffic specialists, office personnel, and representatives of sales, the sponsor and the agency. The miscellaneous personnel that the producer may have in a large station or network situation includes messengers, clerks, typists, mimeograph operators, teletype operators and even a helicopter pilot. All kinds of miscellaneous supporting personnel, depending upon the sponsor of the program and the product being exhibited, may evolve in relation to newscasts.

Organizing the Program

It is the responsibility of the producer to preside at that most important determining session known as the "line-up." This is the meeting at which all members of the news production team, including the newscasters, editor, producer, director, film, art and graphics personnel, and writers appear. Line-up time in large television news centers is usually two to four hours before presentation. The purposes of this session are to examine a suggested routining of the presentation of stories, to choose a lead story and to determine the appeal of particular stories by discussing, examining and listening to an evaluation of the picture material available for each of the news items to be presented. The usual ratio estimate of video to audio material is approximately one-to-one in a 15-minute commercial news program. For example, six to seven minutes will be devoted to film and other visuals and the remainder will be devoted to the "shooting" of the newscaster.

Individual film stories may vary in length. On a 15-minute program, six to seven minutes of film may break down into from four to as many as eight video periods. These periods, properly distributed throughout the entire program, will hold the live camera portions of the program to no longer than 30 seconds or a minute at any one time. A decision to include or exclude specific materials for specific purposes is up to the producer. For example, an unusual news story of above average running time, on film or video tape, may be substituted at the last moment on the decision of the producer made in conjunction with the newscaster and director.

It is not the purpose of this chapter to discuss in depth methods of news selection. It suffices to say, among the most important decisions made by the producer responsible for the all-over newscasting policy of the station will be those of coverage for *particular audiences* at *particular times* of day. For example, the early morning adult audience is in a hurry. It will do more listening than watching. It needs quick, concise coverage. The daytime audience is different. On weekdays, it is largely female and is interested in a slackened news pace and in more features. The early evening family audience desires broad coverage of all the news that has happened within the past 24 hours. As many stories as possible should be covered, and shock and horror stories avoided. Late evening news coverage can be more relaxed in pace. The audience is presumed to be mainly adult and wants news reviews and indications of what may occur the next day—including weather predictions.

Thus, the responsibility of the producer of the news telecast includes the direction of all personnel and elements of the program, intimate involvement in everything from writing to projection, and a tight control over the line-up period.

The Documentary Program

Documentaries generally fall into two major categories: the semi-documentary and the straight documentary. The semi-documentary allows greater latitude for creative approaches in concept and writing. It gives the producer, the director and the writer an opportunity to enlarge, in an imaginative way, on circumstances and persons. It allows more freedom in interpretation—within the limitations of basic fact—and provides a means for bringing alive what could be factually dull if done as a sheer recital of researched material. The producer's responsibility is to provide, within budget limitations, the facilities and writing support necessary to accomplish the pre-determined objectives of such a program.

The pure or straight documentary requires ingenuity in researching files of known visual and audio materials, accurate examination and cataloguing of such available materials, and a planned concept for use. All other production needs and requirements remain generally the same.

There is an important relationship between the news broadcast and the documentary, particularly at the network level. Not all independent producers of documentary film or documentary programs are basically journalists in their training or in their background. But in terms of network documentaries, those done by CBS, NBC, ABC, PBS, Group W and other major organizations, for the most part the documentary producer or the documentary planner has a significant background in journalism and in journalistic reporting. To this he or she must now add a new and different approach which involves the understanding and the in-depth planning concept of the drama. The documentary producer must understand the concept of the well-rounded play because the documentary must tell a story, with a beginning, a middle and an end. It must tell it in a form which will hold, attract and continue to impress upon the viewer that here is something special, here is documented information or a semi-documented approach to information or cultural material which has an interest and an impact.

The major distinction between the producer of the documentary program and the producer of other programs is that the documentary producer has a factual story to tell. The producer of other programs is usually interested principally in the entertainment values contained in the program. Basically, the documentary producer is a journalist. He or she deals with facts. The facts are marshalled in a way which makes sure that the complete sequence of the story is understood and the impact of the results of the story are readily documented and can be factually seen.

Producer-Writer Relationship

The relationship of the documentary producer to the documentary writer is quite a different one from that of the news producer to the news writer. In many instances the documentary writers are their own producers. They conceive the ideas, do the research and investigation and do their own on-site and location shooting with a film team. The conclusions drawn and the statements made are those which have either implications for information, stimulation of new ideas or conclusions which project concepts of the future.

The relationship of the news producer to the news writer is quite different. The news writer conceives the written approach to the news, writes it, places it in proper reportage framework and turns it over to the producer, who then elicits the kind of projection he or she wants from the news reporter who will present it on air.

In many instances the relationship of the documentary writer to the documentary producer depends very much upon whether they are the same person. Sometimes the documentary producer has hired the documentary writer based on reputation and it frequently becomes a matter of the will of the documentary writer being predominant in decision-making situations. But in every instance the final decision as to what to use, what to cut, how to edit, what is in the documentary script must remain the province of the producer of the documentary, who is always the final arbiter as to direction, meaning, inclusion or exclusion of material and ideas.

The way the documentary is produced and finally edited must take into account the fact that it is a product of a tri-partite team. It represents the total feeling, approach, planning and research of the producer, the writer and the filmmaker or cinematographer. It is not an unusual occurrence when a documentary is being shot on location, that frequently things do not develop or appear as they have been planned. The cinematographer may see material which is better suited to revealing the subject. Flexibility is required at this point from both the writer and the producer in terms of their original concept. The final shaping of what is actually available to the camera then becomes important as the final product of what will appear to the viewer. Many decisions must enter into the process of actually shooting a documentary. What is shot, how it is shot and, finally, what is used and what is not used, however, is still up to the final decision of the producer.

THE DISCUSSION PROGRAM

The discussion program is one of the most common types which the producer will be called upon to organize, either at the local or network level. The characteristic of the roundtable discussion is "informality." Do not confuse informality with lack of organization. The word informality, as used here, means a free discussion in which there is an orderly exchange of ideas, in which content is organized, and in which participation by the members of the roundtable is controlled by the moderator.

Choosing Participants

The informal roundtable may be either person-centered or problem-centered in its content approach. Where person-centered, it revolves around the availability of a famous personality in a given field of endeavor. For example, the discussion might be on the changing life styles of young people as a reflection of their attitude toward society. The discussant might be the famous social anthropologist, Margaret Mead. We might have a panel of qualified persons in the field of teen-age development—social psychologists, experts on the drug scene and the influence of drug availability on hyper-sensitive and impressionable teen-agers, or the like. Where a discussion is to be centered on specific medical problems, for example, qualified persons in such fields as cancer research, heart disease or diabetes might be participants.

Preferably, there will be four members on the panel plus a moderator although, frequently, it is perfectly acceptable to have three panel members plus a moderator. Never, only two participants and a moderator. When you have only two participants what you have is a kind of "dialogue" discussion, which is simply an exchange of ideas between two qualified persons who may or may not have different points of view on the problem being discussed.

Although all members of the panel should be qualified in relation to the content, there are degrees of qualification. It is the producer's obligation to find persons who fit categories that can provide a discussion in depth. What categories of qualification are there? First there is the *authority*—the person qualified in both training and experience in the particular problem or area under discussion. The second panelist is usually an *informed* person in relation to the content, someone who will have some training or some experience. The third person represents an audience point of view, is intensely interested in the content areas being discussed and may have some general knowledge of the problem or some training. This person, working with the moderator-producer, helps to elicit the kind of information and reaction that would be of interest to the viewer.

The producer who is also the moderator of the program must acquire some background on the subject of the discussion. He or she must also have necessary background information on each member of the panel and, in presenting them during the broadcast, must make clear the level of their competency and authoritativeness. The producer-moderator must be capable of abstracting ideas from the members of the roundtable, organizing the discussion, routining the presentation and summarizing the ideas presented. If the producer is not the moderator but the director of the program, then a moderator acts for the producer-director, maintaining organizational control over the discussants through agreed-upon signals conveyed through the floor manager of the program.

Procedure and Organization

A good discussion program is not organized in the haphazard manner that sometimes seems apparent when we view such shows on television. Too many discussion programs are organized loosely, planned at the last moment, and if any preliminary warm-up with the participants does take place, it is usually in a very cursory and off-the-cuff manner. Whether or not the producer is also the moderator does not change his or her primary responsibilities. These include:

1) Locating the participants and determining levels of authoritativeness.
2) Interviewing each member of the panel in preparation for a preliminary discussion, to fix areas to be included in the content of the broadcast.
3) On the basis of individual preliminary talks with the participants on the program, tentatively suggesting what shall be the high points of discussion.
4) Planning the first meeting of all of the participating discussants, making sure that each has received a proposed preliminary content outline of points to be included in the broadcast.
5) Taking ample notes during the first group run-through, thus being able to return to the second preliminary rehearsal session with the discussants to effectively finalize an agreed-upon content-approach to the problem under discussion.
6) Determining with the participants the art and graphics materials needed to heighten the visual effectiveness of the program. It must be noted here that most discussion programs, as done today, would be equally effective if aired by radio. One major point of TV effectiveness is the visual impact of the personality of the discussant on the viewer. To simply turn a camera on a discussion, because the place of origin is a television studio, is to make less than complete and adequate use of the medium for heightening understanding.
7) Preparing for the final "warm-up" discussion period—which should desirably take place immediately before the broadcast—and planning a ten-minute period between the warm-up and the actual on-the-air discussion.

Routine Sheet and Visual Materials

The producer must prepare the following materials for use by the director:

1) A complete routining sheet. The routining sheet, which acts as a guide to the director and is used in annotated form by the moderator, will have the following form and parts:

THE ROUTINING SHEET FOR A DISCUSSION PROGRAM

INTRODUCTION   to the program. This should be fully scripted and accurately timed.

OPENING   This is full scripted and accurately timed. It introduces the subject, *briefly.* The opening provides for an introduction to each member of the panel. *Don't* (as is the usual practice) have your panel members sit there, saying nothing, staring vacuously into the camera, while an overvoice describes how outstanding they are because of what they have done or accomplished. *Do* try to involve the discussants in helping to give some of the background about themselves. *Don't* concentrate on the past too long. *Remember,* the good producer wants to get to the discussion as soon as possible.

SEGMENT 1   Note that most discussion programs will conveniently break into three segments—the usual number of segments to be found in most communications, whether good letters, stories, dramas, public addresses, classroom presentations by teachers, or well-organized broadcasts. This should be semi-scripted and in outline form for the points to be covered. SEGMENT 1 should conveniently lead to a . . .

LINK   This should be fully scripted. It may be:
(a) a summary of SEGMENT 1, or
(b) a transitional statement leading to SEGMENT 2, or
(c) a combination of both, an internal summary as
    described in (a) above, and (b) above.

SEGMENT 2   Again, semi-scripted and outlined as in SEGMENT 1. SEGMENT 2 differs from SEGMENT 1 in that it represents a high development or exploration of points introduced under SEGMENT 1. SEGMENT 2 leads naturally to the next . . .

LINK   In form, this is the same as the first LINK, above. Its purposes are also the same, namely, to summarize SEGMENT 2, to act as a transition to SEGMENT 3, or both.

SEGMENT 3   This is semi-scripted and outlined, as are the previous segments, and the points covered are the major points of the discussion. In this segment we bring the discussion to its highest point and conclude it. This leads to our last . . .

LINK   which is a transitional statement, only. The transitional statement (*fully* scripted) leads to a . . .

SUMMARY AND CONCLUSION   This is the final wrap-up summary, or an internal summary, or a concluding statement for the entire content of the discussion, or all of these.

PROGRAM CLOSE   This concludes the program, thanks the guests, contains a statement preparing for the next discussion program, and gives the credits.

2) The producer should indicate, clearly, the places in the routining sheet in which art, graphics, visuals, stills, clips—visual inserts of any kind—are to be incorporated, and should see to their execution.
3) At least one part of a discussion can advantageously use multiple graphics

to aid the understanding of difficult statistical points. A variety of stills, slides or a combination of these may be used in well-organized succession.

4) There should be at least one three-dimensional artifact used in the program. This lends visual variety and can provide a focus for carefully delineated consideration and clarification through visualization.

The above requirements for visuals for a discussion should be regarded not as a definitive list, but as a listing to stimulate the thought and outlook of the producer. With such a list in hand the producer will consciously seek, throughout the pre-broadcast discussions, to find ways to more effectively use the television medium to disseminate the information and philosophical attitudes of the panel.

Variety-discussion Program

A popular offshoot of the standard discussion program is the "talk" show format sometimes called the "variety-discussion" program. This refers to that type of program which one frequently sees during the day, very early or very late in the evening or quite early in the morning (as for example, *The Today Show*). The moderator or presenter of this type of program seems to work in a very loose kind of format. He or she is at ease; rarely seems harried or pushed; seems in complete control of the situation and of the personalities being introduced; and apparently works without stricture of any kind and without a very tight outline format.

In reality, these presenters are quite "old hands" at the game. What seems to be an off-the-cuff introduction is indeed very well planned, frequently rehearsed, and is always a matter of complete briefing of the moderator by the staff. There is always a thorough identification of the individual being introduced, an indication of what will be discussed, what the individual will do, or a combination of these things. Discussions seem "loose." Many of the presenters seem to work without a specific direction in mind. Frequently the best of these people will tell the press that they don't like to be held to a tight outline or a specific series of questions. Those who have done such programs for many years are so well acquainted with the format and the formula that they frequently need no outline in hand. But they must have a careful and thorough briefing. The appearance is that a kind of unconscious preparation has taken place. If the guest is an outstanding individual in a noted field of endeavor, the presenter knows exactly how to handle him or her. If we have a guest who is a show-business type of personality, there is a very carefully structured and complimentary way of handling this kind of individual. The introduction must convey a "he-or-she-loves-everyone-and-everyone-loves-him-or-her" aura.

This kind of variety-interview/discussion type of program, if examined carefully, does have links and certainly has segments as we go from individual to individual, and most frequently has summaries and conclusions. Such summaries may be as simple as, "Well, we've talked with so-and-so and so-and-so and so-and-so today. We talked about such-and-such and such-and such, and I think we have seen that generally this and this happens"—and so on.

True, this may be a very crude kind of summary and conclusion, but it does the trick, and when handled by an old pro, works well and is almost as effective as a thoroughly planned and carefully rehearsed summary and conclusion. Information is disseminated, philosophical attitudes are reinforced, and generally there is a tight and concentrated presentation. But, let us remember, skill for this kind of program handling comes only with a great deal of experience, a retentive eye and ear, and an almost-never failing memory.

Production Techniques

Just as one cannot legislate good citizenship, one cannot dictate the production level to be sought by the honest, thorough-going, involved and concerned producer of the discussion program.

Certain standard methods of physical juxtaposition of panel members in a studio setup have evolved over the years. Most panel discussions are two-camera presentations. One camera must be used as a "cover" camera. The other must be kept completely mobile and, at the discretion of the director, able to go to individual panel members or to the moderator as they move from content point to content point. An aid to the director in predetermining the shots is the routining sheet and its indications of a particular panel member's contributions on a particular point.

An important aspect of graphics preparation is identification boards or slides used for each member of the panel; customarily there is a small name-identification visual on the table area in front of each discussant. Usually, a last name is sufficient. Frequently, it will be preceded by the abbreviation of a title such as "Dr.," "Prof.," or the like. It is usually advantageous to prepare a slide which can be "supered" in a medium shot over the discussant, identifying him or her at key points in the panel discussion. At the beginning of the program, as the camera goes from one member of the group to the other during the introduction, the name is supered over the lower part of a medium shot of the guest. During key points in the discussion itself, the name of the discussant is supered over a medium shot, particularly when the disscussant may be presenting more than two or three points on the topic under consideration.

Finally, the routining sheet should contain an estimated timing of each segment and a specific timing for all fully scripted portions of the program. The timing elements for the "wrap up" at the end of the program will give the director an opportunity (by means of hand signals or an intercom voice signal to the floor director) to convey to the moderator precisely how much time is left to finalize the discussion, make adequate identification at the end of the program and insert promos or commercials.

Summary

The obligations of the producer in relation to a discussion program are, then, the following:
1) Identify the particular content to be discussed, its timeliness, and its application to the interest of the viewers.

2) Identify and commit to both preparation and broadcast, the authorities to be used on a discussion program.
3) Hold preparatory individual conferences with the participants to elicit from them information expressing their attitudes on the content to be discussed, and background related to each discussant and his or her expertise in the subject area.
4) Prepare, first, a rough outline; second, a more detailed outline; and third, a routining sheet of points to be covered, indicated timings for the discussion, the links between segments, internal summaries, final summary, introduction and wrap up of the program.
5) Work closely with the art and graphics people on conceptions of photographic, three-dimensional, slide, film and other material that may enhance the content presentation as well as provide as much visual interest as can be achieved by such a program.
6) Work closely with the engineers in seeing to it that there is adequate in-studio preparation and set-up for the broadcast, taking into account close association with the director in the lighting, camera angles and microphone coverage problems of the broadcast.

THE DRAMA

The drama presents more possibility for imaginative and interpretive production skill than any other program type. It may be argued that the "variety" or "magazine" program type has the advantage of greater latitude in conceiving various portions of the program. One might plan a dance presentation on one part, a specialty act in another. But once the determination of a particular act or performing artist is made, little interpretive latitude or production skill remains to be exercised. The director of the variety program plans the creative aspects of sound and picture. In the musical program much depends upon the ability and musical training of the performers and the conductor or upon the compositions that form the content of the program. In the discussion program the personalities of the discussants, the expertise they have in relation to the subject-content, and their general enthusiasm in conveying information and insights determine the success of the broadcast. The producer of the drama, however, has the opportunity to mold each element of the presentation, changing interpretation, controlling the elements of music, picture and sound, and working with the writer until over-all desired effect is achieved.

As in the news and discussion program types thus far discussed, the drama broadcast product is frequently affected by whether the producer of the drama is also the director. For the purposes of this chapter, let us assume that the producer and the director of the drama program are *not* the same individual.

Procedure

What are the responsibilities of the producer of the drama broadcast? In this respect we are not discussing the daily drama serial, but the full-length original script or dramatic adaptation, usually the once-a-week presentation, a half-hour or an hour or more in length, and a story or dramatic unit that is completed at the time of broadcast.

The producer's first step is either to read the script under consideration for broadcast, or to commission an original or adaptation script to be written. If the script is to be commissioned, the producer must determine what type of play it shall be—comedy, drama, deep tragedy, or possibly a dramatic semi-documentary. The answer to this question will depend very much upon what audience the producer has in mind, whether the program is part of a continuing series with a fixed format, the time of day of the broadcast, and the sponsor—if there is sponsorship. In public educational television broadcasting the answer will depend upon whether we are trying to do direct instructional programming, general informational programming, broad cultural programming, or presenting part of a total series that offers a continuity of insights to a particular event (or events) in a period of history—as does a semi-documentary or documentary.

Once we know the kind of drama, we can determine who shall be asked to write the script. Like skilled artisans in any art or craft, writers, by disposition, outlook, ability and opportunity, tend to specialize. The skilled documentarian will have a highly developed sense of research ability and (frequently) training in one or more aspects of historical scholarship, and an intuitive sense of characterization analysis for the important and common personalities of the past.

Once the script is completed, the detailed work of production planning begins. If the producer of the dramatic program is not the director, the determination of who shall direct the program will have to be made almost at the same time that the writer has been assigned to script the presentation. The producer and the director will work closely together as determinations are made as to who, how many, and what kinds of support shall be needed on the production team to back up the director in the studio.

Analyzing the Script

What happens when the producer finally has a script in hand? First, give the script a quick, complete, uncritical reading. In this first reading, the producer is interested in one thing and one thing only: to seek the same reaction one would expect from a viewer who will see and hear the drama for the first time. When the first reading is completed, only one question should occur to the producer: "will the listener *appreciate* it?" This is a little different from the question, "will the listener *like* it?" Depending upon the nature of the script (and the program and sponsor), it is not always important that the viewer *like* it. Does the drama capture the viewer's interest? Does it hold the attention from beginning to end? Does it fulfill the objective for which it was written—that is, does it move the viewer to action, to a new point of view, or does it attract attention and bring about a phase of new consideration and ideas in the viewer's mind? This is all predicated on the assumption that, in initial screening of submissions, the story editor has approved this script as fitting the basic format requirements of the program on which it might be produced.

Now the producer is ready for the crucial question, "shall the script be produced?" If it is to be produced, are changes needed? If so, what kind? To arrive at a determination of whether the script shall be produced and if so, with or without changes, a critical analysis is important. The following are questions the producer could well raise as a basis for determining the desirability of producing the script in hand:

1) Can the entire drama be produced as written? Is there complicated action which cannot be readily understood by the viewers? Should any of the dialogue be rewritten? Are all the scenes necessary? Do all the scenes contribute to the over-all structure of the drama? Does the drama fit the allowed broadcast time? At this point, the individual who will direct the script on the air should be brought in to read it, to discuss it with the producer, and to aid in making determinations on further questions, below. If the script looks as if it is precisely right in timing, yet subsequent rehearsals prove it overlong, where shall cuts be made? The writer should be consulted as to suggested script cuts. Are any of the speeches too long to be handled by an actor or actress?

2) Are time and place in all scenes clearly delineated? The delineation must be in the form of readily identifable sound effects, visuals, graphics and/or scenic execution. Scene settings must be clearly defined in terms of visuals, music and/or sound.

3) Is there sufficient visual, sound and music support of reaction? Is there too much?

4) The plot, characters, dialogue, exposition, motivation for entrances and exits, and immediate presentation of the interest-holding conflict at the beginning of the drama must reflect the principles of writing the good and effective television play, as delineated in Chapter 4 of this book.

At this point, the producer and director must minutely examine all places where transitions are needed—from scene to scene, from character to character. Indeed, the transitions from a scene to a commercial announcement are of particular importance in commercial television. Although commercial transitions are frequently considered the province of the writer, ideally they should be decided upon jointly by the director, the producer and the writer. If an advertising agency is involved and has indicated that it wants commercials in specific number and in specific places during the time sequence, such request should be honored wherever possible. Much of the time, slight rewriting for timing or for making a smooth and integrated transition with the drama can be readily achieved.

The producer does exercise certain prerogatives over script changes. Unless contractually specified, they may be made without consultation with the writer. Hopefully, the writer will be consulted. They should always be made in consultation with the director so the director will understand precisely what the producer has in mind. Sometimes the addition of music, sound or visual support or the subtraction of these are made by the producer to fit the all-over production idea and concept. Sometimes changes are dictated by budget limitations. For all of these reasons, the producer, in consultation with the director, may make certain transitional changes or small cuts when necessary for timing purposes—or may delegate the making of such cuts entirely to the director. First option for script changes must go to the original writer, but if the writer refuses, rewrites may be done by the producer or director or whomever they designate.

Analyzing the Production Needs

The producer's answers to major questions concerning the program provide the bases for understanding the approach to solving the drama program's production needs.

1) What is the aim of the program? The purpose of most dramatic programs is either to inform, entertain or educate. Sometimes drama programs will attempt to do more than one of these at the same time; in any event, entertainment in the highest sense is always included.

2) What type of drama is this? The producer's answer to this question leads to several considerations.

Characterization. A delineation must be made between characterization in tragedy—which is thoughtful and slow and must be developed in greater detail for the audience—and in farce, in which the character approach is in terms of a rapid tempo and broad interpretation rather than thoughtful depth. Characterization determines the type of talent the producer and director will look for in casting any given part.

Production Treatment. If the drama is tragedy, not only will characterization be more thoughtfully and slowly developed than in farce, but the director's entire pacing will be more deliberate, building to a climax that resolves all the tragic implications indicated in the plot. This very pacing will determine the type of scene-setting, the kind of incidental and background music, the types of transitions, the whole artistic approach to visuals. Conversely, farce will be at a fast pace and the entire production slanted toward rapid exchange of dialogue—in many instances, for gag value—and very much in the manner of farce techniques so well known in the theatre. The important influence in determining production pacing relates directly back to budget considerations. The kind of artistic approach necessary for drama, the kinds of settings this will produce, the entire way in which music shall be composed or sought for in transitions or for backing sequences—all will be directly influenced by the budget for the program.

Interpretation. Although the final on-the-air interpretation of any drama script lies, for execution, wholly within the hands of the director of the drama, the producer must nevertheless indicate clearly, succinctly and with no equivocation to the selected director, precisely the kind of interpretation desired, why, and the way in which this will influence the whole dramatic outlook that the director will bring about. To the extent that the director understands precisely what it is the producer wants, interpretation in terms of taste, good sense and cohesiveness will be achieved. Where the producer and the director are in disagreement as to interpretation, these disagreements must be resolved before rehearsals get under way. Should these disagreements develop during rehearsals, they must again be resolved on a mutually professional basis of understanding. In all cases, the final arbiter of what the interpretation shall be must be the producer. It is up to the director to deliver this. It is also up to the director to have a depth of understanding of the producer's interpretative desire. Only with such interpretation and depth can the director properly motivate the performers to produce the results sought.

3) What is the setting of the play? On the face of it, this may seem like an ambiguous question. However, determining the exact locale is a matter of agreement between the producer and the director. On the determination of such locale will depend the budget allocation for the particular setting desired. For example, it is not enough that the producer, working with the director, shall have as a setting "a street corner." It must be a particular street corner in a particular city before the exact locale can be achieved in scenic design and construction. Once the locale is determined, the next question is, "where precisely is the audience's place in the scene?" Is the viewer with the main character in the scene or with a perspective of what is going on from, for example, the vantage point of a traffic officer in an outdoor setting at the corner of, let us say, 5th Avenue and 42nd Street. The director is responsible for the details of clarity which will move an audience within a scene from one point to another, or from one scene to another. On transitional devices—whether these are visual, or in terms of sound effects, music or dialoque, or some combination of all of these—will depend the quickness and clarity with which the viewers will move from one locale to another.

4) What methods of transition will be used? These will depend upon the type of drama and the kinds of scenes involved. Budget, too, will be a factor in deciding upon the transitional device. On a low budget program, for example, it might be necessary to dissolve to a still shot, with background music and background sound effects making the transition. It might be necessary to go to an in-limbo (a non-representational background) presentation to achieve the transition. In any case, the transitional device must be clearly established and followed through in execution, in terms of music, sound, narration, arts and graphics.

5) How shall the drama be cast? Factors such as the following will influence the decisions: the number of characters in the drama; whether a "name" performer is to be used; whether, because of the large number of parts or the peculiarity of character types, auditions must be held. Until the main characters are cast, minor or supporting roles should not be. Much will

depend upon a balancing of acting talents, voices, physical types, and contrast of such types. If the program is part of a regular series, it will usually have a fairly fixed cast with permanent leads, and with only minor characters changing.

6) What are the production staff requirements? For the most part, dramatic programs require the following: engineers; an announcer or narrator; a music director and orchestra, or organist, or record engineer—depending upon the music to be used and whether the budget will allow for original scoring; sound effects personnel; arts and graphics personnel; studio construction personnel; and other standard studio and technical persons.

7) What are the studio needs? At this point, based on budget, the producer must make decisions on the following: How many microphones and cameras will be used? What kind and amount of sound equipment is needed? What are the accommodations for the size of the cast? Do the director and the engineer have line-of-sight to all studio elements from the control room? If not, are studio elements placed in such a position that these are readily controllable and viewable through the use of monitors in the control room? In setting up the studio plan, the director working with the producer must be ready with alternative plans should changes be necessary because of budget, because of set construction, or because of the non-availability of specific kinds of studio space.

8) What are the special effects problems if any? For example, there may be video or sound effects never before used which require special experimentation. Frequently, such experimentation must be carried out in conjunction with the Engineering Department in order to achieve the effect desired. Occasionally, the special effects problems may involve special orchestration or require a highly specialized original underscoring. Whatever the problem may be, it is frequently up to the producer, in conjunction with the director, to work with the particular departmental chief or chiefs under whom the total effect needs to be worked out.

9) How much rehearsal time is needed for this broadcast? Naturally, the amount of rehearsal time required is entirely in the hands of both the producer and the director. Only one stipulation needs to be made. The broadcast must be prepared so as to be taped or filmed and edited to hit the air at the scheduled broadcast time on the scheduled day. We must recognize that the producer and the director of the drama program, who work for a product of superiority, will never believe that the rehearsal time has been sufficient. Apart from striving for this ideal, however, the following factors determine the amount of rehearsal time that should be planned: If a cast is large, it will take more time to rehearse a program than if the cast is a small one. The complexity and amount of sound and visual patterns sought are determining factors for the amount of rehearsal time needed. Video and sound routines employing standard materials, however, are not difficult to rehearse nor do they necessarily require a great deal of time.

Original background music will take more time to rehearse than music which is standard. It is generally conceded that the amount of required in-studio rehearsal time for the average well-produced drama program is roughly 15 to 20 times the length of the broadcast. Each program presents its own time complications, however, when it comes to setting a rehearsal schedule. It is frequently better to overestimate rather than have a production suffer because of insufficient amount of rehearsal time. It is important to check the AFTRA and other pertinent union contracts to determine how much rehearsal time is allowed before going into overtime.

Summary

What may we best say about the producer of the drama program and the way in which to approach production needs? In reading the script, look for particular things—interest aroused at the opening, whether all characters are necessary, whether time and place are clearly delineated, whether all audio, video and music references in the script are necessary to the action, whether there is a definite progression from minor to major climaxes, whether the drama should be produced as written, whether entrances and exits are properly motivated and whether transitions satisfy the producer's and director's script treatment. The producer must then do the following:

1) See to the duplication of scripts in sufficient number to take care of the cast, engineers, announcing, production, video, sound and music, filing and publicity.

2) Requisition the staff. Final contracts must be drawn where these are necessary. The producer must gather studio staff, engineers and camera operators, and requisition audition and rehearsal space, as required.

3) Requisition studio equipment, including numbers and kinds of cameras, microphones and special effects devices. All of this must be planned well in advance, against a carefully worked out time schedule.

4) If one of the rehearsals is to be video-taped for analysis before going to the final dress rehearsal, this must be arranged for.

5) Set up the rehearsal sequence, including reading rehearsals, blocking rehearsals, the first microphone and dummy camera rehearsal (if required), the music cue rehearsal, the technical and camera rehearsal, the dress rehearsal, the spotting rehearsal.

6) Whenever possible, a second dress rehearsal should be scheduled. Under most conditions this is a luxury that is not often attainable.

The producer approaches air time and must:

7) Check the script for last minute changes and confer on those changes with the personnel involved, including camera operators, floor director and video engineer.

8) At the last minute, rehearse the opening of the program to make sure that all of the elements are ready and in place. Make a final check with the floor director, the video engineer, the musical director or the music engineer, and the sound effects personnel.

9) Make a final microphone check.
10) Provide the announcer or narrator introducing the program with a last minute run-through.

The Dramatic Serial

Some differences between the handling of the regular drama program and that of the serial-drama permit a shortening of time in preparing the latter. In many instances there is a continuity of cast, crew and other production personnel and facilities, reducing the amount and kind of pre-rehearsal work. First rehearsals are usually a combination of blocking and reading. Frequently, these may take place before dummy cameras and either dummy or live mikes. On the serial-drama program, sound and music are brought together in the rehearsal immediately following the blocking rehearsal. Sometimes these elements are not combined until the final "dress," just before video-taping or going on the air. There should always be a run-through for timing of the announcer's opening and closing, as well as for any commercials that may be used. Basically, the producer makes no distinction between the regular drama and serial-drama when it comes to an adherence to principles of organization, pre-planning and budgeting.

OTHER PROGRAM TYPES

By-and-large, all that has thus far been described as the producer's duties and responsibilities, pre-planning requirements and detailed anticipation of in-studio and on-the-air needs, is applicable to all other program types. Some interesting variants that the producer is likely to meet, however, suggest a brief overview of other major program forms.

The Variety and Magazine Types

The variety and magazine types of programs may contain elements of news, discussions and interviews as well as featured performers such as singers, instrumentalists and others. Many such programs include circus acts and similar types. The problems of the producer, while essentially the same as those previously discussed, may be minimized, depending upon the length of each segment of the program. One of the difficulties the producer faces with the variety or magazine type is that if the budget is more or less standard, in many instances it may be necessary to settle for other than "name" talent. Learn how to find and judge new talent from night clubs, off-Broadway theatres and other sources.

One kind of magazine show uses the approach of "stripping." Strips or segments appear in many types of magazine formats and are especially popular in children's or young viewers' types of programming. The magazine show that uses strips combines many different types of materials such as storytelling, animated sequences, sequences on "understandings" or "appreciations." There are also the actuality or on-the-spot types of realistic inserts. These may be anything from an interview which takes place in someone's living room, to a sequence from a musical or ballet, to an on-location nature spot which examines conditions as they are in nature, rainfall, animal environment, and the like. The strip approach has a distinct advantage in that short sequences can be shot on location and used at different times and in different productions according to the producer's all-over design.

Women's Programs

Women's programs before the emergence of the women's liberation movement of the 1960s were largely a special containment of what was then thought to appeal to the singular interest of women. This usually confined itself to such things as cooking and sewing, homemaking, new recipes and fashions. In the broadcast media—in the television discussion program and in the radio program—"women's programs" rarely contained much of anything. They were what they were because women were always conceived to have a secondary place in life. In the total outlook upon the world their job was to be ornamental, "homemakers," the bearers and carriers of children. On occasion a brilliant woman might rise and become something more than just the cliché of the woman with her specialized place in life; occasionally she was indeed a very real person. But this was only if she rose to the fore and became outstanding. Usually this happened in the world of the arts, occasionally in the world of social welfare, but only rarely in the other areas of human endeavor controlled by and jealously guarded by men.

Late in the 1960s a radical change took place in the whole concept of women's programs. Certain women personalities on the air came to the fore. They became the progenitors of at least beginning attempts to integrate women into the mainstream of broadcasting.

In addition to the gradual emergence of women as personalities and subjects in programming in general, so-called women's programs, as discussed in Chapter 4, became oriented to special needs—such as credit, housing, insurance, jobs, medical treatment and similar areas in which women suffer severe discrimination.

The Educational or Instructional Program

As is customary, developments in the field of education lag behind developments in the counterpart commercial fields. This is true whether we are discussing an educational idea, a new concept or a new approach to learning, learning theory, satisfying the continuous learning needs of the individual or providing new and innovative insights. The same has been true in the development of software or media materials for educational and learning needs. Traditionally, a new idea in the field of education takes roughly 50 years from time of inception to time of acceptance at the elementary and secondary level. However, professional colleagues in the field of education frequently suggest that it takes at least 400 years for a new idea to be accepted, tried, used and refined at the post-secondary or college and university level. Such lengthy lags of time are neither needed, tolerable nor acceptable when it comes to television materials. But production in the field of educational television, too, lags by approximately 10 to 15 years. We are all aware of the usual image conjured up by the words "educational television." Such an image is one of the "talking head." The method of vocal delivery is usually even, uninteresting and frequently has been didactic and authoritarian. One might be tempted to suggest that this is a reflection of the teacher-cum-ruler-in-a-classroom. However, the glare of the television tube no longer allows this kind of refuge or over-sanctimonious protection of the less than liberated thought and method of approach practiced in the confines of many elementary, secondary and post-secondary institutions.

The educational television program hasn't the right to be as dull and as drab as the producer of it may wish it to be. The lighted black box in the corner of the living room or at the front of the classroom must not be permitted to be as much of a "boob tube" as it may wish to be. The viewer, whether 8 or 80, is far more sophisticated and demanding of what may or may not be delivered and what he or she will or will not accept.

The principles of production planning and production training enunciated in this chapter apply equally well to the background and training of the producer of the educational television program. The producer of that program, like the producer of the commercial program, must obey the same dicta: 1) think it through; 2) plan it thoroughly and well; 3) research it for internal values; 4) test it thoroughly on the possible recipient; 5) be sure that whatever is in the formative stage holds up after you have subjected it to a summative evaluation; 6) look for thorough-going and dependable reactions and research.

Above all, ask the questions: Does it fit? Does it hold together? Does it hold interest? Does the viewer react effectively? Is it believable? And, most important, does it have the true sense of interest, amusement and reliable understanding?

One major type of instructional broadcast is designed for very specific content information. Disseminating philosophic attitudes and attempting to clarify changes in attitude or outcome are difficult to achieve in the creation and dissemination of television material. Basic information broadcasts should be designed to disseminate information in a palatable, interesting and, at times, amusing form. Where possible, such broadcasts should be designed for both the specific learner group and a broad general audience. This is not always easy to achieve, but where it is done it pays handsome dividends for the producer. There are two separate and distinct audiences: one to learn, one to be informed. In designing material for these two types of audiences, content should not be strained or pulled out of focus.

An important element in the production design is the planning, constructing and packaging of non-broadcast materials. First and foremost among the non-broadcast materials are guides either for the teacher or, more importantly, for the learner. The guide is, in effect, an informational road map which helps the learner to be prepared for what is to be seen on TV, to receive it in an intelligent and informed manner, to be instructed as to the follow-up activity to reinforce the learning that is hoped for and to be prepared for the post-viewing process of examination—normally a part of the total reinforcement pattern.

Depending upon the type of course, slides and films are accompanying materials that can aid greatly. These are especially important materials in the science areas where the demonstration of the object, formula or the scientific process are essential to an understanding of the material that has been presented. The illustrated slide or the film loop will frequently bring details or a reinforcement of details to the eye that could not be managed during the actual television presentation of the material itself.

In certain courses audio recordings are extremely helpful. These are usually available in cassette form and are particularly helpful in the learning of foreign languages or in the reproduction of public presentations such as the speeches of outstanding participants in various public and educational procedures.

One approach to the design and execution of instructional materials is that of consortia planning. In some instances anywhere from 25 to 47 different organizations, state education departments, institutions, and national level professional organizations have combined thoughts, talent and money to bring about the production of a necessary instructional sequence which would have been far too costly for any single member of that consortium to produce by itself. The combination of dollars to bring about this outcome also represents a combination of thinking, approach, educational commitment and recognition of learning need. One of the most important advantages of the consortium is the non-duplicative potential of a pooling of information and resources. Traditionally, institutions of various kinds have resisted the use of materials created by other organizations. For the most part, such organizations and the individuals within them have said, in effect, "Only I know what the student needs," or "Our students and our learners are different from students and learners in other places and, therefore, materials designed elsewhere cannot possibly address themselves to our identified problems and the level of our learner resources." This syndrome of dissembling, known as the "NIH" syndrome—Not Invented Here—has plagued the producer of educational materials. The dedicated educator will say, "There is a universality in all learning needs. There are certain basic pieces of information that all learners may note and share. There are certain approaches to the totality of learning and humanistic needs that exist for all of us."

BUDGETING

The primary concern of all television programming should be the public to be served. Broadcast television, like any other enterprise, is primarily a business. Businesses are concerned with profit and loss. Programs of pure entertainment, seeking huge audiences, usually have strong sponsorship and are profit-making ventures. On the other hand, a program designed to serve a number of needs of the community usually must be produced within the confines of a limited dollar amount.

When budgeting is done for either sustaining shows or non-commercial shows the dollar figure is arrived at on the basis of previous experience and, most important, on the basis of total available budget for all programming needs for the year. In most stations of any size the executive producer works closely with a member of the business staff in preparing the budget. Both are well aware of the outside limitations in terms of dollars. Both are well aware that if the budget for a given program goes over what is anticipated for it, then certain adjustments must be made. It is the job of the budgeting person who, in effect, acts almost like a combination business manager/production manager to determine what are the variations and the limitations which can be approached to achieve what the producer has in mind for the particular program or series of programs.

An overriding need on the part of all persons who prepare a production budget is to *know* all the elements of production. What type of a program is this? Is it a dramatic show? If so, how many sets are involved? How many and what kinds of talent will be involved? What is the general mode of the program? How much time will it take to "light" the program?

One important element in budget planning is referred to as "the spill factor," the unknown factor that is likely to require additional time, and therefore additional concomitant costs such as crew time, recording time, performer time. An example of the "spill" factor, suggested by Peter Calabrese of WNBC-TV Business Affairs, is the situation in which you bring a theatre group to perform scenes from a Broadway production in which they may be involved at the time. The group is unaccustomed to the heat of the studio lights. This may cause their energy levels to change and, therefore, many more "takes" may be required than would be from performers accustomed to the environment of a television studio. Or the cast is unaccustomed to the background music that is inserted. Because of the required additional time, the budget "spills" over, is greater than might initially appear necessary. A good budget would anticipate this possibility and would provide an estimated number of additional dollars for such "spill" circumstances.

When a program is being budgeted, it may be that the total dollar figure arrived at is not within the dollar range limits that are known to the budget-maker or the executive producer of the show. In that case, management must be approached to find out whether there is any latitude or any additional dollar source available. A budget is a reflection of a number of ideas, and it is the way in which the budget translates the ideas of the executive producer that a two-fold plan will emerge.

Therefore, budgeting is an effective instrument not only for measuring the dollar costs of a production but for measuring the approach that will be taken to the preparation of that production and the airing of it. To reiterate, a budget is a plan for achieving that which the executive producer has originally conceived, or that which a freelance writer may have conceived and translated into a script and which an executive producer subsequently takes and converts into a production concept and, finally, a program.

In no way can one section in one chapter attempt to answer all the questions necessary for preparing a television production budget, either for film or videotape. This section will attempt to deal with only some of the basic overviews of budgeting.

Basic Planning

A budget is as much a reflection of the financial circumstances which surround a television station as it is of the production to be achieved in that station's environs. It is impossible to prepare a budget without an adequate background in the field of production. If the budget-maker and the producer are two different people, then the budget-maker must be someone who has spent a number of years in various areas of production, at least a few of which should have been very intimately involved with budgeting for a given production. A budget rundown sheet should actually be a layout sheet of the procedures to be accomplished within a particular budget. It should take into account as many areas as possible and it should try not to "lump" together too many elements of the budget into one generalized concept. It is all well and good to start the budget preparation with the idea that one minute of a half-hour program may cost "x" amount of dollars. However, this is only a generalized figure and, as budgeting proceeds, more detail is necessary, broken down with as many dollar amounts as possible.

There are a number of things of which the budget-maker must be aware. For example, if film is to be shot on-location a wise budget-maker knows that the following elements must be considered: cost of raw stock; cost of developing; cost of location shooting; cost of producing a magnetic track.

But back of all of these and before we even arrive on the scene to do any shooting, one must include the following: the crew—a breakdown of the individual members of the crew; pieces of equipment—are these to be rented? do they exist? are some rented and some to be bought? The location-director costs.

Above-the-line, Below-the-line

Generally, budgets are divided into two main elements, "below-the-line" costs and "above-the-line" costs. The "below-the-line" costs are all those involved with the physical production itself—the things that need to be done in the studio; the costs of set-making; the dollars to be invested in the crew and shooting; the kind of special equipment that may be used for special scenes. "Above-the-line" refers to such elements as talent, director, legal fees, music.

Location Considerations

You need to have information about the location, if you are shooting on location; what the laboratory and sound charges will be; the raw stock to be used; what the equipment costs will be (and whether these must be acquired or rented to take on location, whether they exist at the site or whether they are part of a package-and-crew arrangement); what the amortized costs are.

Unions

Are you in an area where you will be dealing with any of the broadcasting unions? It is important to know what their basic fees are, residuals, rehearsal time specifications, and what overtime, travel time, and other rates are. The major unions to be considered are: AFTRA (American Federation of Television and Radio Artists); AFM (American Federation of Musicians); DGA (Directors Guild of America); SAG (Screen Actors Guild); ASCAP (American Society of Composers, Authors and Publishers); BMI (Broadcast Music Incorporated); NABET (National Association of Broadcast Employees and Technicians); IATSE (International Alliance of Theatrical Stage Employees); and IBEW (International Brotherhood of Electrical Workers).

Film

An important element in developing a production budget relates to the use of film. The question must be answered, "Will the entire program be shot on film or will there be a number of film segments in it?" In developing a film budget, the following factors must be taken into account: the number of shooting days; length of shooting day required by the producer; amount of raw stock; number of crew required; development and processing of the film (will it be at an outside lab, or will it be developed with internal facilities, if such facilities exist?).

It is usually cheaper to use an in-house facility for film processing. However, sometimes the in-house facility may not be available when it is wanted. Therefore, the budget must provide for the use of an outside processor. In subsequent adjustments of the budget, it may become necessary to use the in-house facility on a first-come-first-served basis. The capacity of the in-house facility must also be considered. Can it produce work prints? Does it have the ability to produce an optical track? Not all in-house facilities have such capacity.

If conferencing with the producer or writer of the program or series indicates, for example, that only one day of shooting is required, then such a filming schedule would normally not present a problem. The film could be developed in-house. A work print could be made for the editors to work with. They could cut the work print and then use it to edit the original film. After editing, the film could then be integrated into the final editing of the program with the videotape. However, if the entire program is to be shot on film, the situation is somewhat different. Under the condition in which film becomes the sole means of production, remember that opticals will be needed for credits and titles. With the above in mind, an outside lab should be used for the work print, for the corrected print, and for the final print to be used for broadcast.

It should be noted that once the budget is determined and once the production people are informed that they may use an outside lab for the development of film, they are then expected to use their own judgment. Any money saved on the film development can be used in several ways: to extend aspects of production, to be returned to the administration for future uses, to be applied to other needs related to the program under production, such as promotion.

Let us assume that a certain amount of film will be shot on location and will then be brought into the studio to be edited. Whether the entire program will be in film form or whether part or most of it will be on videotape, we must remember that the chore of editing is a time-consuming one. The cost of the editor and the editing equipment (or use of the editing equipment at an editing house) is an important part of the budget. Editing a half hour of television programming from film usually takes about seven weeks. If it is a one-hour program, it takes about twelve weeks. This is only a "rule of thumb," but it is a good one to follow since this will then determine when you can logically expect to have a program completed and when you can logically plan for an airing. If the editing is to be done by an editing house, ask them to submit a budget in advance and a breakout—as complete as possible—of all the elements for which the budget is proposed, with a dollar figure attached to each element. In this way one can judge whether or not the charge is adequate, is an over-charge, perhaps, or whether some elements that may be necessary are being completely ignored or downgraded.

Budgeting Schedules

The production manager is expected to see that the necessary production elements are where they should be at the proper time. Sometimes the budget coordinator or manager will sit down with the production manager and review the budget to be sure that appropriate measures are being taken to maximize the utilization of funds provided.

In some instances—such as a network serving the rebroadcast needs of some of its affiliates, redistribution by various libraries or centers, or distribution of a public broadcasting program for in-school use—final budgeting for the costs of copies can be considerably reduced if the copies to be provided are to be on some of the excellent ¾-inch or U-matic cassettes, or on some of the compatible EIAJ-I ½-inch videotape formats.

The following schedules, "A," "B," and "C," represent three forms used as basic budgeting approaches to programs, as provided by Peter Calabrese of WNBC-TV Business Affairs and Larry Johnson, Manager of WNBC-TV's Community Affairs, whose insights are principally reflected in this discussion on budgeting. (Keep in mind that such costs are subject to constant change.) In the case of schedules "B" and "C," dollar amounts are attached to specific items. In the case of still other items no dollar amount appears since the particular item was not used for budgeting the program under consideration.

GRAM:	AIR DATE		PRE	POST-TO { DATE COMP	ACTUAL
MGR.	VTR DATE	REPORT DATES:			

BELOW-THE-LINE	BUDGET	PRE-SHOW EST.	POST TO { DATE COMP	SHOW EST.		ACTUAL
STOCK SCENERY						
SCENERY CONST.						
SCENIC ART						
PROPS						
DRAPES						
COSTUME DESIGN						
COSTUMES						
TRUCKS						
SCENIC DESIGN						
GRAPHIC ARTS						
SUB-TOTAL						
STAGEHANDS						
MAKE-UP						
WARDROBE						
ELEC. EQUIP.						
STUDIO FACIL.						
LIVE STUDIO						
FILM STUDIO						
AD/SM						
SPECIAL EFFECTS						
STORAGE						
BASIC ENG.						
PRIOR/POST ENG.						
DRY REH, ENG.						
EXTRA TECH. EQUIP.						
REFERENCE RECORDINGS						
SOUND EFFECTS						
FILM						
VIDEO TAPE						
TAPE EDITING						
KINE						
AMORTIZATION						
CONTINGENCY						
LOW-THE-LINE TOTAL						

RKS:

ACTUAL AND ESTIMATE COST REPORT

PROGRAM		AIR DATE		REPORT DATES:	PRE	POST-TO { DATE / COMP	ACT
UNIT MGR.		VTR DATE					

ACCT. NO.	ABOVE-THE-LINE	BUDGET	PRE-SHOW ESTIMATE	POST TO { DATE / COMP SHOW EST.	AC
300	NBC ORCHESTRA				
301	NON-PROFESSIONAL TALENT				
302	PRIZES				
307	SCRIPT SERVICES				
308	OUTSIDE REHEARSAL HALLS				
311	TALENT				
312	PRODUCTION STAFF:				
313	WRITERS				
315	PRODUCER				
315	DIRECTOR				
316	ANNOUNCERS & COMMENTATORS				
317	PACKAGE PAYMENTS				
319	RIGHTS				
322	MUSIC (OUTSIDE)				
345	ALL ENTERTAINMENT & LOCAL TRAVEL				
346	OUT OF TOWN TRAVEL & SUBSISTENCE				
359	MISCELLANEOUS				
388	EQUIPMENT RENTAL				
	OFFICE OVERHEAD				
699	PRODUCTION UNIT COST				
701	AFTRA, WGA, DGA, AFM - P&W				
	CONTINGENCY				
	ABOVE-THE-LINE TOTAL				

REMARKS:

OVER-NC (10/70)

Schedule "B"

ABOVE THE LINE:

Talent 284
Honorarium 50
Associate Producer 528
Producer 886
Music . . . . –0–
Musicians . . . . –0–
Pension/Welfare 22
Payroll Service Cost 74

ABOVE THE LINE TOTAL: $1,844

BELOW THE LINE:

AD/SM 165
Make-Up 42
Stagehands 1067
Scenic Design . . . . –0–
Wardrobe . . . . –0–
All Other Staging . . . . –0–
Props & Stock Rental 50
Graphic Arts 150
Construction Scenery 20
Sound & Special Effects . . . . –0–
Other Shop Charges . . . . –0–
Studio Engineers 1467
Studio (Live) . . . . –0–
Studio (Film) 225
Audio Recording 16
Video Tape Programs 251
Video Tape Editing 31
Travel & Entertainment 65
Miscellaneous 35

BELOW THE LINE TOTAL: $3,584
*FILM PROVISION $1,376

TOTAL PROGRAMS: $6,806

                                                                       ÷2 Pgms =
                                        TOTAL: $3,403 Per Pgm

Schedule "B"
Film Provision Only

ABOVE THE LINE:

    Talent ....
    Producer ....
    Writer ....
    Director...............................
    Associate Producer......................
    Production Coordinator ....

ABOVE THE LINE TOTAL:

BELOW THE LINE:

    Film Crew............................725
    Equipment Charges 75
    Raw Stock 245
    Processing..........................444
    Sound Services 62
    Optical .... –0–
    Film Studio......................... –0–
    Stock.Footage .... –0–
    Film Editing (Local) 140
    Script Services 30
    Miscellaneous 25
    Travel & Subsistence 45
    Contingency .... –0–
    Other .... –0–

BELOW THE LINE TOTAL: $1,791
                                                         × 20 Sessions
                                                         ─────────────
                                                         $35,820 ÷ 52 Pgms. =
                                                         $689
                                                         × 2 Pgms
                                                         ─────────────
                             TOTAL: $1,378 Per Pgm.

Schedule "C"

ABOVE THE LINE:

Talent 350
Producer/Writer 2750
Writer . . . . –0–
Director . . . . –0–
Associate Producer . . . . –0–
Production Coordinator . . . . –0–
Pension/Welfare 83
Payroll Service Cost 187

ABOVE THE LINE TOTAL: $3,370

BELOW THE LINE:

Film Crew 4869
Equipment Charges 550
Raw Stock 945
Processing 2678
Sound Services 975
Optical 675
Film Studio . . . . –0–
Stock Footage . . . . –0–
Film Editing (Local) 3295
Script Services 200
Miscellaneous . . . . –0–
Travel & Subsistence 700
Contingency . . . . –0–
Other 200

BELOW THE LINE TOTAL: $15,087

TOTAL PROGRAMS: $18,457

The process of budgeting can be either helpful or traumatic. The very concept of a disciplined approach to the use of money to achieve maximal results for that which the viewer perceives has made people weep. In the hands of the wise and alert the budget becomes an incredibly useful planning tool. Where there are severe monetary restrictions, the creative imagination can produce wonders in terms of camera effect. Where monetary restrictions are minor, the imagination can soar. The challenge is to the well-disciplined and dedicated producer. The prepared professional knows no limitations.

One may end this chapter on a note of unwholesome gloom, looking through the crystal ball of impossibility at the tasks that the television producer faces. One might shrug and say that the whole thing is impossible; that surely, there must be a better way to earn a living; surely, one has the right to enjoy a professional existence that doesn't lead to ulcers—the long-accepted hazard of the television profession—fallen arches, prematurely graying hair, sippy diets or the early collapse of the lungs from the overuse of tobacco and hard liquor as professional tranquilizers. But if we pass this professional way only once in our lives, we have a right to expect something more than the mundane, the utterly and reliably dull, dependent things in life. If professionalism cannot bring an air of excitement and constant inconsistency—if we cannot each day turn a new corner and find a whole new set of challenging and interesting circumstances to cope with, what are we doing in broadcasting to begin with?

The maturation of the whole person through professionalism is in itself a growth in learning along a continuum of constant education. Let us not hold a flag-of-cause for the Alice-in-Wonderland way of professional life. We must remember that the way for the producer can be one of excitement in outlook, fullness in accomplishment and rich in personal satisfaction for each positive goal achieved.

BIBLIOGRAPHY

Bermingham, Alan and others. *The Small TV Studio.* New York: Hastings House, 1975. A *Media Manual* of practical information on the operation of small (1600 sq. ft. or less) studios, well illustrated.

Bluem, A. William, John F. Cox, and Gene McPherson. *Television in the Public Interest: Planning, Production, Performance.* New York: Hastings House, 1961. Gives specifics on preparing material for a program before getting to the studio. Dated, but still useful.

Chester, Giraud, Garnet R. Garrison and Edgar E. Willis. *Television and Radio.* New York: Appleton-Century-Crofts, 1971, 4th edition. A general text as well as a production and performance guide. Not in-depth, very broad in coverage.

Costa, S. A., *How To Prepare a Production Budget for Film and Video Tape.* Blue Ridge Summit, Pa.: TAB Books, 1975. Second edition. Excellent practical guide.

Efrein, Joel Lawrence. *Video Tape Production and Communication.* Blue Ridge Summit, Pa.: TAB Books, 1971. Especially good on indicating the difference between live and recorded TV operations; good detail on tape equipment and requirements, dubbing and editing.

Emery, Edwin, Phillip H. Ault and Warren K. Agee. *Introduction to Mass Communications.* New York: Dodd, Mead, 1973. A definitive text for understanding mass media.

Fang, Irving E. *Television News, Revised and enlarged edition.* New York: Hastings House, 1972. Excellent examples of network TV reporting and production.

Green, Maury. *Television News: Anatomy and Process.* Belmont, Cal.: Wadsworth Publishing Co., 1969. Excellent comment on both the role in and the effects of news on society; particularly applicable at the local level.

Lazersfeld, Paul, and Robert K. Merton, "Mass Communication, Popular Taste and Organized Action," in *Mass Culture, The Popular Arts in America,* edited by Bernard Rosenberg and David Manning White. Glencoe, Ill.: The Free Press, 1957, pp. 457–473. Insights in communication theory, practice and psychological investigation.

Marsh, Ken. *Independent Video: A Complete Guide to the Physics, Operation and Application of the New Television.* San Francisco: Straight Arrow Books, 1974.

Millerson, Gerald. 1972. *The Technique of Television Production,* 9th edition. New York: Hastings House, 1972. Informative, with detailed diagrammatic illustrations. Thorough analyses of why production decisions are made.

Peterson, Sheldon, ed. *The Newsroom and the Newscast.* New York: Time-Life Broadcasting, Inc., 1966. An excellent and inexpensive collection of news by practicing newscasters; stresses newsroom operations and staffing; still valid.

Robinson, Richard. *The Video Primer: Equipment, Production and Concepts.* Westport, Conn.: Hyperion Press, 1974.

Spottiswoode, Raymond, Gen. ed. *The Focal Encyclopedia of Film and Television Techniques.* New York: Hastings House, 1969. Deals with both film and distribution production techniques. Well diagrammed; clearly organized. Has more than 1000 pages and 1600 entries.

Stasheff, Edward and Rudy Bretz, *The Television Program: Its Direction and Production,* 5th edition, John and Lynn Gartley. New York: Hill & Wang, 1977. A good intermediate text; emphasizes the aesthetics of production.

Stone, Vernon, and Bruce Hinson. *Television Newsfilm Techniques.* New York: Hastings House, 1974. A project of the Radio Television News Directors Association, it deals with practical professional operations.

"Theatre on Television," in *World Theatre,* Vol. IX, No. 4 (Winter, 1960). A compendium of international thought and reports on producing and directing the drama for television.

Westmoreland, Bob. *Teleproduction Shortcuts: A Manual for Low-Budget Television Production in a Small Studio.* Norman, Okla.: University of Oklahoma Press, 1974.

Zettl, Herbert. *Sight, Sound, Motion: Applied Media Aesthetics.* Belmont, Cal.: Wadsworth, 1973. Basic concepts of the "art" of television.

———. *Television Production Handbook,* 3rd Edition. Belmont, Calif.: Wadsworth, 1976. A standard text on all phases of the production process.

ROBERT L. HILLIARD

*Chief, Educational Broadcasting Branch
Federal Communications Commission*

● *Television Broadcasting* is Dr. Hilliard's fourth book for Hastings House Communications Arts series, and revises and updates his 1964 publication, *Understanding Television*. The latter was translated into Spanish and distributed by the United States Information Agency in Latin America. A companion work, *Radio Broadcasting*, is in its second edition, and was translated into French and distributed in Africa by the U.S.I.A. His *Writing for Television and Radio*, in its third edition, is the leader in its field, and he is co-author with Dr. Hyman H. Field of *Television and the Teacher*. Dr. Hilliard has also published numerous articles on communications and education in professional journals. He has worked in both the commercial and educational mass media fields as a writer, producer and director, has been the recipient of several playwriting awards and has had his plays produced in university and community theatres. His newspaper background includes five years as a drama and film critic in New York.

Dr. Hilliard received the B.A. degree from the University of Delaware in philosophy and political science, the M.A. and M.F.A. degrees from Western Reserve University, and the Ph.D. degree from Columbia University. He began his teaching career in 1950 at Brooklyn College, subsequently taught at Adelphi University and was Associate Professor of Radio, Television and Motion Pictures, University of North Carolina at Chapel Hill, prior to joining the FCC staff in 1964. He has been active in professional associations and has served as chairperson of committees and projects for national and regional organizations. He has been consultant on television in higher education for New York State and special consultant on television for the Council of Higher Educational Institutions in New York City. He is Founder of The International University of Communications, Washington, D.C., the first institution to combine the individualized learning and project approach with the use of communications to directly solve critical human problems. In 1970 he served as a consultant and lecturer on communications and education in Japan, assisting in the planning for the Open University, and he visited officials of eight other Asian nations on behalf of the U.S. government.

In addition to his position as Chief of Educational Broadcasting for the FCC, Dr. Hilliard founded the Federal Interagency Media Committee in 1965, was re-elected chairperson of that organization every year since, and in 1977 became the first chairperson of the board of the Federal and International Media Communicators. Since 1974 he has been serving as chairperson of the Educational Technology Subcommittee of the Federal Interagency Committee on Education, appointed by the Assistant Secretary of the Department of Health, Education and Welfare. He was also instrumental in the founding of the FCC's National Committee for the Instructional Television Fixed Service, of which he served as executive vice-chairman. He is a frequent speaker to professional meetings and citizen groups and has received several awards for his work in education and communications.

*Dr. Hilliard has written this chapter in his private capacity. No official support or endorsement by the Federal Communications Commission is intended or should be inferred.

4

WRITING

BY ROBERT L. HILLIARD

THE TELEVISION WRITER aims at an audience that at one and the same time is very small and very large, that has much in common and almost nothing in common, that is a tightly knit group and a disunified mass.

Millions of people may be seeing the material developed by the writer. Yet, any one group within this vast audience is apt to be a small one—usually a family group, at home, in everyday surroundings. The distractions of everyday life are constantly at hand, continuously operative, and likely to pull the individual viewer away from the program. The writer must capture the imaginations and interests of this undiscriminating audience as soon as possible. Each word, each picture must be purposeful, must gain attention and hold interest. Ideally, there should be no irrelevancies in the writing, no extraneous moments.

To make any single piece of material effective, the writer often tries to find a common denominator that will reach and hold as many as possible of the groups and individuals watching the more than 120 million television sets in use in this country.

Unfortunately, there is an acceptance of the lowest common denominator and a reliance upon a *quantitative* measurement. The cultural contributions of our mass media have become, for the most part, comparatively mediocre in quality and repetitive in nature. An outstanding casualty of this trend has been serious drama.

THE MASS AUDIENCE

Television utilizes many of the techniques of the theatre and of the film, and the audience is directed through sight as well as through hearing. With its use of mechanical and electronic devices, television has more flexibility than the theatre but, because of the limitation of sight as opposed to the unlimited imagination of hearing alone, is not as flexible as radio. Nevertheless, television can combine the sound and the audience-orientation of radio, the live continuous performance of theatre and the electronic techniques of the film. It is capable of fusing the best of all previous communications media.

On the other hand, television also has specific limitations. It is greatly restricted in production by *physical* time and space. Time-wise, the writer cannot develop a script as fully as might be desirable. Actual program length, after commercial and intro and outro credit time has been subtracted, runs from approximately 10- to 12-minutes for the quarter-hour program, 21- to 24-minutes for the half-hour program and 42- to 49-minutes for the hour program. This limitation is a particular hindrance in the writing of a dramatic program. Space-wise, the writer is hampered by the limitation of the camera view, the limitation of settings for live-type taped television (the term "live-type taped television," as used here, refers to the taped program which uses the continuous action, non-edited procedure of the live show; it is done as if it were a live show) and the comparatively small viewing area of the television receiver. The writer must orient the script toward small groups on the screen at any one time and make extended use of the close-up shot in studio-produced taped shows, as differentiated from TV films. Sets and outdoor effects are also obviously limited. These limitations prompted the intimate, subjective approach in dramatic writing.

Television combines both subjectivity and objectivity in relation to the audience, fusing two areas that are usually thought of as being mutually exclusive. Through use of the camera and electronic devices, the writer and director frequently may give the audience's attentions and emotions a subjective orientation by directing them to specific stimuli. The close-up, the split screen and similar devices are especially useful. The television audience cannot choose, as does the threatre audience, from the totality of presentation upon a stage. The television audience can be directed to a specific stimulus which most effectively achieves the purpose of the specific moment in the script. Attention can be directed to subtle reaction as well as to obvious action.

The writer not only faces a problem with the quality level of the material, but faces concrete manifestations of this problem in the selection of specific subject matter. Television writing is affected greatly by censorship. Censorship falls into two major categories: material that is "censorable" and material that is "controversial." Censorable material, as discussed here, is that which generally is considered not in good taste for the home television audience, although this same material might be perfectly acceptable in the legitimate theatre or in films. Profanity, the sanctity of marriage and the home, suicide, unduly provocative sex and other similar items are theoretically governed by censorship codes or, as sometimes called, standards of good conduct.

The Federal Communications Commission frequently acts as an arbiter of public taste. The Communications Act of 1934, As Amended, authorizes fines or license suspension for "communications containing profane or obscene words, language, or meaning. . . ."

Censorship of controversial material is of concern to the writer. Controversial material refers to subject matter which in the broadest sense might disturb any viewer. Such material might relate to any area of public thinking, including certain aspects of political, social, economic, religious and psychological problems. "When a story editor says, 'We can't use anything controversial,' and says it with a tone of conscious virtue, then there is danger," observes Erik Barnouw.

There is a great danger to freedom of expression and the democratic exchange of ideas in American television because many of the media executives fear controversy. On the grounds of service to the sponsor and on the basis of high ratings for non-controversial but mediocre entertainment, anything controversial has been avoided in too many cases. It can be said that if a sponsor permits a product to be identified with a controversial issue that may offend even small groups of citizens, there may be damage to the company's prestige. It can also be said, on the other hand, that anyone using the public airwaves has a responsibility not only to a private company, but to the public as a whole.

The media are powerful. The impact of the media is clearly reflected in the success and importance of Madison Avenue. Commercials *do* sell products and services. The impact of media has enabled news and public affairs programs, even in their frequently limited and sometimes biased coverage of controversial issues, to become significant factors in changing much of our political and social policies and beliefs. Television is credited with bringing to much of the American population an understanding of the violence and prejudice practiced against Blacks, with its coverage of the civil rights movement in the south in the early 1960s. The media brought to people in their homes some of the horrors of Vietnam and some of the actions of millions of Americans in actively opposing the war. The result was nationwide citizen pressure that caused one president to end his political career and another president to ultimately wind down and end most of American war participation in southeast Asia. In the early 1970s the live coverage of the Watergate hearings and the Nixon impeachment proceedings brought sharply to the American people information, ideas, feelings and, in many cases, motivated action that would not have otherwise come.

The writers who prepare continuity and background material for programs dealing with such issues and events can have the satisfaction of knowing that they are contributing to human progress and thought and are directly participating in changing society and solving problems of humanity. There are not too many professions in which one can accomplish this on such a broad and grand scale!

Theoretically, the writer can help to fulfill the responsibility of the mass media to serve the best interests of the public as a whole, can raise and energize the cultural and educational standards of the people and thus strengthen the country. Realistically, the most well-intentioned writer is still under the control of the network and advertiser whose first loyalties seem to be directed toward their own interests and not necessarily toward those of the public. Occasionally, these interests coincide. The writer who wishes to keep a job in the mass media is pressured to serve the interests of the employer. It is hoped that conscience will also enable the writer to serve the needs of the public.

BASIC PRODUCTION ELEMENTS

When videotape came along in the 1950s many people looked for a revolution. Magnetic tape did replace film in many areas of TV production, but film remained dominant in entertainment programs, particularly drama, and in news and commercials. With the refinement of videotape equipment and techniques, some inroads were made, but it wasn't until the early 1970s that something along the lines of a real revolution—or, perhaps, instant evolution—began to be seen. In the mid-1970s a number of stations, and even major production studios, concluded that the advantages of videotape in many ways surpass those of the film and were switching to tape. In the late 1970s the video disc became technologically and economically practical and in the 1980s it might well begin to rival videotape.

The writer must learn what the camera can and cannot do, what sound or visual effects are possible in the control room, what terminology is used in furnishing directions, descriptions and transitions, and what other technical and production aspects of the media are essential for effective writing. There are six major areas the writer should be aware of: the studio, the camera, the control room, special video effects, editing, and sound.

The TV Studio

Studios vary greatly in size and equipment. Network studios, where drama series and specials are usually produced, have not only all the technical advantages of a television studio, but the size and equipment, as well, of a movie sound stage. Some individual stations have excellent facilities, others are small and cramped. The writer should be aware of studio limitations before writing the script, especially where the show may be videotaped or produced live, and it is necessary to avoid too many sets or large sets.

The Camera

Whether the show is being recorded by a film camera or by a television camera on videotape, the basic movements of the camera are the same. Even the terminology is the same. The principal difference is the style: short, individual takes for the film approach; longer action sequences and continuous filming for the television approach.

In either case, the writer should consider the camera as a moving and adjustable proscenium through which the attention of the audience is directed just as the writer and director wish. Camera movement may change the position, angle, distance and amount of subject matter seen. There are five specific movements the writer must be aware of and be prepared to designate, when necessary, in the script.

Dolly In and Dolly Out/Zoom In and Zoom Out. The camera is on a dolly stand which permits smooth forward or backward movement. This movement to or away from the subject permits a change of orientation to the subject while keeping the camera on the air and retaining a continuity of action. The zoom lens accomplishes the same thing without moving the camera.

Tilt Up and Tilt Down. This consists of pointing the camera up or down, thus changing the view from the same position to a higher or lower part of subject area. The tilt also is called panning up and panning down.

Pan Right and Pan Left. The camera moves right or left on its axis. This movement may be used to follow a character or some particular action or to direct the audience attention to a particular subject.

Follow Right and Follow Left. This is also called the "travel" shot or the "truck" shot. It is used when the camera is set at a right angle to the subject and either moves with it, following alongside it or, as in the case of a stationary subject such as an advertising display, follows down the line of the display.

Boom Shot. Originally familiar equipment for Hollywood filmmaking, the camera boom became more and more part of standard television production practices. Equipment, usually attached to the moving dolly, enables the camera to "boom" from its basic position in or out, up or down, at various angles— usually high up—to the subject.

Note the use of the basic camera movements in the following scripts. In the first, using the standard television format, the writer would not ordinarily include so many camera directions, but would leave their determination to the director. They are included here to indicate to the beginning writer a variety of camera and shot possibilities. The left hand column, as shown here, would be written in on the mimeographed script almost entirely by the director.

VIDEO	AUDIO
	DETECTIVE BYRON
ESTABLISHING SHOT.	(AT DESK, IN FRONT OF HIM, ON CHAIRS IN A ROW, ARE SEVERAL YOUNG MEN IN DUNGAREES, LEATHER JACKETS AND MOTORCYCLES CAPS) All right. So a store was robbed. So all of you were seen in the store at the time of the robbery. So there was no one else in the store except the clerk. So none of you know anything about the robbery.

VIDEO	AUDIO
DOLLY IN FOR CLOSE-UP OF BYRON.	(GETTING ANGRY) You may be young punks but you're still punks, and you can stand trial whether you're seventeen or seventy. And if you're not going to cooperate now, I'll see that you get the stiffest sentence possible.
DOLLY OUT FOR LONG SHOT OF ENTIRE GROUP. CUT TO CU. PAN RIGHT ACROSS BOYS' FACES, FROM ONE TO THE OTHER, AS BYRON TALKS.	Now, I'm going to ask you again, each one of you. And this is your last chance. If you talk, only the guilty one will be charged with larceny. The others will have only a petty theft charge on them, and I'll see they get a suspended sentence. Otherwise, I'll send you all up for five to ten.
FOLLOW SHOT ALONG LINE OF CHAIRS IN FRONT OF BOYS, GETTING FACIAL REACTIONS OF EACH ONE AS THEY RESPOND.	(OFF CAMERA) Joey? <div align=center>JOEY</div>(STARES STRAIGHT AHEAD, NOT ANSWERING.) <div align=center>BYRON</div>(OFF CAMERA) Al? <div align=center>AL</div>I got nothin' to say. <div align=center>BYRON</div>(OFF CAMERA) Bill? <div align=center>BILL</div>Me, too. I don't know nothin'. <div align=center>BYRON</div>(OFF CAMERA) O.K., Johnny. It's up to you.
TILT DOWN TO JOHNNY'S BOOT AS HE REACHES FOR HANDLE OF KNIFE. TILT UP WITH HAND AS IT MOVES AWAY FROM THE BOOT, INTO AN INSIDE POCKET OF HIS JACKET. CUT TO MEDIUM SHOT ON BOOM CAMERA OF JOHNNY WITHDRAWING HAND FROM POCKET. BOOM INTO CLOSE-UP OF OBJECT IN JOHNNY'S HAND. (ORDINARILY, A BOOM SHOT WOULD NOT BE USED HERE. A ZOOM LENS WOULD BE EASIER TO USE AND AT LEAST AS EFFECTIVE.)	<div align=center>JOHNNY</div>(THERE IS NO ANSWER. THEN JOHNNY SLOWLY SHAKES HIS HEAD. UNPERCEPTIBLY, BYRON NOT NOTICING, HE REACHES DOWN TO HIS MOTORCYCLE BOOT FOR THE HANDLE OF A KNIFE. SUDDENLY THE HAND STOPS AND MOVES UP TO THE INSIDE POCKET OF HIS JACKET. JOHNNY TAKES AN OBJECT FROM HIS POCKET, SLOWLY OPENS HIS HAND.)

Although the format in the following, a film script, is different, note that the terminology and the visual results are virtually the same. The numbers in the left-hand column refer to each "shot" or "sequence," with film scripts usually shot out of sequence, all scenes in a particular setting done with the cast at that location. The numbers make it possible to easily designate which sequences will be filmed at a given time or on a given day, such as "Barn Set—sequences 42, 45, 46, 78, 79, 81."

FADE IN
1. EXT. BEACH — SUNRISE — EXTREME LONG SHOT
2. PAN ALONG SHORE LINE AS WAVES BREAK ON SAND

3. EXT. BEACH — LONG SHOT
Two figures are seen in the distance, alone with the vastness of sand and water surrounding them.
4. ZOOM SLOWLY IN UNTIL WE ESTABLISH THAT FIGURES ARE A MAN AND A WOMAN.
5. MEDIUM LONG SHOT
The man and woman are standing by the water's edge, holding hands, staring toward the sea. They are about 50, but their brightness of look and posture make them seem much younger.
6. MEDIUM SHOT — ANOTHER ANGLE ON THEM
They slowly turn their faces toward each other and kiss.
7. CLOSE SHOT
8. MEDIUM CLOSE SHOT
Their heads and faces are close, still almost touching.
>GLADYS:
>>I did not feel so beautiful when I was 20.
9. CLOSE SHOT — REGINALD
as he grins
>REGINALD:
>>Me neither. But we weren't in love like this when we were 20.
>CUT TO
10. INT. BEACH HOUSE — ENTRANCE HALL — MORNING
The door opens and Gladys and Reginald walk in, hand-in-hand, laughing.

Types of Shots

Shot designations range from the close-up to the medium shot to the long shot. Within these categories there are gradations, such as the medium long shot and the extreme close-up. The writer indicates the kind of shot and the specific subject to be encompassed by that shot. The use of the terms and their meanings apply to both the film and the television format. Here are the most commonly used shots:

Close-up. This may be desgnated by the letters CU. The writer states in the script: "CU Harry," or "CU Harry's fingers as he twists the dials of the safe," or "CU Harry's feet on the pedals of the piano." The close-up of the immediate person of a human subject will usually consist of just the face and may include some of the upper part of the body, with emphasis on the face, unless specifically designated otherwise. The letters XCU or ECU stand for extreme close-up and designate the face alone. The term shoulder shot indicates an area encompassing the shoulders to the top of the head. Other designations are bust shot, waist shot, hip shot and knee shot.

Medium Shot. This may be designated by the letters MS. The camera picks up a good part of the individual or group subject, the subject usually filling the screen, but usually not in its entirety, and without too much of the physical environment shown.

Long Shot. The writer may state this as LS. The long shot is used primarily for establishing shots in which the entire setting, or as much of it as necessary to orient the audience properly, is shown. From the long shot, the camera may move to the medium shot and then to the close-up, creating a dramatic movement from an over-all view to the impact of the essence or selective aspect of the situation. Conversely, the camera may move from the intriguing suspense of the extreme close-up to the clarifying broadness of the extreme long shot.

Full Shot. This is stated as FS. The subject is put on the screen in its entirety. For example, "FS Harry" means that the audience sees Harry from head to toe. "FS family at dinner table" means that the family seated around the dinner table is seen completely.

Control Room Techniques and Editing

The technicians in the control room have various electronic devices for modifying the picture and moving from one picture to another. The technicians in the film editing room have the same capabilities, except that the modifications are done during the editing process, while in live-type videotaped television the modifications are done during the recording of the program. Further modifications can take place when editing the videotape.

The Fade. The fade-in consists of bringing in the picture from a black (or blank) screen. The fade-out is the taking out of a picture until a black level is reached. The fade is used primarily to indicate a passage of time, and in this function serves much like the curtain or blackout on the legitimate stage. Depending on the sequence of action, a fast fade-in or fade-out or slow fade-out or fade-in may be indicated. The fade-in is used at the beginning of a sequence, the fade-out at the end. The fade sometimes also is used to indicate a change of place.

The Dissolve. While one picture is being reduced to black level, the other picture is being brought in from black level, one picture smoothly dissolving into the next. The dissolve is used primarily to indicate a change of place, but is used sometimes to indicate a change of time. There are various modifications of the dissolve. An important one is the matched dissolve, in which two similar or identical subjects are placed one over the other and the fading out of one and the fading in of the other shows a metamorphosis taking place. The dissolving from a newly lit candle into a candle burned down would be a use of the matched dissolve.

The Cut. The cut is the technique most commonly used. It consists simply of switching instantaneously from one picture to another. Care must be taken to avoid too much cutting, and to make certain that the cutting is consistent with the mood, rhythm, pace and psychological approach of the program as a whole.

The Superimposition. The "super," as it is sometimes called, means the placing of one image over another, thus creating a fantasy kind of picture. This sometimes is used in the stream-of-consciousness technique when the thing being recalled to memory is pictured on the screen. The superimposition may be used for non-dramatic effects very effectively, such as the superimposition of titles over a picture or the superimposition of commercial names or products over the picture.

The Wipe. This is accomplished by one picture literally wiping another picture off the screen in the manner of a window shade being pulled down over a window. The wipe may be from any direction: horizontal, vertical, or diagonal. The wipe may also blossom out a picture from the center of a black level or, in reverse, envelop the picture by encompassing it from all its sides. The wipe can be used to designate a change of place or time.

The Split Screen. In the split screen the picture on the air is actually divided, with the shots from two or more cameras occupying adjoining places on the screen. A common use is for phone conversations, showing the persons speaking on separate halves of the screen. The screen may be split in many parts and in many shapes.

Film and Slides. For live-type television production, such as newscasts and in many college and university training studios which may not have sophisticated film or videotape equipment, film clips (short-lengths of 16-millimeter motion picture film) and slides are important. Films and slides provide visual information not available in the studio for news, sports, feature and documentary programs. The film clip may also be used in live-type videotaped drama to provide background shots necessary to the production which could not be achieved in the limited settings of the studio.

Sound

Sound in television does not convey movement and does not physically orient the audience as it does in radio. The microphone in the television play usually is not stationary, but is on a boom and a dolly to follow the moving performers. In the single-action shot of the film, it may be stationary if the actors do not move. The dialogue and sound on the set emanate from and must be coordinated with the visual action. Off-screen sound effects may be used, but they clearly must appear to be coming from off-screen unless they represent an action taking place on camera. Remember that the sound or music does not replace visual action, but complements or heightens it.

ANNOUNCEMENTS AND COMMERCIALS

Announcements and commercials differ mainly in that most of the former promote not-for-profit ideas, products and services—which may include ideological participation through personal time, energy or money contributions—while the latter sell, for profit, products, services and ideas. All commercials are designed to sell something. It is the existence of these commercials that provide the economic base for the American broadcasting system as it is now constituted.

Some commercials are awful because they insult our aesthetic sensibilities. Some are awful because they insult our logic and intelligence. Some are awful because they play on the emotions of those least able to cope with the incitements to buy—such as children.

Some commercials are good because they are, indeed, more aesthetically pleasing than the programs they surround. Some are good because they are educational and do provide the viewer with informational guidelines on goods and services.

This puts the writer squarely in the middle. On one hand, the writer has a responsibility to the agency and advertiser, creating not only the most attractive message possible, but one which convinces/sells. On the other hand, the power of the commercial charges the writer with the responsibility of being certain that the commercial has a positive and not a negative effect on public ethics and actions.

More and more the pressures of audiences, civic and citizen organizations, some professions and the federal government itself are changing the approaches to commercial writing and presentation. At one time some commercials were blatantly racist. Most advertisers and agencies have recognized the need not only to avoid stereotyped portrayals of minorities, but to include minorities as nonstereotyped characters in commercials. Prejudicial portrayals have not been limited to race. Negative ethnic references, particularly those related to national origins—Italy, Poland, for example—have also needed pointing out and correction. Perhaps one of the most flagrant areas of prejudice has been that regarding women.

Ethical considerations relate not only to portrayals of people, but to representations of products as well. In 1970 ACT (Action for Children's Television) petitioned the FCC to, among other things, eliminate all commercials from children's programming, citing content and approaches which ACT believed were harmful to children. In 1974 the NAB (National Association of Broadcasters) voluntarily amended its TV Code to reduce the commercial minutes in children's programs and to set certain content restrictions.

Lengths

Spot announcements may be commercial or non-commercial. The non-commercial kind are called public service announcements. Commercial spots may be inserted either within the course of a program or during the station break.

Spots may be of various lengths. The overwhelming number are 30 seconds long, although when the economy is up there is a marked increase in 60-second spots. Some advertisers have occasionally attempted the "split 30" commercial—combining two 15-second commercials for two of its products into one 30-second spot. Agencies have generally opposed this, however, believing that most products or services need more than 15 seconds to be effectively presented and sold.

Public Service Announcements

Stations usually receive PSAs already prepared by the writer for the distributing organization. Service groups, government agencies and other organizations devoted to activity related to the public welfare, such as Public Health

Departments, educational associations, societies aiding the handicapped, and ecology groups, among others, have devoted more and more time in recent years to special television and radio workshops for their regular personnel and volunteer assistants.

The good PSA is like the good commercial: it puts the product or service in the setting, using the strongest attention-getting, attention-keeping and persuasive elements, including personalities, drama and other special needs, as in the following example. This provides an example, too, of the format of the television spot.

(60 SECONDS)

VIDEO	AUDIO
FADE UP ON MLS OF WIFE, HUSBAND AND CHILD IN LARGE HAMMOCK. MOVE IN TO MCU OF MOTHER AND CHILD. DISSOLVE TO LEFT SIDE MCU SHOT OF ALL THREE. DISSOLVE TO MCU OF FRONT SHOT OF MOTHER AND CHILD.	JANIE SONG: I want to watch the sun come up another fifty years I want to write a novel that will bring the world to tears And I want to see Venice
DISSOLVE TO CU OF CHILD. DISSOLVE TO CU LEFT SIDE SHOT OF MOTHER AND CHILD.	I want to see my kids have kids I want to see them free
DISSOLVE TO MLS OF ALL THREE — MOVE IN TO MS. DISSOLVE TO LEFT SIDE MS OF MOTHER AND CHILD.	I want to live my only life I want the most of me I want to dance
DISSOLVE TO MS OF RIGHT SIDE OF MOTHER AND CHILD.	I want to love
DISSOLVE TO CU LEFT SIDE OF MOTHER AND CHILD.	I want to breathe
FREEZE FRAME AND DISSOLVE TO B & W.	ANNCR VO: Janie died On an endless road in America
PULL BACK FROM B & W PHOTO IN A PICTURE FRAME AND DOLLY PAST EMPTY BED	Because a lonely man was driving drunk out of his mind
	Problem drinkers who drive are responsible for more than 40 deaths every day Get the problem drinker off the road. JANIE SONG: I want to know what's out there beyond the furthest star I even want to go there if we ever get that far
TITLE: "GET THE PROBLEM DRINKER OFF THE ROAD." FADE TO BLACK.	And I want to see Venice.

C-1 I want to watch the sun come up another fifty years.

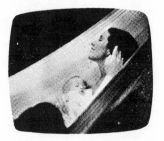

C-2 I want to write a novel that will bring the world to tears.

C-3 And I want to see Venice.

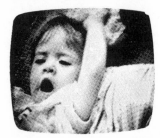

C-4 I want to see my kids have kids. I want to see them free.

C-5 I want to live my only life. I want the most of me.

C-6 I want to dance. I want to love. I want to breathe.

C-7 Janie died. On an endless road in America.

C-8 Because a lonely man was driving drunk out of his mind.

C-9 Problem drinkers who drive are responsible for more than 40 deaths every day. Get the problem drinker off the road.

C-10 I want to know what's out there beyond the furthest star.

C-11 I even want to go there if we ever get that far. And I want to see Venice.

WRITE:
DRUNK DRIVER
BOX 1969
WASHINGTON, D.C.

U.S. DEPARTMENT OF TRANSPORTATION
NATIONAL HIGHWAY TRAFFIC SAFETY ADMINISTRATION

C-12 Help. Do something about the problem drinker. For his sake. And yours.

Techniques of Writing Commercials

Barbara Allen, copywriter and teacher of television and radio writing, sets forth five preliminary steps in putting commercials together: 1.) know the product or service; 2.) pick the central selling idea; 3.) choose the basic appeal; 4.) select the format; and 5.) start writing.

Emotional Appeals. The appeal of the commercial is an emotional one. By emotional we do not mean the evoking of laughter or tears. Emotional appeal means, here, the appeal to the non-intellectual, non-logical aspects of the prospective customer's personality. It is an appeal to the audience's basic needs or wants. There are a number of basic emotional appeals that have been particularly successful and upon which the writer of commercials may draw as the motivating factor within any individual commercial. The appeal to self-preservation is perhaps the strongest of all. Drug commercials, among others, make good use of this appeal. Another strong appeal is love of family. Note the next commercial presented by an insurance company. Other widely used emotional appeals include patriotism, good taste, reputation, religion, loyalty to a group and conformity to public opinion.

Audience Analysis. Before choosing and applying the specific emotional or logical appeals, the writer must know, as fully as possible, the nature of the audience to whom the message is directed. In the mass media it is often impossible to determine many specifics about a given audience at a given air time. The audience is a disunified mass of many attitudes and interests, economic, social, political and religious levels, spread out over a broad geographical area—particularly in television. When advertisers sponsored entire programs and were, indeed, identified with particular programs and personalities, the writer could make some judgment on the kinds of people who watched that particular show. Since the spot ad began to replace the full-sponsor program, it has been harder for the writer to make such an analysis.

There are some basic elements of audience analysis that the writer may apply. These are: age, sex, size, economic level, political orientation, primary interests, occupation, fixed attitudes or beliefs, educational level, ethnic background, geographical concentration, and knowledge of the product. The writer should try to include appeals to all the major groups expected to watch the given program—and commercial. Be careful, however, not to spread the message too thin.

Organization of the Commercial. Inasmuch as the commercial's primary purpose is to persuade, the writer should be aware of the five basic steps in persuasive technique. First, the commercial should get the attention of the audience. This may be accomplished by many means, including humor, a startling statement or picture, a rhetorical question, vivid description, a novel situation or suspenseful conflict. Sound, specifically the use of pings, chords and other effects, effectively attracts attention, too.

Second, after attention is obtained, the audience's interest must be held. Following up the initial element with effective examples, testimonials, anecdotes, statistics and other devices, visual or aural, should retain the audience's interest.

Third, the commercial should create an impression that a problem of some sort exists, related vaguely to the function of the product advertised. After such an impression has been made, then, fourth, the commercial should plant the idea in the audience's mind that the problem can be solved by use of the particular product. It is at this point that the product itself might even first be introduced.

In the famous "try it, you'll like it" Alka Seltzer script, the process is condensed and the problem is quickly and cleanly presented and solved:

30 SECONDS

VIDEO	AUDIO
OPEN MCU MAN SEATED AT TABLE IN RESTAURANT. BEHIND HIM YOU SEE OTHER CUSTOMERS AND WAITER WHO IMITATES THE MAN'S GESTURES.	SFX: Restaurant noises. Low murmur, clatter of dishes, knives and forks. MAN: Came to this little place. Waiter says, "Try this, you'll like it." "What's this?" "Try it, you'll like it." "But what is . . . ?" "Try it, you'll like it." So I tried it. Thought I was going to die. Took two Alka Seltzer.
CUT TO TWO ALKA SELTZER DROPPING IN GLASS OF WATER. PAN ACROSS ASPIRIN BOTTLE AND TWO ASPIRINS. CONTINUE PAN ACROSS ROLL OF ANTACIDS AND TWO ANTACIDS. CONTINUE PAN TO FOIL PACK OF ALKA SELTZER.	ANNCR VO: For headache and upset stomach, no aspirin or antacid alone relieves you in as many ways as Alka Seltzer. For headache and upset stomach.
CUT BACK TO CU MAN IN RESTAURANT.	MAN: Alka Seltzer works. Try it, you'll like it!

Courtesy of Miles Laboratories and Wells, Rich, Greene, Inc.

Writing Styles. The writer constantly must be aware of the necessity for keeping the commercial in good taste. Usually, the writer will avoid slang and colloquialisms entirely unless these forms have specific purposes in specific places in the commercial. The writer should be certain that the writing is grammatically correct. Action verbs are extremely effective, as are concrete, specific words and ideas. If an important point is to be emphasized, the writer must be certain to repeat that point in the commercial, although in different words or in different forms. One exception would be the presentation of a slogan or trade mark; in this case word for word repetition is important. The writer should avoid, if possible, the use of superlatives, false claims, phony testimonials and other elements of obvious exaggeration.

The Television Storyboard

Commercial producers (and account people, sponsors) like to see as fully as possible the visual contents for a prospective commercial in its early stages.

For this purpose a "storyboard" is used. The storyboard usually is a series of rough drawings showing the sequence of picture action, optical effects, settings and camera angles, and it contains captions indicating the dialogue, sound and music to be heard. There are frequently many refinements from the storyboard that sells the commercial to the advertiser to the finished film or tape that sells the product to the viewer. Some producers work from storyboards alone. Others want scripts, either in the Hollywood or New York style, containing the visual and audio directions and dialogue. The U.S. Department of Transportation safety PSA, "Janie's Song," on pages 151–153 provides a comparison between the storyboard and the TV script.

Commercial Formats

There are five major format types for commercials: straight sell, testimonial, humorous, musical and dramatization. Any single commercial may consist of a combination of two or more of these techniques. The straight sell is, of course, the basic commercial approach.

Straight Sell. This should be a clear, simple statement about the product. The straight sell may hit hard, but not over the head and not so hard that it may antagonize the potential customer. The straight sell is straightforward, and although the statement about the product is basically simple and clear, the writing technique sometimes stresses a "gimmick," usually emphasizing something special about the product, real or implied, that makes it different or extra or better than the competing product. A slogan frequently characterizes this special attribute.

The Testimonial. The testimonial commercial is very effective when properly used. When the testimonial is given by a celebrity—whose social and economic status is likely to be quite a bit higher than that of the average viewer—the emotional appeals of prestige, power and good taste are primary. What simpler way to reach the status of the celebrity, if only in one respect, than by using the same product he or she uses? The writer must make certain that the script fits the personality of the person giving the endorsement.

An alternative to the traditional celebrity testimonial is the testimonial from the average man or woman—the worker, the homemaker, the man- or woman-in-the-street with whom the viewer at home can more easily identify.

Humor. Just as public attitudes toward humor change over the years, so do the humorous approaches in commercials. Always an effective attention-getter, humor in commercials, to be successful, must reflect the humorous trends of the time. The use of humor in commercials grew rapidly in the early 1970s and then, suddenly, as inflation, Watergate, industry ripoffs, pollution, impeachment, depression and other grim problems overtook the public, some things weren't very funny any more. A number of advertisers who had used humor heavily began to move away from it, playing it safe with the straight sell, frequently with a personality endorsement.

Satire and parody mark some of the most successful humorous commercials. The most effective parodies have been those which have a story line, even a limited one, in which the situation is dominant. Within the situation are the references to the product.

Music. The musical commercial has always been one of the most effective for having an audience remember the product. How many times have you listened to a song on radio or television, been caught up in its cadence, and then suddenly realized it was a commercial and not the latest popular hit tune? Music has been so effective in writing commercials that many of us have come to identify and remember Coca-Cola, McDonald's and United Air Lines, among others, first with their theme music and only secondarily with a particular sales message. One of the most effective examples, now a classic, is the following:

60 SECONDS

VIDEO	AUDIO
	Song:
CUT TO CU OF GIRL'S FACE AND SINGING.	I'd like to buy the world a home and furnish it with love. Grow apple trees
PB TO REVEAL GIRL SINGING WITH BOY AND GIRL WITH COKE BOTTLE ALSO SINGING.	and snow white turtles doves
DISS TO PAN ACROSS OF BOYS AND GIRLS IN NATIVE DRESS WITH COKE BOTTLES IN HAND AND SINGING.	I'd like to teach the world to sing (sing with me) in perfect harmony (perfect harmony) and I'd like to buy the world a coke and keep it company.
	It's the real thing.
DISS TO SIDE VIEW OF ROWS OF BOYS AND GIRLS IN NATIVE DRESS AND SINGING.	I'd like to teach the world to sing (what the world wants today)
DISS TO PAN ACROSS OF ROWS OF BOYS AND GIRLS IN NATIVE DRESS SINGING.	In perfect harmony (perfectly)
DISS TO PAN ACROSS OF COKE BOTTLES IN HANDS OF BOYS AND GIRLS.	I'd like to buy the world a Coke.
	and keep it company
DISS TO CU OF GIRL'S FACE AND SINGING.	It's the real thing. (Coke is)
DOUBLE EXPOSE CU GIRL'S FACE SINGING OVER CROWD SHOT TO PB TO REVEAL CROWDS OF BOYS AND GIRLS OF ALL NATIONS ON HILL WITH CRAWLING TITLE AND MATTE:	What the world wants today Coca-Cola . It's the real thing. What the world wants today Coke is. Coca-Cola.

SUPER: ON A HILLTOP IN ITALY WE
      ASSEMBLED YOUNG PEOPLE
      FROM ALL OVER THE WORLD
      TO BRING YOU THIS MESSAGE
      FROM COCA-COLA BOTTLERS
      ALL OVER THE WORLD. IT'S THE
      REAL THING. COKE.

Courtesy of The Coca-Cola Company. Words and music by Roger Cook, Roger Greenaway, William Becker and Billy Davis. McCann-Erickson, Inc.

Dramatizations. A dramatization is, in effect, a short play—a happening that creates suspense and reaches a climax. The climax is, of course, the revelation of the attributes of the product. In the classic structure of the play form, the resolution is the members of the audience all rushing out of their homes to buy the particular product. Dramatizations frequently combine elements of the other major commercial forms, particularly music, testimonials and humor.

NEWS

Any real happening that may have an interest for or effect upon people is news. The television and radio reporter has a limitless field. Anything from a cat up a tree to the outbreak of a war may be worthy of transmission to the mass media audience. The gathering of news, however, is not our primary concern here. The writing of news broadcasts is.

Two major agencies, the Associated Press and United Press International, which serve as news sources for the newspapers, also service television and radio stations. The larger networks have their own news gathering and reporting organizations.

All stations of any consequence, even small local stations, subscribe to at least one wire service. The small station also may use more immediate sources for local news, such as telephoned reports from city agencies or even private citizens, special information from the local newspapers, word of mouth communications, and sometimes special reporters of their own. The local news story must be written from scratch and, for television, written to fit in with the available visual material.

In the large station, the news usually is prepared by writers in a special news department. Most small stations do not have separate news departments, so news broadcasts are prepared by available personnel. The continuity department, if there is one, prepares the special local reports.

Styles of Writing

The writer of the news broadcast is, first of all, a reporter whose primary duty is conveying the news. The traditional "5 W's" of news reporting apply. In its limited time, the television report should tell What, Where, When, Who and, if possible, Why. The key word is *condensation*. The writer must be aware of the organization of the broadcast in order to provide the proper transitions, which should be clear and smooth between each story. The writer should also be aware of the content approach, whether it is straight news, analysis or personal opinion, so as not to confuse editorializing with news.

Consider the time of the day the broadcast is being presented—whether the audience is at the dinner table, seated comfortably in the living room, or rushing madly to get to work on time. The writer should think of the news as dramatic action. The story with an obvious conflict (the war, the gang fight, the divorce case, the baseball pennant race) attracts immediate attention. Because action is important, write the stories with verbs. The immediacy of television, as opposed to the relatively greater time lapse between the occurrence and reporting of the incident in print journalism, permits the use of the present tense in stories about events which happened within a few hours preceding the newscast. The television writer should be cautious in the use of questions as opposed to direct statements as the opening element of a story.

The writer should begin the news story with precise, clear information. The opening sentence should be, if possible, a summary of the story as a whole. Be wary of including too many details. Remember that the audience hears the news only once and, unlike the newspaper reader, cannot go back to clarify particular points in the story. The audience must grasp the entire story the first time it hears it. The writing, therefore, must be simple and understandable and, without talking down to the audience, colloquial in form. This does not imply the use of slang or illiterate expressions, but suggests informality and understandability. Repetition must be avoided, and abstract expressions and words with double meanings should not be used. The information should be accurate and there should be no possibility of a misunderstanding of any news item.

Types of Broadcasts

The most common type of television news broadcast is the straight news presentation, usually in 15-minute and half-hour periods. There are also commentator-personalities who present news analysis and/or personal opinions on the news. Sometimes these are included in the straight news show. In recent years news analysis in depth, stressing feature stories and dramatic aspects of the news, has become more common. Networks and stations frequently have "specials" which probe the news.

Most news programs are a combination of the live announcer or announcers, film and videotape and, in some cases where a story is breaking at that moment, live remotes. There can be, as well, multiple pickups from various studios, involving reporters closer to the scenes of the events. Networks frequently present news roundups from various parts of the country and, on radio and through satellite on TV, from various parts of the world. There are also frequent—though, perhaps, not frequent enough—on-the-spot news broadcasts which show or narrate the event actually taking place.

In the straight news program the writer should look for a clear and logical organization, no matter what the topic or approach. One such organization is for the placement of stories to follow a topical order; that is, the grouping of similar stories into sections, although the order of the sections themselves may be an arbitrary one. A geographical grouping and order is another organizational form. For example, the news coverage may move from North America to Europe to Asia to South America to Africa to the rest of the world. Another frequently used grouping organizes the material into international, national and local news categories. Probably the most common approach is to place the most important story first in order to get and hold the audience's attention, much as does the lead story in the newspaper.

The organization is determined, in part, by the audience being reached. In the mid-morning newscast, for example, stories are frequently chosen and placed to appeal primarily to women, the bulk of the listening group at that time. In the early evening the organization usually is one that will reach most effectively the male listener or viewer who has just returned from work. The news broadcast just before prime-time on TV frequently seeks to reach a family group watching together. The time of day is also important in relation to what the audience already knows of the news. In the early morning newscast it is desirable to review the previous day's important late stories. In the late evening broadcasts the current day's news should be reviewed and the audience should be prepared for the next day's possible happenings.

The physical format of the news show may vary. It may begin with an announcer giving the headlines, then a commercial, and then the commentator coming in with the details. It may start with the commentator beginning directly with the news. It may be a roundup of different reporters in different geographical areas.

Rewriting

One of the newswriter's duties, particularly on the local level, is *re*writing. A smaller station without a newsgathering staff is sometimes almost totally dependent on the newswire. The announcer, given sufficient time and energy, edits those stories that can be appropriately adapted to include a local angle, evaluating their impact on the community. In effect, the announcer *re*writes the news. As noted above, news broadcasts are organized into homogenous groupings. Finding a unifying thread that means something special to the listener in that community frequently requires rewriting. For example, segments in a topical grouping of stories dealing with the economy might be rewritten to reflect their relationship to the local unemployment figures.

Perhaps the most common form of rewriting is updating. An important story doesn't disappear after it is used once. Yet, to use exactly the same story in subsequent newscasts throughout the day is likely to turn off those listeners who hear it more than once and conclude that the station is carrying stale news. Updating is an important function of the network newswriter. There are several major areas to look for in updating news stories. First, the writer determines if there is any further hard news, factual information to add to the story. Second, if the story is important enough it is likely that investigative reporting will have dug up some additional background information not available when the story was first broadcast. Third, depending on the happening's impact on society, it will have been commented upon after its initial release by any number of people from VIPs to ordinary citizens. In addition, a story may by its very nature relate to other events of the day, that relatioship being made clear in the rewriting.

Process

Remember that television is visual. The reporter, feeding a remote or in the studio, must have a visual personality. In the past two decades the television news personality—the Murrows, the Huntleys and Brinkleys, the Walters, the Cronkites—have become the stars of television. The physical setting should be interesting and attractive, consistent with the concept of informational and exciting news. Even the presentation of content that in itself may be undramatic should be visually stimulating. For example, watch the techniques and "gimmicks" introduced by weather reporters in the nightly weather segment of the news program. Television news should stress the visual and may use videotape, film, slides, photographs, inanimate objects and, where necessary for emphasis or exploration in depth, even guests in the studio. Except for relatively extensive use of an anchorperson to keep together the physical continuity of the program or, through that person's special personality, to instill confidence or, as a star, to motivate viewing by the audience, the TV news program should *show* the news, not *tell* about it.

Writing the script that appears over the air is only the final stage of a long, arduous and frequently complicated process. Planning and development begin early in the day, even for a program such as "CBS Evening News with Walter Cronkite" which may not go on until early evening. Susan Leavitt of CBS News lists the many preliminary materials preceding finalization of an actual script: 1) CBS Program Log is distributed on the morning of the show, showing all the film pieces used on the Morning News, Midday News, Evening News and even on the other network news programs from the previous day; 2) written about 6 or 7 A.M. and distributed around 8:30 A.M. is a "CBS News Insights" sheet, with logs, which shows who is assigned to what coverage, what the planned assignments are for the day, and with a domestic and foreign "Who's Where" so that any member of the staff is reachable at all times; 3) about 11 A.M. a "Who Does What" rundown is distributed, showing which associate producers and which reporters are doing what and where; 4) about 11:15 A.M. a "Morning Line" is issued, with more information on the big stories and who is assigned to them; 5) about 12:30 or 1 P.M. a "Pre-Lineup" is completed, providing a list of the stories expected to be used on the program; 6) about 3:30 P.M. or shortly thereafter the "Line-up" comes out, listing the stories that will be on, their page numbers and times; 7) about 5. P.M. there is an "Editorial Line-up" with more exact information on what each page will be; 8) up until show time there are "Line-up Revisions," incorporating any changes warranted following the time the first line-up was prepared; 9) the final script itself. Here is the beginning of the final script of one program:

Final   *Final*
FROM CBS NEWS HEADQUARTERS IN NEW YORK
THIS IS THE CBS EVENING NEWS WITH
WALTER CRONKITE . . .
AND . . .
IN WASHINGTON:
FRED GRAHAM
BRUCE MORTON
ED BRADLEY
DANIEL SCHORR
BOB MCNAMARA IN BALTIMORE
BILL PLANTE IN DETROIT
AND BOB SIMON IN HANITA, ISRAEL

2. CRONKITE   Good evening:
                             John Ehrlichman, for four years a powerful associate of
                             President's Nixon's at the White House, was convicted today of
                             conspiracy and perjury.— The verdict for his role in the break-in
                             at the office of Daniel Ellsberg's psychiatrist during the
                             Pentgon Papers controversy.
                             Also convicted:
                             Ehrlichman and 3 co-defendants — G. Gordon Liddy, Bernard
                             Barker and Eugenio Martinez.
                             Fred Graham reports from Washington.

3. Graham VTR   TRACK UP

FRED GRAHAM: After only 3 hours of deliberation, the jury found all 4 defendants guilty of
conspiring to violate the civil rights of Daniel Ellsberg's psychiatrist. Ehrlichman was also
found guilty of 1 count of lying to the FBI and 2 counts of lying to a grand jury. He was
found not guilty of another count of lying to the grand jury.

JOHN EHRLICHMAN [convicted conspirator]: We've just come from a meeting with our
attorneys to review the matter, and I have instructed them to prepare to file an appeal in
our behalf. As I think you know, we've been concerned from the very beginning about our
ability to secure a fair trial in this district and certainly one of the grounds of our appeal
will go to that question. It was also a matter of concern to us that a great deal of the
substance in the background of this entire case was excluded from the evidence by rulings
of the court and obviously that would be another question to be raised on appeal in this
matter.
    I have, and have for many years had, an abiding confidence in the American judicial
system. Nothing that happened today has in any way shaken that confidence, and we look
forward to an eventual complete exoneration as this matter moves through that process.

QUESTION: Do you feel you were betrayed by those at the White House who asked you to
do this?

EUGENIO MARTINEZ [convicted plumbers burglar]: I do not want to use the word
"betray", but it looks like the one that gave the order. — At the time of the trial, everyone
tried to run away. Everyone lost their memory. Everyone — [laughs] No one knew what's
going on. And, really, it looks [MARTINEZ] like the only one who knew were us. And the
little assignment that we had was for certainly — is as our attorney said. I'm sure that the
case didn't have to start in Miami.

QUESTION: You think you got stuck holding the bag?

MARTINEZ: Well, I believed you say it.

GRAHAM: The defendants will remain free without bond until they are sentenced on July
the 31st. Ehrlichman could get a maximum of 25 years in prison; the others, up to 10 years
in prison.

Fred Graham, CBS News, at the D.C. Court of Appeals.

4. Cronkite	On the question of impeachment of the president, a key matter now being examined by the house judiciary committee is whether he illegally received and passed on Watergate grand jury information. And a key figure in that matter is assistant attorney general Henry Peterson who was in charge of that investigation. He was before the committee today. Bruce Morton reports.
Folo 4. MORTON VTR	TRACK UP
VO Peterson silent	Members said Peterson told them it was proper for him to pass information about the grand jury to the President, and for the President to use it. Hogan of Maryland said Peterson said he really only gave the President information about what the prosecutors were doing, not the grand jury. But in at least one case, the President promised not to pass on what Peterson told him . . . and yet the information did get to the President's men.
White House transcripts	The edited White House transcript of a President to Peterson phone call, the evening of April 16, 1973 . . .
Nixon	President: I just want to know if there are any developments . . . anything you tell me, as i think I told you earlier, will not be passed on. Because I know the rules of the grand jury.
Peterson still	Peterson: You asked about Colson. Colson and Dean were together with Erlichman when Erlichman advised Hunt to get out of town . . . so he is going to be in the grand jury.
Nixon	The President repeats, making sure the grand jury will call Colson.
Erlichman	Early next morning. Erlichman called Colson. "My grapevine tells me you are going to be summoned over there today . . . They're going to ask you about a meeting in my office."
on camera	Erlichman reminds Colson of the meeting. Colson says he wasn't there, but is sure he never heard any order to Hunt to leave town and will so swear. A few minutes later, just before ten ayem, the White House transcripts show Haldeman telling the
Haldeman	President: "Colson flatly says there was never anything where he was where there was a discussion of Hunt getting out of the country . . . Erlichman has checked out everyone who was at that meeting and nobody recalls that being said except Dean."
on camera	So Peterson's information was apparently used by the President's men. Peterson testified today he saw nothing improper in that; one Democrat called him "a good soldier," bm, cbs n, wash

4A. Cronkite	Presidential lawyer James St. Clair and White House news spokesman Gerald Warren issued conflicting statements today about whether Mr. Nixon expects the House Judiciary Committee to vote for his impeachment.
	Warren said the President expects a committee vote for impeachment, but also believes the full House will vote in the President's favor.
	St. Clair said he spoke to Mr. Nixon just this morning and didn't hear any such view expressed.
	Later, Warren took the blame for all the confusion and said that actually the President thinks it would be inappropriate to make predictions.
No 5 or 6	
7. Cmcl	CMCL
COML # 1	:60VT
	Clear Eyes/Breakfast Squares

Courtesy of CBS News

Special Events

The special event is usually under the direction of the news department and is essentially something that is taking place live and is of interest—critical or passing—to the community. It is usually a remote, on-the-spot broadcast. Special events usually originate independently and include such happenings as political conventions, parades, dedications, banquets, awards and the openings of new films and supermarkets. More significant kinds of special events, perhaps, are political conventions and astronaut launchings. The assassinations of John F. Kennedy, Martin Luther King, Jr. and Robert F. Kennedy were fully covered by the media although, of course, unanticipated. The first human landing on the moon, the Watergate hearings and the impeachment proceedings in the House of Representatives were also fully covered, but as planned events with time for preparation in depth.

Sometimes special events are merely introduced, presented without comment, and—occasionally—summarized or critiqued when over. Sometimes they are narrated on radio and are accompanied by commentary on television. The opening and closing material and, frequently, transition and filler material are provided by the writer. The latter two are sometimes handled directly by the broadcaster who is assigned to the event and who presumably is an expert on the subject being covered.

For events other than those which require only a short intro and outro, the writer should collect as much material as possible. News stories, maps, press releases, historical documents, books, photographs, locales and similar sources can be pertinent and helpful in preparing continuity. Copy should be prepared for all emergencies as well as for opening, closing, transition and filler uses.

Material should include information on the personalities involved, the background of the event and even on probable or possible happenings during the event.

Usually covered as a "special event" by the news and public affairs department are political speeches, interviews and press conferences. Some elements in such presentations overlap the formats of "features" and "talks" programs. The presidential "special event"—in the positive sense—took on new meaning with the election of Jimmy Carter in 1976. Call-in programs, frequent press conferences, informal "fireside chats," speech-discussions mark President Carter's use of the media, and we may see him following up on recommendations for using the media to bring the public closer to all federal government activities by participation in agency meetings and deliberations through two-way television and radio at media centers throughout the country.

SPORTS

AT ONE TIME the sports department of a station or network was an offshoot of the news department. But the phenomenal growth of live sports event coverage has given sports new status in broadcasting and more and more sports divisions are separate, independent functions from the news division. The smaller the station, of course, the greater the likelihood that sports will be a function of the news department, rather than a separate entity. The writing of sports is similar to the writing of news. If anything, the style for sports broadcasts must be even more precise and more direct than for news broadcasts. The language is more colloquial and though technical terms are to be avoided so as not to confuse the general audience, the writer of sports may use many more expressions relating to a specialized area than can the writer of news.

Types of Sports Programs

The straight sportscast concentrates on recapitulation of the results of sports events and on news relating to sports in general. Some sportscasts are oriented solely to summaries of results. These summaries may come from wire service reports or from other sources of the station. Material which is rewritten from newspaper accounts or which is taken from the wires should be adapted to fit the purpose of the particular program and the personality of the broadcaster.

The sports feature program may include live or recorded interviews with sports personalities, anecdotes or dramatizations of events in sports, human interest or background stories on personalities or events, or remotes relating to sports but not in themselves an actual athletic event.

A sports show may amalgamate several approaches or, as in the case of the after-event critique or summary, may concentrate on one type alone. Many sports news shows are combinations of the straight report and the feature.

The most popular sports broadcast is, of course, the live athletic contest while it is taking place.

Organization of Sports News

Formats for the sports news broadcast parallel those of the regular news broadcast. The most common approach is to take the top sport of the particular season, give all the results and news of that sport, and work toward the least important sport. In such an organization the most important story of the most important sport is given first unless a special item from another sport overrides it. Within each sport the general pattern in this organization includes the results first, the general news (such as trades, injuries and so forth) next and future events last. If the trade or injury is of a star player or the future event is more than routine, such as the signing for a heavyweight championship fight, then it will become the lead story. The local sports scene is usually coordinated with the national sports news, fitting into the national reporting breakdowns. The local result or story, however, will usually be the lead within the given sports category and sometimes the local sports scene will precede all other sports news. Formats vary, of course.

Sports Special Events

The live on-the-spot coverage of an athletic contest is the most exciting and most popular sports program. The newspaper and magazine cartoons showing a viewer glued to a television set for seven nights of baseball in the summer or seven nights of football, basketball and hockey in the winter are no longer exaggerations. The sports special event can be other than a contest, however. Coverage of an awards ceremony, of an old-timer's day, of a Cooperstown Hall of Fame induction, of a retirement ceremony are all special events that are not live contests on the playing field or court.

The sports broadcaster must have filler material; that is, information relating to pre-event action and color, statistics, form charts, information on the site of the event, on the history of the event, about the participants, human interest stories and similar materials which either heighten the audience's interest or help clarify the action to the audience. This material must be written up and must be available to the broadcaster to be used when needed, specifically during lulls in the action, and in pre-game and post-game opening and closing segments. At one time staff writers prepared this material. More recently, sports broadcasters have been expected to be experts in their field and to know and to provide their own filler material.

The primary function of the writer for the live contest is that of a researcher and outliner. The script may be little more than an outline and/or a series of statistics, individual unrelated sentences or short paragraphs with the required background and transition continuity.

FEATURES

The feature or, as it is sometimes called, the special feature, falls somewhere in between the special event and the documentary. While the special event is coverage of an immediate newsworthy happening, sometimes unanticipated, the special feature is pre-planned and carefully prepared. There are special events, of course, such as sports events, which are pre-planned. The special event usually is live, while the feature usually is filmed, taped or, if live, produced from a script or at least a routine sheet or detailed rundown sheet. Special events usually are public presentations that stations arrange to cover. Features usually are prepared solely for television and radio presentation and generally are not presented before an in-person audience. The special event is part of the stream of life while the feature is designed by a producing organization.

Features usually are short—2- to 5- or 15- to 30-minutes in length; the former for fillers and the latter for full programs of a public service nature. The subject matter for the feature varies. Some sample types: the presentation of the work of a special service group in the community, a story on the operation of the local fire department, an examination of the problems of the school board, a how-to-do-it broadcast, a behind-the-scenes story on any subject—from raising chickens to electing public officials.

Writing Approach

Because it does come so close to the documentary, the feature requires careful research, analysis and evaluation of material, and writing based on detail and depth. That does not mean that it requires a full and complete script. Because the feature is composed, frequently, of a number of diverse program types—such as the documentary, the interview, the panel discussion and the speech—it may be written in routine sheet or rundown form. Some features have combinations of script, rundown sheet and routine sheet.

Because the feature is usually a public service presentation it often contains informational and educational content. But it doesn't have to be purely factual or academic in nature. It can even take the form of a variety show or a drama—or certainly have elements of these forms within the program as a whole. The feature is an eclectic form and can be oriented around a person, an organization, a thing, a situation, a problem or an idea. The following example is principally oriented toward an organization (the Red Cross) but also includes a problem (dissaster work) and a situation (a specific disaster in the Harrisburg area and a specific technique, artificial respiration). Note that this feature was produced by a local commercial station as part of a regular public service series and is a live-type program with film inserts.

HOW RED CROSS DOES IT

VIDEO	AUDIO
SLIDE #1 TRI-STATE STORY	MUSIC: RECORD "RED CROSS SONG" IN AND OUT BEHIND STATION ANNOUNCER:
SLIDE #2 RED CROSS EMBLEM	As a public service, WEHT presents TRI-STATE STORY — a half hour prepared through the cooperation of the Springfield Chapter of the American Red Cross. Here to introduce our guests for this evening is Mr. John Smith, Director of Public Relations for the Springfield Red Cross. Mr. Smith:
CAMERA ON SMITH	(MR. SMITH THANKS ANNOUNCER AND INTRODUCES TWO GUESTS, MR. HARVEY AND MR. JONES. THEN ASKS MR. HARVEY TO SPEAK.)
CAMERA ON HARVEY CLOSEUP OF PHOTOS ON EASEL	(MR. HARVEY TELLS OF RECENT DISASTER WORK IN HARRISBURG AREA, SHOWING PHOTOGRAPHS OF SERVICE WORKERS. HE WILL RISE AND WALK TO THE EASEL.)
CAMERA ON SMITH AND JONES	(MR. SMITH INTRODUCES MR. JONES. THEY DISCUSS SUMMER SAFETY SCHOOL FOR SWIMMERS. JONES LEADS INTO FILM WITH FOLLOWING CUE):
	"Now I'd like our viewers to see a film that was made at Lake Roundwood during last year's Summer Safety School."
SPECIAL FILM	(8:35) (SILENT — JONES LIVE VOICE-OVER)
CAMERA ON JONES	(JONES INTRODUCES ARTIFICIAL RES-PIRATION DEMONSTRATION.)
CAMERA ON TWO BOYS	(JONES DESCRIBES METHODS OFF CAMERA.)
CAMERA ON SMITH	(SMITH THANKS JONES AND HARVEY AND GIVES CONCLUDING REMARKS.)
SLIDE #3 TRI-STATE STORY	MUSIC: THEME IN AND UNDER STATION ANNOUNCER: Tri-State Story, a WEHT Public Service Presentation, is on the air each week at this time. Today's program was prepared through the cooperation of the Springfield Chapter of the American Red Cross. *By permission of American National Red Cross*

THE DOCUMENTARY

Many broadcast news personnel say that the documentary, combining as it does news, special events, features, music and drama, is the highest form of the television art. At its best the documentary not only synthesizes the creative arts of the broadcast media, but it also makes a signal contribution to public understanding by interpreting the past, analyzing the present or anticipating the future. Sometimes it does all these in a single program, in highly dramatic form, combining intellectual and emotional meaning.

Form

Although the documentary is dramatic, it is not a drama in the sense of the fictional play. It is more or less a faithful representation of a true story. This is not to say, however, that all documentaries are unimpeachably true. Editing and narration can make any series of sequences seem other than what they really are. The documentary form is flexible. The semi-documentary or fictional documentary has achieved a certain degree of popularity. Based on reality, it is not necessarily factual. It may take authentic characters but fictionalize the events of their lives; it may present the events accurately but fictionalize the characters; it may take real people and/or real events and speculate, as authentically as possible, in order to fill in documentary gaps; it may take several situations and characters from life and create a semi-true composite picture.

Although the documentary deals with issues, people and events of the news, it is not a news story. It is an exploration behind and beneath the obvious. It goes much more in depth than does a news story, exploring not only what happened but, as far as possible, the reasons for what happened, the attitudes and feelings of the people involved, the interpretations of experts, the reactions of other citizens who might be affected, and the implications and significance of the subject not only for some individuals, but for the whole of society.

Procedure

Essentially, the documentary contains the real words of real persons (or their writings, published and unpublished, including letters if they are not living or cannot possibly be reached and there is no record of their voices), the moving pictures of their actions (or photos and drawings if film or video tape is unavailable or they lived before motion pictures) and, concomitantly, the sounds and visuals of real events. These materials, sometimes seemingly unrelated, must be put together into a dramatic, cohesive whole and edited according to an outline and then a script.

First, the writer must have an idea. What subject of public interest is worthy of documentary treatment? The idea for the program frequently comes not from the writer, but from the producer. All documentaries should have a point of view. The writer and/or producer may suggest; the network and/or sponsor have the final word. What is the *purpose* of the particular documentary? When the subject and the point of view are determined, the real work starts: from thorough research in libraries, to personal visits to people and places, to investigations of what video and audio materials on the subject are already available. When the research is completed, the writer can prepare a more definitive outline.

After all the materials have been gathered and have been reviewed, usually many, many times by the writer, the development of a final script can begin in earnest. The final script is used for the selection and organization of the specific materials to be used in the final editing and taping of the program. It is significant, in terms of the high degree of coordination and cooperation needed to complete a good documentary, that in a great many instances the writer also serves as the producer and even as the director and editor.

The picture may be the primary element in any given sequence in the television documentary, with the narration and taped dialogue secondary. The people and their actions may be actually seen and thus understood, rather than being imagined through verbal descriptions of what they did and saw. On the other hand, the words of the people and the narrator may be the prime movers, with the pictures merely filling in visually what is being described in words.

A frequent approach to the television documentary is that which concentrates on narration and interviews and does not attempt dramatic technique. The visuals may be little more than graphics relating to the subject, plus actualities with interviewees. Such a documentary is the CBS News Special Report, "What's Going On Here?—The Troubled American Economy." Note the simple format: John Hart, anchorperson, introduces through narration different aspects of the troubled economy and then switches to a correspondent who conducts the actualities for that segment. Excerpts from the first part of the program follow, illustrating the organization as well as the approach.

HART:	Good evening. As it turns out, six weeks ago were the good old days. When our brand new President told us our political nightmare was over. And now we were going to work on our economic one.
FORD: VTR:	My first priority is to work with you to bring inflation under control. Inflation is domestic enemy number one.
HART:	He called for an economic summit meeting where the best brains from labor, industry and agriculture would help him plan the attack. That meeting begins this Friday in Washington. In the six weeks we have been waiting for — and the brains have been preparing for — the summit, these things have happened. The stock market slid to its lowest value in 12 years. Homebuilding to its lowest point in 4 years. Wholesale prices made their biggest jump in one year. Tonight we are going to look at our economy and the summit and what to expect from both of them.
ANNOUNCER:	This is a CBS News Special Report . . . WHAT'S GOING ON HERE? . . . THE TROUBLED AMERICAN ECONOMY . . . With CBS News Correspondent John Hart.

Ist Commercial

ANNOUNCER: Here is John Hart.

HART: What is going on here is more than one thing in more than one place.
                        We have a mixture of troubles. We have inflation. It is everywhere. We
                        have stagnation, in a number of places where things just aren't
                        moving much, forward or backward. We have recession in places
                        where things have been going backward for sometime. We have
                        depression in places where things are going straight down. We even
                        have some strengths left, here and there. It is not ALL bad. Just mostly.
                        There are a number of what the economists call indicators — trends
                        they look at at to see where the economy is weak and where it is
                        strong and how much.

RP LIST: We are going to look at 12 indicators, of what has been going on
                        since the first of the year.

CONSUMER PRICES: The obvious indicator is prices. They have been going up on an
                        average of one per cent a month. 12 per cent a year. This is a
                        weakness in our economy. A clear minus.

POP ON   Wholesale prices are another indicator of inflation. They have gone
WHOLESALE   up more than two per cent a month on the average, or 27 per cent
PRICES: per year. Another weakness.

POP ON MINUS: Another minus.

RETAIL SALES: Retail sales indicate how people are reacting to prices. Dollar
                        volume has gone up every month this year, except in June.

POP ON PLUS: In one way that is a strength, in that it helps keep business in
                        business.

POP ON MINUS: But in another way these retail sales dollars hide weakness. In many
                        cases we are buying fewer things and simply paying more for what we
                        buy, as with cars.

PROFITS: The profits picture is a plus. Corporate profits after taxes grew at an
                        annual rate of 55 per cent over 1973, keeping well ahead of inflation.

WAGES: Wages went up at an annual rate of 4.4 per cent, but did NOT keep
                        up with inflation.

POP ON PLUS: Real income went down for the millions of people living on wages
                        but ironically, a plus for the economy as a whole, in that wages are
                        not giving a big push to inflation.
                                          * * *
                        The reasons are that the three things we cannot do without — food,
                        shelter and fuel — are things this economy is rationing by inflation.
                        Bernard Kalb reports on food.

VTR

KALB: You can't do without it, it should be a pleasure. But what you're
                        eating is costing you more, and more, and more. The bad news on
                        food prices from Secretary of Agriculture Earl Butz.

BUTZ: Our estimate is that the average of 1974 will be approximately 15 to

16 per cent over the average of 1973. It would be approximately a 30 per cent jump in two years. It's been severe, there's no question about that.

KALB: No question either about the shock among consumers. A trip to the supermarket these days can be a little like walking through a mine field . . . new prices exploding everywhere. All this has made a mockery of earlier official forecasts that food prices during this period would remain steady . . . and even decline slightly; once again, a case of governmental optimism outrunning reality.

Ellen Zawel, President of the National Consumer Congress on the mood of consumers.

ZAWEL: Most people are depressed. They just don't know what to do. It becomes scary and you don't know where you gonna cut down next. Everybody feels they're being shafted. Somebody's taking advantage and they're not sure who.

*   *   *

Courtesy of NBC News
Leslie Midgley, Executive Producer; Hal Haley and Bernard Birnbaum, Producers

You don't need a major network in order to produce a first-rate television documentary. With careful planning and imagination local stations can produce dramatic and pertinent documentaries. Though not usually controversial, the subject of libraries is a significant one in most communities, and Barbara Allen of WGAL, Lancaster, Pennsylvania, decided that it was pertinent to viewers in the many cities within her station's signal. Her approach was to take an ostensibly inanimate thing and humanize it. In doing so she captured many of the aspects of libraries that relate to human drama—in this case those of a worrisome nature that require action on the part of the viewers. Her approach was to dramatize the problem, but in the form of a factual statement, not a semi-documentary. Here is a portion of her script:

LIBRARIES: BRUISED, BATTERED AND BOUND

VIDEO	AUDIO
CU OF INITIALS CARVED IN TABLES, WALLS, ETC., FOR EACH LOCATION	MUSIC UNDER — LOVE THEME FROM "ROMEO AND JULIET"
	BARB: This is a love story with an unhappy ending. In Harrisburg, R.P. loves B.L. In Lebanon, A.M. loves P.S. In York, it's M.O. and S.T. In Reading, C.K. loves P.R. and in Lancaster, Brenda loves Bill. START TO FADE MUSIC
COVER SHOT OF TABLE TOP	But love is a very private relationship and these intials are written in very public places. MUSIC OUT

SUPER TITLE SLIDE OVER TABLETOP	They are your public libraries and they are Bruised, Battered and Bound.
DISSOLVE TO COVER OF BARB AND LIBRARIANS AT TABLE	Hello, I'm Barbara Allen. With me around this bruised and battered library table are five librarians from the Channel 8 area.
ZOOM IN TO BARB	They're not here to tell you about what your local library has to offer. They're here to talk about larceny, decay, suffocation and rape. These things are happening in your library right now. If you don't stop them, the next time you visit your library, you may be greeted by this.
:05 FILM PERSON PUTTING CLOSED SIGN IN WINDOW	
BARB, THEN MR. DOHERTY	(INTRODUCE MR. DOHERTY, CHAT WITH HIM ABOUT CLOSED SIGN AT READING PUBLIC LIBRARY AND ASK HIM ABOUT THE PROBLEMS AT THE READING LIBRARY THAT YOU CAN SEE)
1:15 FILM SHOWING EXTERIOR OF LIBRARY AND VISUAL PROBLEMS INSIDE	MR. DOHERTY VOICE OVER FILM
MR. DOHERTY	(CHAT WITH BARB ABOUT ONE PROBLEM YOU CAN'T SEE)
BARB, THEN MISS YEAGLEY	(ASK ABOUT PROBLEMS YOU CAN SEE AT MARTIN MEMORIAL LIBRARY, YORK)
1:15 FILM SHOWING EXTERIOR OF LIBRARY AND VISUAL PROBLEMS INSIDE	MISS YEAGLEY VOICE OVER FILM
MISS YEAGLEY	(CHAT WITH BARB ABOUT ONE PROBLEM YOU CAN'T SEE)
BARB INTRODUCES MR. GROSS	(ASK ABOUT PROBLEMS YOU CAN SEE AT THE HARRISBURG PUBLIC LIBRARY)
1:15 FILM SHOWING EXTERIOR OF HARRISBURG LIBRARY AND VISUAL PROBLEMS INSIDE	MR. GROSS VOICE OVER FILM
MR. GROSS	(CHAT WITH BARB ABOUT ONE PROBLEM YOU CAN'T SEE)
BARB INTRODUCES MR. MARKS	(ASK ABOUT PROBLEMS YOU CAN SEE AT LEBANON COMMUNITY LIBRARY)

* * *

Courtesy of Barbara Allen and WGAL-TV, Lancaster, Penna.

Talks Programs

"Talks program" is used sometimes as an all-inclusive term, encompassing virtually all program types that are not news, documentaries, drama, music or commercials. Included in "talks programs" are interviews, discussions, speeches and, in many instances, quiz, audience participation and celebrity panel shows. Interview and discussion programs are outlined, either in rundown or routine sheet form. A principal reason they cannot be prepared in complete script form is that the very nature of an interplay of ideas and, sometimes, feelings among people requires extemporaneity. Another reason is that the participants, excluding the interviewer or moderator, usually are nonprofessionals and cannot memorize or "read" a prepared script without seeming strained and stilted.

Nevertheless, the writer should prepare as much of the script as necessary—whether a detailed routine sheet or a simple outline—for the best possible show. Why take a chance with an unprepared question or sequence when the chances of success are better with prepared material? The rundown sheet is the key for most talks programs. The rundown sheet is a detailed listing of all the sequences in a given program, frequently with the elapsed time, if known, for each item. Rundown and routine sheets sometimes include alternate endings of different lengths so that the extemporaneous nature of the program can be maintained and still end on time through the choice of the proper-length sequence for the final item in the program.

The Interview

The interview may be prepared completely, with a finished script for interviewer and interviewee; it may be oriented around an outline, where the general line of questioning and answering is prepared, but the exact words to be used are extemporaneous; it may be completely unprepared, or ad-lib. Very rarely are interviews either completely ad-lib or completely scripted. The unprepared interview is too risky, with the interviewee likely to be too garrulous, embarrassing or embarrassed, or just plain dull, and the interviewer likely to be faced with the almost impossible task of organizing, preparing, and thinking of appropriate questions on the spot. The prepared script usually results in a stilted, monotonous presentation except when both the interviewer and interviewee are skilled performers who can make a written line sound extemporaneous, a situation not often likely to occur.

The written material for the extemporaneous interview is the rundown and/or routine sheet, a step-by-step outline of the program which includes a list of questions and content of answers as determined in the pre-interview session. Sometimes, of course, the interviewee will not be available for a conference before the show, and the interviewer and staff must guess at the probable answers to their questions—based on thorough research of the interview.

In all interviews—prepared, extemporaneous, ad-lib—the writer, ideally, prepares at least the opening and closing continuity, introductory material about the interviewee and for each section of the program, lead-ins and -outs for commercial breaks and an outline of the questions and, if possible, answers. The closing continuity should be of different lengths in case the program runs shorter or longer than expected. The writer should be certain that the background of the guest is clearly presented. Except where the interviewee is very well known, it is sometimes helpful to begin with questions of a human interest nature so that the audience gets to know something about the personality of the guest before the interview is too far along. Even with a well-known guest this sometimes is advisable. In the strictly informational, newstype interview this approach could be distractive, although even in such programs the interviewer frequently asks "personality" questions.

There are three major interview types: the opinion interview, the information interview and the personality interview. Any given interview can combine elements of all three.

The opinion interview concentrates on the beliefs of an individual. However, inasmuch as many of the interviews of this nature are with prominent people, usually experts in their fields, such interviews are not only opinion but, to a great extent, information and even personality types.

The information interview usually is of the public service type. The information may be delivered by a relatively unknown figure or by a prominent person in the field.

The personality interview is the human interest, feature story. The format of the program may be oriented toward one purpose—to probe or to embarrass or to flatter—or it may be flexible, combining and interweaving these various facets.

We usually think of the interview as static: two or more people talking at each other. However, even in the simplest question-and-answer process, some visual interest can be injected. The visual movement may be of a subjective nature, with the camera probing the facial expressions and bodily gestures of the interviewee. The visual approach may be broader and more objective, with film clips or photographs of places, events or personalities referred to by the interviewee. Because television is visual, the interviewer (and writer-producer-director) must be cautioned about misleading the audience, even unintentionally. One classic story is about the television interviewer who made much in pre-program publicity of a forthcoming interview with a famous stripper. Although the audience should have known better, many viewers were quite disappointed that she didn't do what she obviously couldn't do on television.

Format is paramount. Each interview program has its own organization and the writer must write for that particular format. Some interview shows open with an introduction of the program, introduce the guest and then go into the actual interview. Others open cold, with the interview already under way, in order to immediately grab and hold the audience's attention, with a subsequent cut-in for the standard introductory material. The following script for "Face The Nation" illustrates the latter approach.

HERMAN TEASE QUESTION _____

SEN. JACKSON ANSWERS _____

(ANNCR: V.O.)

FROM CBS NEWS WASHINGTON . . . A SPONTANEOUS AND
UNREHEARSED NEWS INTERVIEW ON "FACE THE NATION", WITH
SENATOR HENRY JACKSON, DEMOCRAT OF WASHINGTON.
SENATOR JACKSON WILL BE QUESTIONED BY CBS NEWS
DIPLOMATIC CORRESPONDENT MARVIN KALB, DAVID S. BRODER,
NATIONAL POLITICAL CORRESPONDENT FOR THE WASHINGTON
POST AND CBS NEWS CORRESPONDENT GEORGE HERMAN.
"FACE THE NATION" IS PRODUCED BY CBS NEWS, WHICH IS
SOLELY RESPONSIBLE FOR THE SELECTION OF TODAY'S GUEST
AND PANEL.

BILLBOARD _____ 10 sec. _____
  (IMBB   1801)   (VTR)

COMMERCIAL _____ 1:40 _____
  (SRA MATH   IMSR   5112)   (VTR)

(HERMAN CLOSING)
I'M SORRY GENTLEMEN, BUT OUR TIME IS UP. THANK YOU VERY
MUCH FOR BEING HERE TO "FACE THE NATION".

COMMERCIAL _____ :36¹/₂ _____
  (THIRTY SECONDS   IMCO   3312FN)

(ANNCR: V.O.)

TODAY ON "FACE THE NATION", SENATOR HENRY JACKSON,
DEMOCRAT OF WASHINGTON, WAS INTERVIEWED BY CBS NEWS
DIPLOMATIC CORRESPONDENT MARVIN KALB, DAVID S. BRODER,
NATIONAL POLITICAL CORRESPONDENT FOR THE WASHINGTON
POST AND CBS NEWS CORRESPONDENT GEORGE HERMAN.

(BILLBOARD   IMBB   4806   6 sec.)

"FACE THE NATION" HAS BEEN SPONSORED BY IBM.

(ANNCR: V.O.)

NEXT WEEK, ANOTHER PROMINENT FIGURE IN THE NEWS WILL
"FACE THE NATION". THIS BROADCAST WAS PRODUCED BY
CBS NEWS.

(ANNCR: V.O.   CREDITS)

VISIT SAUDIA ARABIA — ONE OF THE STOPS ON PRESIDENT
NIXON'S UPCOMING TRIP TO THE MIDDLE EAST — AND MEET THE
KING WHO SITS ON TOP OF ONE THIRD OF THE WORLD'S OIL,
ON 60 MINUTES LATER TODAY.

(ANNCR: V.O.)

"FACE THE NATION" ORIGINATED FROM WASHINGTON, D.C.

Courtesy of CBS News

The Discussion Program

Discussion programs are aimed toward an exchange of opinions and information and, to some degree, toward the arriving at solutions, actual or implied, on important questions or problems. They should not be confused with the interview, in which the purpose is to elicit, not to exchange.

The writer of the discussion program has to walk a thin line between too much and not enough preparation. It is not possible to write a complete script, partially because the participants can't know specifically in advance what their precise attitude or comment might be on any given issue or statement brought up in the discussion. On the other hand, a complete lack of preparation would likely result in a program in which the participants would ramble; it would present the moderator with the impossible task of getting everybody someplace without knowing where they were going. To achieve spontaneity, it is better to plan only an outline, indicating the general form and organization of the discussion. This is, of course, in addition to whatever standard opening, closing and transitions are used in the program. This might include opening and closing statements for the moderator, introductions of the participants, and general summaries to be used by the moderator in various places throughout the program.

GAME SHOWS

The mid-1970's saw the Game Show become a staple of commercial television, starting early in the morning and filling program schedules through the afternoon and into prime time. The formats for the game show are many, ranging from the quiz of a contestant or an entire panel, to the performance of an audience member, to the participation of a celebrity. In all formats the participant is put into competition with another person or persons or with a time or question barrier. In each case someone is expected to solve some problem in order to achieve the specific goal of the game—that is, win money or goods. The problem may be to stump a panel of experts, guess what someone else is thinking, answer extremely complicated or extremely elementary questions about some subject, or hit one's spouse in the face three out of five times with a custard pie.

Most of the TV game shows fit into one of five major formats: celebrity participation, word games, variations on gambling, straight question-and-answer games and non-games. The variations are virtually endless.

Game Shows are invariably spontaneous—or made to look that way. Because the participants are in part or totally non-professionals in the acting field, it is not possible to write out a complete script. The "readings" would come out stilted. Yet, as with any well-prepared program, as much of the continuity as possible is written out, and the routine or rundown sheets for many game shows are quite detailed.

Opening and closing continuity, introductions, ad-lib jokes, questions, commentary introducing and ending sequences and similar material are written out. The material should be flexible and adaptable to the spontaneity of the participants. The prepared material should be designed to fit the personality of the person hosting the show and should be developed in consultation with him or her. In some audience participation shows virtually all of the dialogue, except that which will be given by the non-professional participants, is scripted. In many instances even the participants' supposedly ad-lib dialogue is prepared, even if only in outline form. Sequences—including routines, stunts, matches or whatever the particular game show calls for—should be timed accurately beforehand so that the basic script fits into the required time length. Alternate material of different time lengths may be prepared in case the show begins to run too long or too short.

The visual elements of the particular game should be stressed. Charts, pyramids, curtains, models, all bigger than life, are some of the set pieces for game shows. As the years progress they and the games seem to become more and more complicated. Yet, a game show can be simple. For example, one of the most effective formats in the entire history of game shows was that of an individual grimacing and sweating in the confines of a glamorized telephone booth with tens of thousands of dollars seemingly hanging on his or her answer to a question.

Music and Variety Programs

Television has not utilized the musical program to the same degree that radio did. There have been some successful series of musical personalities and orchestras, such as Liberace and Lawrence Welk, and occasional attempts at adapting the radio disc jockey program—in effect, on the-air discotheques with youngsters in the community dancing to the TV deejay's records and commentary. Dick Clark's success with this format in Philadelphia and then nationally led to similar shows in many cities. Popular entertainers who are primarily singers, such as Carol Burnett, have been successful with TV variety, rather than with strictly musical shows. With the phenomenal overnight popularity of rock groups, large audiences have watched TV specials featuring some of the better known bands. Continuing series of music programs of special quality have occasionally proven popular, such as Leonard Bernstein's children's concerts and Arthur Fiedler's Boston Pops concerts on public television.

The job for the scriptwriter in the area of music and variety is principally in preparing continuity for the TV variety show. The variety program depends greatly on humor, and you will notice that the credit crawls at the end of such programs frequently contain long lists of names of comedy writers. That kind of writing is a craft in itself and, according to most producers and writers in the field, can't really be taught.

Techniques of Writing the Music Program

One of the reasons that musical programs have not been especially popular or successful on television is that music is not a visual art form. Attempts to make visual action the focal point of musical programs on television often have defeated the purposes of musical presentation and have resulted in unfulfilled goals, both aurally and visually. The action must remain secondary to the sound. Yet, the action must be of sufficient interest to make worthwhile the audience's full attention and time to the television screen. Otherwise, the listener might just as well hear the music on radio or on a phonograph.

The success of the "rock" specials on television illustrate the importance of the visual action. It is not the music that the audience looks for as much as the gyrations of the personalities, some of them demi-gods and -goddesses to the younger viewers. For the first time, they can get extreme close-ups of their heroes and heroines, who heretofore they worshipped from the cavernous recesses of a stadium.

The first thing the writer must ask is: "What will the picture add to the sound?" Avoid gimmicks, strange angles and bizarre shots which may be exciting in themselves, but which have no integral relationship to the music. If you first develop a central theme, such as a relationship to a locale, an interpretation or representation of a situation, or the conveying of a mood, it will be easier to find the specifice visual elements for the program.

Other art forms, specifically pantomime and dance, may provide interpretive visualizations of the music. Inanimate objects and forms, such as photographs, paintings, slides and film, can also illustrate realistic and nonrealistic interpretations. Landscapes, people, places, actions and events may be shown, indicating various environmental and psychological meanings and moods of the music.

Techniques for the Variety Program

The term, variety, implies a combination of two or more elements of entertainment and art: a singer, a dancer, a stand-up comic, a comedy skit, a Shakespearean actor, a puppeteer, a ventriloquist, a pianist, a rock group. Depending on the personality who is the principal figure in the program, several of these elements would be incorporated in a manner that shows off the star to the best advantage. The basic variety show types are the vaudeville show, the music hall variety, the revue, the comic-dominated show, the personality (usually singer or dancer) program with guests, the musical comedy approach and the solo performance.

The most important thing for the writer of the variety show to remember is that there must be a peg on which to hang a show. You must develop a clear, central theme, capable of being organized into a sound structure, with a unity that holds all the parts of the program together. Otherwise, each number will be a number in itself, and unless the audience knows what the next act is and especially wants to watch it, it would feel free at any time to tune in another station at the end of an act. The theme could be a distinct one or the continuity factor could simply be the personality of the star.

Within each separate type of variety show there are distinct orientations that must be determined by the writer. Will the musical portions stress popular or novelty numbers? Will the dances be classical in style? Modern? Presentational? Representational? Interpretive? The comedy must be written to fit the personality of the comic, and it must contain a sufficient amount of ad-lib material to forward the public concept of the comic's spontaneous talents. What kind of comedy will be emphasized? Simple good humor? Wit? Satire? Slapstick?

When planning a variety show consider the intrinsic meaning of the term "variety." There must be a differentiation between each successive number and among the various segments of the program. Contrast is important—not too great a contrast to disturb the viewers, but enough so that there can be no feeling of sameness, a feeling too easily transferred into boredom.

In programs that use outside acts—that is, those that cannot be scripted and timed exactly, as with vaudeville or with late-night talk/variety programs, the final number or act should have two versions, a short one and a long one, so that the proper one can be called for depending on the time remaining when that act is about to begin.

See page 181 for part of the rundown sheet for "The Tonight Show."

THE TONIGHT SHOW
TAPED: THURSDAY, MAY 9, 1974
AIRED: FRIDAY, MAY 10, 1974

6:00:00   (12:00:00)

	9. STARRING SL
GUESTS: JACK PALANCE (PAPUSH)	
JOANNA CASSIDY (SAM)	
JOSE MOLINA (DOLCE)	9A. ANNOUNCE UPCOMING GUESTS
ORSON BEAN (DOLCE)	
	10. ORSON BEAN
HOST: JOHNNY CARSON	
ANNCR: ED McMAHON	
	11. COMML: SUNBEAM/ROCKWELL — LCI
	(FM/VT) — MTC SL)
NOTES:	
	12. JOANNA CASSIDY
	13. COMML: WAMSUTTA/SIMMONS — LCI
	(VT/FM — MTC SL)
	14. JOANNA CASSIDY
	15. COMML: SEARS — LCI
	(FM — MTC SL)

5:30:00 (11:30:00)	16.	STATION BREAK 6:30:00 (12:30:00)

1. THEME AND OPENING TAPE	17.	STARRING SL
2. JOHNNY MONOLOGUE	18.	JACK PALANCE
3. COMML: DUPONT/CLOROX — LCI (VT/RM — MTC SL)	19.	COMML: WINTHROP/GLENBROOK — LCI (VT/VT — MTC SL)
4. MATERIAL	20.	JACK PALANCE
5. COMML: VICK/SIMMONS — LCI (VT/FM — MTC SL)	21.	COMML: KENTUCKY FRIED CHICKEN — LCI (CHICKEN BUCKET) (VT — MTC SL)
6. ORSON BEAN	22.	JOSE MOLINA (Dance to Panel)
7. COMML: NO. AMERICAN SYSTEMS/ J & J — LCI (VT/FM — MTC SL)	23.	MTC VT & NET FILL & LOGO SL
7A. CONTINENTAL SL	24.	PANEL
	25.	DISC SLS & LOGO SL / STATION BREAK
8. STATION BREAK		

Courtesy of NBC Television Network

CHILDREN'S PROGRAMS

The face of children's programs on television changed greatly in the 1970's. The concept of the writer developing a good action program to keep the kids at home on the edge of their seats, glued to the violence and, not incidentally, to the hard-sell commercials is, hopefully, a thing of the past. The writer of children's programs must, first and foremost, keep in mind the effect of the programs on the vulnerable minds and emotions of the child-viewers. The writer must be socially aware and, hopefully, have a social conscience. Even unintended violence, prejudice or sexism is inexcusable.

Approach

Imagination is the key word in the preparation and writing of programs for children. The imaginations of children are broad, exciting, stimulating. It is only when we approach adulthood that we begin to conform, to restrict our minds and thoughts, to dry up that most precious of creative potentials. The best format is of a level of intelligence that respects the child who is watching. For the pre-school child the activity program featuring some elements of fantasy, such as Mother Goose rhymes, as well as the use of things familiar to the child's world, is common. The child in the first few grades of elementary school is able to relate to material containing beginning elements of logical thinking. Sketches with simple plots, and fairy tales, are usually successfully appealing. Activities with which the child can get involved, if not too sophisticated or complicated, are effective. The child over eight or nine years of age is able to respond readily to the activities and accounts of the outside world. At this age drama begins to be very effective, particularly stories of adventure and individual action, where the child can identify with the heroine or hero. The mid- and upper-grade elementary school child is ready for elements of reality, through drama, discussion, documentary, and participatory and observational activity. The reality may relate to political and social events of the contemporary world or it may deal with scientific and environmental history and happenings.

Writing Techniques

The child should be reached in a direct manner. The presentational approach is most effective, with the narrator or character relating to the viewer candidly. The children must be able to understand the ideas presented. Be simple and be clear. This does not imply that children should be talked down to. Too much dialogue is not advisable, either in a dramatic or non-dramatic program. Action and vivid, colorful presentation of ideas are most effective. This implies an adherence to a simplified plot in the dramatic story. Material of a light nature should be featured on children's programs or, if the material is serious in content, it should not be morbid and it should not contain the sometimes disturbing psychological probing often found in the better adult programs. This is especially true of programs oriented primarily for younger children. The resolutions should not be ambiguous and the characters, though not necessarily real, should be believable.

The child identifies to an extraordinary degree with those dramatic elements that are within his or her own realm of experience and understanding.

If you wish to present a program of an educational nature, avoid the simple repetition of material that children viewing the program may have gotten in school. Known material may be used in the educational program, but it should be used to stimulate the child to participate in the program through thinking and applying the knowledge already learned, and to learn more. Some programs go beyond the schools in quality and teach what most schools never taught but which capable parents always taught—self-esteem and self-ego and a relationship of self to the social, political and environmental ideas and happenings of the real world.

Several techniques have been especially successful in the story or drama for the child audience. First, there must be suspense. Children, like adults, should be caught up in a conflict, no matter how simplified, and should want to know what is going to happen. Children should be let in on a secret that certain characters in the play do not know. And, finally, children always love a good "chase" no less than the adults who assiduously followed the "Keystone Cops" in silent films and who follow the crime and action shows on television today. Keep in mind, however, that there must be a believable base and that slapstick for slapstick's sake usually ends up as low-level violence, as evidenced in too many of the Saturday morning cartoon programs over too many years!

The visual element of television can be used very effectively in children's programs. On any show, in any format, the writer can use actors, special set pieces, puppets and marionettes, film clips, interesting makeup and costumes, attention-getting camera angles and movements and, particularly enjoyable for children, special electronic devices and effects.

The presentational approach, mentioned earlier, is important. On television the performer can play directly to the camera and to the child-viewer. Care must be taken not to overdo this because children know when the performer is fawning or condescending.

Television is particularly good in illustrating visual elements and experiences in society and in involving children in some kind of activity. Pre-school programs frequently use this approach, emphasizing painting, construction, dancing, cooking, and other arts and crafts and visual-action games. Television also can introduce ideas and sights beyond the games and art activities through such things as visits to museums, demonstrations by artists, an inside view of a fire station, backstage at a theatre, in the dressing room or on the playing field at an athletic event, on the assembly line at a factory, in a courtroom—the possibilities are unlimited.

Many children's shows are written out completely. In many situations, particularly for non-dramatic programs that use a "live-type" production approach, detailed outlines or routine sheets are written. The following script excerpts from "Sesame Street" present the material in non-condescending terms, using varied forms of audience persuasion and motivation. Some segments in the usual "Sesame Street" production are in variety-show form; others are in audience-participation form; still others use the dramatization or skit. Comedy, ranging from gentle satire to farce, is also used. Drawing on the persuasive impact of commercial writing, "Sesame Street" frequently captures and holds its audience's attention by adapting the form of the commercial.

SHOW #494

CHILDREN'S TELEVISION WORKSHOP

SESAME STREET

Final Air Version

1.   Film: Show Identification   :15

2.   Film: Opening Sesame Street Theme   :50

3.   DAVID IS STUDYING (SOCIAL ATTITUDES)   2:02

HOOPER DRESSED IN DAY OFF OUTFIT ENTERS NEAR FIXIT SHOP. HE
GREETS AND THEN GOES INTO STORE. DAVID IS BEHIND COUNTER.
HE IS READING A BOOK AND TAKING NOTES.

HOOPER: Hello David.

DAVID: Oh hi Mr. Hooper. What are you doing here? This is your day off.

HOOPER: I know but I just happened to be in the neighborhood and I thought I'd drop by. (NOTICES DAVID WAS READING) Reading huh?

DAVID: Uh . . . yeah I was.

HOOPER: (LOOKS MIFFED) Reading on the job?

DAVID: Hey wait a minute. I know this looks bad . . . but there were no customers in the store and I just . . .

HOOPER: (CUTS HIM OFF) Yes I know . . . but the floors could use a sweeping . . . and the shelves could be straightened. I don't know . . . in my day when I was young like you . . . when i worked . . . I worked.

DAVID: (A LITTLE MIFFED) Listen Mr. Hooper. I know I shouldn't be reading when you're paying me to work, but I wasn't just reading. I was studying.

HOOPER: Studying?

DAVID: Yeah, I have a big law school test tonight.

HOOPER: A test? Why didn't you say so? Studying is very important. It's a good thing I came by. You shouldn't be here in the first place. (STARTS USHERING DAVID OUT OF THE BACK INTO THE ARBOR) Come on come on. You gotta study. I'll work today.

THEY GET TO ARBOR . . .

DAVID: Wait, Mr. Hooper, That's not fair to you. It's your day off.

HOOPER: So you'll work on your day off and make it up. You want to be a big lawyer some day no?

DAVID: O.K. If you say so. Thanks a lot, Mr. Hooper, I appreciate it. (SITS AND STARTS TO READ, AT TABLE)

HOOPER: My pleasure, Mr. Lawyer, my pleasure.

SCENIC: Street, Arbor, Store

TALENT: David, Hooper

PROPS: Constitutional Law Book, note book, pencil

COSTUMES: Hooper in regular clothes

4.   VTR: BEAT THE TIME-TRAIN (GUY, CM, AM) (446) (33a)   3:03

5.   BB STUDIES WITH DAVID   3:03

BB ENTERS ARBOR AREA CARRYING A SCHOOL BAG. DAVID IS STUDYING. THERE IS A STOOL AT TABLE OPPOSITE DAVID.

BB: Hi David. Do you mind if I study with you?

DAVID: What are you gonna study BB?

BB: (REACHES INTO SCHOOL BAG AND TAKES OUT LETTER "U" AND PUTS IT ON TABLE) The letter "U." It takes a lot of study you know.

DAVID: O.K. BB go ahead. (GOES BACK TO READING)

BB: (GETS CLOSE TO LETTER) U . . . U . . .

DAVID: (LOOKS UP) BB quietly.

BB: Oh sorry David. (TAKES A UKULELE OUT OF SCHOOL BAG, PUTS IT NOISILY ON TABLE THEN DOES THE SAME WITH AN UMBRELLA.

DAVID: BB what now?

BB: Oh these are just some things that begin with the letter "U." A ukulele and an umbrella. See it makes it easier to learn a letter if you know a word that begins with that letter.

DAVID: I know . . . I know. But listen BB. You can't be putting all kinds of things on the table. It bothers me.

BB: Oh sorry Dave. Well then how about if I do something that begins with the letter "U"?

DAVID: (WILLING TO AGREE TO ANYTHING BY NOW) O.K. Sure. As long as you're quiet.

BB: I'll be quiet.

DAVID GOES BACK TO READING
BB: (GETS UP AND TIPTOES TO SIDE OF TABLE . . . BENDS OVER AND
PUTS HIS HEAD UNDER THE TABLE AND TRIES TO GO UNDER IT . . .
POSSIBLY KNOCKING IT OVER)
DAVID: BB what now?
BB: I was going under the table. Under starts with the letter "U."
DAVID: BB you're driving me crazy.
BB: Gee it's not my fault the letter "U" is a noisy letter to study. Well anyway
I'm finished studying it.
DAVID: Good.
BB: Are you finished studying your law book?
DAVID: No.
BB: Well don't feel bad. Not everybody is as fast a learner as me. (STARTS
GATHERING HIS STUFF TOGETHER)
DAVID: (BURN)

SCENIC: Arbor
TALENT: BB, DAVID
PROPS: BB school bag, letter "U", a ukulele, umbrella

6. FILM: U IS FOR UP   :34

7. FILM: DOLL HOUSE #2   1:32

8. FILM: U CAPITAL   :46

9. BB AND SNUFFY STUDY WITH DAVID   2:57

BB AND SNUFF NEAR 123. BB HAS A #2.
BB: O.K., Mr. Snuffleupagus, are you all set to go study with David?
SNUFF: Sure Bird. I'm ready. What are we gonna to study?
BB: The number two. (HOLDS UP NUMBER)
SNUFF: Oh goody. Let's go.
BB: O.K., but be very quiet. Don't make a sound. We mustn't bother David.
SNUFF: O.K. Bird. I won't even say a word.
THEY GO TO ARBOR . . . SNUFF SITS IN BACK OF DAVID WHO IS READING
INTENTLY. . . . BB GOES TO STOOL OPPOSITE DAVID.

*   *   *

WOMEN'S PROGRAMS

As the impact of communications on human change is more and more understood, more and more minorities are joining the society-wide revolution for individual rights and self-realization. Media, particularly television, comprise a significant part of the women's revolution.

The negative images of women in television and radio are legion. From the soap opera to the dramatic series the woman usually is portrayed as either incompetent or overbearing. Even in programs where women behave in adult, responsible, respected ways, there is always the tragic (or, more accurately in terms of media practice, "comic") flaw that makes the woman less than the ideal image presented of the male.

A study by the National Organization for Women (NOW) of 1241 TV commercials showed women's place as in the home in almost all. In 42.6% of the commercials women were doing household work; in 37.5% their role was to provide help or service to men; and in 16.7% their main purpose was for male sex needs. In only 0.3% of the commercials were women shown as independent individuals. It is not surprising that a *Good Housekeeping* survey found that one-third of the women have at one time or another turned off commercials because they found them offensive.

Mary Ellen Verheyden-Hilliard, director of the National Organization for Women's National Task Force on Education stated, at a Senate hearing:

> Why is such pervasive demeaning of females shown on network television? Why do the networks allow it? Is television simply a mirror of society? Can it be, should it be more? No network would, any longer, put on five hours of programming (every Saturday morning) in which Blacks acted dumb, fell over their feet, and were happy as long as their white friends loved them. Why have Blacks been able to change this kind of TV image and females have not? Why should girls be portrayed this way? Is it imperative that the television networks recognize their sensitive role in the socialization of our children. Sex discrimination and stereotyping must be eliminated on television and superseded by a reasonable, balanced presentation of women in the wide range of roles we do, in fact, hold.

Approaches to programming have been changing, and in the early and mid-1970's women were presented more and more in unstereotyped roles. Not only is the image of women changing in dramatic programming and on commercials, but the approach to the daily "bread-and-butter" women's programming is also changing. The so-called women's programs have principally been those which primarily attracted women viewers and listeners because of the time of day during which they were presented and those which carried content traditionally deemed of interest primarily to women regardless of the time of presentation. Women's programs have begun to add or substitute topics that are vital to women and to society, such as equal opportunities, job training, rape, abortion, birth control, financial dependence and legal discrimination.

Essentially, writing the women's program is not any different from writing other program types, as far as basic form is concerned. The news program or panel discussion or feature which considers the needs of women does not change in its essential technique. What it does is to be sensitive to the needs of the women, to the kind of content and words that reflect women's achievements and aspirations and are not insulting to or stereotyping of women. How many commercials have you seen that relate to women, sell a product and do it without suggesting, for example, that the woman's principal function in working for the advertisers is to show a sexy body which somehow promises a form of mental and emotional fornication while flying through the air and reinforces the stereotypes of stewardesses which suggest that the passenger will get more than an airplane ride for *his* money?

Gertrude Barnstone, broadcast writer and producer, believes that the principal need is, within any program approach or format, to keep in mind the specific points of view which reflect the needs and interests of women:

> In many program areas we find it helpful to include a redefinition or articulation of the subject from the women's—the feminist—point of view. For example, in sports, write materials not only on the health and physical well-being aspects of athletics for women, but on the sense of one's own body gained from such involvement. Be sensitive to news items about women otherwise ignored in standard news coverage. Investigative reporting and features should be aware of the special problems relating to women—such as rape, child care, women alcoholics, sexism in schools and in toys. Women's programs should provide answers to problems plagueing women that are not easily obtainable elsewhere, such as unemployment, credit discrimination, loan discrimination, real estate and housing practices, among others. Open up the audience's minds to alternative life-styles, those which provide the women with an alternative to the traditional non-paid concubine-housekeeper and, in some cases, additionally, a breadwinner role.

Among the women's programs that have shown in their choice and treatment of topics that men are also adversely affected—psychologically, physically, economically—by the sexist problems they inflict or condone is Washington, D.C.'s WTOP-TV's "Everywoman."

Shirley Robson, producer of "Everywoman," explains that the program, with a specific orientation toward those subjects primarily relating to women and with impact of the subjects on all of society, encompasses all kinds of formats. "This is a program about those things that concern and that can help women. We are not afraid to take a strong editorial stance and cover such topics as rape, divorce, economic discrimination and prostitution. We have interviewed a rapist and shown the stark degradation of a woman alcoholic. We showed in the program on "The Great American Breast" an actual breast implant operation—which many people, including one of the program's personalities, were too squeamish to watch."

Robson stresses a need for thorough research, as for any well-prepared script. "Don't leave a stone unturned in doing research because the aspects of any situation, particularly topics of immediate public interest or public controversy, may change from minute to minute."

Here is a rundown sheet and script excerpt from "Everywoman's" "The Great American Breast."

Clock Time	Dura- tion	Topics and Guests	Audio	Video	Area/Prop
	0:30	Tease (8 cleavage)	Music	Slides	
	0:15	Open	v/o		
	0:05	Title . . . sound			
	2:20	Intro Rene & Carol	In key slides		
		Bump	Music		
0-:10		Bump (Great American Breast)	Music		
	:22	Rene & Carol lead to girlwatchers & blue denim	(Cleavage in key)	Film	
	:42	How sexy is flat-chested woman Comment (Rene & Carol)	(Cleavage in key)		
	1:13	Why flat chested women feel cheated Comment (Rene & Carol)		Topless stillframe	
	2:15	Topless routine Comment (Rene & Carol)	Audio tapes	Topless stillframe	
	:45	Breast animation Carol . . . Billboard & Bump		(Great American Breast)	
		Bump (E.W. . . . Great American Breast) Rene & Carol . . . ad lib setup Black & white breast surgery, psychology	Music		
	1:45	Lead to operation			
	7:26	Operation	Audio w/carts		
		Bump (we'll be right back)			
		Bump . . . (E.W. . . . The Great American Breast) Rene & Carol in limbo	Music		
		Commentary			
	:47	Credits w/ bandaging breasts			
		Brill	Bye Bye Birdie Music		
			RENE:		
			THE GREAT AMERICAN BREAST . . PHOTOGRAPHED . . . MEASURED . . . INJECTED . . . EXPOSED . . . PADDED AND PUSHED UP . . . RESTORED WITH COCOA BUTTER . . .		
			A HYBRID OF CROSS BREEDING UNLI ANYTHING IN THE ANNALS OF AN ANATOMY TEXTBOOK. OUR GUEST ON EVERYWOMAN.		

RENE & CAROL INTRO
RENE & CAROL — GENERAL HELLO TO
AUDIENCE

RENE:
SOMEWHERE ALONG THE WAY TO
MAIDENHOOD WE BECAME AWARE OF
BREASTS. USUALLY OUR OWN . . . HERS
IF THEY WERE BIGGER.

CAROL:
AND IN THE SEVENTH OR EIGHTH
GRADE GYM CLASS THE SLOW BUDDING
AMONG US CLUTCHED TOWELS TO OUR
CHESTS AND DRESSED BEHIND LOCKER
DOORS WHILE SISTERS OF AMAZING
GRACE WHIPPED "C" CUPS ON AND
OFF FOR SHOWERS.

RENE:
IN HIGH SCHOOL THE BOYS IN THE
CAFETERIA BEGAN THE SERIOUS
MEASUREMENT . . . WE HAD KNOCKERS.

CAROL:
OR GOURDS.

RENE:
OR TITS.

CAROL:
OR JUGS.

RENE:
OR BOOBS.

CAROL:
OR WE WERE WELL STACKED.

RENE:
NO ONE SEEMS TO KNOW WHY A
LARGE PROPORTION OF OUR MALE
POPULATION BECAME BREAST
WORSHIPPERS. MAYBE THE PILGRIMS
DONE US WRONG . . . THE LEGACY OF
THOSE ROUND WHITE COLLARS AND
HIGH BUTTON SHOES WERE JUST TOO
MUCH MODESTY FOR ONE PEOPLE TO
TAKE. AFTER WORLD WAR I WHEN THE
BOYS HAD SEEN "PAREE" . . . GIRLS
CHANGED INTO SOMETHING MORE
COMFORTABLE. STILL BREASTS DID NOT
GET A LOT OF ATTENTION BECAUSE
WOMEN WERE BUSY BINDING THEM UP
TO GET THAT STYLISH "FLAT" LOOK
TO GO WITH THE NEW CHEMISE.

*   *   *

RENE:
AND THE MAJORITY OF PATIENTS SEEK-
ING A BREAST OPERATION ARE IN-
VOLVED IN MAJOR LIFE CHANGES . . .
USUALLY A READJUSTMENT CONCERN-
ING MARRIAGES . . . WOMEN WHO ARE
MOST FREQUENTLY SEEN JUST BEFORE
OR AFTER A DIVORCE OR SEPARATION.

WE'RE GOING TO SHOW YOU A
BREAST IMPLANT OPERATION . . . IF
YOU ARE SQUEAMISH YOU MAY NOT
WANT TO SEE THE FIRST PART. CAROL
WATCHED IT . . . I COULD NOT. THE
VOICES YOU WILL HEAR ARE THOSE OF
THE SURGEON WHO PERFORMED THIS
OPERATION AND A WOMAN WHO HAS
HAD THE SURGERY.

COMMENTARY CLOSE FOR BREASTS

RENE:
WELL . . . CAROL . . . IF THIS PROGRAM
WAS DESIGNED TO ANSWER THE QUES-
TION "HOW DID A NICE GIRL LIKE YOU
END UP IN SURGERY?" THEN THE
MEDIUM GAVE YOU ONLY PART OF THE
MESSAGE. SOME OF THE RAUNCHIER
CONDITIONING . . . YES . . . BUT THE
SUBTLETIES OF SEXUALITY HAVE BEEN
CONFUSED WITH A WORD THAT CREPT
INTO OUR LANGUAGE . . . "SEXY" . . .
AND THAT IS HARDER TO NAIL DOWN.

FROM THE TIME SHE WAS CON-
STRUCTED FOR ADAM . . . EVE HAD
FEW EQUALIZING WEAPONS TO KEEP
HERSELF OPERATIVE. WAS THERE AN
APPLE HANDY? SHE USED IT. WOMEN
USED ANYTHING THAT WORKED. THEY
RESPONDED WITH A VENGEANCE . . .
PUTTING TOGETHER ALL THE SIGNALS
AND DEVICES THAT SAID "COME AND
GET ME . . . CROWN ME QUEEN OF THE
MAY." MAKING IT AS PAINLESS AS
POSSIBLE FOR THE MAN TO SINGLE
HER OUT FOR HIS PROTECTION AND
CARE AND MATING . . . THUS INSURING
HER SECURITY . . .

BUT . . . ALAS . . . ! THE MORAL OF
THIS STORY . . . ANGELS . . . IS THAT IT
TAKES MORE THAN CHEMISTRY AND A
"C" CUP TO SURVIVE.

CAROL:
RIGHT ON OR AMEN . . . OR SOMETHING
LIKE THAT.

*Produced by Shirley Robson, written by Rene Carpenter, starring Rene Carpenter
and Carol Randolph, WTOP-TV, Washington, D.C.*

Minority and Ethnic Programs

The truism that a writer writes best out of his or her personal experience is particularly applicable to minority and ethnic programs. This applies across the board, whether in news, documentaries, features, talks, drama or commercials. The orientation of the material must be in terms of the feelings and attitudes of the minority audience—which are to greater or lesser degrees different than those of the majority audience for whom almost all other program materials are written. It is not simply a matter of "thinking" what a particular minority group may be interested in or affected by. It is a matter of "knowing" and "feeling." Unless the writer has been part of the minority experience, there can be only the superimposition of understanding, no matter how sincere or talented the writer. In the mid-1970s this was evidenced in a number of "sitcoms" oriented around minority group characters, but either decried or taken with a grain of super-fiction salt in the super-fly manner by the minorities viewing the programs.

The principal problems minority, ethnic, nationality and religious groups have had with the media are the same as those described for women earlier: either denigrating stereotypes or unrealistically sympathetic portrayals. Consideration of and sensitivity to minority and ethnic needs in writing applies to all formats and program types. In commercials, for example, minorities have served as convenient stereotypes for humor for decades. On any television day you can see the Hispanic, the Oriental, the Native American, the comically-accented "foreigner," the ethnically-identified worker and others as naive/too sophisticated, stupid/scheming, dull/violent, overbearing/underbearing or with some other characteristic that the writers of the commercials would strongly object to if applied to them or to their own relatives. The fact that the portrayals are meant to be funny and that one presumably should have a sense of humor and overlook the stereotyping for the laughs does not eliminate the derogation and the negative impact on the population as a whole.

A most important concern of minority and ethnic groups is the lack of adequate news coverage. The writer should be aware of the special needs, attitudes, feelings and motivations of the minority-ethnic group newsmakers and news viewers, as well as those of the non-minority audience. News impact of a particular event on minorities—such impact is, by the nature of our society, different than that upon the majority—is usually ignored, except where the happening directly and strongly includes a minority issue.

Throughout the country, on majority-owned stations and on the gradually increasing number of their own stations, minority and ethnic groups are presenting news programs which interpret and include those events they deem of interest that are not included in the regular news programs.

Although in the mid-1970s minorities, particularly Blacks, began to appear more and more on entertainment programs, especially sitcoms, and in commercials, writers and producers did not include much minority representation on news and public affairs programs. The public affairs and documentary series oriented solely to minority and ethnic concerns provided the most significant coverage for these groups. Some of the programs were continuing series on local television and radio stations, produced by members of the minority and ethnic communities who were provided free air time or who purchased time. A most significant national series was Public Broadcasting Service's "Black Journal."

The following excerpts from one "Black Journal" program presents a minority viewpoint which at the same time reflects majority concerns about a topic of general interest.

WNET/13 — BLACK JOURNAL #408

"We, The Enemy"

VIDEO	AUDIO
Studio — TONY BROWN (O/C): Chromakey Cards: New York Times Headline Amsterdam News Headline Militant News Headline Government Surveillance of Private Citizens	On May 16, 1972, one year before the White House Enemies' List was made public by John Dean, Jack Anderson exposed in his syndicated column the existence of a computerized list compiled by the Secret Service of 5,500 Black Americans which it labeled "The Black Nationalist File." Everyone in this file is "of protective interest" to the Secret Service. What this means is that, in the opinion of the Secret Service, they either bear ill will toward the President, another government official, have demonstrated at the White House, have a criminal record or a record of mental instability. Access to a series of documents about the counter-intelligence operations of J. Edgar Hoover's FBI was gained because Carl Stern, a reporter at NBC, sued the Justice Department under the Freedom of Information Act. The Washington Post, in an editorial of March 15, 1974, said: ". . . Mr. Kelley might take a close look at the Bureau's methods of seeking information from Black Communities as disclosed in those papers and in comments by former agents. Bookstores, churches, saloons, store-front community organizations, campuses and student organizations all seemed to be fair game for the FBI if they had the words Afro or Black in their titles. In fact, one former agent who had been assigned to racial matters here in the district told a Post reporter, 'The bureau was interested in anything or anyone that said Black' . . ."
Chromakey Card: Congressional Black Caucus	On Tuesday, June 27, 1972, in Washington, D.C., the Congressional Black Caucus held an ad hoc hearing on governmental lawlessness. Jack Anderson, syndicated columnist and winner of the 1972 Pulitzer prize for National Reporting, was a witness. During his testimony, Mr. Anderson brought out some very vital and enlightening facts about intelligence activites aimed at American citizens, particularly Blacks. Mr. Anderson's testimony was as follows:

*   *   *

	(MUSIC)
V/O ANNOUNCER:	From Washington, D.C., BLACK JOURNAL presents "We, The Enemy." When BLACK JOURNAL originates in various cities, viewers in that area can participate by calling in. This edition, from Washington, D.C., features Jack Anderson, syndicated columnist, and Dick Gregory, political satirist. And now, our host and moderator, Tony Brown.
TONY BROWN:	I think it's very important to place a lot of those statistics, particularly those that you brought out, Mr. Anderson, in historical perspective. That information, or the FBI surveillance — and correct me if I'm incorrect — began in 1961 when John F. Kennedy, a Democrat, was President; it continued under Lyndon Johnson, and into the Nixon administration. And recently, in 1971 according to the FBI director, the new FBI director Clarence Kelley, he no longer is using "lawlessness to fight lawlessness." Is that accurate?
JACK ANDERSON:	Yes I think it's accurate. I would make this clarification. This was done by the late FBI chief, J. Edgar Hoover. There was no evidence at any time that it was ordered by John Kennedy or Lyndon Johnson. There's not even a great deal of evidence that they were aware of the scope of it. They certainly were aware that Black leaders were in the FBI files. But I don't think that they were at any time aware of the scope of it. The late J. Edgar Hoover had a fixation about Blacks, and this — these files I think reflect that fixation, reflect his own personal attitudes, much more so than official policy.
TONY BROWN:	Now, Dick, you were on the famous — or infamous — Watergate or the White House Enemies List. What is your personal reaction to having been placed on that list?
DICK GREGORY:	Well, when the press got in touch with me — I think it was Bob Johnson of Jet Magazine called me when the news broke, and told me I was on Nixon's Enemy List, did I have any comment. And I told him, "Yeah, call him up and tell him I accept before he changes his mind." (LAUGHTER)
	* * *
TONY BROWN:	Hello. You're on BLACK JOURNAL, go ahead please.
VIEWER:	Yes, I'd like to know how both guests feel about affirmative action. There's a Supreme Court case on affirmative action right now, and does society owe the Blacks
	* * *

Courtesy of Tony Brown, Executive Producer, Black Journal

The question of language and terminology is a critical one in writing minority and ethnic programs. Loraine Misiaszek, Director of Advocates for Indian Education and a television producer, stresses this point as a part of the understanding and sensitivity the writer should have. She finds that non-Indian writers frequently use words such as "squaw" and "breed" and similar terms, perhaps not realizing how derogatory they are. She cites news programs which almost always are "put-downs" to Native Americans.

Thomas Crawford, writer-producer of Native American-oriented programs, states: "In considering writing and producing scripts with/for/about Native Americans, one must first of all become familiar with the idioms, patterns of expression, turns of thought, and pronunciations of the particular Indian community with which one is dealing. This kind of background will enable a scriptwriter to deal with the subject in a way that will interest and be appropriate to the people. The writer must also be willing to shift the topic to one that has more immediate interest and appeal." Crawford stresses the need for personal experience and empathy on the part of the writer.

The special background and history as well as the immediate needs of a particular minority or ethnic group help determine the writing approach. Russ Lowe of the Chinese for Affirmative Action Media Committee describes one program as a combination of news, commentary and satire which reflects the perspectives and viewpoints of the Chinese-American that are not otherwise usually broadcast. Lowe notes that the script writers choose words especially carefully, with the vocabulary frequently referring to different parts of the community or to certain events or actions that may have explicit meaning only to the Chinese-American listener.

Dr. Palma Martinez, director of Detroit's "Project: Latino," advises writers of programs for and about Hispanics to keep in mind that they are dealing with people and not with a strange segment of society. "Too many writers," she says, "because of a lack of understanding, are either prejudicial or condescending. In writing about Hispanics, or creating Hispanic characters, make them a part of everyday society and not an excluded group." She advises writers that even when depicting the unique problems Hispanics face, the Hispanic should be shown as a responsible person who is an integral part of society.

There are many more diverse minorities who need to be served by television. Special interests of comparatively small audiences may range from planning herb gardens to making leaded glass to learning Sanskrit to protecting water environments to listening to Kabuki performance background music. The interests may be those of growing minorities who have been largely neglected, such as the aged. The mentally retarded are a minority whose needs can be served by the public airwaves. Programming can serve the physically handicapped, such as the blind. Many other segments of our population can be considered minorities in terms of television programming.

EDUCATION AND INFORMATION PROGRAMS

Education and information programs cover many areas: formal instruction to the classroom, informal education to adults at home, technical updating to professionals, vocational preparation, industry training, and many others. Some of the programs are purely or principally instructional in nature. Others are primarily informational. Still others, with elements of education and information, are public relations oriented.

A principal form of the educational-instructional program is the formal lesson designed for classroom use. Another important form is the training program, principally for government and industry use. Also prominent are programs updating professionals in their fields, particularly in the health sciences. Public information programs which at the same time promote an organization, product or idea—in essence, public relations—are a staple with both government and industry.

Formal Education

The writer of the formal education program is, above all, a planner. The writing of the program begins with the cooperative planning of the curriculum coordinator, the studio teacher, the classroom teacher, the educational administrator, the producer, the TV specialist and the writer. The writer must accept from the educational experts the purposes and contents of each program. The writer should stand firm about the method of presentation; educators, by and large, are too prone to use television as an extension of the classroom, incorporating into the television program the outmoded techniques of teaching in most classrooms. The most important thing to remember is to avoid the "talking head."

After determination of learning goals and contents, the length of individual programs and of the series is determined and the programs are outlined. The outline should carefully follow the lesson-plan for each learning unit as developed by the educational experts. The important topics are stressed, the unimportant ones played down. The educational program does not have to be fully scripted, however. It may be a rundown or routine sheet, depending on the content and whether you use a studio teacher—and to what degree that studio teacher is a professional performer.

Even in the outline stage you should explore the special qualities of television that can present the content more effectively than in the classroom, even when there is a competent classroom teacher. Infuse creativity and entertainment into the learning materials. The TV lesson can use humor, drama and suspense and borrow liberally from the most effective aspects of entertainment programs. Don't be afraid of a liberal infusion of visuals. Even with limited budgets, you can use film clips, slides, live actors, close-ups of graphics, photos, demonstrations, detail sets. Good use of visual writing permits more concrete explanation of what is usually presented in the classroom. The classroom teacher frequently presents principles and explains with examples. Through television the examples can be infinitely more effective than the usual verbal descriptions. You can, in fact, show the real person, thing, place or event itself.

The sequences in the script follow a logical order, usually beginning with a review and preparation for the day's material and concluding with introductory elements for follow-up in the classroom, including review, research, field projects and individual study. Before you begin your script and before you incorporate all the imaginative visual stimuli and the attention-getting experiences, you have to know what is available to you in terms of the program's budget.

The word "motivation" is mentioned so often in education that we have become inured to it. Yet, it is still the key to TV watching and to learning. The better a "show" you have, the better the student will learn. To make learning exciting, the material must be pleasurable and stimulating. Teaching is a form of persuasion. The instructional script should be developed as much as possible for a target audience. Be carefully guided by the educational experts you are working with as to the degree of complexity of concepts you can present, what can be presumed to be already known, and the language level required for comprehension by the students in the particular grade the program is designed for. Although for different persuasive purposes, the instructional program may follow the organization of the commercial: get the students' attention, keep their interest, impart information, plant an idea, stimulate thinking about the subject and, most important of all, motivate the students to create through their own thinking something new. The instructional program, like the good play, should increase in interest and intensity.

One of the simplest and most-used ITV formats is the direct presentation of views and sounds of people, places and things that otherwise would not be available to most students. Science experiments, biographical interviews and geographical descriptions are among the topics that fall into this category. Often the TV presentation may physically resemble a travelogue, with the TV teacher, voice-over, commenting on the filmed or taped material. The material, its sequence and the descriptive information is, of course, carefully planned in terms of curriculum and learning requirements.

Training—Government

Writing educational scripts for government training purposes varies with the size and production budgets of each individual agency. But whether a high budget or a low/no budget situation, the basic element of the program, the script, has got to be as good as possible. Eileen McClay, writer-producer-director of television training materials for the Federal Trade Commission, notes one of the important considerations to the writer:

> You may find that your product must be reviewed (for content, format, policy, security) by so many layers of authority that you despair of ever getting a program out on a timely basis. Also—and this may be one of the most substantial differences between you and your counterparts in commercial or public television—the persons who will rule on your product may have little knowledge about either the limitations or the special capabilities of audiovisuals and may, in fact, have little sympathy with the concept of instructional television. To many people, television is associated with, and thereby ineradicably tainted by, "show biz."

McClay describes her approach to one particular project:

> Because of the time pressure, I decided not to write complete scripts, but to use improvisational techniques and to schedule short but intensive rehearsal periods with staff members who were directly involved in the kinds of situations to be dramatized and who would, therefore, be able to talk spontaneously and knowledgeably on the subject. Also, because of lack of time, I made no attempt to use music or graphics. The script I wrote was more of a detailed routine sheet, in which I prepared as much of the introductory, ending and transitional continuity as possible, but left the analyses and discussion of specific problems in the improvisational form. Also, as writer-director I prepared the video portion of the script, as well.

Training—Industry

Instructional training programs for industry follow the basic approaches and forms of the formal instructional and government training program. Scripts do vary in terms of content and, as in low-budget government operations, in terms of time and facilities requirements, and, especially, in terms of technique required to get across some of the complicated and detailed industrial information. Donald S. Schaal, TV producer-director for Control Data Corporation Television Communications Services, states that "when you come to grips with scripting for industrial television, for the most part you might just as well throw all your preconceived ideas about creative/dramatic and technical writing in the circular file." Schaal states that attempts to transfer the classroom teacher to television have failed and that "unfamiliarity with what television could or could not do . . . resulted in a product which left just about everything to be desired. It lacked organization, continuity, a smooth succession of transitions and, in many cases, many of the pertinent details. . . . Since we think so-called 'training' tapes should *augment* classroom material and not supplant it, we soon realized that we could gain little but could lose everything by merely turning an instructor loose in front of the tube to do exactly what he does in person in the classroom. . . . The videotape he needs for his classroom *must* provide something he cannot conveniently offer his students in person."

Professional Updating

In providing an example of instructional/informational programs for the various professions, Dr. Sandra W. Bennett, Deputy Director of the Ohio Nurses Association, stresses the need for writers of health education programs to work very closely with health professionals. She states that although it sometimes becomes a sensitive area,

> . . . most professionals involved with television production require the assistance of a television writer. Depending on the format and objectives,

the health professional may be supplying the largest percentage of the content for the production. That professional must be made to understand and appreciate the limitations as well as the boundless opportunities television offers.

That's where television writers combine their skills with professionals. All the principles of television writing still apply. Good television writing should not be compromised. (The pressure to abandon what you know to be good writing, however, may be great, especially if you are working with people inexperienced in television.)

Writing for health education requires a few other basic principles:

(1) Give yourself twice as much lead time. Too many professionals are not at all concerned with your time or television's deadlines. Even those who are knowledgeable about TV have patients whose health care needs take priority over your time schedule. Allow for it.

(2) Identify your intended audience and the specific objectives at the outset. Television writing for closed-circuit or VTR distribution is different from open-channel commercial broadcasting.

(3) Slides and audio references to patients need to be carefully screened for public viewing. While this may seem obvious, TV writers must double check to be sure that the information they've been given has protected the privacy of the health care consumer.

Public Information

Sid L. Schwartz, Motion Picture and Audiovisual Officer for the Energy Research and Development Administration, likens the government public information message to the Public Service Announcement:

> The writer's primary task is to find the kernel of the message so that when produced as a PSA it can be compressed to fit a very brief period of time and still make a point in the show-biz presentation that will make more than a mere statement. That is why the successful PSA script must be produceable as an entertaining, interesting, startling or beautiful moment for the radio ear or the television eye and ear—otherwise the effort will be a failure.

> Writing a PSA is like designing a billboard and reducing it to seconds of sound or seconds of sight and sound. Catching an audience's attention, holding their interest and imparting a message in 30 seconds is like a billboard that succeeds in imparting a message to traffic passing at 55 miles per hour.

Mr. Schwartz notes that one popular type of PSA mainly urges the audience to write for more details.

ENERGY I
TV PUBLIC SERVICE ANNOUNCEMENT
30 SECONDS

VIDEO	AUDIO
1. CU hand with quill pen, period coat and cuffs, signs Declaration of Independence.	(FX: Room noise . . . crowd murmurs, etc.) ANNOUNCER: PHILADELPHIA . . . JULY 4TH . . . 1776! A REVOLUTION TAKES PLACE THAT CHANGES THE COURSE OF THE WORLD.
2. Dissolve to traffic montage.	(FX: Traffic noise) TODAY, 200 YEARS LATER, ANOTHER REVOLUTION . . . THIS ONE CONCERNING ENERGY.
3. Dissolve to scientist in lab with test equipment.	(FX: Fade traffic) THE NEW BATTLEFIELD IS THE LABORATORY . . . THE PRIMARY WEAPON, THE HUMAN MIND! WE'RE WORKING HARD TO DEVELOP NEW ENERGY SOURCES.
4. Dissolve to logo: ERDA WASHINGTON, D.C. 20545	TO LEARN HOW, WRITE: *ERDA*, THE ENERGY RESEARCH AND DEVELOPMENT ADMINISTRATION, WASHINGTON, D.C. 20545.

Written by Jack Moser, U.S. Energy Research and Development Administration

Schwartz adds:

More popular and effective are those PSAs that carry the burden of the entire message in their brief exposure. For example, the U.S. Forest Service campaign where Smokey Bear says: "Matches don't start forest fires—people do. Next time think before you strike."

PSA script writing should relate to the client's current campaign or herald the next one. The script should develop empathy and involvement by signalling the audience to use its memory, understanding, ambitions and fantasies. The writing of TV PSAs, for government or nongovernment information purposes, generally follows a written concept, a treatment, a shooting script and, in many cases, a story board.

THE PLAY

The rules of playwriting are universal. They apply generally to the structure of the play written for the stage, film, television or radio. The rules are modified in their specific applications by the special requirements of the particular medium. Don't assume that because there are rules that playwriting can be taught. Genius and inspiration cannot be taught, and playwriting is an art on a plane of creativity far above the mechanical facets of some of the phases of continuity writing.

Sources

The writer may find the motivating ingredient for the play in an event or happening, in a theme, in a character or characters, or in a background. The writer may initiate the preliminary thinking about the play from an idea. Another source for the play may be the social environment. The character may be several people rolled into one. The sources of the play usually are only germs of ideas. The writer should write, ideally, out of personal experiences or knowledge so that the play may have a valid foundation. However, if the writer is too close, either emotionally or in terms of time, to the life-ingredients of the play, it will be difficult to heighten and condense and dramatize.

Play Structure

Modern drama has emphasized character as most important. The actions which determine the plot are those the characters *must* take because of their particular personalities and psychological motivations. The dialogue is that which the characters *must* speak for the same reasons. The three major elements in the play structure—character, plot and dialogue—all must be coordinated into a consistent and clear theme. This coordination of all elements toward a common end results in the unity of the piece, a unity of impression. The characters' actions and the events are not arbitrary, and the audience must be prepared for the occurrence of these actions and events in a logical and valid manner. "Preparation" is the term given to the material which thus prepares the audience. The background and situation also must be presented; this is the "exposition." Another element the playwright must consider is the "setting," which the playwright describes in order to create a valid physical background and environment for the characters.

After you are certain that you understand and can be objective about the characters, theme, situation and background, you can begin to create each of them in depth. Do as much research as necessary—or, perhaps, as much as possible—to acquaint yourself fully with the potentials of the play.

After the characters have been created, you are ready to create the situation, or plot line. This should be done in skeletonized form. You need, first, a conflict. The conflict is between the protagonist of the play and some other character or force. A conflict may be between two individuals, an individual and a group, between two groups, between an individual or individuals and nature, between an individual or individuals and some unknown force, or between an individual and the inner self. The nature of the conflict will be determined largely by the kinds of characters involved. After the conflict has been decided upon, the plot moves inexorably toward a climax, the point at which one of the forces in conflict wins over the other. The play reaches the climax through a series of complications. Each complication is, in itself, a small conflict and climax. Each succeeding complication literally complicates the situation to a greater and greater degree until the final complication makes it impossible for the struggle to be heightened any longer. Something has to give. The climax must occur. The complications are not arbitrary. The characters themselves determine the events and the complications because the actions they take are those, and only those, they must take because of their particular motivations and personalities.

Concepts of Playwriting

Unity. One of the essentials that applies to all plays, regardless of type or style of production, is the unity of action or impression. There should be no elements within the play that do not relate in thorough and consistent fashion to all the other elements, moving toward a realization of the purpose of the playwright.

Plot. The plot structure of a play is based on a complication arising out of the individual's or group's relationships to some other force. This is the conflict, the point when the two or more forces come into opposition. The conflict must be presented as soon as possible in the play, for the rest of the play structure follows and is built upon this element. Next come a series of complications or crises, each one creating further difficulty in relation to the major conflict, and each building in a rising crescendo so that the entire play moves toward a final crisis or climax. The climax occurs at the instant the conflicting forces meet head on and a change occurs to or in at least one of them. This is the turning point. One force wins and the other loses. The play may end at this moment. There may, however, be a final clarification of what happens, as a result of the climax, to the characters or forces involved. This remaining plot structure is called the "resolution."

Character. Character, plot and dialogue comprise the three primary ingredients of the play. All must be completely and consistently integrated. In modern dramaturgical theory character is the prime mover of the action, and determines plot and dialogue. The character does not conform to a plot structure. The qualities of the character determine the action. The character must be revealed through the action; that is, through what the character does and says, and not through arbitrary description or exposition. Character is delineated most effectively by what the individual does at moments of crisis. This does not imply physical action alone, but includes the concept of inner or psychological action.

Dialogue. Inasmuch as the play does not duplicate real people or the exact action of real life, but heightens and condenses these elements, the dialogue also has to be heightened and condensed rather than duplicated. The dialogue must truly conform to the personality of the character speaking it, it must be completely consistent with the character and with itself throughout the play, and it must forward the situation, the showing of the character and the movement of the plot.

Exposition. Exposition, the revelation of the background of the characters and situation and the clarification of the present circumstances, must not be obvious or come through some device, such as the telephone conversation, the servant or the next-door neighbor. It must come out as the action carries the play forward and must be a natural part of the action. The exposition should be presented as early as possible in the play.

Preparation. Preparation, too, must be made subtly. Preparation, or foreshadowing, is the unobtrusive planting, through action or dialogue, of material which prepares the audience for subsequent events, making their occurrence logical and not arbitrary.

Setting. Setting is determined by the form of the play and the physical and mechanical needs of the play structure. Setting serves as locale, background and environment for the characters of the play.

Television's Special Characteristics

The special characteristics of the television audience require a special approach on the part of the playwright. You may combine the subjective relationship of the viewer to the television screen with the electronic potentials of the medium to create a purposeful direction of the audience's attention. You may direct the audience toward the impact of the critical events in the character's life and toward the subjective manifestations of the character's existence. The ability to focus the viewer's sight, attention and even feeling so specifically permits the writer to orient the consciousness of the audience closely to the inner character of the person on the screen.

The Hollywood-style taped or filmed TV play permits a great expansion of action over the stage play and can include a greater number of transitions. Through cuts, dissolves, fades and other electronic devices there are no restrictions of time and place.

Time and space are two more special characteristics of the television medium which the writer must understand and apply. One of the most important problems of all for the television playwright is that of time. The hour drama is really only about 42 minutes long, the half-hour drama 21 minutes in length. Even the hour-and-one-half dramatic program permits only about 63 minutes for the play. The television play should be extremely tight; it should have no irrelevancies. It should have as few characters as possible, and one main, simplified plot line, containing only material relating to the conflict of the major character or characters.

Space limitations are of two major kinds in television. First is the physical size of the room within the studio in live-type TV drama. Second is the decreasing smallness of the objects in a picture picked up by an increasing camera distance, and viewed over the narrow and constricting viewing area of the relatively small television screen.

The limitation of space suggests two major considerations for the writer: the number of characters on a screen at any one time, and the number and scope of sets. In order to avoid a situation where the small television screen is choked with a mass of humanity, the writer must be sure that only a few characters are on camera at the same time. Stage convention permits ten people to represent a crowd. Except in the film-for-TV play, ten people on television (in sitcoms, for example) likely would appear too small individually and too jumbled as a group.

Dramaturgical Concepts for Television

Unity. The most important changes in the unities as applied to television relate to time and place. Television can transcend boundaries of time and place that even the most fluid stage presentation cannot match.

Plot. The dramaturgical rules relating to plot apply to the television play as to the stage play. The problem of time, however, necessitates a much tighter plot line in the television play, and a condensation of the movement from sequence to sequence. The short time for the television play requires the plot to be the essence of reality, to contain only the heightened extremities of life. Aim for the short, terse scene.

Although the emphasis on plot, because of the time factor, seems to make this the motivating factor in the television play, the exploration of television's intimacy and subjectivity potentials enables the writer to delve into character and to use it as a plot-motivating element.

Character. Do not use unneeded people. A character who does not contribute to the main conflict and to the unified plot line does not belong in the play. If a character is essential, put it in the script. If there are too many essential characters, then rethink the entire approach to the play.

Dialogue. Television requires one significant modification in the use of dialogue to forward the situation and to provide exposition. The visual element can often substitute for the aural. If you can show the situation or present the expository information through action instead of through dialogue, do so. The long shot as well as the closeup has made it possible to eliminate time-consuming dialogue in which the character describes things or places. You can concentrate not only on action but on "reaction," keeping the dialogue at a minimum and the picture the primary object of attention.

Exposition. The short time allotted to the television play permits only a minimum of exposition. Because the conflict should be presented almost as soon as the television drama begins, the exposition must be highly condensed and presented with all possible speed.

Preparation. The writer should prepare the audience in a subtle and gradual manner for the subsequent actions of the characters and the events of the play. Nothing should come as a complete surprise.

Setting. Television drama essentially conforms to the play of selective realism in content and purpose, and realistic settings usually are required. Both the limitations and the potentials of television have combined to modify the realistic setting, however. First, the live-type TV setting usually must be smaller than the writer might wish it to be. Second, live-type TV drama makes it difficult to have very many exteriors or large nature effects. On the other hand, the fluidity of teleivison through film and tape makes up for these restrictions by permitting a greater number of changes of setting and a considerable broadening of setting, with frequent changes of time and place.

The Scenario

It is called the scenario, the treatment, the outline, the summary. What it does is give the producer and/or script editor a narrative idea of what the play is about: the plot line, the characters, the setting and maybe even bits of dialogue. Most producers/editors can tell from this narrative whether the play fits the needs of the particular program. The scenario and treatment are usually longer than the outline and summary, perhaps as much as a fifth of the entire script. The summary and the outline may be only two or three pages, in effect providing a preliminary judgment prior to a preliminary judgment. Some producers/editors want to see a summary or outline first, then a scenario or treatment and, finally, the complete script.

The Manuscript

The television manuscript should have all the characters clearly designated, the dialogue, the stage directions, the video and audio directions and, in the Hollywood-style filmed play, the shot designations.

The most frequently used form for the live-type taped play is the two-column approach: the right hand column containing all of the audio—that is, the dialogue plus the character's movements—and the left-hand column containing the video—that is, the mechanical and electronic effects. The left-hand column may also contain special sound effects and music. In some cases the columns are reversed.

Another manuscript approach is to place all of the material, video and audio, together, right down the center, similar to the stage play form, or solely in a left-hand column or right-hand column, leaving the other side free for the director's notes. The names of the characters should be typed in capital letters in the center of the column, with the dialogue immediately below. Video and audio directions and author's stage directions are usually differentiated from the dialogue by being in parentheses and/or in capital letters and/or underlined. Script editors prefer that dialogue be double-spaced, with double-spacing between speeches.

An example of the live-type taped script form is the following opening excerpt from one of the programs of the "Good Times" series.

Note the compactness of the writing and how in the first few minutes of the opening scene 1) the background for the characters and general plot line is established, 2) the characters begin to be delineated and character relationships are shown, 3) the exposition for this particular story is established, and 4) the conflict begins to be introduced.

GOOD TIMES
"The Dinner Party"

ACT ONE
FADE UP:
INT. EVANS' APARTMENT — DAY
(JAMES IS GOING OVER SOME BILLS AT THE TABLE. MICHAEL IS DOING HIS
HOMEWORK. THELMA IS COOKING. J.J. IS AT HIS EASEL PAINTING. FLORIDA
ENTERS FROM BEDROOM)

FLORIDA:	Anybody seen my pin cushion?
J.J.:	I hope you don't mind, Ma, I used it for a still life of a bowl of fruit I just painted.
FLORIDA:	(REACTS — CROSSES TO J.J.) You used my pin cushion in a bowl of fruit?
J.J.:	It is a prime example of ghetto artistry. You make the most of what you got. Your pin cushion as the apple, Michael's basketball as the pumpkin, Dad's socks as the avocados and Thelma's face as the lemon.
THELMA:	Just bend a little and you can throw your body in as a banana. (THEY HASSLE)
JAMES:	Hey, you two, knock it off. I'm trying to figure out these bills.
FLORIDA:	(CROSSES TO CHEST) What's our financial position this month, James?
JAMES:	Well, we ain't in a position to threaten the Rockefellers . . . but we ain't heading for the poor house either. For once we are in the black.
J.J.:	(LOOKS AROUND) What do you mean, for once?
FLORIDA:	J.J.! (PUTS PIN CUSHION DOWN — CROSSES TO SINK TO WASH HANDS) Is everything paid for, James?
JAMES:	(INDICATING ENVELOPES) Everything . . . rent . . . utilities . . . and luxuries.
MICHAEL:	Dad, you didn't mention food.
FLORIDA:	(CROSSES TO JAMES WIPING HANDS ON TOWEL) These days that comes under luxuries. (JAMES COUNTS A FISTFUL OF DOLLARS)

The filmed play does not have the continuous action that still marks many taped plays. The filmed play has a break at each cut or transition. That is, each sequence may last two seconds to two minutes or longer. Between sequences the director can change sets, costumes, makeup, reset lights and cameras, and even reorient the performers. The filmed play is not shot in chronological order, as the taped play usually is. All the sequences taking place on a particular set or at a particular locale, no matter where they appear in the script, are shot over a contiguous period of time. Then the entire cast and crew move to the next set or locale and do the same thing. Instead of writing scenes, write shots. Each shot is set in terms of a picture rather than in terms of character action, although the latter should, in all plays—filmed or taped or live—be the motivating factor. The writer states the place, such as INTERIOR or EXTERIOR, and the shot, such as FULL SHOT or CLOSE-UP. The writer also describes the setting, states the characters' physical relationships to the set and their proximity to each other, and then presents the dialogue for that shot. The individual shots are numbered in consecutive order so that the director may easily pick out any sequence(s) desired for initial shooting, retakes or editing.

An example of the Hollywood-style filmed TV script form is the following opening excerpt from one of the programs of "The Waltons" series.

THE WALTONS
"The First Day"

ACT ONE

FADE IN:

1   EXT. WALTON'S MOUNTAIN — DAY   1

It is dawn –– the first gray light — and there's the suggestion of autumnal
crispness in the air, the first blush of fall colors in the underbrush.

JOHN-BOY (v.o.)
(as a man)
When you're growing up, Septembers have a special
feeling. Another carefree summer is too quickly ended
and a new school year is about to begin.

2   EXT. WALTON HOUSE & YARD — DAY   2

In the dawnlight, we make out the faintly yellow glow of a lamp burning
in John-Boy's room.

JOHN-BOY (v.o.)
(as a man)
There was an extra excitement for me in the September
of 1935. My years at Miss Hunter's school on Walton's
Mountain were over and I was ready to take those first
faltering steps into the strange world outside.

3   INT. JOHN & OLIVIA'S ROOM — DAY   3
In the dim light, we see OLIVIA lies beside JOHN, who appears to be asleep.

JOHN-BOY (v.o.)
(as a man)
How vividly I recall the edgy excitement, the awful
exhilaration of preparing for my first day at college.

Olivia reacts to a MUFFLED BUMPING SOUND.

JOHN-BOY (v.o.)
(as a man)
A day which showed me how little I knew about some
things . . .

Olivia begins to get up. John reaches out and stops her. She looks at him,
surprised. She didn't know he was awake.

JOHN-BOY (v.o.)
(continuing; as a man)
. . . and how well my parents had prepared me for others.

Olivia kisses John and reaches for her bathrobe.

JOHN
Where you going?

We HEAR the muffled sound again, coming from John-Boy's room.

3   CONTINUED: (2)   3

                                    OLIVIA
          John-Boy's up.

                                     JOHN
          I hear. I guess he's anxious to get going.

                                  *   *   *

Rod Serling, who was one of television's most articulate as well as prolific writers, called TV a medium of compromise for the writer. He was concerned that the writer cannot touch certain themes or use certain language. He criticized television because of "its fear of taking on major issues in realistic terms. Drama on television must walk tiptoe and in agony lest it offend some cereal buyer. . . ." Despite these restrictions, he felt that "you can write pretty meaningful, pretty adult, pretty incisive pieces of drama."

As a writer you are, with relatively few exceptions, dependent on the commerical mass media for your existence; yet, you can take comfort in the fact that despite the restrictions put upon you by sponsors, networks and production executives, your play is still the prime mover, the one element upon which all other elements of the production must stand or fall. With a script of high quality, with writing of ethical and artistic merit, you may at least take pride in knowing that you have made a significant effort to fulfill some of the mass media's infinite potentials.

SELECTED BIBLIOGRAPHY

Bliss, Edward, Jr. and John M. Patterson, *Writing News for Broadcast.* New York: Columbia University Press, 1971. Various approaches to writing radio and television news, with good descriptive examples including comparison of same evening newscasts of the three major networks.

Bluem, A. William, *Documentary in American Television.* New York: Hastings House, 1965. Creative approach to form, function and method.

Bluem, A. William and Roger Manvell, eds. *Television: The Creative Experience.* New York: Hastings House, 1967. Includes aesthetics and the writer's viewpoint.

Connochie, T. D., *TV for Education and Industry.* New York: William S. Heinman, 1969.

Cousin, Michel, *Writing A Television Play*. Boston: Writer, Inc., 1975.

Dary, David, *How to Write News for Broadcast and Print Media*. Blue Ridge Summit, Pa.: TAB Books, 1973.

Effron, Edith. *The News Twisters*. New York: Manor Books, 1973.

Elliott, Philip, *The Making of a Television Series*. New York: Hastings House, 1972. Examines the making of a seven-part controversial documentary series, including conceptual work, gathering of materials, preparing outlines and scripts.

Fang, Irving, *Television News,* 2nd Ed., Rev. New York: Hastings House, 1972. Deals with principal problems in writing and reporting news on TV, including editorials, fairness doctrine, libel, election coverage, access, equal time and privacy. Includes a chapter on radio.

Field, Stanley, *Professional Broadcast Writer's Handbook*. Blue Ridge Summit, Pa.: Tab Books, 1974.

Gordon, George N., *Classroom Television: New Frontiers in ITV*. New York: Hastings House, 1970.

Gordon, George N., *Persuasion: The Theory and Practice of Manipulative Communications*. New York: Hastings House, 1971. Basic concepts are applicable to commercial persuasion.

Greenberg, Bradley S. and Brenda Dervin. *Uses of Mass Media by the Urban Poor*. New York: Praeger Publishers, 1970. Findings of three research projects.

Hall, Mark W., *Broadcast Journalism: An Introduction to News Writing,* Revised edition. New York: Hastings House, 1978. A basic introduction to radio-TV news-writing, including style, techniques, sources and types of stories covered.

Herman, Lewis, *Practical Manual of Screen Playwriting for Theatre and Television Films*. New York: New American Library, 1974.

Hilliard, Robert L. and Hyman H. Field, *Television and the Teacher: A Handbook for Classroom Use*. New York: Hastings House, 1976.

Hilliard, Robert L., *Writing for Television and Radio,* Revised 3rd edition. New York: Hastings House, 1976.

Jennings, Ralph and Carol Jennings. *Programming and Advertising Practices in Television Directed to Children*. Newtonville, Mass.: ACT, I-1970, II-1971.

Kaye, Evelyn. *The Family Guide to Children's Televison*. New York: Pantheon Books, 1974. An approach to regulating viewing time, contents of children's programs and what you can do about advertising, sexism and violence aimed at children.

Lawson, John Howard, *Theory and Technique of Playwriting and Screenwriting*. New York: Hill and Wang, 1960.

Lewels, Francisco J., Jr. *The Uses of the Media by the Chicano Movement*. New York: Praeger Publishers, 1974. A study in minority access.

Peck, William A., *The Anatomy of Local Radio-TV Copy*. Blue Ridge Summit, Penna.: Tab Books, 1968.

Rilla, Wolf P., *The Writer and the Screen: On Writing for Film and Television*. New York: William Morrow, 1974.

Shamberg, Michael. *Guerilla Television*. New York: Holt, Rinehart and Winston, 1971. Some non-establishment approaches to bringing minority views to TV.

Small, William, *To Kill A Messenger: Television News and the Real World*. New York: Hastings House, 1970. The day-to-day decision processes of selecting, analyzing and presenting news, from his viewpoint as Vice President and Washington Bureau Manager, CBS News.

Stone, Vernon and Bruce Hinson, *Television Newsfilm Techniques*. New York: Hastings House, 1974. A project of the RTNDA, this is a manual of practices and trends at TV stations.

Surgeon General's Advisory Committee on Television and Social Behavior. *Television and Social Behavior*. Washington, D.C.: U.S. Government Printing Office, 1972.

Television in Instruction: What Is Possible. Washington, D.C.: National Association of Educational Broadcasters, 1971.

Terrell, Neil, *The Power Technique for Radio-TV Copywriting*. Blue Ridge Summit, Penna.: Tab Books, 1971.

Trapnell, Coles, *Teleplay: An Introduction to Television Writing*. New York: Hawthorn Books, 1974.

Tyrrell, R. W., *The Work of the Television Journalist*. New York: Hastings House, 1972. A primer describing every job from writer and producer to camera operator, recordist, film editor, newscaster. Compares British and American television news.

Wainwright, Charles Anthony, *Television Commercials: How to Create Successful TV Advertising*, Revised Edition. New York: Hastings House, 1970.

Willis, Edgar E., *Writing Television and Radio Programs*. New York: Holt, Rinehart and Winston, 1967.

TOM C. BATTIN

Professor of Communications (retired)
University of Houston

● Dr. Battin has been active in television for 30 years, including 20 years experience in producing and directing in both commercial and educational television. He joined the University of Houston in 1954, where he was a member of the staff of KUHT, the nation's first ETV station, and he held the rank of full Professor of Communications. His 30 years of university teaching included the University of Michigan, and the University of Florida where he initiated television production and wrote, produced and directed numerous educational television series through the facilities of commercial stations in Jacksonville. At one time he was associated with the production staff of General Electric Television in Schenectady, New York.

Dr. Battin received his B.A. degree from the University of Ohio and his M.A. and Ph.D. degrees from the University of Michigan. His dissertation was the first doctoral level research in the nation in the field of TV. He has published numerous articles on television in educational and trade journals. He has been very active in professional associations—among the offices he has held are those of Chairman of the RTVF Interest group of the Speech Communications Association of America, Chairman of the RTVF Interest Group of the Southern Speech Association, and Chairman of the RTVF Interest Group and Director of Public Relations of the Texas Speech Association. He has conducted workshops and presented numerous scholarly papers at national, regional and state conventions over the past 25 years. In addition to television, Dr. Battin has had many years of experience in university and semi-professional theatre. He has also worked in motion picture production and has played character roles in several major feature films.

5

DIRECTING

BY TOM C. BATTIN

TELEVISION DIRECTING is one of the most exciting, most challenging, most demanding and, frequently, most frustrating activities in which any individual can participate.

Television is a combination of three means of communication: sight, motion and sound, in that order of importance. Most people think of television as being essentially photographic. Think of television, however, as "sight in motion" and recognize the fact that motion adds impact to the already powerful combination of the "sight and sound" medium. It is a medium working with time, light, space, motion and sound, all of which make television an efficient instrument which can distribute messages simultaneously to millions of individuals all over the world. The television director must, above all, be visually minded.

Too often television directors become "button punchers." They become technicians. Television is an art form which requires an artistic approach. The director must use the equipment and not be used by it. The director must understand human nature and know how to relate to people. A background in psychology and sociology is valuable.

The good director has a keen sense of continuity; he or she sees and not only looks. The director has a strong sense of form and structure, a highly developed sense of timing, and a perceptive sense of hearing; he or she listens and not only hears. The director should have a sense of the whole, understanding mood and how long mood should be held.

When you look, see; when you hear, listen.

It is said that a picture is worth a 1,000 words. Under the eye of an artistically skillful director this becomes literally true in television. The camera and microphone are selective tools. Each shot is a picture. Remember that you are working in a medium of intimacy and immediacy. Sets, props, lights and talent are your palette and cameras are your brushes. You literally paint a picture in color on the home receivers. The director must think in terms of pictures. You must visualize detail and analyze so that you don't see one picture alone, but as a part of many individual pictures which produce the visual continuity. Each picture is just one of many frames which combine to make the whole. When you analyze your visual continuity you should literally see hundreds of frames, each a portion of one larger picture of pictorial continuity.

The director should be especially well acquainted with the camera, with its potentialities and limitations, with its flexibility. The best place to learn directing is behind the camera. When you know what the camera can do, you are better able to experiment successfully and not be content to conform to what already has been done.

Be aware of the importance of sound. Sound must balance the picture; sometimes one or the other may dominate, but most of the time they balance each other. Because television is a medium of action, both sight and sound must have motion and movement.

In sum, the director must be able to tele-visualize a script or sequence when reading it, must think in terms of pictures, action and movement, must be sensitive to the selectivity of the human ear, and must have knowledge of sound perspective—all of this in order to balance picture, sound and motion successfully.

THE DIRECTOR'S RESPONSIBILITIES

In many local TV stations a director generally assumes also the responsibilities of a producer along with those of a director. In the local station many of the responsibilities in producing and directing overlap and become a combined task for one person, who then becomes a producer-director. The job, then, becomes a dual activity which requires a broad working knowledge of all studio and control room equipment, coupled with an equally broad knowledge of the programming and production side of television. A producer-director must be a person of many talents and qualification. The producer's role is discussed in Chapter 3 of this book.

The producer-director in the role of director has the sole responsibility for putting the television program on the air. All the efforts of the production staff and talent reach a climax in the performance as a director. Since all programs are telecast for a viewing audience, a most important directorial responsibility is to the audience. The director must understand its needs and wants and be capable of fulfilling them. The director is a conductor whose symphony is one of picture, language, music and motion. All these things the director molds into moving patterns which are readily understood and enjoyed by the audience. It is the director's task to present visually, as closely as possible, the work of the writer as the latter visualized it while writing.

Personal Qualities

The director must be able to communicate instructions rapidly and clearly, must be definite and decisive and, due to the pressure of time, must not hesitate in making decisions. Put thoughts into as few words as possible for easy and quick comprehension.

The director must be adept at exhibiting things effectively and without "gimmicks" or through "unorthodox" methods, must have an instinctive sense of good taste and must never intentionally offend in what is visually presented. The director should have the ability to recognize a good script and its potential for the TV medium.

The director must be stern, but sternness should be seasoned generously with understanding and tact. Remember you are working with human beings and recognize when performers and staff are tired and need a rest period. You must, however, adhere to rigid deadlines and rehearsal schedules if you are to make a success of the on-the-air presentation. The director commands the respect of the technical staff and talent by the way rehearsals are handled, and accomplishes what must be done without waste of time.

The director must have a keen sense of observation in order to recognize those things which add to the quality of a show as well as increase viewer interest. You must be able to recognize the need for any necessary last minute changes.

The director must be a person of foresight, one who anticipates problems before they occur, thus avoiding what otherwise could develop into major difficulties.

The director must be alert to the pressures and strictures of time, for time in television is evanescent. Be alert to the many and varied details inherent in any TV production, and be capable of making fast and correct decisions.

The television director is working with a great many different persons involved in many different individual tasks. Although participating in what appears to be "organized chaos," working under tremendous pressure and nervous tension, the director must remain calm and not reveal tension, for tension is contagious.

The director must be able to work under extreme pressure—the pressure of numerous responsibilities being carried out simultaneously. To the director, speed is of the utmost importance.

The director must be able to memorize the many details of the directing assignment, and be capable of quickly recalling any or all details at a moment's need. The director must be able to rapidly learn an entire script, all movements, camera shots, business, cues and other details. During the on-the-air telecast the director cannot afford to be imprisoned by the script, but must know it—forward and backward.

The director must be a strong self-disciplinarian and entirely self-dependent in the directing of the production. No one tells the director what to do. While constantly telling others what to do, the director must adhere religiously at the least to the standards and demands being made of others.

The director has a responsibility to the station and must do the very best job humanly possible for the station. Your goal should be for quality and perfection; never settle for mediocrity.

The director must be able to evaluate a script well enough to determine the good from the bad. As you read the script, tele-visualize it; be capable of mentally telecasting the content. This visualization of script content is extremely helpful in determining the value of the material relative to its production.

The director is the pivotal figure around which the production revolves. It is the director's task to coordinate the many elements of production while functioning as an on-the-air director. The director is working in a highly technical medium and must be skilled enough to use it artistically.

Control Room Activities

Most of the time the director will be in communication with many members of the technical staff involved in the on-the-air telecast. This is done through an inter-com system consisting of head phones and a small microphone. The director is involved in many activities, most of which are going on simultaneously. Some of these activities are:

1) Talking with members of the technical staff such as those in the control room and master control room, the audio engineer, technical director (if there is one), VTR operator, film and slide projectionists.

2) Conversing with the light director relative to any special lighting effects during the show.

3) Talking with the production crew in the studio: floor manager, camera operators, microphone boom operators. (The inter-com is vital here.)

4) Watching, depending upon how many cameras are being used, at least three monitors almost simultaneously: two camera monitors and the program line monitor. Frequently an eye is also kept on the film and/or VTR preview monitors.

5) Listening to all sound: speech, music and sound effects.

6) Maintaining contact with announcers, narrators and any other persons involved in any off-camera speaking.

7) Following the script, routine sheet or whatever type format is used. An alert director will memorize basic elements in script material.

8) Finally, keeping an eye on the control room clock for the overall timing of the show. Some directors use a stop watch for keeping check on certain portions or segments of the show such as commercials, opening and closing announcements, and so forth.

If the director is going to do the switching, and in most local stations this is so, then he or she must be a very alert individual who can set up camera shots, call them, switch them and, at the same time, maintain all communications necessary with the various members of the technical staff.

Preparation

The director much check the availability of all equipment to be used before going into any rehearsals. It usually is necessary to set up rehearsal dates according to when equipment is available. Make a check on all equipment that will be used during rehearsals and for the on-the-air telecast, including cameras, lens complements, special lenses, special effects equipment, all audio equipment such as microphones, live sound such as music and sound effects, films and slides and film and slide projection equipment. Make a request for all such equipment well in advance of the dates of rehearsals and telecast.

The director should be familiar with the NAB TV Code. Determine whether or not the program is in good taste. Is the material suited for the mass audience of TV? Check for any objectionable material before going into rehearsals.

Plan every moment of rehearsal time; see that not any of it is wasted. Utilize the cast and staff efficiently. If someone is not needed for a particular rehearsal or segment, do not ask that person to appear. Determine if there is something else he or she should be doing to help prepare for his or her part in the production.

A broad, humanistic background becomes most significant when preparing the most important part of the production: translating the characters, plot and dialogue of the author into living beings and action. In addition to helping the performers understand the motivations of their individual roles and their relationships to the other roles, the director has to be ready to direct movement, business, line-readings, expression and all the myriad techniques that go into effective interpretation of the characters and the script. Don't jump into a production without first making a complete diagnosis—a complete analysis of every detail of the production from beginning to end. An improperly placed set piece, an incomplete costume may distract from the continuity of the whole.

The director may be an artist, but must also be a technician. Learn the mechanics of the television medium: how to handle a camera, hang lights, operate an audio console, run a film and slide projection system, operate a VTR, a television electronic programmer, editec, slo-mo and all the other technical aspects of a production for which you, as director, have the ultimate responsibility.

During rehearsals be an active director. You need to move around, playing the role of the camera, seeing the production as the cameras will see it and relay it to the audience. There are many types of viewfinders you can buy. Use one during rehearsals, adjusting it as you move around to determine the best picture and the best distance. Some directors even use a child's wagon, sitting in it and being pushed around by the dolly-pusher. Even though all cameras are of the zoom type, don't let this make your show a static one. Don't be afraid to move the camera itself, fast or slow, in any direction. And don't forget that all such movement, as well as that of the performers, is motivated by dialogue and business. Create pictures. Be an artist.

The beginning director frequently marks up the script very little. This is a mistake. Record numerous notes on the script or copy sequence sheet. These are the road marks which will permit you to conduct meaningful rehearsals. These, changed and translated as rehearsals go on, eventually enable you to execute directorial duties in the control room quickly and skillfully. The mark of an amateur director is an unmarked script.

TELE-VISUALIZATION

The director must learn to think in terms of pictures, images or shots. The camera is a relatively flexible and mobile piece of equipment which, when handled by an imaginative and skillfully adept person, can make a viewer feel actually present at the scene of action. Carroll O'Meara, former producer-director for NBC, writes in his book, *Television Program Production:*

A person attending a three-ring circus has an over-all view of a vast panorama of assorted action and sights. But he does not watch the over-all performance at all times. Instead, he alternately concentrates on one ring at a time, focusing his attention on a nearby clown, looks at the trapeze performers on their lofty swings, then turns to see the face of the friend seated next to him. With nature's magnificent optical system and perception senses, he is in effect constantly cutting from one shot to another, instantly and automatically focusing at will. He sees what he wants to enjoy, what he accidentally discovers, or what attracts his attention.

The director must select shots according to their interest value, their significance, their dramatic impact. Look for unusual composition which will attract attention to the subject and not away from it. Select shots which visually tell the story and which enhance the action and the speech or sound. Add variety by introducing varied camera angles and levels in shots, but don't cut for the sake of cutting. Each shot should be selected for its importance in adding to the viewer's pleasure and interest in watching the program.

As a director, use the cameras as you would use your own eyes when viewing a scene. Be cognizant of the fact that the viewer actually sees everything through the eyes of the director; therefore, the director must think of the camera as the eyes of the viewer. The director must judge what the viewer wants to see, and when. Select the best camera angles as motivated by the action and/or dialogue of the performers. Vary those angles and movements, creating dramatic emphasis and emotional impact which will arrest and sustain viewer interest.

No two directors will "shoot" a program alike. The shooting of any show is determined by the individual director's ability, imagination, judgment and good taste, coupled with an understanding and knowledge of the medium. The director is dependent upon a knowledge of the equipment and an ability to use such equipment in producing the very best possible results. Creativity and imaginative skill, united with ingenuity, will enable you to present program content significantly and effectively.

The director must know when and how to use wide shots, close shots, close-up shots, and understand the importance of the necessity to modify and to use the many variations of such basic shots for purposes of visual continuity. There must be a reason for showing a certain view (shot) of a subject or object in a certain way at a given time or moment. There must be a premise, a motivation, a purpose behind such a shot. For example, suppose the director has a waist shot of a person. As viewers watch, this person looks off camera or out of the frame of the picture toward the left, and suddenly reacts to something seen. The viewers now are curious about what it is off camera which causes the strange reaction. The director immediately cuts to another camera which reveals the picture of what had caused the reaction. The cut to the other camera was motivated by the reaction, which in turn aroused the viewers' curiosity and desire to see what that person had seen. In other words, the director had a motivation or purpose for cutting to the other camera.

Points of View and Impact

Cameras provide the director with several physical points of view. You can view the scene from as many angles as you have cameras. The director must establish the setting or locale of the show to orient the viewer as to where the action is taking place. This should be followed by a closer view of certain parts of the setting as motivated by the action. At times it is necessary to go to close-up or tight close-up views, depending upon how minute the detail, how intimate and dramatic the scene, or how important the specific information may be.

When setting up or plotting shots, the director should keep in mind the impact of effectiveness of each individual picture or shot. Each shot must be meaningful. Each shot must have a relationship to the visual continuity, and relate to or affect the shot which precedes it and the one which follows it. Dollying or zooming to change angles of view may take place while the camera is on-the-air or when repositioning for a new shot. Camera movement is based on the psychological effect it will have on the viewer. Regardless of the type of program being telecast, there should be dramatic value in any and all camera movement—movement based on motivation or purpose relative to the continuity of the program. Movement should never be done or used just for its own sake—unless, as a last resort, to give life to an otherwise dead show. However, proper directorial preparation, analysis and diagnosis can avoid what could be a dead show.

Pictures—Images—Shots

Before the director can know and use even the basic shots in TV, it is necessary to understand what is meant by the term "shot." A shot is a picture which appears on the TV screen and which may last for a few seconds or for an indefinite period. It is the picture or image created by a camera and it is usually held as long as the director feels it is effective or motivated. The shot is the director's building block, the bricks and stones which, when put together, create visual continuity. A series of shots builds sequences. When the shots are integrated intelligently the end result should be effective "image story telling."

The television program is usually made up of a series of different shots which result from combining a long shot, a medium shot and a close-up shot. There must be a progression of shots—related pictures—if the program is to have visual continuity. The basic technique is cutting or switching, changing picture size through changing lens size. This type of cutting or switching should give the viewer a feeling of smooth movement from one picture to another and should impart a close relationship among the various shots being used. Of course, there are times when the director wishes to alert or shock the viewer. This may be done by cutting from a long or wide shot to a close or close-up shot, which achieves the desired dramatic effect. Or by cutting from a medium shot to a close-up. However, never cut from a long shot to a close-up unless there is a very special reason. You may be on a side shot, then dolly or zoom in to a close or medium view and then cut to a close-up. This gives the same relative effect as a progression of lenses.

The most frequently used shots in television are the close and close-up shots, reflecting not only a consideration of the size of the TV screen, but the fact that television is an intimate medium requiring the intimacy of the close and close-up shot. This is not to indicate that the long shot is not valuable; on the contrary, the long shot is the only means by which the setting, locale or environment of the drama or show can be established for the viewer. The wise director, the thinking director, will never repeat the same shot set-up from the same angle—except on occasions when there may be a very special reason to do this for dramatic emphasis. The thinking director will hold a shot only as long as the viewers need it to quickly and clearly grasp its visual significance. The director must remember that varying the angles and size of the three basic shots is actually the only way to add visual interest; the various changes of angles change the viewpoint and accentuate important detail.

Identification of Shots

Let us visualize the human body as the subject relative to the identification of shots (see Fig. 1):

ILLUSTRATION OF APPROXIMATE POSITION
OF BASIC CAMERA SHOTS.

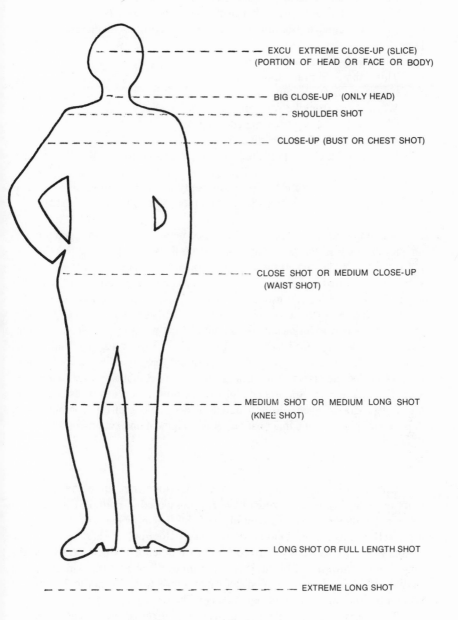

EXCU EXTREME CLOSE-UP (SLICE)
(PORTION OF HEAD OR FACE OR BODY)

BIG CLOSE-UP (ONLY HEAD)

SHOULDER SHOT

CLOSE-UP (BUST OR CHEST SHOT)

CLOSE SHOT OR MEDIUM CLOSE-UP
(WAIST SHOT)

MEDIUM SHOT OR MEDIUM LONG SHOT
(KNEE SHOT)

LONG SHOT OR FULL LENGTH SHOT

EXTREME LONG SHOT

Fig. 1

Call your shots by body identification, such as bust shot, waist shot, etc.

Long shot—a wide, full length shot of the person.

Medium shot—a close shot, usually from the waist up.

Close-up shot—usually a shot of the head and shoulders.

Many directors use terminology relative to portions of the body, as follows:

Knee shot—from the knees up.

Thigh shot—from the thighs up.

Hip shot—from the hips up.

Waist shot—from the waist up.

Chest or bust shot—from the chest up.

Shoulder shot—from the shoulders up.

Head shot—a close-up of the head, often referred to as a Big CU or Tight CU.

Face shot—extreme close-up, shows only a certain portion of the face as indicated by director. Some directors call this the "slice" shot.

It is important to indicate the difference between a close shot and a close-up shot. The close shot is usually a shot from the waist up, while the close-up is from the shoulders up. If the director is on a waist shot of a person, a closer shot can be created by moving the camera or zooming unobtrusively until it is reached. The director can use a full range of shots from the long shot to the close-up, and the extremes of both. The close-up shot and the long shot offer the director a wonderful means for dramatic effect when the two shots are combined into what is termed the close-up-long shot. This is a shot set up on one camera combining a close-up of a subject in the foreground and a long shot of another subject or object in the background. This combination shot has many variations, particularly for dramatic programs; however, it can be used on other types of programs when wisely handled. The variations of this combined shot depend entirely upon the imagination, good judgment and common sense of the director.

Zoom

One of the most important technical developments, from the director's point of view, has been the zoom lens. It is composed of multiple, movable elements. By moving a simple control the focal length of the lens may be progressively changed from long (wide) to short (close-up) or short to long. The majority of color cameras use 10 to 1 ratio zoom lenses, which means that the longest or narrowest end of the lens is ten times the size of the widest end, in millimeters. For example, a zoom lens may range from 35 mm to 350 mm or 40 mm to 400 mm. Recent developments include a 15 to 1 zoom.

The zoom is easily operated. It gives the effect of movement toward or away from a physically distant object or subject with considerable speed and smoothness. It permits a rapid, dramatic movement, one which literally sweeps the viewer's eyes from a wide view to a tight view, or vice-versa. It has become a substitute for the dolly shot, particularly in commercials and in similar situations when the director wishes to emphasize detail or arrest attention quickly. Be aware, however, of an aesthetic artificiality of the zoom which may prove to be a limitation. Because of the zoom's adeptness, unless you fully understand its use you may carried away by it and over-use it. The beginning director is tempted to zoom instead of dollying. The former moves the object closer or farther away; the latter moves the viewer in or out, creating a more realistic psychological effect. Practice using the zoom until you can recognize the difference between the perspective and movement of objects on the zoom and on a dolly shot. Some directors have let the zoom become a "gimmick" and have earned the title of "zoom-happy."

The zoom is a combination of many fixed focal length lenses. On the back of the camera, usually near the viewfinder, a gauge indicates which focal length lens is being used on any given zoom shot. To set up the zoom lens so that it will always be in focus as it is zoomed in and out, set the camera at a desired distance from a subject, zoom in to get the tightest shot possible, focus it sharply, then zoom out to the widest shot and check it. If the lens is functioning properly the wide shot will also be in focus. Each time the camera breaks set the camera operator must "run the focus." Zooming-in to a tight shot is referred to as the "front-focus" and zooming-out is the "back-focus."

Motivation and Editing

The director may do his or her own switching or may use a technical director. Regardless of method, as director you are your own editor—decide what shots to set up and which to select to maintain good visual continuity. When you plot the shots in the camera rehearsal, you will discover as you progress that you become highly selective relative to the shots you will call during the on-the-air telecast. You may also plan shots before rehearsals begin, in the very early stages of rehearsal or, as in the "winged" show, on the air. Whatever the method of planning, the selection and use of planned shots is termed "editing."

The director has the opportunity to select from a variety of images or shots and to determine which shot will be the most effective when sent out over the air. In this act of selection the director becomes, as well, the "editor." Selectivity determines the strength of the visual continuity which must sustain the interest of the viewer. The director guides the attention of the viewer by varying angles and sizes of a scene or subject action during the show. Ingenuity in editing will determine the effectiveness and quality of the visual aspect of the show. There must be a succession of closely related shots which create a progression of closely related pictures telling a moving visual story. The manner in which the director edits the shots will determine the relative progression of pictures.

In most producer-director situations, the director is also the editor. Regardless of how many takes in a program, all of which may be later physically edited by a VTR operator who understands all the technical intricacies of editing, the director still has the final responsibility. In many local station situations, in which the nature of the program or the budget permits no time for rehearsals, the director edits while the show is being done, on-the-air. Where rehearsals are possible, the director will block out movement of the talent and potential camera shots and movements. In actual camera rehearsals, the final shot continuity is determined, that which eventually will be put on tape. During this entire process, the director has been editing.

There must be a premise, a reason or purpose for setting up a shot in a certain way. There must be a motivation for every shot set up and sent out over the air. The director's premise indicates the what, how and why of the shot. Let us assume it is a shot of a person, a certain portion of that person. The shot is set up at a certain direction from the camera, forming a particular angle from which the viewer will see the person. The shot of the subject is well framed, sharply focused, and clearly visible to the viewer. The shot is well composed, with good balance to itensify interest and pleasure. The shot is determined by motivation. What is motivation? It is the reason why the particular shot was set up by the director. For example, let us assume it to be a close-up shot, a shot of a name-plate on an apartment door. Prior to this close-up shot, the director has a shot of a young man moving down the hallway of the apartment house searching for this particular name-plate. He stops and looks at the plate. As viewers, we wish to see the name-plate too, so the motivation for the cut to the close-up is quite obvious.

Movement

Regardless of the type of program, the director must achieve some kind of dramatic effect. There are many techniques which may be used: camera angles, composition, lighting, setting, sound, music, and movement involving talent and/or camera or both. The director has three basic movements with which to control visually the continuity of the program: 1) the subject moves on-camera, the camera and dolly remaining stationary except when necessary to pan or tilt; 2) the camera moves in or out, pedestals up or down, or perhaps moves in an arc around the subject, who remains relatively stationary; 3) both the subject and camera participate in the movement. For example, the subject walks toward a window and the camera dollies in or tightens up the subject during the movement. The director draws upon imagination and technical skill when using any or all of the basic movements.

It is quite possible for a TV program to become static because of a lack of movement or too little movement. Since TV is such an intimate medium, the performers are working in what we think of as the natural environment or setting. The space is usually comparable in dimensions to those of the actual living room or office. The performers' movements, then, are extremely natural and permit the director a lot of freedom in setting up shots. For example, two performers are talking in the family room of the house, one of them gets up from a chair and goes over to the fireplace to get something. The other performer watches every action and makes some move or does some bit of business, all of which helps to keep the scene moving and interesting. At the same time, such movement and business give the camera new angles and a new point of view, enabling the director to achieve visual continuity. However, a director must sense when a movement is good or bad and must know why it is good or bad. Remember that TV is an action medium, as well as photographic, and you will always be able to visualize movement in a relative manner.

A good television show has movement because that movement is paced by the tempo of the story or other program content. The movement is paced by dialogue or by just plain conversation. The director must use movement with discretion and taste. Don't become so interested in movement that you will cause your viewers to lose contact with the story or basic content of the show. Beware of becoming involved in the "technique" of movement. Frequently the director wishes to make transitions by other means than the cut, the dissolve or the fade. You will find, by experimenting, that camera movement often offers wonderfully effective ways of making transitions. For example, suppose you are doing an interview and have a close or close-up shot of the interviewee. It is time for a commercial or a promo, so you cut to a waist shot of the interviewer and as the interviewer orally cues the announcer, who is doing a live studio presentation, have the camera move in slowly and tilt up. The camera loses the interviewer as it tilts up to the light background of the setting. A cut is then made to the camera positioned in the area where the announcer is located; this camera is already tilted up. As it tilts down the announcer comes into view in the same manner as the interviewer was taken out of view. Experimenting with camera movement is fun, but do not overwork it.

Camera Movement

There are 12 basic movements of the camera that all directors should become expert with:

1) Dolly-in: Camera moves toward a stationary subject or object. Usually limited to narrowing attention of viewer in order to concentrate on a particular item without changing that subject's position on the set.

2) Dolly-out: Opposite of dolly-in. Sometimes this movement is used to open a sequence when a certain subject or object has a basic significance to the scene, action or sequence to follow, with the camera opening on a tight shot and pulling out for a wider view.

3) Walk-in: Subject moves into a closer shot. For example, subject is in a waist shot and moves in toward camera until subject forms a shoulder shot. The camera remains stationary.

4) Walk-away: Opposite of walk-in. For example, begin with shoulder shot of subject, who then moves away from camera for a wider shot.

5) Follow-shot: Both subject and camera move. Generally, the subject moves away and the camera follows, trailing behind. For example, subject gets

up from a chair, moves to get coat from a closet, while camera remains wide; as subject puts on coat and moves to the door, camera follows, moves along behind subject, keeping a steady distance; as subject goes out the door and closes it, camera faces the closed door.

6) Following one subject to reveal and concentrate on another subject: Camera follows one subject until a new subject appears from background or foreground, then picks up and centers on the new subject and lets the original subject go. Effective in transferring interest smoothly from one subject to another.

7) Following one subject to include more subjects: Camera follows one subject's movement into a group of subjects and includes both individual and group in one shot.

8) Transition from a group to an individual: Camera on group, individual of importance walks from group toward camera into sharp-focus close-up. Similarly, camera may be on follow-shot of a moving group and as group moves toward camera, camera concentrates on individual and follows that subject within the group with a relatively close shot.

9) Following a subject leaving a group: Camera on group, one subject walks away from group and camera follows this subject until subject appears alone.

10) Correcting for composition: Camera must either pan, tilt, truck or dolly to maintain composition on one or more moving subjects. For example, subject is seated in a chair, seen in a waist shot, gets up, camera gets up with subject to maintain balance and framing; or, camera can loosen up into wider shot as subject rises.

11) Subjects reversing: Camera shoots past subject A and features subject B, B walks toward camera, passes subject A, turns to face A, B's back toward camera; subject A turns toward camera to follow movement of B and is now featured.

12) Countering: One subject moves and another subject "counters" —moves into a pre-determined position which will maintain video composition.

In order to execute almost any of these basic moves, there must be perfect timing among performers and crew. The movement becomes more difficult when it requires a dolly or truck. Camera operators, particularly those who move their own pedestals, must time the moves with those of the performers. Performers must time their moves with each other. Timing is critical.

COMPOSITION

The viewer's acceptance of any picture is dependent upon the composition of that picture.

Composition is the result of the combined efforts of the director, camera operator, set designer and lighting director. Let us assume the scene is a modern living room which is lighted to create the illusion of late evening. The director calls for a full length shot of the subject standing by the fireplace in the room. The camera operator sets up the shot relative to a personal visualization of composition. However, the director may wish to modify the shot a little or may wish to change the angle of the shot, and makes suggestions to the camera operator who adjusts the shot according to the director's instructions. The result is a picture composed through the combined efforts of the director and camera operator. The director may have some suggestions for certain changes in arrangement of furniture and props, and possibly in lighting. All such combined efforts result in good composition.

The general layout, positioning of talent, scenery, props, mike booms and lights have all been carefully planned and set up relative to composition. The director and camera operator must think of the position and movement of the subject in relation to the camera, lights and scenery. The composition of any TV picture is never constant, but is always changing. Talent moves, scenes change, lights change, cameras move, all effecting a change in composition. It is easy to see how a static picture can be made to come alive, be given movement by simply changing the angles from which the camera shoots or views the subject.

If you study any picture carefully you will note there is an arrangement of shapes made up of line, mass and form. Instinctively, the human being has a marked emotional reaction to shape—for example, one's reaction when first viewing the Grand Canyon or the Washington Monument. Pictures must be composed to motivate a definite emotional response from the viewer. Any well composed picture has, or should have, a center of interest—a focal point— which is determined by the arrangement of the subjects in the picture. The director should concentrate on that center or focal point of interest when setting up shots. Since every television picture or shot should be motivated, then the picture should be composed to accomplish a specific purpose. Composition must contribute to the telling of the story.

A director who thinks about composition must think of depth. Without depth there is no composition; the picture becomes flat. Television is a two-dimensional medium and the director must give it depth by creating the illusion of a three-dimensional medium. If depth is to be achieved, there must be a balance between the foreground and the background. To create a feeling of great depth, of three-dimensions, there must be a foreground, a middle-ground and a background. It is very important to pay particular attention to the distance between each of the three things used to create foreground, middle-ground and background.

For example, the background could be rear-screen projection of a scene of the ocean with the surf rolling in, while the middle ground could be sand on the floor of the studio with a blanket spread out with one or two persons sprawled on it, and the foreground could be a prop rock with some pieces of driftwood to add the final bit in creating the three-dimensional aspect.

Composition should never distract. It must arrest attention and be pleasing to the eye. Try to avoid using the straight line arrangement, for example, in setting up products for commercials. Experiment with the triangular, the semicircular, the circular, and even the square arrangement of objects being displayed. The broken-up arrangement of objects or subjects is always most appealing to the eye.

The director who is creative and artistic, who is imaginative and observant, generally is aware of good composition. Although that director may not know all the artistic rules and theories of good composition, the manner in which visual aspects are related provide enough valid clues to create good composition. The arrangement of shapes in any picture—the line, mass and form—directs our attention to a specific object or subject which influences our emotions. In the final analysis, composition is the placement of subjects or objects within the picture frame in a way which will affect us emotionally. We know that physiological stimulation of the eye will affect the heart, lungs and glands. The director's job is to stimulate the eye of the viewer in order to achieve effective and appropriate empathic response.

TRANSITIONAL DEVICES

The Cut

The quickest, simplest and most frequently used method of transition from one camera to another is the straight or direct cut. It is instantaneous and definite. It is the fastest means by which two scenes can be joined or related and which can show the viewers what they want to see when they want to see it. When a change is made from one camera to another is is usually done for the purpose of giving the viewer another look at the action from a different angle or view. This is what we think of as an immediate substitution of one picture for another.

The impact of the cut should not be underestimated. The direct cut can be used effectively in several ways: 1) As an excellent device for creating sudden shock by cutting from a long shot to a close-up, or from a medium shot to a tight close-up. The sudden cut creates a dynamic impact upon the viewer. However, this must be used wisely and sparingly for a very definitely motivated purpose; otherwise, the visual continuity will be interrupted. 2) By fast cutting the director can create the illusion of increasing the tempo of an otherwise slow pace. 3) Cuts can be done to the rhythm of a dance or musical number. Short, quick cuts, when used wisely, can be exciting. 4) Cutting on action must be done so the visual shock of the cut will be unobtrusive. Generally, the shot is either held for the duration of the action or it may be completed in following cuts. Unless there is a very definite motivation for cutting away from the action, it is much wiser to remain on the first shot. 5) A direct cut from black to a picture of full intensity is frequently used to open a scene. It is dynamic and can be a very strong attention getting device. A direct cut from a picture to black has a very definite feeling of finality.

When to cut:

When action calls for a cut—when there is obvious motivation.
For variety. Keep continuity interesting. Cut to different angles.
For dramatic emphasis.
At the end of a sentence or phrase, not in the middle.
At the end of a musical phrase. Pace cuts according to pace of music.
On action or movement, within the action or movement.
For reaction, cut should be made a split second ahead of reaction of person.

When not to cut:

Don't overcut. A series of fast cuts are meaningless. However, if paced properly, cuts cometimes can be used to create the illusion of stepping up a slow pace.
Don't cut blindly. Always be aware of the need to cut.
Don't cut to identical shots. If you get "trapped" go to black and work out fast.
Don't cut to extreme angles (e.g. from a profile to a front view or long shot).
Don't cut from a pan to a stationary shot. This is disturbing to the eye.
Don't cut on a pan shot unless the cut is to another pan shot moving in the same direction as the one from which the cut was made.
Don't cut to extremely different angles. Subject must always be recognized immediately in any shot.
Don't be afraid to stay on one camera, even for a long period of time, unless there is a very definite reason for cutting to another camera.

A director who is aware of the fact that the cut is an abrupt transition from one picture to another will recognize that the sudden change created by the cut produces a subconscious shock in the mind of the viewer. If the director selects the two pictures involved in the cut with great care, then there will be an immediate association of ideas which takes place in the mind of the viewer and the resultant emotional effect is that which the director wishes to achieve when shooting the program. Used wisely, the cut is exciting and stimulating.

There are times when a director wants to build suspense by holding a shot on the air when viewers would like to see what is going on off-camera. This is particularly useful in drama. For example, the director will use this "delayed cut" method to achieve greater suspense by holding a shot just a second longer than usual before cutting to another camera. By the time the cut to the other camera is made, viewer empathy is usually much greater. Generally, viewers anticipate the director's cutting to new shots. When the director intentionally withholds cutting to another shot, it increases interest and suspense.

The director should tell the floor manager to cue talent first before the switch is made to another camera, in order to insure a smooth transition by talent from one camera to another. To ready talent to "look" from one camera to another, the floor manager usually gives a "standby" cue first. As soon as the talent has reached the end of a sentence or phrase, the floor manager cues talent to the other camera. The cut from one camera to the other must instantly follow the cue to talent.

A director selects and changes shots when the new shot gives welcome relief, stimulates and increases interest. Action of any kind generally motivates a change of picture and new angles of view. To prevent a picture of the same subject or object from becoming monotonous, it is necessary to vary the angle and composition of shots of the subject. However, use these changes sparingly, and primarily to prevent the program from becoming static. Remember, too much cutting results in confusion, annoyance and a jumpy effect on the screen.

The Fade

Fade is a term which means a major change is being made in the visual continuity of the show. If a "fade-in" is used, it means the picture is being brought in from a black screen to the picture's fullest intensity. The fade-in means "curtain going up"—beginning of action—opening of a scene or act. The fade-in should be done at a normal speed to insure the feeling of introducing the action without shock. However, sometimes a fast fade-in does a relatively good job of shocking if that is the effect desired by the director.

The "fade-out" is the reverse of the fade-in—it fades out the picture from full intensity to black. This indicates "curtain coming down"—end of scene or act or show. Here again the important factor is the control of the speed of the fade-out. A restful reaction can be created by the slow fade-out, while the fast fade-out has a tendency to destroy some of the feeling of whatever suspense may have been built up during the scene. Sometimes the fast fade-out can help strengthen suspense.

The Dissolve or Mix

The dissolve is blended transition, somewhat like the cross-fade used in radio. Two cameras are in action at the same time, each with a picture framed and focused for on-the-air. One camera is on the air while the other is ready and standing by. The two cameras are, in a sense, cross-faded. The camera on the air is faded-out as the other camera is faded-in simultaneously. The two pictures must pass on the way out and in. For a brief, split second the two cameras' pictures are on the air at the same time, thus assuming the role of a momentary superimposition.

The dissolve can be used to indicate a short lapse of time, a minor change of locale. It can mean a very smooth transition from one angle to another if proper attention is then given to such things as changes in angles, changes in movement, and changes in size of shot. Otherwise, at the moment of the dissolve when the two pictures are mixed there will be an unrelated conglomerate of images appearing on the screen. The dissolve can create a very nice, easy, smooth transition, one which is restful to the eye. The viewer does what we might think of as a mental dissolve as he or she witnesses the visual dissolve done by the director. The beginning director, by practicing with the dissolve, will note it has rhythm, a rhythm which is easy and smooth and has great harmony. The dissolve should blend one train of thought into another. The speed of the dissolve is pertinent to how well it fulfills its purpose. It must be done wisely and carefully; otherwise, it distracts.

The Matched Dissolve

This transitional device involves two cameras with shots of closely related subjects or objects. It is excellent for transitions in drama. Of course, it can be used effectively in other types of programs, too. For example, the director may dissolve from a shot of a professional baseball player in the batter's box to a shot of a small boy in baseball uniform standing in the batter's box on the local sand lot; or from a close-up of a model jet airliner to a shot of a real jet in flight. The speed of the dissolve determines its effectiveness. Content motivation will indicate whether the dissolve should be fast, slow, gentle or even rhythmic (try it to music sometime!).

Defocus to Refocus

This technique can be used in a number of ways (e.g. dream sequences, suggesting a person losing consciousness, creating a misty or hazy effect). It is an excellent device with which to change or move from a present day scene to one in the past—the flashback. This is done by defocusing the camera on the pivotal character at the end of a scene. During this action another camera, defocused, has been framed upon the character or on the area in which the flashback action in the next scene is to take place. The first scene ends as the camera is taken completely out of focus, the director dissolves to the second camera, also out of focus. Since both cameras are out of focus during the dissolve the viewer is never aware of the dissolve technique. As soon as the dissolve is executed, the second camera is refocused and the viewer is transported to the scene of the flashback. The return to the present or first scene is done with the same technique. There are a number of ways this technique can be used in the production of commercials.

The Super

This term is derived from "superimposition." The effect is comparable to the double exposure in photography. In television the picture from one camera is superimposed over the picture from another camera, blending the two pictures into one meaningful visual. The use of the "super" is left up to the discretion of the director. Great care must be taken in selecting the correct background for the supered material. In using a super all subject material must be easily identifiable and meaningful to the viewer.

When using a super the director should inform the camera operator by saying "going into super," "super is on," "coming out of super full into camera 1" (or whichever is free).

Whatever method of transition is used, the director must remember its use is governed by motivation and not to use it as a "gimmick."

DIRECTING APPROACHES

Pattern Shooting

When shooting newscasts, interviews, panel shows and other programs which are usually unrehearsed, many directors set up a "pattern." Most of these types of programs are on the daily schedule and generally follow the routine sheet script format (see Chapter 4). Camera shots seldom deviate from the three basic shots—the long, medium and close-up. The director sets up an "editorial pattern" for a given program and then "wings" it with a variation of the basic pattern.

Winging, Ad-Libbing, Free-Shooting

These terms are synonomous and refer to a method of directing in which the director sets up and edits the shots while the program is on the air. This method is used when there is no time available for rehearsing. When a show such as an interview is to be aired, the director usually does a short run-through rehearsal of the beginning and ending of the program to assure a smooth opening and closing as well as a means of setting up back-timing for controlling the close.

Instructions and Conduct

There are three basic terms used to get cameras ready for a "take" during a program: "ready," "standby" and "hold." Ready is the most commonly used, but take your choice. Just be sure that you make clear to your staff your particular method of setting up and calling shots. For example, let us assume you want to execute a dissolve between camera 1 and camera 2. You would instruct both cameras to "ready for dissolve" or "standby for dissolve" or "hold for dissolve," and follow with "dissolve to two." As soon as the dissolve is completed you indicate that the other camera (in this case number 1) is free to break set and reposition for the next shot. Set shots during the camera rehearsal so that each camera operator clearly understands the type of shot, lens to be used, composition, movement and position. See that each operator has an individual list of shots. This list usually is attached to the back of the camera, on the left or right side, where it is clearly visible. This "cue sheet" has shots numbered for each individual camera according to the shot number in the shooting script. The lens is indicated either as a zoom or by millimeters or inches. Here is an example of a "shot sheet" for two cameras for a taped or live program:

CAMERA CUE SHEET—CAM #1   CAMERA CUE SHEET—CAM #2
(SHOT SHEET)

NOTES	LENS	TYPE OF SHOT (DESCRIPTION)	SHOT #	NOTES	LENS	TYPE OF SHOT (DESCRIPTION	SHOT #
	10-1 ZOOM	Waist of Matt— high angle	6		10-1 ZOOM	TCU – HEAD – JANE FRONT SHOT	3
		Waist shot of Chester stand- ing by wagon	7			Long shot of Jack as he walks toward Jane. Let him walk up to Jane creating med. 2-shot.	4
		Zoom out to full length shot of Matt as he walks toward wagon and joins Chester	8			Waist shot of Jane, obviously irritated at Jack	5
						Shoulder shot of Jack he is upset	6
		2-shot of Matt and Chester as they talk	9			Waist shot of Jane as she backs away and runs from Jack	7

It is important to keep a running commentary of instructions for the camera operators, so there is no chance of a mistake. If there is one, it should not be because you did not give the right instructions. For example, always let the camera operator know when a subject is going to get up and walk to some object, and vice-versa. You might say: "Camera 1, watch performer, he is going to get up, get up with him (or tilt up or come up or bring him up), follow him." And the reverse: "watch him, follow him, sit down with him (or go down or tilt down)." When a performer is featured, such as in an interview or talk program or for a featured singer or similar act, it is a good idea to place the talent on six-inch risers. This enables the camera operator to keep the camera at "eye level," which provides good visual results. When talent on such programs are placed on floor level, the camera sometimes must tilt down to get the shot, giving the appearance of a slant. In such shots it is also hard to avoid including the floor in the picture—which frequently is not the most attractive decor in most stations. Avoid profile shots—simply because they usually are unflattering. The exception is in the drama where they may be used to achieve specific empathic responses. Always protect yourself during a show by keeping a "cover-shot," which is simply a wide shot covering everything of importance relative to the subject on camera. This will prevent getting caught with close or close-up shots on both cameras, if you are working in the local station situation of two or three cameras. Don't be afraid to move cameras on the air as long as the movement is meaningful. Movement is the essence of successful television. Remember that TV is a medium of action and that for every action there must be a reaction.

Terminology is constantly changing. Keep abreast. As noted above in the use of "ready" and "tilt" there are equivalent terms that are used. For almost every technique there are several terms. For example, "dolly out," "dolly back," "pull out," "pull back" all mean the same thing. From an artistic standpoint, add to that a virtually equivalent substitute technique, "zoom out."

The director is responsible for the interpretation of dialogue, copy and narration and must express good judgment and taste in the selection of shots which visually interpret the author's purpose. At the same time the director must simultaneously listen to all sounds such as dialogue, music and sound effects, watch all monitors, carry on conversations with the camera operators, floor manager, audio engineers, boom operators and technical director, and possibly roll film and/or video tape when needed. And if the director also performs the duties of the technical director, as is frequent in many small stations. . . . You have to be able to anticipate any difficulties which might arise while you are on the air and to be prepared to meet such situations without falling apart. Every program becomes a challenge to a combination of your many abilities.

Regardless of the pressures, you must always think about your staff. Be polite. Say "please" and "thank you." You might even want to replace the terms "good" and "bad" with something like "effective" and "ineffective." Always compliment a camera operator when a shot is well composed or a movement is well executed. Note the good work of people in the control room with you, as they perform their duties. Compliment other deserving members of the staff, cast and crew, particularly at the end of a program. This all helps for morale and cooperative action on the next show.

The Control Room

The control room is the nerve center of television production. In Chapter 2 of this book is an analysis of control room equipment. The director is the pivotal figure in this nerve center and is in touch with the studio floor, announce booth, film and/or slide projection room, master control, video engineers, audio engineer and video tape recording room. The director's video switcher is located in the control room. During rehearsals and on-the-air telecast the director sits in the control room facing a line of TV monitors, each with a picture from some video source (Fig. 2). In most control rooms there is, at least, one monitor for each camera for preview, one for each camera for video control, one for film, one for the program line, and also one for general previewing. The

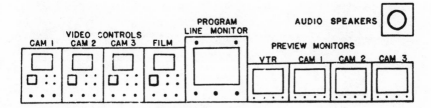

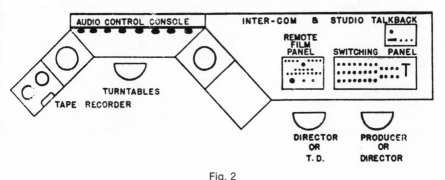

Fig. 2

A basic control-room setup for the beginning director.

director communicates via the inter-com with the camera operators to set up the shots to put on the air. On the program line monitor is seen the picture (shot) which is being telecast and which also appears on one of the camera monitors, depending upon which camera shot is being sent out on the air. On another camera monitor is the shot or picture being set up, checked and readied to be taken next by the director. When the director feels it is the moment to "take" this next shot, he or she or the technical director punches the button on the switcher which controls that camera and the shot or picture is switched to on-the-air position on the program line monitor. The director then sets up the next shot and gets ready to take it. The director must see the shots from several different angles. This offers an opportunity to better select the shot which will present the subject most effectively. This activity continues throughout the show as the director interprets the script and transforms it into series of related visual images.

Video Switcher

In the control room is a special panel of buttons and levers with which the director or TD (technical director) controls all picture aspects of the program. This video switching panel may be relatively simple or it may be extremely complicated, depending upon the system used by the individual station. Regardless of the system, every video switcher must provide three possibilities: 1) switching between studio cameras; 2) special effects such as fading, dissolving

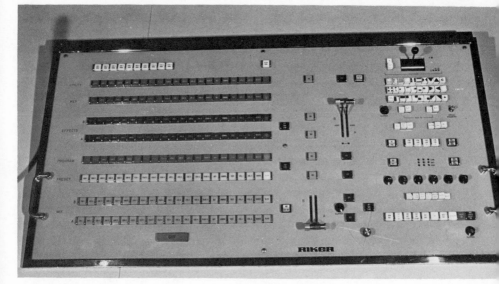

Fig. 3-A
The Video Switcher

and superimposing; 3) program monitoring and previewing. (See Chapter 2, pp. 79–86.)

The buttons used for switching are set up in parallel rows called "banks" or "buses." The simplest of switching systems usually has three banks or buses. One bank is for direct or instantaneous switching while the other two banks are used to create such effects as fading, dissolving and superimposing. The buttons are used for "punching up" shots during camera rehearsals or the on-the-air telecast.

A more sophisticated video switcher is illustrated in Fig. 3-A. In most modern studios you will use a switcher similar to the Riker.

General Use. For simple switching, the desired source may be "punched up" on the PROGRAM line bank. To preview the next shot prior to airing or taping it, the PRESET bank is used. To cut between the PROGRAM bank and PRESET bank, punch up the CUT bar and the PRESET bank becomes the PROGRAM bank and vice-versa. This is called the "flip-flop" switcher. To DISSOLVE, punch up MIX on the right of the PROGRAM line. This affects the MIX (A&B) banks. To FADE from one source to another, the FADER bar at the right may be changed from A to B and vice-versa. To use any of the SPECIAL EFFECTS, punch the green EFF button on the right. This affects the EFFECTS bank (A&B). SPECIAL EFFECTS also has its own FADER bar, located at the far right of the EFFECTS line bank. UTILITY and KEY involve special effects use of varying colors, operated on the lower right of the switcher. To CHROMA KEY, punch the CHROMA button and the EX-TERNAL KEY button and work out of an appropriate camera in the UTILITY

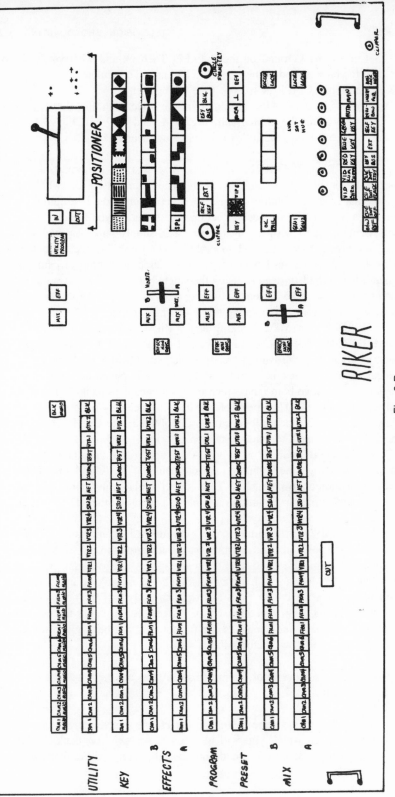

Fig. 3-B

Diagram of the Riker Video Switcher

bank. Set up the background on the B EFFECTS bank and what you want to KEY over the background in the A EFFECTS bank. To regulate the intensity of the KEY there is a CLIPPER to adjust the KEY level.

Specific Techniques. After running over the basic operation above, try out on a switcher (or on the photograph, Fig. 3-A, and diagram, Fig. 3-B, if a switcher is not available) the following switching techniques:

DIRECT or STRAIGHT switching: The first, or bottom bank, is used only for direct or straight switching. The buttons used for switching are the flat-type push buttons. Camera 1 is activated by the first button on the left, Camera 2 by the second button, and so on. If you are on the air with Camera 1 and wish to cut to Camera 2, simply punch up button 2 and you have cut from CAM 1 to CAM 2. The small flat-like bar below bank 1 is called the cut-bar and is used for direct switching of cameras when it is punched, instead of using the single button for a camera on the direct bank. Using the cut-bar, a director may cut back and forth at will; however, be careful of overusing this kind of switching.

DISSOLVE or MIX: Looking at the Riker switcher in Fig. 3, assume that CAM 1 is punched up on bank 1 and that both faders are in the back position opposite bank 1, ready to activate CAM 1 on bank 1. To execute a dissolve or mix from CAM 1 to CAM 2, punch up CAM 2 on bank 2. Then move both faders forward from bank 1 to bank 2. The dissolve is completed. The speed of the dissolve depends on how fast or slow you move the faders forward. To dissolve back to CAM 1, simply move the faders back to bank 1 position.

FADE TO BLACK: You're on CAM 2 and you wish to fade slowly to black. Punch up the B button opposite bank 1. Then move the faders back to position opposite bank 1. To go direct to black, instead of fading, you can cut. Punch up B button on bank 1. The cue to the TD is "black it."

SUPERIMPOSE: Assume CAM 1 is punched up on bank 1, with faders in back position. You wish to "super" over picture on CAM 1 the information in picture on CAM 2. Punch up CAM 2 on bank 2, then move the faders forward to halfway position between banks 1 and 2. Both cameras are then on the air, although each has only half the normal picture strength. To control the intensity of a super, you can split the faders. That is, move only one handle of the faders until you have given dominance to one of the two pictures in the super.

Special Effects. Several of the most-used effects are the wipe, the chroma key and colorizing.

WIPE: Punch the wipe button on the effects generator. Set up the two sources from which you will be wiping, source 1 on bank A and source 2 on bank B. Choose the design desired, such as a vertical wipe, usually used for wiping in titles or names, or a circle wipe, used to highlight special subjects. Push or pull the effects bar or mixer, located next to the effects generator, thus wiping from one bank to another. Above the effects designs is the positioner or, as sometimes called, the joy stick. This is used to position the effects design chosen to any desired location on the screen. The "in" button by the joy stick engages it; the "out" button disengages it. Under the effects design is a circle symmetry, which permits the creation of an ellipse shape out of the circle effect design.

CHROMA KEY: This is often referred to as "krokey." When chroma-keying, one of the cameras must be used for the krokey, which effectively isolates that camera, preventing it from being used to cover the program during the chroma-keying procedure. In chroma-keying, the differences between foreground action and the background are effected by the differences in hue rather than by those in darkness or lightness. Blue is always used as a background color and the most satisfactory seems to be ultra-marine blue. The blue background should be flat-lighted white light, usually by scoops. In such cases the performer or subject should have no blue. If the performer or subject is to be shot full-length, the floor must also be painted blue and lit with blue light. The switcher procedure is to first press the EXT button on the effects generator, then to punch the KEY WIPE button. Press the appropriate button (i.e. FILM 4) on the key bank of the switcher to activate the chroma-key. Set up the effects banks on the switcher for the desired sources. For example, bank B for the background, which might be a slide, and bank A for the foreground, which might be a camera live on the talent. CLIPPER, located at the bottom of the switcher, selects the color to be chroma-keyed. To KEY in words such as names or titles, first press the SELF KEY button on the effects generator, then punch the KEY button. Set up the effects banks for the desired sources, such as bank B for background, providing the names being keyed, from a slide or graphic, and bank A for foreground, providing the video source, either a camera, VTR, film or slide. Then adjust the CLIPPER to clean the key.

COLORIZING: Follow the same procedures in setting up keying. Then punch up the EXT button. If background, for example, is on bank B of effects bank, move it to key bank, just above. Punch appropriate CAM on bank B of the effects bank. This engages the colorizer. To adjust the color, press the manual (MAN) button at lower right of the switcher and turn the HUE knob to the color desired.

Ideally, an instructor will provide you with exercises on a switcher in which you will practice the basic techniques above and move into more complicated approaches and combinations of switching. The photograph and drawing in Fig. 3, however, should provide you with a basic familiarity with the switcher before you actually use one.

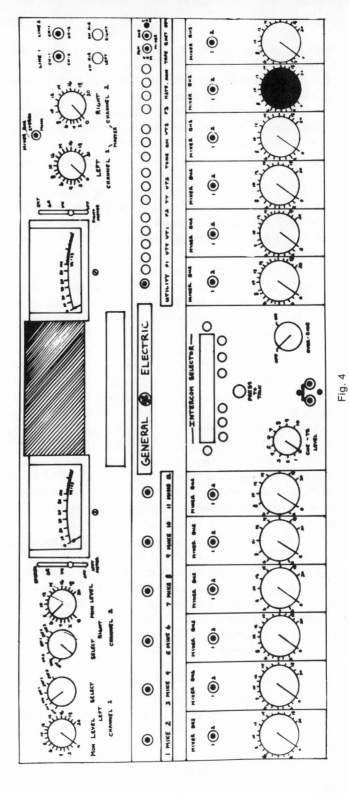

Fig. 4

General Electric Audio Console

Audio Console

Too many directors forget that television is also an audio medium. Be aware not only of the aesthetic uses of sound, but the basic elements of sound production, including the audio console. If you do not have radio experience, a review of control room equipment and procedures in RADIO BROADCAST-ING, the companion volume to this book, will provide a good introduction. Fig. 4 is a diagram of a General Electric console, of the type you will find in a television control room. All microphone selector switches, located in the middle left of the drawing, are activated by moving them in a vertical manner, the upper position for odd numbers, the lower for even. The channel selector switch for each pot moves from left to right. The tone for video tape operators, to enable them to set their audio levels, is activated by pushing the button marked tone, at the center right of the board. A channel with an equivalent line work together to send audio to the VTR.

Intercom

The director, via the intercom system in the control room, can simultaneously contact the camera operators, floor manager, light director, film chain operator, VTR operator, shading engineer and (if separated from the control room) audio engineer. An announcer who may be in an isolated announce booth can also be contacted through the intercom. (See Fig. 5).

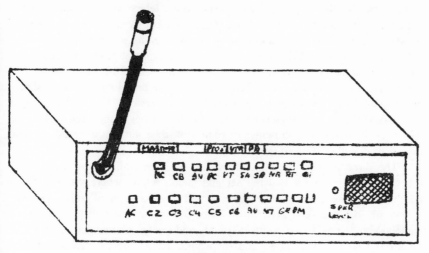

Fig. 5

To activate the Intercom system there is a switch which is located, usually, just under the table or console on which the Intercom is placed. It is always next to the switcher for the director's convenience. To operate, select switch, turn to red position for tempory communication, turn to green position for continuous communication. Speak into microphone, adjust return level by control near speaker.

PRE-PLANNING

The director must have some type of format which will provide direction. This format is the road map, guide, blueprint which facilitates movement from one point to another, namely, from the beginning to the end of the program. The format is a guide by which to develop smoothly the visual and aural continuity of the program and may take several different forms. It may be elaborate and very meticulously planned and set up, such as a complete script in "story board" form; it may be partially scripted; or it may be only a routine sheet. Regardless of which approach or method the director uses, it is necessary to pre-plan in one way or another. There must be something tangible from which to work as a director; otherwise, valuable time will be wasted and the end result, generally, will be a somewhat "sloppy" production. Examples of each of the above types of format are indicated later on in this chapter. Remember, however, that television is a "committee art." The director should discuss the aesthetic objectives with the members of the production team.

Any television program is an expensive and complex operation. Meticulous, thorough pre-planning is necessary before any rehearsals begin. The director must be aware of any visual and/or aural problems during the pre-planning stage and resolve them before rehearsals get under way. There are several reasons why pre-planning is of such great importance: 1) to meet rigid time schedules; 2) to reduce production costs; 3) to create a sense of direction and security for the director when going into the rehearsal stage; 4) to enable the director to gain the respect of the staff and talent by showing a knowledge of where he or she is going and how he or she is going to get there.

The director is called upon to do a variety of types of program, such as interviews, commercials, public service, children's, audience participation and drama. Regardless of the type, there must be some pre-planning. Some directors go into what others might consider elaborate planning, that of setting up a story board layout of their script: a script with sketches using stick figures, or with very carefully done drawings of each shot to be sent out over the air. The degree of planning is up to the individual.

The director must pre-plan the set-up for rehearsals. Know how much space you will need for housing set and talent. Know where you can place boom microphones, how much space you will need for cameras and movement. If you are to use easels, know how many and where you will place them so cameras can be positioned on them quickly and easily. Know what props are to be used, where, when, how, and by whom. Know the lighting set-up and whether or not any special lighting effects are to be used. To have everything arranged and in proper order, have a floor plan on which to sketch such arrangements. Have a light plot worked out so lights will be placed exactly as you want them. This pre-planning assures that things will be done correctly and in time for rehearsals. Such pre-planning is a time saving device, which you will find invaluable when you begin rehearsals, particularly in the studio. You will find that you need every second of time available.

Working With the Script

As indicated in Chapter 4 in this book, script formats differ, depending on the kind of show, whether the Hollywood or New York dramatic form is used, the requirements of the individual program, and the techniques of the author. Usually the director prefers to get a script with two distinct columns: audio and video. When the director gets the basic script duplicated for distribution to cast and crew he or she frequently will transfer certain information into the appropriate columns, if it is not already there. For example, camera, set and stage directions, movements and "business" may be put on the video side; and characters' names, dialogue, music and sound effects, and interpretations may be put on the audio side. This varies with the individual director. Most directors prefer to have the timing indicated on the script, sometimes a timing for the whole, sometimes a timing of sections in minutes. Some directors number the dialogue lines to enable them more easily to indicate to a performer where a line or cue should be picked up during stops in a rehearsal. For similarly easy identification, directors prefer that all pages are numbered clearly at the top left or top right, such as 2/2/2/2.

Marking the Script

It is said that the stamp of an amateur director is a script free of notes or marks. Of course, individual directors differ in the manner in which they mark their scripts or sequence sheets. However, they do mark them in order to have a means by which they can memorize the pattern of the show, a blueprint from which to maintain visual and/or aural continuity. A director should be thoroughly acquainted with the script or sequence sheet and should use it as an aid and not be imprisoned by it.

How elaborately marked a script may be is the result of the individual director's own approach to marking. Most directors use a shorthand or abbreviated method of marking. That is, instead of noting on the script, "dissolve to camera #2—long shot of patio," the director might mark it "DISS 2—WIDE PATIO." Mark the script and standardize symbols, but because elaborate marking often is confusing and time consuming, use markings wisely and do not overmark. The director should indicate information for all shots, movements of talent and cameras. Some directors go so far as to include the lens to be used on each shot. Cues for talent, music and/or cues for sound must be noted. Many directors like to set up both front- and back-timing indications. This makes it much easier to follow the control room clock. Everyone involved in the on-the-air telecast should have a copy of the final script, marked exactly as the director will use it. One example of a director-marked script is shown on pages 243–244.

In marking the script, some directors "color code" it. For example, each camera for each shot is given a number in some bright color. Camera 1 may be RED, camera 2 may be BLUE, camera 3 YELLOW, etc. This makes it possible for the director to quickly identify each camera and each shot. A competent and meticulous director becomes thoroughly familiar with every infinitesimal detail of the script, and color coding makes it even easier to follow the progression of the shots.

Symbols

As previously stated, the director must tele-visualize the script as he or she reads it. Think in terms of shots you would like to have relative to the action, dialogue and movements, and write these in the video column of the script. Circle or underscore audio cues such as those for music and sound. Mark where the talent is to be cued. Generally, the audio aspect is marked in red or blue pencil or in ink. All marks must be clearly visible. Some writers indicate camera shots or directions in their scripts, but usually this is only when it is something very specific or critical which they wish to make certain the director will get. If such shots or directions appear, the director usually circles or underscores them.

It is not possible to list all symbols and cues being used today in all TV stations, but the following are examples of some that are most commonly used in the industry.

T-1	Take 1	Switch to camera 1.
DISS-1	Dissolve 1	Dissolve to camera 1.
DI	Dolly in	Move in close to subject.
DB	Dolly back	Dolly out to a wider shot.
Tight CU	Tight close-up	Very tight shot of subject or object. Usually a head shot.
Loosen up	Wider shot	Usually given when camera is off air. A change of lens is in order.
CU-LS	Combination close-up and long shot	Shot of two persons, one seen in close, other seen in distant background.
OS	Over shoulder shot	Shot taken from over the shoulder of a subject and including another subject in background, or over shoulder as subject is looking in close at some object such as newspaper.
SUP	Superimposition	A super is to be done at this point in the program.

F-I	Fade in	Means to fade from black to a live scene. Fade in the film, the VTR, etc.
F-O	Fade out	The opposite of fade-in.
Pan-L Pan-R	Pan left or right	Pan the camera to left or right.
Tr R Tr L	Truck right or left	Camera and dolly moved in a horizontal direction to the right or left.
Tilt up Tilt down	Tilting action	Camera is moved vertically on axis up or down.
FL	Flip card	Cue floor manager to flip card.
SL	Slide	A slide is to be used at a given time in the program.
CUE or Q	Signal to talent	The word cue or letter Q is usually written in video column right next to line of copy or dialogue to indicate when to cue performer.
THEME	Music	The word theme is usually written above the word music, which is circled in ink.

The Dramatic Script

Some directors set up a dramatic script in the following manner, while others use the film or Hollywood format. This is one example of a dramatic script with the director's prepared shots, movements, cues and symbols. Examples of symbols are in parenthesis. Note that a filmed opening is used on this live production.

THE TIN STAR

By Lou Brown

VIDEO   AUDIO

FADE IN: FILM
EXT: DAY LONG SHOT
THREE COWBOYS ON HORSES RIDING INTO
TOWN. MARTY IS DRESSED IN BLACK
HAT. NICK IS TALL, THIN, DIRTY, MEAN
LOOKING. RIO, MEXICAN
AND TOUGH, HIS TEETH SET
IN A PERPETUAL SMILE.
THEY RIDE DOWN THE CENTER OF THE
STREET, THREE ABREAST, TOWARD THE

VIDEO	AUDIO

CAMERA . . . PASS IT AS IT PANS AND
FOLLOWS THEM TO THE FRONT OF THE
SALOON. THEY DISMOUNT, TIE UP
HORSES AND LOOK AROUND.
CLOSE THREE SHOT . . . .
WAIST SHOT — MARTY

MARTY

Just like I told ya . . . this town's gonna be
easy . . . take a look around . . . no one
out . . . the bank over there just waiting to
be knocked of . . . . Come on . . . let's get
a drink . . . I'm dry . . .

THREE SHOT   *3 -SHoT*

THEY MOVE AROUND HORSES UP STEPS
AND THROUGH SALOON DOORS. CAMERA
PANS ACROSS STREET TO DOORWAY OF
STORE NEXT TO BANK. DEPUTY NED
STEPS OUT OF THE SHADOW OF THE
STORE DOORWAY. HE STEPS OUT INTO
STREET TOWARD SALOON . . . STOPS
CLOSE SHOT.   *C U*

NED

Q

(MUMBLING TO HIMSELF) Those three
the ones on the wanted posters Sheriff
Marsden was showing me yesterday.

NED TURNS AND HURRIES TOWARD
SHERIFF'S OFFICE . . . .
LIVE STUDIO:
CUT TO INTERIOR OF OFFICE AND SHOT
OF SHERIFF JOEL MARSDEN AT HIS DESK
LOOKING OVER WANTED POSTERS.

Q THEME

(MUSIC:) THEME IN FULL . . .
ESTABLISH . . . HOLD

SUPER 1—TITLES   *SUP 1 -TiTLEs*
AS TITLES END DISSOLVE 2 WIDE OF
JOEL   *DIS - 2 WIDE JoEL*
TIGHTEN OF SLOWLY TO DESK SHOT. *TiGHTEN*
TAKE 1 OF POSTER . . . SET UP IN *T-1 PosTeR*
HANDS OF ONE OF CREW OFF SET.
2-WIDE INCLUDING JOEL AT DESK
AND DOOR OF OFFICE AT HIS RIGHT.
TAKE 2 AS NED BURSTS INTO OFFICE
AND UP TO DESK   *T-2*

Q

MUSIC: SNEAK OUT AS NED ENTERS.

Q

JOEL

Where are they?

TIGHTEN 2—   *2 -SHoT*

JOEL RISES . . . MOVES TO SIDE OF DESK
ON NED'S LINES. TAKE 1—OVER SHOUL-
DER   *T-1 - OS*
SHOT NED AND JOEL

NED

Over at the saloon . . . three of 'em, rode
about ten minutes ago.

JOEL

Well, it had to come to this some day. Gu
I've been a sheriff too many years.

TAKE 2—CU NED   *T-2 – CU*   <u>NED</u>

(VERY CONFIDENT) What do ya mean?
There's only three of 'em . . . you and me,
we can . . . .

TAKE 1—OVER SHOULDER   *T-1 – OS*   <u>JOEL</u>

(STERNLY) We can do what? Walk across
the street, put the cuffs on them . . . and
that's it. Sure . . . things are not always
that simple, Ned.

In the dramatic script some directors like to have every shot, action and movement indicated by some identification symbol or illustration which can be easily and quickly interpreted. However, there is seldom enough space on the original script for such elaborate markings. Some directors use a looseleaf binder or notebook with a page of the script on the left and a blank sheet of paper on the opposite side at the right on which to put a "story board" layout of the shots, actions and movements. Some directors draw small 3:4 aspect ratio boxes in which to make sketches (often using stick figures) which represent the types of shots or movements blocked out. This is one method. Other directors have their own techniques of marking scripts, standardized to their individual directing assignments. Some directors use a double number on scripts such as $①_3$ (camera #1, shot #3) for an easy reference to the order of shots.

The Semi-script

Many non-dramatic scripts are fully written out, with complete dialogue and author's directions. The director's approach to marking follows that for the dramatic script above. In the semi-scripted or detailed routine-sheet kind of program, the director's markings may not be quite so detailed, although an attempt should be made in pre-planning to make them as complete as possible, as exemplified in the following.

WO SHOT   *2-SHOT*   Dr. Jenkins, why was Andrew Jackson considered such a great soldier and statesman?

U JENKINS   <u>JENKINS</u>

EXPLAINS THAT JACKSON WAS A MAN OF
THE COMMON PEOPLE, NOT A LEARNED
MAN, BUT A MAN OF COURAGE, STRONG
BELIEFS . . . .

WO SHOT   *2-SHOT*   <u>JONES</u>

Then he was not an educated man, that is, a
man of formal education?

CU JENKINS	JENKINS
	EXPLAINS HOW LITTLE EDUCATION JACKSON ACTUALLY HAD, HOW AT TIME HE WAS EVEN UNWISE . . . .
TWO SHOT *2—SHOT*	JONES
	Is it true that he was a rough, often crude type of person?
CU JENKINS	JENKINS
CU PICS OF JACKSON	REPLIES THAT HE WAS A MAN OF PRO-FANITY WHO OFTEN LIKED TO DRINK . .

Routine or Rundown Sheet

These types of formats are usually used in programs having established patterns or routines, shows which are telecast five days a week. These shows are done by what might be termed "pattern shooting." A set pattern of camera coverage is set up and then a form of "free shooting" or "ad libbing" or "winging" is used in directing the program. In this type of script most directors will indicate the continuity of the show in segments, the set areas in which each segment takes place, and the over-all running time, time of each segment, and whatever back-timing they feel necessary, as exemplified in the following rundown sheet.

11:07:30	Jud Welcomes Sen Smith	(10:00) (Center Area)
11:17:30	Jud Cues	(0:30)
11:18:00 SOF	Fluorox COM	(1:00) (SOF)
11:19:00	Teddy Hart Sings	(3:00) (Band Area)
11:36:30	Jud Intros Barbara	(1:00) (Center Area)
11:37:30	Barbara Welcomes Playwright, George Alfred	(6:00) (Corner Table)
11:43:30	Jud Reads Some Anncts and Goes Into News	(3:00) (Center Area)
11:46:30	Jud Closes Out News and Intros	(3:00) (Center Area)
11:49:30 SOF	*A.D. Remedy* Com	(1:00) (SOF)
11:50:30	Jud Welcomes Red McGuire and Guest	(6:00) (Center Area)
11:56:30 SLIDE	Booth Does *Moonglow Bread* Com	(1:00) (Booth)

11:57:30	Jud Wraps Up Show	(0:30) (Center Area)
11:59:00	Marvin and Band	(1:00) (Dome Area)
11:59:00	Super Credits Over Band	(0:30)

11:59:30 FADE PIC AND MUSIC

THE DIRECTOR IN ACTION

Most directors work in local TV stations where there is always the problem of inadequate rehearsal time. The director must make profitable use of every moment and, therefore, should be familiar with several methods of rehearsing. After the director has the complete script, the first responsibility is to analyze it. While reading, the director must be able to visualize every infinitesimal part of it and know it from beginning to end. The next steps are to cast the show and to set up the first rehearsal.

Rehearsals

If a play, at the first full cast rehearsal the script is read through and discussed in terms of theme, mood, atmosphere, characterization, plot and plot development, character relationship to plot movement, and relation of character to character, among other dramaturgical elements. Next, a dry-run rehearsal is conducted, usually in a large room or a rehearsal hall where the director can work freely in working out business, movement and action. The rehearsal room may be set up in the following manner:

1) Mark off the floor using masking tape to outline walls, doors, windows, furniture, set pieces, and any other details which should be represented. The outside area should be taped to the dimensions of the studio space in which the show will take place.

2) Chairs may be used to represent davenports, tables, floor lamps, doorways, etc. This enables the director to work out details of action, business and movement.

During this rehearsal period the director begins to think in terms of pictures and sets up tentative shots at various angles and positions where the cameras will be placed. Make notes of possible shots, movement, business and action. Since there are no cameras at this stage, you may make use of your hands in framing a picture by placing the two thumbs together, end to end, forming a horizontal base, and with the two index fingers in vertical position you have a rectangular frame through which you may view a scene or subject. You can move closer to the subject to simulate a closer shot or move back from the subject to simulate a wider or longer shot. Most of the problems and details of action, business and movement can be worked out here. This makes camera rehearsals much easier and faster since there would be little need for the trial and error method.

Dry-run. When the cast has all lines memorized and can move through rehearsal without scripts in hand, the dry-run takes place. This is frequently done in the studio and is a walk-through of the entire show. No facilities are used, although camera operators, crew, engineers and other key technical personnel are present to get an idea of the complete show well in advance of air time. The director walks through all camera positions and shots as set during the earlier rehearsal period and is able to get a rough over-all timing. All cues are given aloud, and positions of the boom microphones in relation to action areas and camera placement are anticipated.

Camera Blocking. Everyone concerned with the production telecast is present, including camera operators, technical director, audio engineer, lighting director, floor manager, boom microphone operators, script assistant, and all crew members involved in handling props, set changes and other technical movement. Camera blocking—all shots, camera positions, angles and camera movement—must be established. Coordination of camera and performer movement must be set. Some directors move through the entire show, setting up shots as they go. Other directors use the stop-start method in which each shot is set before going to the next. Many directors take the show scene by scene, working out all shots in each scene or act and, after setting up each shot in a scene, run the scene again to assure a visual continuity in the mind of each person concerned with the telecast. Some directors like to plot shots in the studio, viewing each shot through the camera viewfinder. The choice of method is up to the individual director.

Critical shots and special shots must be carefully established in this rehearsal. Boom microphones are set in their relative positions. Use of props and scenery and any set or prop changes must be rehearsed at this point to clarify camera and mike positions and performer movements. Lighting and special effects must be checked out on camera monitors to assure any necessary changes before dress rehearsal.

Camera Rehearsal. Quite different from the camera blocking rehearsal is a complete run-through of the show without stopping. This can be done several times. It gives the director, camera operators, talent and crew a chance to set all shots, cues and movement before the dress rehearsal. It also provides a relatively accurate over-all timing of the show. All props, business, movement and scene changes are carried out without stopping. However, the emphasis is on camera continuity.

Dress Rehearsal. Usually there is time only for one dress rehearsal. All video and audio elements are included, such as music, sound effects, film, slides and video tape. All costumes, make-up, scene changes, props, lighting and special effects are utilized. This is the time for minor changes to be made; *never* make any major changes during this rehearsal. An accurate check on over-all timing must be made. This rehearsal should be conducted as if it were an on-the-air performance.

The director should be wise enough to finish "dress" early enough to allow time to permit a rest period before air time and to make last minute security checks.

Short-cut Rehearsal Plan. The preceding rehearsal method is ideal; in most stations, however, there seldom is time for this. The director must establish a "short-cut" method of rehearsals, such as the following:

1) Read through.
2) Stop-start, by scenes or acts. Re-run of scene to crystallize.
3) Complete run-through several times, checking for over-all timing, audio peaks, mike placements, coordination of camera and performer movement. Make notes of mistakes which can be cleared up on the next run-through.
4) Dress rehearsal, complete with all video and audio elements, scenery and scene changes, props, make-up, costumes, lights, titles and credits. Make final security checks on everything involved in the production, then see that everything is set up again ready to go for on-the-air telecast.

Regardless of the type of rehearsal method used, the director must set deadlines for memorization of script material such as lines, movement and business. Set up and rigidly enforce rules for promptness—there is no place in television for the "late-comer." Have the visual and aural aspects of the production definitively planned on paper before you call the first rehearsal.

Check-out Procedure

You and your staff and crew are set up in the studio ready to begin a "stop-and-go" rehearsal. This involves every member of the production staff and crew, as well as the video engineer and the VTR operator. Your talent coordinator must have the talent ready in the studio and in proper position for rehearsal. Before beginning, be sure of the following:

1. Check out the studio: lights, mikes, sets, graphics, among other items. Be certain everything is ready for rehearsal and for either recorded or live performance.

2. Ready cameras. Check to see that they are matched. Operators should be on cameras and have them ready for use; go into the studio and check with each camera operator, then check each camera on its control room monitor.

3. Check out all mikes with the audio person in the control room. Be certain that all talent is "miked"—wearing a mike or covered by a boom mike. Hear all mikes being checked—for example, have talent speak a few words on cue from the floor manager. Check on any music you will be using, including a theme for the opening and closing, and be sure it is cued exactly as you want it to be for the program.

4. Check out projection. Be certain all film inserts and slides are set up in order, ready for use, and check on the cue number of each film insert. Do a run-through on all film and slide inserts while watching on the control room monitors. Check on which preview monitor each will be seen. Place a studio monitor where talent can see the film and slides if they are to refer to them on the air.

5. Check with the VTR operator to be certain all tape is ready to roll. Check on the use of color bars. (See *Tape Procedure* later in this chapter for description of color bars as cueing device.)

6. Check on the slate or marker (see *Tape Precedure*), an electronic device shaped like a box on the front of which is milk-colored glass which has permanently printed categories for Program, Producer, Director, Air Date, Air Time and Program Length information. A grease pencil is used for marking the slate. On the front wooden framing of the glass plate are 10 small cue-time lights. When the marker is switched on these lights begin to flash, one at a time, from the left bottom to the top, across to the right and down to the bottom, creating 10 individual flashes resulting in a 10-second time cue. On the tenth flash the light goes out. The slate must be placed in a convenient place in the studio. A camera frames the entire front of the slate, picking up all information and the flashes of the cue lights. This is fed through the studio control room into the VTR. (A "home-made" slate may be made with a menu board, with the 10-second cue clocked by a stop-watch.) The slate information must be recorded immediately after recording the color bars. After color bars and slate have been properly recorded, the director is ready for the opening of the program, either using a taped opening (standard for program series), or a title slide or film strip with music and announcer's voice-over.

Timing the Script

The timing of any program has to be accurate to the "split second." There are two methods. In "front-timing," programs are usually timed in segments: the opening, the program content up to the first commercial break, the commercial, the program content up to the next commercial break, etc., and the close. The director adds the time of all program segments and the result is an over-all timing from the top of the show to the close. For example, suppose you have a panel type program such as "Meet the Public" with an over-all timing of 29:30, including opening, program content, several commercials and the close. The program is to begin at 5:00:00 P.M., the first break for commercial comes at 5:13:00 and finishes at 5:15:00.

Running time	Segment	Time of segment
5:00:00	Opening	00:30
5:00:30	Panel	12:30
5:13:00	Commercial (LV)	2:00
5:15:00	Panel	13:00
5:28:00	Commercial (LV)	1:00
5:29:00	Close	00:30
5:29:30	(Station break)	

A regular timing clock and a stop watch are used, the former to keep an accurate time check and the latter to clock each segment or scene in a program. Before airing or taping a program a director may ask the projectionist or VTR operator something like "what's the clock on the third commercial we will be airing?"—meaning: what is the time length of the spot? The director also frequently asks that a spot which is to be used later in the program be clocked to provide accurate information for the over-all timing.

As director, it is your responsibility to close the show on time, and "back-timing" is a device many directors use. To back-time, first check the station log to determine the time the next program begins. Then count back the number of minutes and seconds necessary to pace the last few minutes of the show. Usually, most directors back-time three to five minutes, giving cues at five minutes, four minutes, two minutes, one minute, and the last 30 seconds.

For example, suppose your "Meet The Public" program is followed by a special announcement for the U.N. at 5:29:30. Your moderator wants a five-minute cue to be followed by one-minute cues. You, as director, must know at what time in the program to give the desired cues. You would begin with 5:29:30 and count back in minutes to the place in the script where the front timing indicates there is only five minutes time remaining in the program.

Your back timing probably would be indicated on the left of the script and should look something like this:

```
5:24:30   . . . . . . . . . . . . . . . 5
5:25:30   . . . . . . . . . . . . . . . 4
5:26:30   . . . . . . . . . . . . . . . 3
5:27:30   . . . . . . . . . . . . . . . 2
5:28:30   . . . . . . . . . . . . . . . 1
5:29:00   . . . . . . . . . . . . . . . 30 seconds
5:29:30 (The U.N. announcement and station break)
```

Cueing

The director must have some means by which to cue performers while the program is on-the-air so that the action and speech may begin at the exact moment needed to insure proper over-all timing and closing of the program. All cueing in the studio is done by the floor manager who receives cues from the director via inter-com and who "shoots" hand-signal cues to the performers to begin speaking, to make an entrance, to stop, speed up and so forth. The performers should know all hand-signal meanings. Many of the cues used in TV are a carryover from radio. Examples of hand-signals used by the floor manager to cue talent are shown in Fig. 6.

The Telecast

The beginning director will learn the "what" and "why" in a course in beginning directing and/or production. You will not really learn "how," however, until you join the staff of a station, either commercial or educational, and begin real experience in directing.

Prior to Air Time. The director's final security check should include the following:

1) With floor manager, on studio: setting, props, lights, microphones, easels, graphics, charts and other visuals.

FLOOR MANAGER SIGNALS

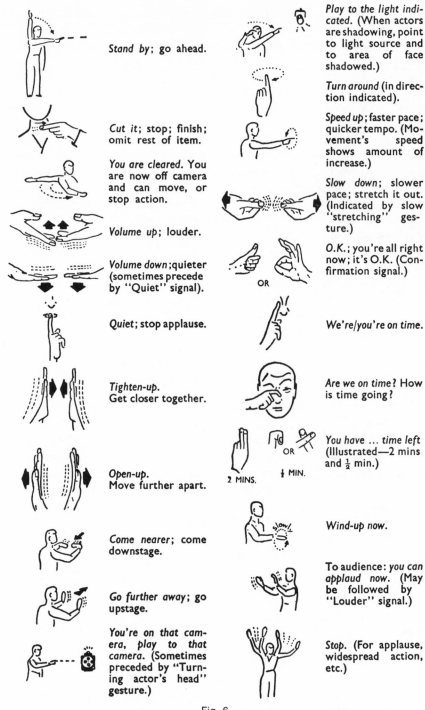

Stand by; go ahead.

Play to the light indicated. (When actors are shadowing, point to light source and to area of face shadowed.)

Cut it; stop; finish; omit rest of item.

Turn around (in direction indicated).

You are cleared. You are now off camera and can move, or stop action.

Speed up; faster pace; quicker tempo. (Movement's speed shows amount of increase.)

Volume up; louder.

Slow down; slower pace; stretch it out. (Indicated by slow "stretching" gesture.)

Volume down; quieter (sometimes precede by "Quiet" signal).

O.K.; you're all right now; it's O.K. (Confirmation signal.)

OR

Quiet; stop applause.

We're/you're on time.

Tighten-up. Get closer together.

Are we on time? How is time going?

Open-up. Move further apart.

2 MINS.   OR   ½ MIN.

You have ... time left (Illustrated—2 mins and ½ min.)

Come nearer; come downstage.

Wind-up now.

Go further away; go upstage.

To audience: you can applaud now. (May be followed by "Louder" signal.)

You're on that camera, play to that camera. (Sometimes preceded by "Turning actor's head" gesture.)

Stop. (For applause, widespread action, etc.)

Fig. 6

From Gerald Millerson, THE TECHNIQUE OF TELEVISION PRODUCTION

2) With floor manager, on talent: all present, make-up, costumes, ready for places.
3) With audio engineer: theme, other music, recorded sound effects.
4) With video engineer: film, slides, video-tape, use of supers for proper shading and focusing.
5) With film projectionists: projectors and cues.

The floor manager must know how he or she is to receive and give opening cues, and then must relay this information to the talent. The talent must know their positions and which cameras are to be used for the opening shots. Camera operators are similarly alerted to their first few shots. The count-down varies with directors, but the general approach is the same. Some directors will indicate a five-minute period remaining before air time, announcing the passing time at one-minute intervals: "five minutes to air, places everyone, four minutes, three minutes, two minutes, one minute, 30 seconds, 10 seconds, stand by." Other directors give only a one-minute cue after the initial five-minute announcement. The following is a typical count-down and opening by a director:

"One minute. Pictures please. 30 seconds. 15 seconds, quiet in studio please. Stand by theme, stand by announce booth. 10 seconds. Ready theme. Ready slide. Hit theme. Up on slide. Theme under. Cue booth. Ready 1 on title card. Take 1. Ready 2 on host. Ready to cue host. Cue host, take 2. Trim head room. 1 on model car. Hold for dissolve. Dissolve 1. Ready 2 on host, take 2. Tighten up a hair, two." (And so on, until the close of the show.)

On the Air. To apply this procedure to a specific instance, let us see what occurs when a director does his or her own switching, using the script, "The Tin Star," which begins on page 243. The five-minute cue is given either by the director through the "talk-back" system to the studio or via inter-com to the floor manager, who relays it to those in the studio. "Five minutes to air—everybody in places." At three minutes the cue is given, "Three minutes—stand by in studio, please." The director contacts the camera operators via inter-com, asking for "Pictures, please." The camera operators rack over into "take" positions the lenses to be used and "frame-up" the first two pictures for opening shots. As soon as the camera shots are set or lined up, the camera operators half-rack to prevent any possibility of "burn-in" before the show opens.

It is now two minutes to air time, the director calls it and the floor manager relays the signal, "Two minutes." Final security checks are made at this time. The control room clock shows one minute to air time and the director shoots the cue to the floor manager, who calls "One minute—stand by, and quiet in the studio, please." At the same time, the director asks for opening shots, calls the projectionist for a last-minute check on film and checks which projector is being used for the opening. The director watches the preview line monitor and sees the close of the preceding show, which indicates there is just

30 seconds before the new show hits the air. The director calls "Stand by and ready to go" to all those involved in the telecast. The ID slide is up and the audio operator is ready to roll the theme as the director says "Stand by music and film." The director then calls "Stand by to roll crawl with opening titles."

As the ID slide fades out, the sweep hand on the control room clock indicates it is air time and the director calls "Roll music—fade in film." The music is up, the film is up, and the opening of the program is established. The director says "Ready 1 for super" and "Ready to roll crawl." As the exterior scene at the opening of "The Tin Star" is established by film, the director says "Super in camera 1 over film," and the titles and other opening information appear on the program line monitor. The director cues the floor manager to "Stand by to cue performers" and gets ready to dissolve to camera 2 for the first live studio shot. The director calls "Dissolve to 2" and executes a dissolve to camera 2 on a shot of Sheriff Joel Marsden seated at his desk. The director then tightens up on camera 2 by indicating "Tighten up 2," and then instructs camera 1 to set up on the "wanted" poster being held off by a member of the crew. (Joel is looking at a wanted poster and to make it possible to see the poster and create the illusion of looking over Joel's shoulder, this sytem is used rather than having to position a camera behind Joel.) As Joel is looking at the poster, the director calls "Take 1" and a picture of the wanted poster appears on the program line monitor.

The director now sets up camera 2 on a wide shot showing Joel at the desk and including the door to the left of the desk. The director "Takes 2" as Ned bursts into the office and moves to the edge of Joel's desk. As Joel speaks, the director tightens up camera 2 for a two-shot. The camera moves in, creating a loose two-shot. As Joel rises from behind the desk, the director instructs the camera operator to "Ease back" to hold the two-shot. The director sets up the next shot, an over-the-shoulder shot on camera 1 which shoots over Ned's shoulder to pick up Joel, too, as he turns to speak to Ned. As Joel turns, the director "Takes 1." While Joel speaks his lines, the director sets up a shoulder shot of Ned on camera 2 and as Ned picks up his line, the director "Takes 2." The director follows this shot with a cut to camera 1 again, which is the same over-the-shoulder shot used before—and so on to the end of the drama.

There are several techniques of good operation to remember while on the air. Always tell the camera operator when his or her camera is on the air by saying something like "one, you're on" or "one has it" or "you've got it, one." This is a security factor important to both the director and the operator. Be prepared to give the operator a "ready" signal or cue on time, preferably a second or so before the take. Be fast. Ready and take cues must be close together time-wise, with no lag. If you ready a camera and then decide not to take it, immediately tell the camera operator to ignore the cue. Know the numbers of the cameras and call cameras by number and not by the names of the operators. Keep the cameras on the move; do not let the show become static. Check the time and communicate with the floor manager relative to remaining time so that he or she will be ready to cue talent when they need time cues. Always cue talent before taking a shot. This avoids having on the air a picture of a performer obviously waiting for a cue. The cue to the performer and the take are almost simultaneous.

The close. The closing of a show follows a rather standard procedure, too. Consider the example given earlier using a host. Assuming the host has been given proper cues up to the last minute for winding up the program, the final director's instructions might go like this:

> "One minute to close. 30 seconds. 10 seconds and wind up host. Ready theme. Ready 1 on crawl and credits. Ready floor to roll credits. Ready booth. Hit theme. Take 1. Roll crawl. Theme under. Cue booth. Theme up. Fade pic and music. All clear in studio. Thank you, everyone. Very nice show. Secure everything."

For best results, be courteous, be thoughtful, and be thankful!

Tape Procedure

Prior to taping a program the director should check very carefully with the VTR operator and the shading engineers to make certain the tape is ready to be used. Every tape should have "color bars" put on it at the very beginning of the tape recording. Every tape must be "marked" before the director takes the opening shot.

Check with the VTR operator as to how long color bars will be held. The marker, sometimes referred to as the "slate," contains all information relative to the content such as title, producer, director, date recorded and time length. The marker or slate is an electronic device which, when picked up by the camera, indicates all the information and shows, in seconds, the time the marker is to be held on the camera to record such initial information. Color bars and marker are recorded at the front of the tape.

When ready to begin taping, indicate to the floor—the studio—that you are ready. Give a standby cue, either by intercom to the entire studio or by relaying it through the floor manager. Give a ready cue to the VTR operator to roll tape. Always get confirmation of such readying directions. When the tape begins to roll, request the color bars. You will see them on the line monitor in the control room and they will be held for some 20 to 30 seconds. Then ask the VTR operator to take out the color bars and go to the marker, which is held for about 10 seconds. Then you go to black and then into the opening shot of the show.

When taping a program with several individual segments, you will probably "bust" the tape at the end of each segment. The director, via intercom, calls "bust it" to the VTR operator. The tape stops. Each segment must fade to black at the end to permit editing. Editing requires an "edit point." This is simply a cue point set up on the tape near the end of the segment so the director can time the roll of the tape in order to take the first shot in the next segment. The edit length is usually 10 seconds. This means the tape can roll for the last

10 seconds of the first segment before the director calls for the first shot to open the next segment. An efficient VTR operator must have at least 5 seconds roll so the VTR will lock sync. This is a part of the 10-second edit cue.

During taping, a good director will go to the VTR room to help set up the edit point. Back up the tape, by hand, to the end of the segment into black. Then, watching the counter on the VTR, continue to back up the tape into the program content for 10 seconds. The VTR operator then sets the controls relative to the desired editing. The edit point is now ready. The director is now ready to tape the next segment of the program from the studio control room. On one of the control room monitors you can see the last part of the tape of the previous segment rolling by. In the tape room the VTR operator is watching the timer and relays a count down to the director. This enables the director to be ready and to take the first shot on time for the next segment.

APPENDIX A.

The Television Log

The director would have a difficult time knowing when to start a program and end it, when to break the station, insert commercials, do public service announcements and promos without a television station log. The TV log is a schedule of the daily on-the-air programming of the station. Television logs differ in their arrangement of the various items listed. The basic content, however, is the same in any station.

The following is an example of the content portion of a typical log used at KUHT, the University of Houston Educational TV station.

KUHT DAILY PROGRAM SCHEDULE AND LOG

DAY: DATE:

TIME	TYPE	ORIG.	PROGRAMS & ANNOUNCEMENTS	ON	OFF	ANNCR
4:44:00	SP-MU	SL-AT-RC	Sign On Announcement SL 201	60 sec.		
4:45:00	SP-ED	SOF-NET	The Friendly Giant		14:21	PROJ-A
	CH		(8006-SOF)			
4:49:21	SP-PS	SOF	Keep Amer. Beautiful		20 sec.	PROJ-B
4:49:41	SP-PR	SL-AT	Promo & ID	SL 177 SL 347	19 sec.	
5:00:00	SP-CH	VTR-NET	What's New		29:02	VTR-1
	ED					
5:29:02	SP-PR	SL-AT	TV Promo	SL N-369	00:22	
5:29:24	SP-PR	SL-AT	Red Cross	SL X-208	00:26	
5:29:50	SP	SL-AT	ID-Preview	SL 106	00:10	
5:30:00	SP-ED	SOF	KUHT Travel Club		27:45	PROJ-A
5:57:45	SP-PR	SL-AB	The Museum of Fine Arts SL 207	00:60		
5:58:45	SP-PR	SOF	NASA		1:15	PROJ-B
6:00:00	SP-PS	VTR-NET	Industry On Parade		14:00	VTR-2

APPENDIX B.

Director's Vocabulary: Terminology, Language, Cues.

The terminology of the director varies from station to station; yet, there must be a basic language upon which the director can draw to communicate all needs to the technical staff during a telecast. Some directors coin new words, expressions or phrases derived from the existing language and terminology. To indicate the vocabulary used and/or coined by all directors would be an interminable task, so let us take a look at those words, expressions, phrases and cues most commonly used. Note the variations of some terms which have the same relative meaning.

Video Cues

Dolly in Move in Push in Go in	Camera moving in for a closer look at subject.
Dolly out Dolly back Pull out Pull back Come out	Camera moves away from subject, creating a wider angle shot. Often used because the field of interest is broadened by the movement.
Pan	A horizontal movement of the camera on the friction head without any dolly movement. Either to left or right.
Tilt	A vertical movement of camera on the friction head without any dolly movement. Either up or down. Some directors say "pan up" or "pan down" instead of using the word "tilt."
Truck Travel	Usually a lateral movement of the dolly and camera. A shot which is not toward or away from the moving subject. Camera movement which parallels the scene.
Arc	A truck or curved dolly which travels a curved path or arc. Either left or right.
Follow shot	May be defined in several ways. In the true sense of the term it means to follow by moving both dolly and camera with performer movement. It may be a shot in which the camera pulls back as the performer moves toward it, the distance between performer and camera remaining relatively constant in the movement. It may be the reverse of this, the performer walking ahead of the camera as it follows from behind in the direction of movement. The director must be cognizant of the basic difference between a pan shot and a follow shot. In the pan shot the dolly and camera remain in a fixed position while the cameras pan either left or right. In the follow and/or truck shot the dolly and camera both move with the performer or subject.

Zoom shot		The zoom shot most certainly can be related to the dolly shot. In the case of the zoom shot the difference is speed. Usually the zoom shot is created by moving the dolly and camera in or out fast.
1-Shot	One shot Single shot	A shot of an individual.
2-Shot	Two shot	A shot of two individuals.
3-Shot	Three shot	A shot of three individuals.
	Group shot	A shot of more than three individuals.
LS ES	Long shot	A shot of the full figure of the person or persons, in which much of the setting is seen behind and beside them. Often called an establishing shot (ES).
ELS XLS	Extreme long shot	A very wide shot of a large area or setting.
FS	Full length shot	Generally a shot of a subject from head to feet.
MS	Medium shot Close shot	Generally a shot from the waist-up, unless otherwise specified.
CU	Close-up shot	Generally a shot of the head and shoulders, unless otherwise specified.
BCU TCU	Big close-up Tight close-up	A shot of only head and face.
ECU XCU	Extreme close- up	A shot of a portion of the face or head. A "slice" of the face or head.
CS	Cover shot	Usually a wide angle shot covering a relatively large area in which action is taking place.
CU-LS	Combination close-up and long shot	Usually a shot of two persons, one seen close to camera while other is seen in distant background.
OS	Over-the- shoulder shot	A shot of two persons taken over the shoulder of one of them. For example, in an interview situation involving two persons, we see one person over the shoulder of the other. Quite frequently this type of shot comes in pairs, in which case the over-the-shoulder shots are matched. For example, we see Mary over the shoulder of Jane and when the cut is made to the other camera we see Jane over the shoulder of Mary. The over-the-shoulder technique is very effective when used in dramatic shows.
Imaginary line		In an interview situation, for example, the director may visualize an imaginary line joining two people conversing. Be cognizant of this line so you will not make the mistake of positioning one of the cameras on the opposite side of the

imaginary line. If you do position one camera on the opposite side, then the cut to that camera will reverse the direction in which the subject is looking.

Defocus

The camera is cranked all the way out of focus by rotating the optical focus control.

Soft focus

The camera is cranked slightly out of focus until the subject appears to be in a hazy atmosphere. This is excellent for drama.

Other ways to
   indicate shots

Knee shot.
Thigh shot.
Waist shot.
Chest shot or bust shot.
Shoulder shot.
Head shot.

All shot descriptions, particularly close-up variations, apply in analogous form to non-human and inanimate subjects and objects, as well.

Audio Cues

Ready audio

Standby cue to audio engineer.

Standby music, theme

Cue to audio engineer to standby with turn-table going and ready to slip cue record of theme or music being used in program.

Hit theme, music
Roll theme, music

Cue to audio engineer to bring in music at full peak or volume and hold until established.

Music in full

Music is brought up to normal peak set for the introduction of program or at any other specified spot in the program.

Music under
Take music under

Volume of music is taken down under the dialogue or sound being used, usually for background purposes.

Sneak in music

Music is rolled with volume either all the way down or very low. Then the volume is gradually increased until desired peak is reached. Generally used to bring music into BG as a scene is progressing.

Music down and out
Fade out music

Music is taken down and faded out completely, according to speed desired.

Music up
Bring music up

Increase volume of music. For transitional purposes, at the end of a scene, and usually at the end of the program.

Sneak out music

Music is being used in BG and director wants it to fade out completely. It may be faded out slowly or rapidly according to effect desired.

Fade music and pic

At the close of the program the music (audio) and the picture (video) are faded out simultaneously.

Open mike	Cue to audio engineer to throw switch which controls the particular mike to be used.
Mike check	Director or TD asks audio engineer to have all mikes checked to make certain they are functioning properly before program hits the air. Usually an assistant on the studio floor does this with a "count down" technique.
Mike level	The mike is opened and the talent speaks relative to placement of mike, exactly as if on the air. Director often wishes to hear this level check.
Mike talent	Making certain the person or persons who are to appear on camera have a mike which will pick up their speech.
ID mikes	Audio engineer must check out position of mikes relative to who is using each mike. Audio engineer marks the pot (fader) on audio console for each user.

Variations of Cues to Announcer

Cue booth Cue announcer Announce Read	Cue booth announcer in announce booth, either by intercom system or hand cue. Method of cueing depends upon where booth is located relative to control room. It is possible the announcer may take cues by watching TV monitor in booth. Such cues are arranged prior to on-the-air telecast.
AB (Announce booth)	In some stations this type of cue is used.
Take it from the top	During rehearsals such an instruction might be given the announcer and/or cast relative to the script or announce copy. Means to begin at the beginning of the copy or script material.

Film or VTR Cues

Ready film Ready A or B (projectors)	If film is being rolled from the control room it is wise to make certain the audio operator knows which projector is being used in order to punch up the correct button on the audio console to put sound on film on the air.
Ready VTR Stand by VTR	Used when the video engineer rolls the VTR.
Roll tape Roll VTR	To video engineer to roll VTR.
Out cue Roll cue	When talent gives a cue for a cutaway from the program to insert a commercial, a station break or some other relative material which is not a part of the main program content. The "roll cue" is another way to indicate the cutaway. This gives the director a means of knowing when to go to the insert, whatever it may be.

Scenic crawl	A large crawl used in a program as set background, usually a scene painted on canvas and stretched over two large cylinders (vertically placed); performers appear in front of such a crawl.
Hit film Roll film	Cue to start film projector.
Fade in film	Film is faded in by using fader levers on video switcher. Done by director or TD.
Take film	Direct cut to film, may be from studio to film, etc.
Dissolve film Dissolve to film	By using fader levers director dissolves from studio to film, or from slide to film, etc.
Video feedback	When a picture is being fed from a certain source, usually outside the studio where program is originating, to the studio monitor, and one of the cameras in the studio is shooting a scene in which the monitor and it's picture is being used.
Drop in	One meaning is to drop in a card during a program. Another is when taping a program and a live studio visual is missed, later it can be dropped in or edited in by using a live camera in studio shooting the pic, and as tape is rolled on VTR the pic is inserted at the spot where it was indicated in the copy. The pic or visual could be a "slide" and inserted from the projection source. This drop in technique takes place after the program has been taped.

Examples of How Some Directors Give Instructions

Frame up	Means to center subject or object.
Move in to lose him/her	Camera moves in closer until subject indicated is out of frame.
Follow subject	Usually means to pan with subject as he or she moves about. Camera operator should always lead the subject a little in executing the pan.
Ease in Move in slowly Go in slowly Tighten up slowly	Camera is dollied in slowly.
Dolly out fast Pull out fast Pull back fast	Camera is dollied out from subject as fast as indicated by director.
Trim head room Trim head	Cue to camera operator to decrease the space between the top of the subject's head and the top of frame.
Trim head a hair	Means to trim head room slightly.

Pedestal up Pedestal down Boom up Boom down	This applies to the pedestal type dolly or mount. This cueing means camera is raised or lowered by raising or lowering the pedestal itself. Director indicates how high or low it should be done.
Fade to black Black it Go to black	Cue to fade out picture to black screen.
Cut	In rehearsals the director will call "cut" to all involved in the rehearsal in order to stop everything.
Zoom in	Camera with zoom lens. Director indicates to the camera operator to zoom to the desired shot, e.g. zoom to waist.
Zoom out	Same as above, only the zoom is out to the desired shot indicated by director.
Check focus Focus up Sharpen focus	Obvious meaning. Sometimes directór or TD must check camera operators on this.
Split focus Pull focus	When the camera is focused on a point somewhere between two subjects and they both fall within the depth of field and are acceptably in focus.
Tighten up one lens (or two)	Camera is not on air. Camera operator racks over one lens longer than was used on previous shot.
Loosen up one lens (or two)	Just opposite of above.
Winging Ad-libbing Free shooting	Refers to director planning, setting up and editing shots while on the air. Show has not been rehearsed.
Widen out	Camera is dollied back to a wider shot while on the air. If off the air, the camera operator may rack to a shorter lens.
Ready for super Hold for super	Director must ready cameras before going into a super. This provides assurance that camera operators know they are to hold their shots steady for super.
Going into super Supering	To let camera operators and engineers involved in the execution of the super know the super is being aired.
Coming out of super Supering out	To let camera operators and engineers know director is taking out super.
Supering out full into 1, or 2	To let camera operators and engineers know which will be on the air when super is out.
Standby for dissolve Ready for dissolve Ready to dissolve Hold for dissolve	The two cameras involved in the dissolve must hold (freeze) their shots while the dissolve is executed.

Dissolve to 1 (or 2) Dissolve 1 Dissolve 2	Directions for dissolving. Depends on the individual director's method of giving instructions.
Cheat to light	Floor manager cues talent to turn or angle head or body toward a particular light. The movement should not be discernible to viewers.
Cheat to camera 1 (or 2)	Same as above, only direction or cue is to a particular camera.
Open up Pictures, please	Cue to camera operators to open lens by removing lens cap and shooting a picture of subject or object so director may check out the cameras. These cues are frequently given just prior to air time so director may view the first shots of the opening of the program.
Cap up and secure	After a program has been taped it is wise to secure cameras. In most studios cameras are pulled into designated spots for securing. Here the camera cables are either coiled or placed in a "figure-eight" position on the floor by the camera. When secured, all cameras must have their lenses capped. This is done either electronically or by a metal cap put over the front of the lens. A "cap" button is located at the bottom of the viewfinder. This simple push-button is handled by the camera operator. The metal cap is usually located on a shelf near the securing place. In some stations both the metal cap and the electronic cap are used for each camera. For security purposes, all stations have cameras capped electronically by the video engineer in the video control room.

BIBLIOGRAPHY

Bare, Richard L. *The Film Director: A Practical Guide to Motion Pictures and Television*. New York: Macmillan, 1973.

Bermingham, Alan. *The Small TV Studio: Equipment and Facilities* (a *Media Manual*). New York: Hastings House, 1975. An in-depth look at the features and amenities that typify the small TV studio (1600 sq. ft. or less).

Bluem, William A. and Roger Manvell. *Television: The Creative Experience.* New York: Hastings House, 1967. Provocative essays and dialogues by leading Anglo-American writers, producers, directors, performers and technicians.

Lewis, Colby. *The Television Director-Interpreter*. New York: Hastings House, 1968. Describes how the director is the interpreter of the program action to the audience.

Millerson, Gerald. *The Technique of Television Production*. New York: Hastings House, 9th ed., 1972. A thorough, exacting text with clear, detailed sketches to illustrate theory. Excellent book for reference and background material. (The hand-signals on page 252 of this book were sketched by Mr. Millerson and reproduced from his book.)

————. *Effective TV Production* (a *Media Manual*). New York: Hastings House,

1976. Covers all the fundamentals of TV directing techniques. Valuable for both small and large TV producing situations.

Robinson, J. F. and P. H. Beards. *Videotape Recording*. New York: Hastings House, 1975. A *Media Manual* providing comprehensive coverage of the entire field for the student and the professional.

Stasheff, Edward, Rudy Bretz, John and Lynn Gartley. *The Television Program:* *Its Direction and Production,* 5th edition. New York: Hill and Wang, 1977. Thorough text, covering all the basic facets of television. Well written and organized. Practical illustrations accompany theory principles.

Zettl, Herbert. *The Television Production Handbook*. Belmont, Cal.: Wadsworth Publishing Co., 3rd ed., 1976. A good, basic text of practical application. Well written and organized.

Rehearsal for "Target: Delinquency," a series of nine videotaped programs on juvenile delinquency, written and produced by Tom C. Battin for the University of Houston under a joint grant from the Health, Education and Welfare Department, Washington, D.C., and the Citizens Committee of the City of Houston. These programs were telecast over the University's station, KUHT-TV, and the three commercial television stations in Houston.

VERNE W. WEBER

Assistant Professor, Head of Media Services
Associate Director, Center of Educational Resources
Eastern Michigan University

● Dr. Weber received his degrees from the University of Michigan. Prior to his appointment at Eastern Michigan University he was staging supervisor at the University of Michigan Television Center with responsibility for settings, lighting, properties, makeup and costuming for all television productions. He is featured in the 30-minute, nationally distributed television training film *Staging for Television* made by the Ford Foundation for distribution to educational television stations. He has been consultant to public broadcasting stations, to the National Association for Educational Broadcasters Conference on Staging and Lighting, and to the Ford Foundation Television Workshop. Dr. Weber is a contributor to the *Production Handbook* issued by NET and has published articles on television in professional journals. In addition to the University of Michigan, he has taught at New Mexico State University and is at present teaching in the Educational Media Division of the Department of Curriculum and Instruction of the College of Education of Eastern Michigan University.

6

STAGING

BY VERNE W. WEBER

TELEVISION IS *the* media of communication. It is the effective combination of both aural and visual information. Radio is an effective *aural* communications device—the pictures of radio are built on the imagination of the listener. Television must provide visual images with the sound. The question, "What is the viewer looking at now?" must always be in the mind of the television scene designer.

DESIGNING THE SETTING

The purpose of the television setting is to provide physical space and environment. It is the space (area, locale) to which the performer can relate as an actor or actress. In children's programming, for example, the form of the performer is limited only by the imagination of the effective costume designer. For the actor or actress the setting provides a scene for the action. It becomes a location within which the characterization can find expression. It may be dimensioned to permit the performer and the audience to associate the setting with a human scale. For the performer the setting must be usable. It must be possible to move about in, easy to enter into and exit from, spacious enough to manipulate television paraphernalia around in. Not only is a TV setting physical space, it must be a visual representation of the thoughts, imagination and purposes of the script.

The Designer and the Setting

The scenic designer for television, as for films and stage, must be a skill-ful blend of artist, crafts expert, home decorator, architect and art historian. He or she must insure that there is a picture suitable to the script, idea, content or intent of the presentation at all times on the TV screen. The TV designer, in visualizing the entire presentation must think in much broader terms than the stage designer. The designer must think not only of wide shots, including entire settings, but must provide for extreme closeup shots of fine detail.

The television designer uses the same elements as does the stage or film designer: *line, space, mass* and *color*. In addition, light and lighting effects are an important part of TV scenic design.

Line is the delineating device used to indicate the contour or shape of an object. Lines may be used in combination to provide a realistic form (one taken from nature or realia), a stylized form (one having a basis in realism but altered through stylization), or an abstract form (one whose basis is solely in design). Space is the area encompassed within the setting. The need for space is com-pensated for or eliminated in many instances by the use of the wide angle lens. The technique of utilizing a lens with a shallow depth of field, thus throwing the background out of focus, may provide in individual shots a feeling of space not achievable with realistic space delineating devices. Whereas space is area in a setting, mass is the bulk. Because all objects occupy space, size determines the mass. The limitation of the TV optical system often precludes the need for three-dimensional mass, permitting two-dimensional or even painted mass to be used. Color in all scene designs, but especially in the highly imaginative set-tings for children's programming, is a most important element in the successful programming for television.

A clarification of the term "setting" is important. The television camera is a limiting factor in design—not in a restrictive sense, but limiting in an em-phatic sense. In essence, because each camera shot is different (that is, because the information of each shot is different), we have a different setting for each shot angle. The television camera, through its complement of lenses, limits the amount of information being viewed. A wide-angle shot may reveal, as in the theatre, a great expanse of scenery. Such a shot may permit the designer to utilize all of the design elements available. But the next picture we see may be of an object in sharp focus large in the foreground before a blurred, out-of-focus and indistinguishable background.[1] Or, the background may be only a small portion of a large expanse of setting. The viewer will see only the infor-mation contained in that one shot at that one moment. The designer, con-sequently, must think in terms of a setting (background) for every shot used in the program. The information and detail required in a wide-angle view of an

---

[1] The use of split-focus and other specialty lenses presents additional opportunities and challenges to the TV scene designer.

expanse of scenery is minimal. Therefore, the designer has the opportunity and the obligation to emphasize those areas of setting which come under the close scrutiny of the TV camera—the close-up shots. In this respect, the TV scene designer has an advantage over both the stage and film counterparts. In the theatre, the viewer who becomes bored can look at will about the setting—unconsciously subjecting the scenery to a great degree of scrutiny. Not so the TV viewer! In the movie theatre, the screen may be 50, 75, 100 or more feet wide. In some instances the screen may almost surround the viewer. All details are magnified and available in a large scale for the viewer. In television, however, how much can the eye wander over a 23-inch screen? Or a 5½-inch screen? What a pleasure it is for the TV scene designer to develop those details of setting which will be seen!

The use of highly sophisticated "chroma-key" special-effects generation equipment provides additional scenery design potential for the designer who can utilize carefully planned and shot photographic slides. (Chapters 2 and 5 explain *Special Effects* equipment and use.) "Keying" the performers into slides offers an almost unlimited opportunity for varied backgrounds.

Kinds and Types of Settings

The five common television program types (other than commercials which, by and large, utilize the other program types for their formats—see Chapter 4) are illustrative of the most frequently designed television settings: dramatic, interview, news, variety and children's. All five program types are found in television network studios. Television settings in most local TV stations, on the other hand, are restricted to news (weather, sports), interview programs, commercials and occasional quiz and variety programs.

Televison, whether dramatic or non-dramatic, can be classified as: realistic, abstract or stylized.

The realistic setting, although originally derived from a combination of naturalistic elements, has become highly selective in its composition. The judicious combination of properties (props) and furniture (highly realistic) with the scenic elements (very often painted) results in what today is called a realistic setting. Certainly no one today (as was done on the theatre stage many years ago) would advocate the use of real bricks in brick walls of settings in the TV studio. Why, when the plastic-sheet vacuum-forms of today (bricks, moldings, motifs, etc.) cannot be distinguished by the TV camera from the real object? Realism in TV, most faithfully duplicated in dramatic settings, is usually simplified to facilitate the design and construction and to reduce cost. (See Fig. 1.)

The use of scenic elements solely as backgrounds has resulted in a strong reliance on abstract forms, shapes or designs to achieve simple, yet attractive settings. Abstract design is particularly popular in music and variety programming. (See Fig. 2.) Abstract elements in scenic design are also utilized frequently in public broadcasting stations, in settings which are simple backgrounds behind the performer or teacher. Whereas abstract settings are often

Fig. 1 *Realistic Setting.* A combination of realistic elements to achieve a small, comfortable conversation area. *Courtesy of The University of Michigan Television Center.*

based solely on elements of design conceived by the artist, symbols or motifs derived from the content of a program or series are usually used by the scene designer as the basis for stylized settings. (See Fig. 3.)

Design Influences

The television scene designer, in common with the stage and film designer, is influenced by various stimuli in the process of creating settings. A few of the more important factors can be discussed briefly.

The script of a single presentation, or the format of a series, will influence the design of the setting as the production demands are indicated. The obvious script requirements are those of time (day, season, year), place (city, country, apartment, interior, exterior), situation (wealth, poverty), and mood (comedy, tragedy). These are the influences which give an initial impetus to the design of a setting. The more subtle determinants are concerned with interpretation of the author's writing. The director or producer selects a style of production which is felt will be successful. The style of the setting may be any one of the three we have previously discussed.

Fig. 2 *Abstract Setting*. A television setting for a panel/conversation group using curving panel shapes in front of a cyclorama. With careful lighting control, shapes can appear lighted against a black background, or silhouetted without light against a lighted background.

Fig. 3 *Stylized Setting.* A setting for a television program about the painter's art. The realistic artist's clutter in the foreground is framed by a stylization of the traditional garret window and stylized sections of wall as backing for the model.

The physical space (studio) within which the presentation is to be produced will determine the size and complexity of the setting(s). The production facilities available within major network centers provide equipment and space sufficient to meet the demands of any presentation. At the local station, however, the TV designer must often work within the confines of a small space. The height of the studio—from floor to the grid arrangement of pipes from which the lighting instruments (luminaires) hang—is a consideration. Satisfactory results for a setting can be achieved with minimal 8′ scenery, if the program is a panel or interview type with limited movement. Shooting patterns differ between a studio with 10 feet of clearance to lights and one with 20 feet of clearance.

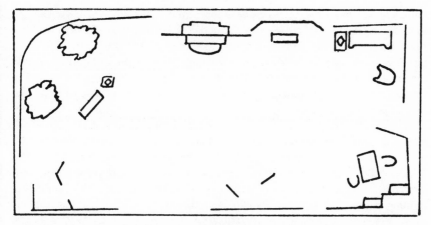

Fig. 4   A rectangular TV studio with small settings spaced along the walls.
Space in the center is for cameras and equipment.

Not only must the amount of the floor space available for settings be taken
into account, but even the shape of the studio (rectangular or square) is important. The rectangular studio shape can permit two elaborate settings—one at
each end—with equipment space in the center or a number of small areas along
the walls with camera and audio equipment space in the middle. (See Figs. 4
and 5.)

The television equipment and the personnel available for production influence design, too. The number of cameras, microphone booms and operators are
important factors influencing the size and number of scenic elements. A studio

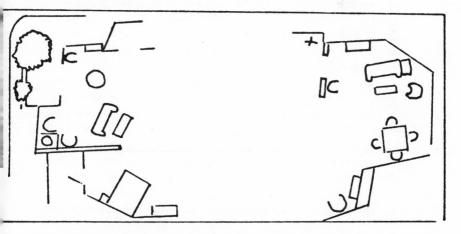

Fig. 5   A rectangular TV studio with settings at the ends of the studio. Space
for TV cameras and equipment is in the center of the studio.

with one perambulator microphone boom[2] must have settings close enough together to enable a short swing of the boom or movement of the perambulator to permit the transition from one setting to another. The settings must be few in number, if the studio equipment includes only two or three cameras, to enable the cameras to maintain a shot sequence.

The lighting capabilities of the studio, including total wattage capacity and instrumentation are all important to the effective visualization of the scenic elements. If the "rule-of-thumb" instrumentation and electrical service of 50 watts per square foot of studio space for black-and-white TV prevails (100-200 watts per square foot of studio space for color), this will be no problem. The 8-inch, 1,000-watt fresnel spotlight should be the minimum front lighting instrument used in combination with scoops. (See Chapter 2 for additional lighting information.) As already indicated, the height of the light pipes from the floor is a very important consideration for the designer. A low grid height forces the wide angle or cover shot to include either lights or a lot of floor.

In addition to budget limitations which must usually be observed in connection with scenic design, other considerations for the designer are:

1) *Size and kind of audience.* The designer working with settings for a religious program recognizes that the audience is a minority one and therefore must provide a setting suitable to the type of program and to the audience. Programs often are designed for special audiences. Women's shows, sports shows, children's shows, music shows are but a few examples.

2) *Age level (adult, child, teenager).* The settings for many youth-oriented programs should reflect the tastes, habits and fads of that age group. With the young child the elements of fancy, imagination and scale are important ingredients for successful TV design.

3) *Network or local station origination.* Most local station live programming is composed of news, sports and weather shows, commercials for syndicated shows, and hosts for "movie" shows. In most instances, once designed and constructed, these "bread-and-butter"'settings remain in position and are used over and over again. This type of setting, because of its continual re-use, requires extra-careful design and execution.

4) *Time slot.* If a single-studio station is in the position of having live programming "back-to-back" (one show following another with only a station break or commercial between), design is affected. Such a situation demands either two simple settings easily exchanged, or settings within which replacing a few elements achieves a distinctive change. Ideally, the program schedule will be planned so that this condition does not exist. The problem is considerably simplified if two studios are available for alternate use.

5) *Staff.* The designer must plan on simple sets when the number of personnel

---

[2] Mole-Richardson Co., Hollywood, California sells a microphone boom capable of being extended, horizontally positioned and aimed by the operator who rides on a rubber-tired, height adjustable, steerable perambulator.

available is small. More elaborate settings are possible when more persons are on hand for setting them up.

These factors are all important and must be given due consideration by the scenic designer and all members of the production team in the planning, preparation and presentation of the television program.

Public Broadcasting Station Scenery

Public broadcasting warrants special mention regarding the design of settings because of many considerations distinctive to its programming. Because the *raison d'être* of the noncommercial station is to provide educational, instructional and cultural programming to a limited audience, the problems of scenery and design are peculiar. Public broadcasting station television scenery must be economical—in terms of size (scale and elaborateness) and in terms of the number of elements or settings. In addition, such settings should be simple, functional and aesthetically pleasing.

1) *Simple.* Time, personnel and money are not always available to permit elaborate, completely detailed settings. The solution is simplicity. The elimination of unnecessary detail, the substitution of one or two elements for multiple units, the planning of shots to reduce the required scenery backgrounds or to simplify them are all part of achieving simple settings. Reducing the number of cover or wide angle shots results in fewer scenery requirements. The judicious use of single elements within the shot composition, and reinforcing the emphasis on the talent or performer will also reduce the need for scenic units.

2) *Functional.* Budgeting restrictions require that all elements of staging must achieve a maximum of flexibility. Flexibility of design means planning for multiple use of staging elements. Flexibility of use means easy adaptation of these elements through slight changes. A table base becomes a desk, a two-person interview table, a conference table or demonstration table by the addition of differently shaped, finished and designed tops. Conversely, a well designed (and constructed) top becomes everything from a coffee table to an interview desk by use of different bases. A section of set wall becomes a blackboard, a magnet board, a display board or a rear projection area by the insertion of functional plugs. The designer hopes to create a series of pieces of furniture and a series of scenic units which will provide imaginative staging personnel the opportunity to combine elements over and over again in almost endless fashion.

3) *Aesthetically pleasing.* The elimination of excessive detail, of arriving at a setting composed of a few, simple, well-designed, functional scenic elements will achieve, as the primary goal of the designer, a visually pleasing, attractive setting for the performance of the TV production. The low budget simplicity of the non-commercial station situation should produce a product which is both mentally and strongly visually stimulating. Public TV cannot compete with commercial TV if poorly designed, weakly staged and visually unattractive programs are transmitted.

BUILDING THE SETTING

Construction

The basic unit for TV, as for the stage, is the flat. This muslin- or canvas-covered frame of white pine, when properly painted, hinged or rope-lashed to other flats, becomes the walls and scenic portions of most of the realistic drama settings we see on TV.

The flat is a simple unit to construct. The frame of the typical 10′ flat is of 1″ × 3″ white pine (#2 white pine or better grade). The two vertical side pieces (stiles) fit between the ends (rails). At the midpoint in the flat is a horizontal member (stretcher). The flat is joined at the corners by butt joints and held in place by corner blocks. (See Fig. 6.) Corner blocks and keystones are made of ¼″ plywood.

The surface of the flat is covered with a heavy unbleached muslin or light duck, stapled and glued down. The finished paint job is applied over a prime coat. Canvas covered flats under 3′ in width are called jogs. Some flats are constructed with openings to accommodate ready-made doors and windows. A single flat can be easily and quickly changed by inserting different architectural period styles of doors or windows or by inserting solid plugs to make the opening disappear. A system of multiple-use units results in a flexible combination of scenic elements.

Television, however, does not rely wholly upon stage construction techniques. A combination of theatre and movie methods of scene construction are used. In many instances, canvas-covered flats may suffice, but the setting for a continuing drama series may demand plywood and canvas-covered solid flats which are more typical of the movie set. Sheet plywood is nailed and glued to 1″ x 3″ white pine on edge and then covered with canvas. Because of the 1″ x 3″ edge thickness, it is a simple matter to erect walls of this type utilizing clamps for fasteners.[3] Although this type of scenery is more rugged and durable, it has disadvantages. It requires more space for storage; the 1″ x 3″ on edge plus the plywood covering results in units almost 3″ thick. The space occupied by one such unit will accommodate three "stage" flats. In addition, the plywood units are much heavier and require more personnel to handle.

Standard scene construction methods are appropriate for most scenic elements used in the TV studio. It is wise, though, to adopt a standard height and modular system to enable the interchange of all elements. Platforms, parallels (collapsing or folding units with solid plywood tops) and step units are easily worked into a modular system.

[3] See the January, 1975 issue of *Popular Science* for a display of most of the currently available clamps. The author recommends the eccentric cam clamp available from Colt's, Batavia, New York.

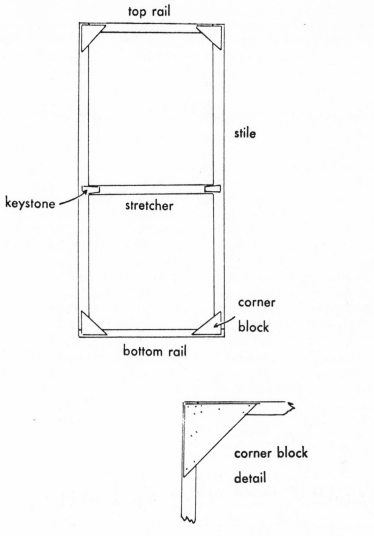

top rail

stile

keystone → stretcher

corner

block

bottom rail

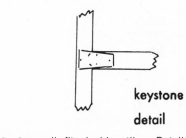

corner block
detail

keystone
detail

Fig. 6 *Standard flat nomenclature.* Note top rail fits inside stiles. Detail sketches show nailing patterns in cornerblocks and keystones.

Painting

The most commonly used paint for the TV studio is a rubber base (latex) paint. Various techniques exist for breaking up large areas of flat color. *Scumbling* is accomplished by brushing with various contrast-colors applied in brief, fairly dry brush strokes in various directions. The blend of colors and strokes will break up the base color and result in a texture effect. *Spattering,* the most frequently used technique, is accomplished over a base coat by striking a paint-laden brush against the hand, causing spatters of paint to land on the base coat color. *Rolling* is accomplished by taking a piece of heavily textured cloth such as burlap, dipping it into the paint and gently rolling the loosely rolled-up cloth over the painted surface. Interesting textures are achieved. *Sponging* is the result of dipping sections of sponge (cellulose or natural) into the paint and gently and softly touching the sponge to the surface of the flat. Care must be taken not to fall into repeated rhythm with any of these techniques. A repeated design will be the result of such carelessness. *Spraying* textures can be made by the use of an air compressor and a spray gun. Various sprays can be achieved by adjusting the opening of the gun, from heavy spray to fine mist.[4]

The ease of using pre-painted or pre-finished materials permits plywoods and other surfaces to be used as manufactured. It is possible, thereby, to obtain—at a somewhat higher initial cost—many scenic materials which require no finishing. Many plywood veneers, formicas and linoleums fall into this category. An abundance of moldings and joint covering items are available to match just about any wood grain or vinyl covering produced. Surfaces covered with carpet offer the imaginative scene designer other excellent texture and color possibilities.

The Cyclorama

The well equipped television studio should include as a basic scenic element a scrim cyclorama (cyc), an open weave cloth available in 30' widths and any length which, when dyed a light blue, can be used easily and effectively.[5] The cyc adapted for television use provides a suitable background, when properly lighted and controlled, for scenic elements. Tightly stretched, it becomes an excellent surface for the projection of light patterns and designs to achieve varied and inexpensive backgrounds. With full light the cyc can become a sky or void background. With no light it becomes a dark background suitable for silhouetting scenic elements or for cameo staging (use of simple painted scenic units against a black background).

---

[4] Brookstone Co., Peterborough, New Hampshire offers a hand-operated texture tosser machine for creating texture on painted surfaces.

[5] Cyclorama is a U-shaped, seamless, loosely woven cloth expanse enclosing three sides of the playing area on the stage or in the TV studio. Use as a sky or void background.

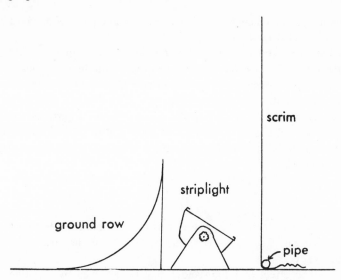

Fig. 7 Sketch of relationship of curved ground row, striplights, and scrim.
Note pipe on excess scrim to stretch it tight.

The scrim cyclorama when hung on carriers on a track along the studio walls can be easily and quickly moved into position behind scenery or scenic elements. One method for blending the scrim cyc in with the floor without a sharp line is to have a foot or more of excess material at the bottom which can be tucked under sections of pipe weighing the cloth down. Bicycle inner tubes inserted over the pipe provide a friction surface. A second method, which demands more floor space, is to utilize a contoured ground row as masking. This method has the advantage of providing a place for lights at the base of the scrim. A skillful paint-job will blend the ground row in with the scrim. (See Fig. 7.)

Floor Patterns

The restriction of inadequate height in many television studios often forces the TV director to shoot either "lots of floor" or "lights." This choice of shots often requires the scene designer to utilize the floor area and by various means to integrate it into his design. There are several possibilities for decorating the floor to make it visually more attractive.
1) Simple or elaborately painted designs can be applied. Unless adequate floor washing equipment and personnel are available, however, this is not a satisfactory solution.
2) Interesting effects can be achieved by using patterns of light projected on the visible floor areas. A variety of punched steel patterns are available from the major lighting instrument companies, or may be made from light

aluminum stock (such as TV dinner trays). These patterns are used in ellipsoidal reflector spotlights.[6]

3) The use of several sizes of colored tape (masking or mystic cloth) applied to the floor in perspective lines or in simple patterns is a quick and inexpensive way of breaking up the expanse of floor and of making it part of a designed picture.

4) A supply of 9″ x 9″ and 12″ x 12″ rubber, plastic, asphalt or carpet floor tiles in several colors, patterns or textures can be placed upon the floor. Care must be taken to restrict their use to the areas where cameras will not be moving.

SPECIAL EFFECTS

Many special scenic or staging effects are required for effective visualization. Such natural effects as snow, rain, fog, smoke are produced in the studio in various ways.

Snow: The effect of falling snow may be achieved by shooting a drum covered with black paper with white dots on it.[7] Slowly rotating the drum gives an impression of snow falling when keyed over a scene. A fast moving drum results in a rain effect. Similarly, it is possible to indicate a night sky by keying stars over a scene. Care must be exercised to properly spot the stars so they do not travel through objects. A very satisfactory snowfall may be obtained from the use of Styrofoam or plastic snow available at the Christmas trimmings counter of stores, or in bulk from window display supply houses. One method of dropping the snow is to use a snow cradle—two battens of wood (1″ x 3″ white pine) with a piece of canvas about 3′ wide fastened to them. One-third of the canvas width is slotted to permit the snow particles to fall through as the cradle is rocked. For small areas, plastic snow may be dribbled slowly through the fingers in front of the camera lens for another snow effect.

Rain: Can be achieved by running water through a pipe drilled to permit the water to run out. Such a pipe hung over and outside a window will give a realistic rain effect. The most difficult part of a realistic rain effect in the studio is getting rid of the water. For large areas, a sheet of plastic, used in home construction as a vapor or condensation barrier, can be banked up to collect the water.

Fog or mist: A piece of gauze (mosquito netting, scrim) or a smoked glass or acetate sheet placed over the camera lens can give a soft diffused effect

---

[6] Kleigl Bros. and Mole-Richardson are two sources of luminaires and accessories for light pattern projection.

[7] A motor-driven rotating drum with variable speed control suitable for this effect and for rolling credits is available from Salescaster Displays Corp., Linden, New Jersey.

which can simulate fog. Commercial fog, smoke and dry ice machines are available to achieve these effects.[8]

The success of any special effect is heightened by combining the visual with the aural. The sound of sleigh bells with a snowfall effect will much more quickly establish the desired illusion. Similarly, the foghorn sound with the mist or fog will most quickly create the illusion. The use of recorded sound effects can effectively aid in establishing a mood or atmosphere. The designer can plan on the use of sound to help in creating an illusion.

PROPERTIES

"Properties" (a carry-over term from stage and film) is the designation given to furniture and set dressing in the television setting. Properties are of two general kinds, "hand props" and "set props."

Classification

Hand props are used by the actor or actress during the performance. Some examples of hand props carried or handled by the performer are: firearms, letters, drinking glasses, dishes, packages, billfolds, knives.

Set props (or dressing) include the furnishings of the setting—furniture, floor coverings, wall decorations. Examples of set props are: rugs, pictures on the wall, tapestries, other wall hanging decorative devices, table coverings, flowers in vases (unless it is a bouquet carried on by a performer), books in shelves, pillows on furniture, guns on display, lamps.

At times the distinction in classification is determined by how an object is used. If a necklace is worn as part of a costume it is classed as costume; if the necklace is displayed on a board on the wall it is a set prop or dressing; if it is carried on set or handled it is a hand prop.

It is possible to classify properties as decorative or functional. The purpose of *decorative* props is simply that of providing attractive, visually pleasing elements to complete and complement the television setting. Just as a home or room is not "lived-in" without the addition of plants, pictures, knick-knacks and many other items, the setting is not finished until the set is dressed with many utilitarian and decorative pieces which combine to achieve a complete picture. The decorative props which a designer incorporates into a dramatic setting may importantly affect the viewer. The number of objects in a setting, the tasteful selection of objects displayed, the quality and finish of the furniture can all combine to give a feeling of wealth, luxury, a definite idea of the people who inhabit the setting. In reverse, a room sparsely furnished with tattered wallpaper on the walls, cracked windows or mirrors, battered chairs and furni-

---

[8] Fog, wind and cobweb machines are available from Mole-Richardson and other motion picture and TV equipment suppliers.

ture may immediately indicate very poor living conditions. The designer has the opportunity to reveal in the setting and dressing the mood of the play and many of the characteristics of the characters in it.

The purpose of the *functional* property is often dictated by the medium. Television, more so than stage or film, has been forced to design and provide many functional properties peculiarly adapted to its shooting patterns and formats. Some of the programs requiring special functional props are panel and audience participation shows such as *What's My Line?*, *To Tell the Truth*, *High Rollers*, *Name That Tune*, and *The Magnificent Marble Machine*, and news shows such as *Meet the Press*, *Face the Nation*, and national network and local news programs.

Undoubtedly the most impressive functional prop in recent television programming was the huge pinball machine on *The Magnificent Marble Machine*. This "machine," with approximate dimensions of 18' wide x 30' long x 16' high, was a functioning pinball device for toting up points for which prizes and cash were received. It dominated the setting of this popular daytime program and required two persons to operate the "playing" parts of the machine.

Some programs not only require specifically functional props and settings, but in many instances also need specially designed seating arrangements. For example, Fig. 8 shows a desk top, designed by the author for a special television program, which serves as a functional and flexible piece of furniture.[9] Multiple seating arrangements around this one piece are possible because of its design. As originally conceived and constructed, the centered legs provided leg room on all sides, thus making it available for a variety of uses. A number of different bases with varying heights offers the opportunity for wide usage. Flexibility and functional qualities are designed into many unique and attractive property elements of television settings.

Furniture

In selecting furniture for use in television settings, function is most important. Furniture (chairs, sofas, stools) designed for office or commercial use fits the requirements of non-drama TV better than furniture designed for the home, for several reasons: it is an inch or two higher at seat level, which makes it easier for the performers to rise and move; it usually has firmer or more serviceable upholstery; it is simpler and cleaner in design, and will combine with many different motifs and styles of settings. Additionally, many pieces of furniture designed for commercial or office use are of modular design and can be flexibly combined into a variety of shapes and combinations.

Furniture selected or purchased for permanent use in non-drama TV should be simple in design, modern or contemporary in style, functional in use, easy to maintain and attractive in appearance.

---

[9] See *Staging for TV*, a training film produced by the National Educational Television and Radio Center (now part of WNET, New York, N.Y.).

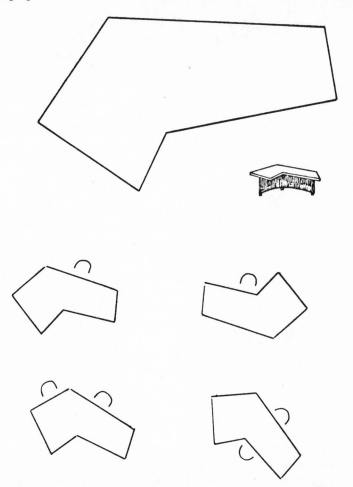

Fig. 8   Top view of specially designed desk-table, and several possible seating arrangements. A Formica top can provide color and beauty; bases of different height and styles can provide additional flexibility.

The most satisfactory seating for TV shot patterns is the open inverted "V" or "L" arrangement, illustrated in Fig. 9. There are, of course, many variations possible in the basic V and L shapes to accommodate different numbers of participants. Although the shot patterns and demands of the program format may dictate the shape of a piece of furniture, the detail, material and finish of the piece are a reflection of the designer and the budget. The not-uncommon practice of utilizing, for interview and talk programming, the furnishings and furniture provided by commercial accounts has helped many local TV stations overcome the need to maintain a large stock of furniture in their prop rooms.

Fig. 9   Inverted "V" and "L" seating arrangements, and variations.

TELEVISION LIGHTING

As was pointed out in Chapter 2, there is a minimum amount of light required to produce acceptable pictures on the TV cameras. The position and aim of the lighting instruments may also be influenced by the audio pick-up of the microphone and by the necessary movements of the microphone boom and of the cameras. Television lighting must achieve aesthetic and artistic goals. Lighting can help to establish time, mood, place and atmosphere. Lighting instruments and mechanical and electrical controls are the tools available to the designer to reach the design goals. The final proof is the picture on the TV screen.

Functions

The primary functions of television lighting are:
1) *Visibility*—sufficient illumination to activate the camera and to enable the viewer to see all the viewer is supposed to see. The amount of light required to achieve optimum pictures varies considerably with the kind and quality of equipment. It may range from less-than-normal room light to the

250–300 foot-candle[10] reading required for some color TV. It is not sufficient only to create visibility in the studio; TV lighting must ensure that
the viewer clearly sees all that is supposed to be seen. This means well-
lighted cover shots as well as properly illuminated fine detail in close-up
shots.

2) *Modeling*—sufficient illumination to create shadows and to develop the
dimensionality of the object or scene. The human face consists of a
number of surfaces and in natural light has illuminated planes and shadow
areas. The TV lighting specialist attempts to light the face and figure just
as nature does and, in doing so, develops shape and form. The lighting instruments are hung at 45° above and in front of the performer to produce a
natural look of highlights and shadows. The light, directed on the subject,
is aimed, focused and controlled in intensity in order to effect a natural appearance.

3) *Reality* (illusion)—sufficient illumination to create an illusion of reality in
the scene. To create this, motivated light is used. Light streaming through
a window to simulate sunlight is motivated light. The flicker of light from
a fire or flame is motivated light. Moonlight, the pool of light beneath a
street lamp, light reflecting from a mirror under rippling water are motivated light—all aid in creating and maintaining an illusion of reality. The
proper illusion created by lighting in combination with other visual and
aural sensations will result in atmosphere.

4) *Mood* (atmosphere)—sufficient illumination to create, establish and maintain an effect consistent with the intent of the scene. A setting of a forest of
trees with patches of sunlight on the grass creates an illusion for the
viewer. Add to this the croakings of frogs, the songs of birds and light,
gay music, and a mood is established. Take the same setting, subdue the
lighting, add to it some wisps of fog or smoke, ominous, eerie music,
stillness broken only by the hooting of an owl, and an entirely different
mood is created. Mood is more than an illusion of reality; it combines psychological overtones which act and react to produce in the viewer an atmosphere which can be at one moment sweet, light and gay, and at the next
moment weird, ominous and mystifying.

5) *Performer*—add beauty and glamour to the face or figure through the use
of diffused or soft light. Control attractive features by playing up the good
and playing down the bad. Should it be desired to make a person unattractive, the combination of harsh, unflattering light, distorting makeup, facial
contortion and unusual shooting angles can effectively destroy the most
perfect features.

[10]To obtain an accurate foot-candle reading, stand in the position of the subject and read
on an incident light meter scale the level of illumination with the meter pointed toward
the camera position. Repeat this procedure for each camera position.

Types of Lighting

The principal illumination on the subject is called "key" light and the spotlight instrument is its source. There are two kinds of spotlights used in television: the fresnel lens and the ellipsoidal reflector spotlight. The general practice is to use fresnel lens spots for key lighting. The fresnel lens provides a soft-edge circle of light in contrast with the sharp-edged light from the ellipsoidal reflector spot. Light from a spotlight is classified as specific or shadow-producing illumination. All spotlights have reflectors and lenses which focus the light rays. Fresnel lens spotlights can be adjusted from a tiny spot position to a broad flood position. Ellipsoidal reflector spotlights emit light rays which are parallel to one another. This feature permits this type of instrument to be used for projecting light patterns or shadows. Focusing this instrument produces little change in the size of the lighted area.

Another characteristic of light is called "quality." Light can be sharp in quality, or soft and diffused.[11] Key light is sharp in quality. It may be reduced in intensity, but it is never softened or diffused.

Lighting used to enhance the appearance of a subject or to create effect may be called "modeling," "dimensional" or "accent" lighting. Spotlights are used for this type of light, too, the quality of which is usually harsh and undiffused. Other lights are "eye" and "kicker" lights; usually spotlights, they are highly specialized in their use. The eye light is used in a close-up face shot to highlight the eyes or to induce a sparkle of light in the eye. The kicker light is a special light which can be used on any subject to add an emphasis or "kick." Very often a tiny fresnel lens spotlight of 75–100 watts, called an "inky-dinky," is used for these purposes. The reason a small instrument is used is because it can be easily concealed within the set.

A flat or even amount of light, often used to eliminate or soften too-black shadows or to fill in dark areas, is called "fill" (base) light. Instruments called "scoops" are usually the source of fill light, the quality of which is soft, with no direction and no shadows. The non-directional, soft light from a scoop is called general illumination. This general illumination instrument, the scoop, has no lens and the distribution of light is controlled only by the parabolic shape of the instrument. General illumination is often considered non-shadow producing light. This is achieved by either of two methods: use of a diffusion medium (fiberglass cloth or silk) or an interior quartz-coated lamp. Both methods will produce an almost shadowless picture.

Light used to eliminate shadows on the scenery, to show the scenery or background or to create silhouette effects is called "background" or "scenery" light. Care must be exercised that the performers remain away from walls or scenery so that they do not come into range of this type of light. If scenery light

[11] Diffusion in light may be achieved by use of any of a variety of diffusion material. Olesen Co., Hollywood, California catalog lists 8 different materials.

is separate and controllable, the problem of unwanted shadows can be minimized. The microphone boom is the source of many unwanted shadows. Spotlights producing such shadows can be "barndoored" (one shutter of a barndoor closed in) to remove the shadow. The "barndoor" is a device that fits into the gelatin frame holder on the front of spotlights. It has either two or four hinged shutters which can be adjusted to control the amount and to confine the direction of the light. It is especially effective for control of unwanted shadows.

Sometimes a small piece of spun glass can be inserted in the frame holder to reduce or eliminate the undesirable shadow. Scenery or backgrounds may be lighted by scoops or spotlights from above, or, optionally, by light from below. Silhouette effects can be achieved with similar light on a plain, smooth surface. If a translucent surface is available for silhouette, the lights may be placed behind, lighting the surface evenly. Sources of background or scenery light may be scoops or spotlights, and may be harsh or soft in quality as the occasion demands.

Light coming from behind the subject on the axis of the camera, used to separate the subject from the background and to create a halo of light about the head and a rim of light along the top of the shoulders, is called "backlight." Backlight is not a natural light. However, it achieves the effect of giving contour to the figure. It also enhances performers by highlighting the hair with sparkle and lustre. The spotlight (or reflector lamp) [12] is the source of backlight. Usually a 500-watt, 6″ fresnel lens spotlight is sufficient to add the backlight effect for monochrome TV. For color an 8″ 1000-watt spot would be used. Care must be taken to attempt at all times to keep the backlight 45° above the floor and 180° from the camera position on an axis with the camera. Backlight is high intensity light, never diffused.

Controllable Factors

The distribution of light in the TV studio can be controlled by the number of instruments, the focus (spot or flood), and the use of barndoors on fresnel spotlights and shutters on ellipsoidal reflector spots. For example, if the studio has five 1,000-watt spotlights, a greater distribution of light is possible than with one 5,000-watt spot. The quantity (amount) of light is controllable by the number, type and size of the instruments.

The intensity of TV light can be controlled by use of a dimmer. A commonly used dimmer is the auto-transformer type. In principle, a single transformer coil (primary) around a soft iron core is supplied with full voltage. A portion of this coil between a movable brush and a common neutral constitutes a secondary coil. The brush movement varies the amount of voltage going to the lamp and so dims the light output. This is an efficient type of dimmer which is not too expensive. Other types of dimmers available include electronic and

[12] Lamps (bulbs) with glass-shaped and mirror-coated elements as reflectors are available in spot and flood types of reflector lamps. "Birdseye" is one of this type of lamp.

Fig. 10   Most commonly used TV lighting instruments —

the scoop or floodlight

the pattern spot or lekolite

the spot or fresnelite

Courtesy of Century Lighting, Inc., New York – California.

silicon core rectifier dimmers. Innumerable preset features and punch card controls are available. Often, to conserve studio or control room space, three elements are utilized for light control: dimmer modules (often located outside the production area), control modules to actuate the dimmers, and remote extension cables to transmit the commands from control to dimmer. Utilizing solid state components permits the control panel to be in the control room with other production elements. The TV studio does not require elaborate lighting controls unless the program schedule includes a variety of programming atypical of the usual local station operation.

The quality (harshness or softness) of the light is controlled by use of silk over scoops or spun glass (fiberglass) over fresnel lens spotlights. Because of the characteristics of its soft-edge light beam and focus ability, the fresnel spotlight is the most frequently used. The soft-edge light permits areas of light to be blended together. The 500-watt 6" lens fresnel is commonly used for backlight in small studios. The 8" 1,000–2,000-watt fresnel usually is used for back light in large studios, and for color. Eight-inch, 2,000-watt (deuce) or 5,000-watt (5 KW), 10" or 12" fresnels are used for front (key) light in large color production centers. The ellipsoidal reflector spots (6", 500–750-watt and 8", 1,000–2,000-watt) are usually used as light pattern projector instruments. (See Fig. 10 for the pictures of instrument types.)

Application

Television lighting is applied in areas or spaces. Utilizing a minimum of three instruments, any one camera "shot" or position can be lighted. The three basic types of lighting (key, fill and backlight) are used. The inverted Y with the subject at the midpoint is the pattern most frequently used. (See Fig. 11.)

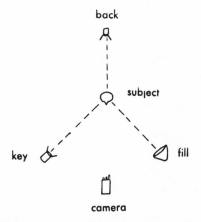

Fig. 11 The instrument, camera and subject positioning for the inverted Y television lighting method.

The spacing of the key and fill instruments is approximately 45° from center, with the backlight on the axis of the taking camera. This light arrangement, adapted to multiple positions or to two- or three-person situations, will satisfy most basic lighting requirements. Additional types of lighting can be added to this basic lighting set-up for accent or scenery emphasis. Subtle controls can be effected in the basic light plot through the use of dimmer circuits or some of the special controllable factor devices.[13]

It is entirely feasible in lighting for TV to address most effort to area lighting. A scene which includes three positions for a performer would be carefully lighted at the three important areas or positions. The space between these important positions is adequately lighted for the cross-movements. While the performer is moving, the viewer will not be able to distinguish detail, nor even expect the lighting polish of the important action areas. On occasion, scoop (fill) light may suffice for the walk-over movements. This technique permits the lighting technician to devote time to completing and polishing the important action areas.

Special Lighting Effects

There are many unusual methods available to the lighting designer to achieve special effects on the TV program. Ellipsoidal reflector spotlights can be used as "pattern" projectors. A metal pattern can be inserted into the focal plane of the instrument and the pattern of light projected onto background surfaces—an effective way of adding visual interest to the picture. It is a simple matter to use aluminum frozen food pans and to cut unique appropriate designs for such patterns. Cucalorus (cookie) patterns cut out of wood or cardboard may be suspended in front of a fresnel spot (with the lens removed) and the pattern can be thus projected. Barndoors, top hats[14] and snoots[15] are available in different sizes and shapes to provide special light patterns. Clouds silk-screened on heat-resistant glass are available for use in ellipsoidal reflector spotlights. The ellipsoidal reflector spot also has framing shutters which can be adjusted to form several light patterns.

Light provides the imaginative, resourceful person with an outlet for creative ideas which can contribute strongly to achieving interesting, attractive and effective pictures in this visual medium.

[13]Ordinary screen door wire inserted in the frame holder of a fresnel spotlight will reduce the intensity of the light by some 10–15%, but will not change the quality of the light.

[14]A top hat is a section of stove pipe or vent pipe spot-welded to a flat metal piece sized to fit the frame holder of a spotlight. In silhouette, the shape of the device resembles a top hat.

[15]A snoot is a conical-shaped metal tube fastened to a flat metal piece to fit into the frame holder of a spotlight. The tip of the cone is removed to allow light to pass.

GRAPHICS

The purpose of any graphic card is to take certain information and convey it in a clear, concise, visually interesting way. The elements which combine to achieve this are: words, ideas and design.

Types

There are two basic types of graphics or visuals common to television: the visual designed to relay *identification,* and the visual designed to relay *information.* Station identification cards, title cards, credits and product identification cards are common to the first classification. Without doubt, the most frequent TV use of the informational visual is in the "super" or "key" card.[16] In baseball, for example, the super provides the viewer not only with the name of the batter but, often, also with his batting average and RBIs.

The production of effective visuals is the responsibility of the graphics designer, who must be not only an artist but also an expert in the visual media. The graphic designer's background and training should include experience in all drawing media: chalk, conté crayon, tempera, pencil and ink (including felt-tip pens), among others. Also essential is a knowledge of film techniques, especially slides, slide cameras and Polaroid cameras. Versatility coupled with the knack of speedy work are a prime combination for the graphic artist.

The television picture has an "aspect ratio" of 3 : 4—three units high by four units wide. All pictures should be composed with this relationship in mind. The most frequently used card size for television studio graphics is 11 x 14 inches. An 11" x 14" card will provide an information area of 7" x 10". The space between the information area and the edge of the card is called "safety." Safety must be provided on all graphic cards to permit some degree of leeway in "framing" the picture.[17] Usually, the object being televised on any camera is centered in the frame.

The lettering requirements for television graphics are: size, clarity and spacing. *Size* of lettering should be $^1/_{10}$th the vertical size of the graphic card, or $^1/_7$th the size of the information area of the card. *Clarity* of lettering will be achieved if the graphic artist relies on simple, clean-of-line letters. Elaborate letter styles have a specialized use on television. Proper *spacing* of the lettering and restricting the width of the type font will remove the likelihood of "smeared" or "streaked" letters running together in the TV picture. The use of "extra-condensed" type styles frequently results in these problems.

[16] "Super" refers to superimposition, a double exposure providing a background picture with secondary information electronically superimposed over the primary picture. "Keying" refers to the insertion of specific information into another background picture. This is achieved through use of the special effects generator.

[17] "Framing" refers to the effective composition of any shot to achieve a pleasing, balanced and effective picture.

In black-and-white TV, the "gray-scale" guides the graphic artist. Even though the camera may be a color camera, the viewfinder and the CCU (camera control unit) monitors will be black and white for control-room personnel. The television system reproduces only a 10-step scale—black (step 10), white (step 1) and 8 shades of gray between. All television pictures are made up of these 10 steps of the gray scale. The use of white lettering on a black card is best restricted to "key" and "super" cards. Good design and visualization result from wise use of 2- to 3-step minimum separations of the gray scale in television graphics.

Although hand lettering lends character to television visuals, the most frequently used printing device is the "hot press" printer. A hot press printer uses heated type and foil for printing purposes. The set-up type is heated and, when pressed down on the selected foil, prints on the surface of the material used. This process results in a quickly made, instantly dry and immediately usable product. The less expensive but quite versatile "magnetic press" has the type set and locked in working position on bars secured to the layout surface by strong magnets. In addition to a variety of type faces (fonts), each of these two printing presses is capable of producing many different printed cards, all in perfect registration (alignment). Both of these presses are simple to operate, making them widely used by television stations.

Noncommercial television operations place special demands on graphic arts departments because of broadcasts designed for instructional purposes. Teaching requires greater use of special illustrations, cartoons, maps, graphs and charts. All such two-dimensional materials are the responsibility of the graphic artist. Frequently, teaching programs demand the use of three-dimensional and/or animated visual materials. The graphic and visual requirements of the noncommercial station quite often exceed those of the commercial TV station, and the former's graphic artist often must produce working scale or simplified, but functional, models of objects, processes or machines on a miniscule budget.

Studio Display

Many methods of displaying graphics in the studio are available. The easel with an adjustable ledge is one basic graphic display device. On an easel, graphic cards can be pulled away to the side or flipped down to change. An easel with a ring binder mounted on it provides an easy method of flipping cards for fast, smooth, guided changes. (See Figs. 12a, 12b.)

Other methods of displaying title cards are available. One is the parchment scroll, a device reminiscent of the Middle Ages, which is opened and unrolled slowly, revealing the information. Another is the circular drum, with a strip containing the information slowly turned past the camera lens focused on one area. As the drum turns, the information appears and disappears from view. The drum rotates vertically (ferris wheel or paddle wheel effect) or horizontally (merry-go-round effect). The information may be printed white on black for

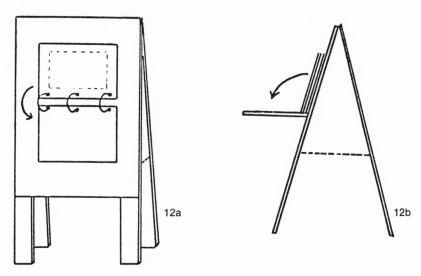

Fig. 12a shows a ring binder mounting flip card easel. Cards can be dropped *out of* camera view, or *into* camera view if focus is on the lower card. Fig. 12b is a sketch of a variation for changing a series of graphics—they are tipped and floated down to reveal next in sequence. Usually for on-the-air movements for both examples.

keying. An electrically operated drum provides flexibility of speed control. An inexpensive book of blank pages with titles and information is another effective method. The pages can be turned remotely by affixing very thin wires; it is equally effective to have a hand turn the pages. For a drama, the title might be put on the cover of a book. Other devices include umbrellas with printing on top of the panels, parts of the body with printing, guillotines with the lettering on the blade readable when the blade drops into view, trays of water with lettering beneath the surface, and sand-covered cards from which the sand is blown to reveal information. The imagination of the graphics designer is the only limiting factor.

Video Display

Most TV stations utilize video character generator equipment to provide titling and captioning at low per-hour labor costs. Available in different type fonts are a number of features possible in high quality character generator equipment: multi-page, multi-color, multi-line, multi-characters per line storage (memory) capability, character underline, flashing, instant entry, horizontal and vertical crawl, automatic centering, key (insert) output, output speed control, and many additional features.

Random access memory (storage) equipment can be utilized for instantaneous recall and storage of often used titles and captions. Computers, for storage and retrieval of graphic and other visual information, are used by the networks and other major production centers.

Special Devices

Television production problems, including many relating to graphics, have resulted in unusual, unique and interesting devices being developed as solutions. The following are a few of the most commonly used special production techniques or devices:

Super pointer. The inability to point or focus attention on film-chain originated pictures can be solved by placing a large black card next to the speaker or performer, who holds a pointer (painted dull black) with an arrow or dot of white on the tip. By supering or keying the white tip held in front of the black card over the film-chain camera picture, the performer can, by watching a studio monitor, indicate or point to any part of the screen with the pointer and emphasize aspects of motion picture film or slides at will.

Pull-up unit. To provide a method of revealing visuals, yet concealing them until the proper moment, the pull-up unit was developed. It is a narrow box which is no higher than and may be concealed by a desk. The box has a number of grooves into which individual graphic cards can be placed. Spring metal leaves pressing against the sides of the cards, when raised into view, hold them in position. A simple lift by the performer reveals the graphic which, when no longer needed, is pushed down out of sight.

Spring tension pole. One of the most versatile graphic display devices developed is the spring tension pole, which follows the basic design of the "polecat." [18] This pole, extendable from 10'6" to 19'6", can be spotted anywhere in the studio playing area. A number of display devices which can be used on this pole or on the pole-cat are adjustable in height to fit the performer and can be easily produced. Variations on this device permit two visuals to be used on a two-sided holder, or three or four. A further variation constructed with a number of grooves permits a series of graphics to be inserted and pulled to be revealed.

COSTUMING

One purpose of the costume designer is to portray visually, through the costumes of the characters of a drama, the prevailing design of clothing worn in any period of our civilization. The costume designer, utilizing the principles of costume design, selection of fabrics, color and style, achieves in the clothing of the characters visual reinforcement of the dramatist's ideas.

As with all visual aspects of dramatic presentation, television costuming must contribute information about the character. The age of a person may be reflected in the cut or style of the clothes. The type and quality of material might indicate economic status. The use and selection of color and accessories

[18] See *Staging for TV* film.

might indicate taste and refinement—or lack of it. The way the clothes are worn and look may reflect social standing. What a person wears and how the person wears it are reflections of characterization.

Basic Costume Rules

Most television stations today are rarely concerned with costuming actors, inasmuch as virtually all drama and documentaries are network-produced and distributed, or syndicated. Most station-produced programs are news, interview and talk shows, and these stations' concern is with the everyday clothing the performers wear. A list of do's and don'ts pertaining to television dress and accessories provide a basic guide:

1) Test fabrics on camera whenever possible to determine the transposition from the fabric color to the monochrome television gray scale. (This is important even though color TV broadcasting dominates.)
2) Avoid flamboyant extremes in contrasts and patterns of cloth.
3) Avoid excessive use of black and white in single costumes. Work as much as possible in 2-3-step gray scale contrast separations.
4) Learn the gray scale. Develop a color sense to be able to transpose from color into the 10-step gray scale.
5) Avoid extremes in accessories. Do not use highly reflective jewelry, pins or similar items.
6) Avoid small repetitive patterns in cloth, which tend to become "busy" before the camera.
7) Avoid hard surface (chintz, glosheen, fiberglass, rayon, sateen), highly reflective costume materials.
8) Advocate the use of off-white or pastel shades in solid-color shirts for men.
9) Lapel pins, pens and pencils in breast pockets of coats, and highly reflective tie pins are not desirable for the male performer.
10) Do not depend on the performer to follow the basic rules of dress for television—be prepared by judicious use of lighting and video control to compensate for and correct costume errors.

MAKE-UP

There are two basic types of make-up application for television—*straight* (non-dramatic) and *dramatic*.

The primary purposes of straight make-up are: to cover the dark beard on male performers; to reduce the reflection of light from the nose, forehead and bald head; when necessary, to "play down" or reduce skin texture. Television pancake make-up is most commonly used. The range of skin tone make-up (from very light to very dark) is available from several manufacturers.[19]

[19] Both Max Factor and Stein's manufacture make-up for television use.

Application of straight make-up for men usually consists of: 1) applying sufficient pancake with a moist sponge on the beard areas to smooth out and cover the face—the make-up should blend down over the jaw and chin line into the upper neck regions; 2) touching up the nose and forehead (head, if bald) to reduce shine; 3) if eyebrows are pale, a small touch-up with brown or black eyebrow pencil may be necessary to provide contrast with skin tone; the same slight touch-up may be required on the hairline area at the temples; touch-up with light colors would be appropriate for dark skin-tones.

Women require special attention in only one area—the lips. Street make-up for skin and eyes—provided there is a pancake or powder base make-up—will usually suffice. Test street make-up on camera for suitability, especially the lipstick. Many of the popular shades of lipstick fail to provide sufficient absorption of light to give the slightly contrasting effect desired for a good picture. For best results, extremes of straight make-up must be avoided at all times. During the first on-camera rehearsal check for the need of make-up, it may not be required.

Dramatic make-up has as its primary purposes (in addition to the same uses as straight make-up) the creating and aiding of characterization. The fundamentals of effective stage character make-up generally apply to television. Television requirements differ from those of the stage primarily in emphasis. On the stage the projection of the characterization across the footlights demands strong, bold and often "contrasty" make-up. The make-up must be effective for the many hundreds of spectators seated near and far from the stage actor. Television, on the other hand, is an intimate, close-up medium and the make-up must, therefore, be more natural and subtle. The viewer is, in effect, the television camera and very often views the performer from extremely close range.

In all matters relating to staging, local commercial and noncommercial television stations may have a special advantage that frequently is not fully utilized. If they are close (in the former case geographically, in the latter also administratively) to a dramatic arts or radio and television department of a college or university, they have good sources of advice, materials and assistance in regard to staging, properties, effects, lighting, costuming and make-up.

BIBLIOGRAPHY

Barton, Lucy, *Historic Costume for the Stage*. Boston: Walter H. Baker Co., 1961. Hundreds of sketches illustrating all periods of costume. Additional valuable information on accessories and construction.

Bretz, Rudy, *Techniques of Television Production*. New York: McGraw-Hill, 1962. Excellent, thorough treatment of subject. Technical and detailed for the professional television worker. Well illustrated with pictures and sketches.

Burris-Meyer, Harold, and Edward C. Cole, *Scenery for the Theatre*. Boston: Little, Brown & Co., 1972. Excellent reference for the standard methods and techniques used in the construction and handling of scenery for the stage.

Corson, Richard, *Stage Makeup*. Washington, D.C.: American Theatre Association, 1975. Good treatment of basic makeup techniques applicable to television. Good beginning reference book.

Gillette, Arnold S., *Stage Scenery: Its Construction and Rigging*. New York: Harper & Bros., 1972. Very well illustrated text in the construction and rigging of scenery for the stage.

Journal of the Society of Motion Pictures and Television Engineers. (Monthly) Articles on lighting, gray scale, color response, and technical information on film and television.

Kehoe, Vincent J. R., *The Technique of Film and Television Make-up*, Revised Edition. New York: Hastings House, 1969. Excellent reference book for the professional or well informed.

Herdeg, Walter, *Film and TV Graphics 2*. New York: Hastings House, 1976. Examples of film and television graphics the world over. Lavishly illustrated.

Millerson, Gerald, *Basic TV Staging*. New York: Hastings House, 1974. A thorough survey of the basic principles of TV staging. Demonstrates effective labor-saving approaches for small-budget productions.

——. *TV Lighting Methods*. New York: Hastings House, 1975. Good book for experts as well as beginners. Easily understood illustrations.

Parker, W. Oren, and Harvey K. Smith, *Scene Design and Stage Lighting*. New York: Holt, Rinehart, and Winston, 1974. Brief but good section on properties. Well illustrated.

Wade, Robert J., *Designing for TV*. New York: Pellegrini and Cudahy. Good reference for problems of designing and executing the television setting. Well illustrated. (Now out of print.)

——. *Staging TV Programs and Commercials*. New York: Hastings House. Coverage of visual aspects of television from the scenic and graphic designer's viewpoint. How to plan and execute settings and props. Includes a chapter on graphics. (Now out of print.)

Wilcox, R. Turner, *The Mode in Costume*. New York: Charles Scribner's Sons, 1974. Well illustrated reference for costumes through the years. Standard reference in costuming.

Wilkie, Bernard. *Creating Special Effects In TV and Films*. New York: Hastings House, 1977. A basic guide to the design and use of special effects and props.

WILLIAM HAWES

● William Hawes is professor and head of the radio-television-film area in the new School of Communications at the University of Houston, where he is involved in the construction of a CCTV facility—completion date 1978. He teaches courses in TV and film performance and production. He has been executive producer and frequent anchor of a weekly TV series over KHTV, Houston, since 1967. He conducted a senior research seminar which resulted in the publication, *Recommendations for the Establishment of Community Antenna Television (CATV) in the City of Houston, Texas* and is currently studying the uses of TV in industry. Dr. Hawes is also professor in the program in Biomedical Communications at the School of Allied Health Sciences, The University of Texas Health Science Center at Houston. He has been employed in various audio-visual capacities for Maxwell House, Variable Annuity Life Insurance, *The Houston Post,* and WTOP-TV, Washington, D.C. Though serving from time to time as an administrator, radio station manager, TV and film producer, Dr. Hawes prefers his role as an educator developing talented performers and writers. Since receiving the B.A. from Eastern Michigan University and the M.A. and Ph.D. degrees from the University of Michigan, he has taught at Eastern Michigan University, Texas Christian University and the University of North Carolina at Chapel Hill. In 1972 he and his wife opened a pre-school where several international youngsters learn English as a second language. Dr. Hawes is author of one Hastings House publication, *The Performer in Mass Media,* contributor to another, *Radio Broadcasting,* and has had articles published in several leading journals. He is listed in ten national and international biographies.

7

PERFORMING

BY WILLIAM HAWES AND ROBERT L. HILLIARD

THE PRINCIPAL MEANS for the presentation of the writer's ideas, toward which all elements of television production focus, is the performer.

Without effective interpretation on the part of the performer or performers, the best script, the most innovative producing, the most creative use of equipment, the most artistic setting, the most imaginative directing do not reach ultimate fruition. Although the performer the audience sees may not be in human form—animation, electronic effects, puppets, animals and other means have been most effective in television—this chapter concentrates on the human performer. Included in this category are actors, actresses, announcers, newspersons, singers, dancers, comics, conductors, interviewers—any and all persons who appear professionally on our television screens. Some are household words, stars of network or nationally syndicated programs. Some are known only in regional or local markets, but frequently are celebrities in a particular town or area to the extent that a nationally known performer might be. Some performers are not TV professionals in the usual sense, but are known in other fields. By virtue of their status they appear frequently on television, either on network television (usually on interview shows) or, as is the case with most, as local celebrities on local stations. Such people include sports figures, politicians, ministers, citizen advocates, industry representatives, teachers, student activists and artists.

Television, like the movies, tends to cast performers by type. Ability frequently is incidental. Does the actor or actress have the right look, the right voice, the right movement for the particular role? Does the news announcer or anchorperson seem as if he or she will elicit a sense of confidence and a high rating from the viewing audience? Most performers start out as actors or actresses. Johnny Carson did not start out to be an interview-variety show host; he is still an actor, but in a non-drama format. Many newscasters were in acting first, just as many began as newspaper journalists. Both groups gravitated to bread-and-butter jobs in broadcasting, frequently at small radio stations, doing disc-jockey, news announcing and commercial spot work. Some eventually moved into television. The television performer appears in any and all kinds of format: drama, news, sports, announcing, commercials, game shows, interviews, panel moderating, music shows, variety programs, children's programs, women's shows, instructional programs, minority and ethnic programs, features, documentaries—every conceivable format in which a live performer may appear.

THE MEDIUM

A distinct opportunity for the good television performer is the chance to utilize, by the very nature of the medium, a combination of both representational and presentational acting techniques. Even as the close-up permits a delineation of the intimate, subjective thoughts and actions of the character, the opportunity and sometimes the need to work directly to the camera results in the person-to-person presentational effect. On occasion the performer is required to combine both techniques virtually at the same time—a fine means for effective communication to the audience, but a not inconsiderable task.

Concentration is one of the key disciplines of the performer—and probably the most difficult thing to achieve in television. It is not possible to isolate oneself as on the stage and use "inspiration" or to "lose" oneself in the character. Even while having to understand, believe and feel the character's motivations and actions in the creation of the role, the performer—and this includes non-drama situations, such as news announcing—must be aware of the cameras, the directions, watch the floor manager for cues, look out for the mass of equipment and numerous technicians running back and forth, and constantly be ready to adapt motivation and action to the exigencies of a technical medium. The television performer must develop intense concentration and full awareness of the outside surroundings at one and the same time. The problem is to remain calm and collected—and, sometimes, sane—in the midst of the confusion and mechanism—and madhouse—of TV.

The Studio

The performer works in an environment of cameras, microphones, lights, other technological equipment, and innumerable technicians and performers.

The performer must adapt to the technical requirements of the electronic medium. For example, one must be aware of the placement of the microphones and of the carefully lighted areas designated on the studio floor in chalk or masking tape—the "marks." Being off one's mark, even slightly, may sometimes make a substantial difference in the light level or composition of the shot. Studios which do not have enough sound equipment or lighting instruments to cover the entire floor create electronic problems: a performer may come out in deep shadow or a distorted color, or may sound as if he or she is speaking from another part of the scene. Unless the electronic results from the cameras are identical, a performer may look good on one camera and poor on another.

The quality of the studio and the amount of equipment available frequently determines whether a program is to be done live, on tape or filmed.

Makeup

Beyond the type-casting approach, in which many producers and directors select performers on the basis of how closely their physical appearance approximates that of the character or job-role being auditioned, makeup is an important factor in achieving the appearance desired on the TV screen. The performer must develop on the outside, particularly through the face, that which expresses the inside: the wise, knowledgeable and serene national newscaster, the open, friendly and honest commercial announcer, the rugged and hard-headed "Kojak," the good-hearted, unsophisticated, tolerant "Edith Bunker."

Facial makeup is somewhat like the lights and setting of the stage: highlights, shadows, lines, angles. The key is in application. Some performers, because their role-personalities call for it, use heavy makeup—Liza Minnelli and Alice Cooper, for example. Others, such as newscasters, use comparatively little. For most TV performers, most of the time, makeup is used to give the skin a healthier tone and smoother texture under studio lights.

A water-base solid, cream stick or grease paint blends the skin color into the hairline, back to the ears and slightly under the chin. Light complexioned men frequently use a tan or rose hue one or two shades darker than their natural skin. Light complexioned women frequently use a pink hue. Black and dark brown complexioned performers usually use only a powder to reduce any facial gloss to a matte. Caucasian performers who seek a medium gray-scale tan may sit in the sun or under a sunlamp to obtain it. There is no ideal answer for makeup; each performer has different requirements, depending upon that person's natural skin, lips and hair coloring and the needs of the TV role. Many performers prefer to apply makeup with a brush, to protect the skin tissues from rubbing, while others blend in makeup with their fingers.

As noted earlier, the performer must be aware of lighting patterns and "marks." That is because lighting and, in many instances, camera angles and distances affect appearance as much as does makeup. The performer's appearance relies, therefore, not only on a makeup expert and the performer's own knowledge and skill, but on many technicians involved in the entire production.

Voice

There are many regional dialects in the United States and, according to many specialists, three major speech types: New England, Southern and Midwestern. Midwestern speech is generally accepted as the most desirable for national performers, based on the theory that no member of the audience should have any difficulty in understanding everything the performer says. Local and regional stations, however, may prefer local and regional dialects, to establish closer identification with the audience and more credibility in announcing commercials. It has been said that President Lyndon B. Johnson could speak with or without his Texas twang, depending upon the audience he was addressing. A growing school of thought is that multi-dialects on TV lend variety and richness to the language and speech patterns of the country. President Jimmy Carter's speech is an example of this.

Some performers have speech styles resulting from a functional or organic defect; one network newscaster has a faulty "l," another has a slight lisp. Such defects may be the result of psychological causes, functional causes such as improper use of the tongue, or organic causes such as missing teeth or improper overbite. Obviously, one can reach the top of the profession with such a defect. But young performers should be aware that it is easier without one. A speech psychologist, voice coach or speech pathologist should be consulted if a defect is suspected. Many a beginner does not realize that he or she may have a speech defect or severely pronounced regional dialect. Dialects are preserved by the speech patterns of the teachers and friends in the beginners' home areas. A young performer may even work successfully in TV in his or her region, but unless there is something special about the performer's personality that obviates a well-defined speech localism, moving to national network performing will be difficult. A Cotton Bowl Princess was once told by a producer of TV commercials: "You're beautiful and photogenic, but we can't use you until you've learned how to talk."

Awareness of the defect or dialect is the first step. Hearing the desirable model after correcting any psychological, functional or organic problem is the second step. Third is repeating the model at the conscious level until the difference is learned. The final step is to allow the desired speech pattern to sink into the unconscious level so that during the pressure of an on-the-spot newscast or a controversial interview or a dramatic scene at some later date the performer does not revert to a prior speech mode or dialect. The procedure may take a long time, and there is no easy substitute for the hard work required with specialists, listening to models, and hours of self-evaluation with a tape recorder.

Movement

Because television is a close-up medium, movement is minimal. That is, facial expressions must be carefully controlled, hand, arm and body movements should not be broad and sweeping, unless specifically called for by a director for a long shot, and walking or running have to be oriented to the movement of the camera and the size of the TV screen.

Any movement which is not absolutely essential to get across the idea, feeling or message should be eliminated. Unnecessary movements distract the audience. Except for acting situations where they fit the character, movements such as finger-tapping, ring-twisting, eyebrow-raising, ear-pulling, squinting should be avoided. That does not mean that a performer should be stiff and stilted. The key is to convey a sense of comfortableness, relaxation and trust to the viewer. Practice being graceful and fluid, with good posture. For non-acting performances, remember that there is a back to your chair. Sink back a trifle, combining a sense of relaxation while retaining high levels of energy and stature.

Studying theatre movement, dance and gymnastics can be very helpful. Remember that although some performers are presenting their own personalities to the audience, most performers are interpreters, presenting the purpose of the writer, with mental attitude and movement oriented toward that goal.

PERFORMANCE TYPES

All performers, including entertainers, journalists and announcers, combine a certain amount of acting ability and technique with their special expertise. Even performers who ostensibly are portraying themselves are creating roles. The host of the talk show may personally and privately not be outgoing, warm, witty and charming; the stand-up comedian may in reality be depressed and introspective; the announcer of commercials may spend long hours practicing how to convey a sense of personal trust and wisdom to the audience; the newscaster has to develop a style that reflects what the audience most respects and appreciates in a news reporter or commentator.

The principles of acting provide a base for all television performances. The basic material presented in the section below on acting applies to all performers; the sections following it reflect specific considerations relating to nondramatic types of television performance.

Basic Acting Techniques

The best training for the television performer is the stage. The basic elements of acting are learned in the theatre and if any talent does exist, it is there that it has a chance to come to the fore. (It is a peculiarity of film technique that although there are many fine performers in that medium, the ability of the medium to edit, create and recreate both visual and sound aspects of any performance permits a person of virtually no acting talent to become a successful star.) The stage performer will find that his or her abilities are transferred to television, insofar as character interpretation and development are concerned, almost in toto. The peculiar characteristics of the medium, however, require special adaptations for most effective use of its potentials and most efficient adjustment to its restrictions.

For the theatre-trained performer, television lacks most importantly an interaction with the audience. The performer cannot feel the audience response and play the subtleties of character delineation accordingly. Everything must be fixed beforehand, in anticipation of what the reaction of the small group watching in front of any given television set is likely to be.

Filmed or taped (with film-technique) television production—that is, where the scenes are shot individually, usually out of sequence—prevents the performer from building or maintaining a rising intensity of continuity of character development. On the other hand, live (or live-type taped) television does permit this and, in addition, provides the performer with the continuity of stage acting and the close-up intimacy of the film at the same time. Even here, however, the performer's advantages are complicated by restrictions. Because the sustained performance is in a close-up medium, the performer must never for a second step out of character. He or she must be acting, or reacting to the other performers, every moment, not knowing when the camera may pick him or her up—even when supposedly off camera, but still on the set. He or she must "freeze" in character before the next scene in case the camera comes in a second earlier. We have all watched the embarrassment of a performer who suddenly leaps into the characterization and scene after the camera has unexpectedly come on. We frequently see this happen with newscasters. The television performer must always be in the scene, listening, feeling and conveying the feeling.

The technical needs of television and the necessity of the director to have every shot planned clearly beforehand, with no unwarranted deviations once on the air, require the performer to make frequent compromises in motivations, interpretations and movements. For example, to meet the requirements of a particular shot, the performer may have to make a movement that is not clearly a part of the character being portrayed. Accordingly, he or she may then have to adjust character interpretation to find valid motivation for that particular movement. Usually, this kind of adjustment is made during the rehearsal period. Sometimes it is more difficult. For example, in one television production the actress was supposed to jump out of the armchair in which she was seated and cross the room to her injured husband. The camera, however, instead of getting the previous close-up on her from a distance with a long lens, as planned, had dollied in with a short lens and was completely blocking her way out of the chair. She had to change her character's motivation and action for that moment to justify her staying in the chair until the camera could be pulled back and an alternate shot pattern ad-libbed by the director.

Because of the impact of television's special characteristics, it is important that the performer become acquainted not only with the director's approaches and problems (see Chapter 5), but with the technical needs and potentials of camera movement, switcher-fader transitions, lighting, sound and special effects (see Chapters 2 and 6). A familiarity with the terminology and uses of equipment and directorial techniques can be of immeasurable help.

Pointers for Television Acting

The following are some of the more pertinent considerations for the television performer in making the most of the medium's potentials and at the same time adjusting to its restrictions.

The first five items are especially basic in their applicability to all types of television performing:

1) Television, as a close-up medium, requires movement, gesture and expression to be both natural and restrained at the same time. The performer must use the face and body with the fullest control, scaling down the entire pattern of movements and conveying all things with the minimum specific motion possible—unless told otherwise by the director. An economy of movement is important and each cross, gesture or move should be purposeful and the performer should clearly validate the reason for it. Make every action count. Excess movements are especially distracting because they are so close to the audience. The slightest facial expression can often serve for what would have to be a gross movement or gesture on the stage. A facial expression that conveys something at all times is important—and so is an avoidance of grimacing. In a close-up, if the audience either gets nothing or too much from your face, then your best solution as a performer may be to try to learn scene designing. Arm and hand movements must be carefully controlled or the gesture may go right off the edge of the television screen. Nose-to-nose playing may be required in two-shots of what may otherwise be natural conversation between two people; on the television screen the distance will look normal. Because of close-ups, not only must the performer avoid artificial and exaggerated movements, but must have an ease, a grace and a naturalness, as opposed to giving the audience the feeling that he or she may be ill at ease, awkward or self-conscious. Even static pictures can be given the essence of movement sometimes by the change of camera angle or distance.

2) Be aware of the mike placement and pick-up patterns so that you can help maintain the proper level of vocal reception while retaining a well-modulated tone. For example, in moving across a set you not only have to walk to the pattern set up for the camera, but you must time and space your vocal delivery to fit the microphone pick-up pattern.

3) Although you must always be aware of the location of the camera (the tally light on a camera tells you that it's the one that's on), never look directly into it unless so ordered by the director, or by the form of the program. Most TV dramas are representational in style; the commercial, the panel show and variety program, among other types, are presentational in nature and demand direct rapport with the cameras. In some

instances, in the representational drama, the performer is required to "cheat"—that is, for the purpose of an effective close shot, to turn somewhat away from the character with whom s/he is performing and toward the camera, so that s/he still seems to be in direct relationship with the other actor while at the same time the camera can pick up the desired shot of the face or body.

4) Because of the comparatively little rehearsal time in the pressure- and budget-controlled commercial television field, the performer must memorize quickly and adhere to what has been agreed upon.

5) Learn to take cues from the floor manager without looking directly at him or her and without being distracted from the business under way.

The following items apply more specifically to the dramatic performance situation:

6) The first sign of the professional performer is that he or she is constantly writing—making clear notes of all the directions given by the director and making certain that they can be executed with precise detail.

7) Precision is important. Because a specific shot has been prepared by the director, the performer must be able to repeat on cue the exact spatial position and bodily relationships set up during rehearsals. All directions must be memorized as accurately and fully as the character's lines.

8) Learn to "hit the chalk mark," the term applied to the exact place the performer has been rehearsed to be in for any given shot. The slightest error may throw off the entire composition of the shot. Yet, the actor or actress must hit the mark without being obvious or mechanical about it.

9) Never drop out of character.

10) Remember that the director is always with you—unlike the theatre where, after the curtain goes up, the director is gone. In TV the director is still there, calling the shots. Since the director controls the cameras, the performer must follow directions explicitly. If the performer is unhappy with any direction or acting requirement, he or she must say so during an early rehearsal before the pattern of the show is set.

11) Although the performer in commercial television usually does not have to oversee his or her own costumes or apply his or her own make-up, the good performer always works as closely as possible with the costumer to see that the costume fits the needs of the characterization; and he or she should know enough about makeup to clarify the character's needs to the makeup person or to put on his or her own, if necessary. (Many experienced performers insist on applying their own make-up.) As noted earlier, makeup for television must be extremely light and subtle. Be careful of aging during a show, of beards, wigs and the use of

lines. Usually, only a lightly applied base with light and shadow tones, as opposed to lining, is effective. Avoid extremes of black and white in costumes. Stick to the middle tones and avoid clashing colors, striped or wavy lines. (For a clarification of costume and makeup needs, see Chapter 6.)

12) While the above principles apply primarily to television acting technique, as exemplified by live or live-type taped television production, many of the points made here are applicable or adaptable to film acting. Inasmuch as films comprise such a large part of the drama presentations on television, it is desirable for the potential performer to become fully familiar with film acting requirements as an important supplement to a knowledge of television acting techniques.

Announcing

The television announcer needs the desirable vocal qualities of the radio announcer: control of volume and pitch, pleasant quality, clear diction and accurate pronunciation. The addition of sight, however, necessitates special adaptation. The television announcer's vocal qualities should match his or her physical appearance—an appropriate, optimum pitch, for example. The announcer must not only know the proper use of the microphone, but also the proper use of the camera. More than any other type, this requires the presentational approach—talking directly to the audience, coming directly as a visitor into the home.

In addition to knowing how to "read" well—that is, to present the ideas smoothly and with effective interpretation—a television announcer must have a broad background. This background should include a knowledge of his or her duties, limitations, and impact on the audience as a part of the television process (see Chapter 1); function in relation to the producer and director and to the artistic and routine processes of production (as described in Chapters 3 and 5); place in terms of the technical and staging potentials and needs of the program (as delineated in Chapters 2 and 6); and familiarity with the various commercial announcements, forms of presentation and program types (see Chapter 4). In addition, inasmuch as television is in great part a medium of news and public affairs, the announcer should have a broad background in the philosophical, historical, social, economic and political influences of our time. In fact, most networks and stations now require a college education or its equivalent as a condition for employing announcers.

Above all, the announcer must remember that he or she is a guest in someone's home, not portraying a fictional character. Behave with the kind of honesty and sincerity that you would expect from a guest. Inasmuch as, most of the time, you are persuading people of something to believe or do, speak and behave with good taste. Be aware that no matter how good and effective your vocal presentation, the slightest disconcerting facial or physical movement, the smallest note of falsity in a gesture may obviate all of your words. Much television commercial announcing is done "voice-over," so in some instances the visual aspects do not apply.

The announcer conveys not only ideas, but feelings and personality. In that respect he or she is also an actor or actress, and should be thoroughly familiar with the special requirements of television acting for a basic development as an announcer.

Newscasters

The media have gone through periods in which the news was presented by people who may or may not have been journalists, but attractive personalities. These "readers" do not gather or edit news, but deliver a prepared script. In the early days of radio, newspaper and wire service journalists brought their investigative and reporting abilities to the sound medium, but the visual appeal of television tended to concentrate on personalities who drew larger audiences than the news itself. Some newscasters, such as Walter Cronkite, David Brinkley and Barbara Walters, share equally with movie stars as the dominant national personalities.

Some news formats deemphasize the newscaster by concentrating on film or tape of the actual event, featuring the participants in that happening, with an unseen announcer doing voice-over narration. Some news programs have concentrated on newscasters who are strong as journalists, with the attractiveness of their voice, appearance and manner secondary. Ideally, of course, the most desirable newscaster is one who is a good reporter, editor *and* personality.

Specific backgrounds and kinds of personalities differ with the kind of news presented: straight news, interviews, sports, weather, human interest features, among others.

Entertainers

Singers, dancers and other variety artists usually have developed their particular acts in night clubs and principally adapt them to television. Some have created new personalities particularly effective for television and have developed reputations through TV far exceeding their previous work. A few performers, like Carol Burnett, have become fixtures on the TV screen. Some older, established personalities as well as some new rock stars are in great demand and require large fees for appearing on TV specials or as guests on regular variety programs.

Personalities

The performers who host talk shows, quiz and audience participation programs, interview programs, panel shows and similar programs are attractive, frequently unique personalities. Performers such as Tony Brown, Merv Griffin, Dinah Shore, Mike Wallace and others already mentioned come across as strongly as the people who perform on their programs or whom they interview. They specialize in being themselves—or, rather, the public image of themselves that they have developed for the television audience. Although not trained as journalists, they may broadcast the news; although not trained as entertainers, they may sing, dance and tell jokes; although not trained as political scientists, they may interview politicians and other public figures. As with newscasters, the ideal personality is the one who has training and/or ability in the particular subject field as well as appealing to the audience through his or her individual attractiveness. Some of the more successful ones have this combination.

Their strongest ability is to bring out the feelings and ideas and personalities of their guests. They are good catalysts and are able to keep a program running fast and smooth and to make it exciting. The audience finds them fun and/or stimulating to be with. They are usually well-versed on a great many subjects. They are able to improvise in extemporaneous situations. These are the superstars of television and the ones the audience usually feels closest to as individual human beings.

Non-professionals

With television providing a forum, principally through talk and interview shows, for experts and human interest experiences from all fields, more and more non-professional performers who are professionals in other areas are becoming media performers. Politicians, executives, physicians, educators, consumer advocates and clergy are among those who are becoming, for large and small audiences, TV stars. Although these people are respected for their knowledge of a particular subject more than for their performing ability, the infrequency of their appearances and the genuineness of their appeals attract an audience. A few years ago these non-professionals paid little attention to the performing aspects of the TV medium; but with the increasing realization that the public identifies their causes in terms of their personal TV impact, they have begun to use the media more and more effectively.

Many representatives of various professions are successful in person or on speaking platforms, but are not able to carry a favorable public relations image to television. It frequently takes some time and some unfavorable publicity before organizations, particularly business and industry, select as their TV representatives people who come across well in the medium.

Some professions provide the media with entertainment as well as personalities. The clergy have been particularly successful in this regard, with ministers as dramatic as any actor and with religious rallies approaching the level of entertainment spectaculars.

For years educators have preferred to believe that instructional television programs should be taught by teachers. Unfortunately, not all—or, indeed, many—teachers on TV are also performers, and we find many educational TV programs dull and boring. Coupled with unimaginative production aimed at merely duplicating on TV the kinds of materials found in the classroom, too many ETV programs are of the "talking head" variety. More and more, ETV producers are becoming aware that TV teachers must be attractive performers. With the proper materials and a script, the good performer, even knowing nothing about a given subject, can make a more effective impact on the student then can the knowledgeable teacher who cannot perform. As instructional TV programs become more sophisticated and take advantage of the medium itself, most important are the teacher-performers who can interact with the student-viewers in direct or indirect participation in discussions, projects and other means of personal involvement. As in other performance types, ETV needs people with a combination of educational expertise and personal charisma. This applies as well to closed-circuit television, used not only in schools, but to a large degree in business and industry training programs.

No matter what the performance type, however, the goal is to bring credibility to whatever message is presented. Hopefully, the performer will not only bring attractiveness to the presentation, but judgment, responsibility, fairness, honesty and perspective as well.

Procedure: Rehearsal and Performance

Some stars have such strong egos or confidence or both that they sometimes think they don't need much rehearsal time. They forget that it was long preparation and practice that made them stars in the first place. (There are a few stars who are overnight fads and whose success is based on a quirk of audience need and public relations; because they may not have any talent to sharpen, they don't need rehearsals in terms of their personal art.)

But television is a group effort. There are not only a great many performers in any given show, but a large technical crew. All of these people need adequate rehearsal if the program isn't to be in chaos by the time it is filmed or taped for air presentation. If you become a big star, remember that the other people associated with the show need rehearsal, even if you think you don't, and they can't rehearse unless all the elements in the show, including your part, are there.

Types of Rehearsals

Dramas, variety programs and shows with detailed and complicated segments and complete scripts need complete rehearsals. The drama, for example, may begin with script interpretation, with the director and all the performers present, then character analysis and development, followed by blocking, with camera and other technical personnel observing, and gradually moving toward run-throughs with costumes, makeup and all the technical effects, by which time all personnel associated with the program will be involved. The final rehearsals are on camera, in the studio, ironing out all problems before taping or filming or, in some small, local or public stations, a live performance.

Rehearsal hours are limited by union contract and are expensive, and it is critical that all performers (and other personnel) be precisely on time.

Some programs, such as panel shows, audience participation programs, interviews and similar productions which do not have complete scripts and include some extemporaneous (although carefully planned) sequences, have what are called abbreviated rehearsals. This includes the opening of the show, transitions between program segments, and the closing of the program. Occasionally, in small stations without adequate personnel and on programs involving non-professionals from the community, there is no time for rehearsal. If you are the station announcer assigned to host such a program, you simply do your best to practice the opening, transitions and closing on your own, and to communicate some basic instructions to the non-professionals when they arrive at the studio.

With the increased use of film and tape editing techniques in television, some performers rehearse and perform only those parts of the script in which they appear, and sometimes do not see the entire production until they watch it on television with the rest of the audience. Some programs, such as situation comedies, are frequently shot in New York-style continuous-action sequence in front of live audiences. Audience participation quiz shows may be shot in multiples, that is, several programs in one day in front of different audiences.

The performer should be so well-prepared, thoroughly rehearsed and confident in his or her role or job that he or she can be flexible and adapt to any form of final performance and to any emergency.

For a detailed rundown of rehearsal and performance procedures, see Chapters 3 and 5.

Cueing

When a performer arrives at a studio for a performance, preparation should be complete. The script has been memorized or is on cue cards. The blocking has been rehearsed or is generally understood. If there have been sufficient rehearsals, the performer is already acquainted with the performing area and with costumes and makeup. Usually, a final technical rehearsal precedes the taping or filming. Once the performance is under way, the director is in the control room, separated from the performers. Yet, there is a continuing need to communicate. This is where cues come in. During the rehearsal period and before the airing or taping, the performer has been given visual and verbal cues or check-points. These continue during the performance.

Oral and visual cues are given by the director through someone on the floor, usually the floor manager or the camera operators, who have intercoms linking them with the control room. A performer must know who is giving the cues, where that person will be, and how visible the cue will be. Once cued, the performer must react instantly. In stop-and-go taping and filming situations following the Hollywood style of production, the director may halt the action and give directions through a studio loudspeaker or even leave the control room or film control area and meet directly with the performers.

Typical oral cueing prior to the beginning of a TV program is announced by the floor director: ''One minute to air (or tape) . . . 30 seconds. Quiet in the studio . . . Ten seconds. Stand by. (A countdown may begin: "Five, four, three, two, one—) Cue."

At the ten-second "stand by," the floor director raises a hand with the flat of the palm toward the talent or points an index finger toward the on-air lens. On cue from the director, received via a headset, the floor director points directly at the performer, who responds instantly. Most visual cues concern timing—the minutes or seconds remaining before the program is over, wrap up, stretch, or speed up; some deal with movement—the floor director waves the performer from one camera to the on-air lens of another, especially if the talent cannot tell from the tally lights which camera is on the air. A performer may cue the director by placing the palms of the hands on a desk in front, or on top of his or her thighs to indicate that he or she intends to stand. Some cues have to do with transitions; if a floor director taps the palm of one hand with the index finger of the other, this signals the talent to go to a spot announcement or commercial; if the FD assumes the pose of looking through a lens while cranking a camera, this means go to film. For the most part, as long as the performer remains on his or her marks, sticks to the script or program outline and performs as the program was rehearsed, cueing is minimal.

At the show's conclusion, the talent does not move until the floor director gives the cue, such as "That's it. Good job. Thanks a lot," or until the cameras have obviously broken to another set. A common error for a novice is to move, especially to take one's eyes from the camera lens, or grimace prematurely. Such action might ruin the take.

Illustrations of cues may be found in Chapter 5, page 252.

The Camera

The camera shows everything in its field of view. Whether a performer is scratching a leg or adjusting a microphone or making an unpleasant expression, the camera will show it. Performers must assume that they are on the air all of the time during the airing or taping of a program; therefore, they never do or say anything that could not go over the air.

Cameras are frequently big and clumsy. They may move slowly from set to set. Nowadays the zoom lens adds fast and fluid variation from a wide shot covering the entire set to an extreme closeup of the performer. No matter how many lenses are visible, a camera has only one that is "hot" or on the air. This hot lens is in a different position on different cameras depending on the model. The performer should know, from rehearsals or briefings, which lens is hot. Each camera has a red tally light indicating when it is on the air.

Generally speaking, except in a dramatic program or an interview, a performer looks directly into the hot lens when he or she is on. Performers relating directly to the audience (such as singers, newscasters and speechmakers), frequently perform for a mythical person fixed somewhere in the dark space above the TV camera. Frequently performers who must look directly into the lens transfer their gaze from one camera to another as the shots are changed.

Such movement should be signaled in advance by the floor director by waving a hand from one hot lens to another. Prompting devices—scripts from which performers are reading, cue cards and electronic devices—are commonplace and performers should get used to working skillfully with them.

The Microphone

The engineer will adjust the level of the various microphones on the console so that every performer's voice blends in with the rest of the program. It is important to cooperate with each request for a "level check, please." There are some general techniques performers should know for the most effective use of microphones.

If you must have a microphone around your neck, place it under your clothing—a tie or scarf will do. If the clothing muffles the sound, the engineer will tell you. Fasten the lavalier. If it moves, it may hit buttons or jewelry; even swinging over the surface of a shirt may be noisy. A jacket or patterned blouse helps women, particularly, to draw attention away from the microphone. To minimize its visibility, attach it to your belt, being certain to leave enough slack so that it will not pull on your clothing. If you must hold a microphone while standing, remember that the long cable will show. It is distracting to see a performer wrestling with a long microphone cable or being trailed by a long black cable resembling a rat's tail. Preplan so that you have ample cable to go wherever you must during the performance.

If you are working with a microphone stand, remember that it causes a resounding thud if accidentally kicked. If the microphone is suspended on a boom or is overhead, avoid the temptation to move out from under the beam.

In general, if you are singing or speaking, one microphone, preferably unseen, should be enough. If you use a musical instrument, mike it separately. If you are part of a round-table discussion, one good omnidirectional microphone is adequate. If you are on a panel, seated in a straight line, usually one microphone for every two or three people is satisfactory. Do not attempt to pass the microphone, because it will make noise. If you are in a musical group, all principal singers and instruments must be miked separately. If you are in concert, however, the orchestra may be picked up on one microphone suspended in the center of the auditorium, in addition to personal microphones for selected participants.

UNIONS

Networks, recognized film companies, larger stations and, in some parts of the country, smaller ones, are generally unionized. Some sections of the country which have strong anti-union traditions or laws do not have performers' unions in broadcasting. The nation's fifth largest city, Houston, is primarily a non-union market. Non-union talent get whatever compensation the highly competitive performers' situation will allow. Union performers get no less than the minimum agreed to by union-station contract, and this is virtually always higher than non-union fees.

Many performers belong to more than one union. The American Federation of Television and Radio Artists (AFTRA) and the Screen Actors Guild (SAG) represent media performers. Actor's Equity Association (AEA) represents performers on the legitimate stage, in stock companies and industrial shows; the American Guild of Variety Artists (AGVA) covers nightclub performers. AEA and AGVA members who perform on television join AFTRA and/or SAG, as appropriate. In the early 1970s many Black broadcasters, particularly D.J.-announcers, became members of the National Association of Television and Radio Announcers (NATRA).

SAG, originally the theatrical motion picture performers union, retains jurisdiction in that category and represents performers in all TV shows and commercials made on film. AFTRA covers the non-film categories. AFTRA and SAG contracts establish minimum wages called "scale." Scale is tied to the lengths of the programs and to use—whether local, regional, national or international use. Contracts also cover residuals for re-use of programs. There are different scales for principal performers, for those speaking under five lines, for non-speaking roles, for extras, for specialty acts, for voice-over, for dancers, singers, groups, and the various other performer categories. AFTRA and SAG contracts define rehearsal hours and days, guaranteed days of employment, meal and rest periods, credits, wardrobe, hair and make-up requirements, retakes, understudies, stand-ins, vacations, holidays, overtime, remotes, auditions, travel requirements, dressing rooms and other working conditions. AFTRA and SAG have won for their members a pension and welfare plan and a health and insurance plan, both paid for by the producers.

In 1977 the initiation fee for AFTRA was $300 and $44 for first-year dues; for SAG it was $500* and $50. In subsequent years dues are paid according to income. One cannot become a member of either professional union until one has been offered and accepted a contract to perform in a program or at a station covered by union contract. Membership, therefore, is limited to bona fide professionals. In 1977 AFTRA minimum scales included the following: half-hour program—principal performer, $260; under five lines, $125.75; extras, $70.75; one-hour program—principal performer, $350; under five lines, $155.25; extras, $90. (* Varies with region where performer joins.)

A PERFORMING CAREER

Every performer has three primary concerns: "How do I look? How do I sound? How good is my material?" Good material can make a performer. Conversely, an exciting personality can enhance mediocre material. Because television is essentially a "personality" business, the performer is usually more marketable than the material. The person—that is, the sound, the look, the image—can be "packaged" and "delivered" to an audience over and over again until the right wrapping has been found. If the audience likes the performer's image and sound, that performer might have instant and overwhelming fame through a single TV appearance. Such situations, despite the glamour stressed in fan magazines, are extremely rare. Most performers who make it have done so through years and years of study, practice, struggle and failure.

If you have a unique look, if you have a unique voice, if you have some unique talent, if you have the capacity for hard work, if you have sufficient ambition to prevent you from being easily discouraged, if you have great patience—then it's worth a try. And you must also have foresight. You must be able to recognize your opportunity when it comes along and drop everything else to take it. And then you must work inexhaustibly, often without reward, often with criticism, to remain in competition for professional status.

There is no certain or single way to become a successful performer in television. You can go to school, take courses in communications, speech, drama, journalism, music, art and other subjects. You can be on the debate team, have leads in plays and achieve recognition in related fields. You can go to college, vocational school, professional schools and universities. You can gain professional experience in summer stock, nightclubs, radio and TV stations and pizza parlors. All of these can be helpful and you can do them all and still not make it.

Performing is unstable. Only a small percentage of professional performers—those in the professional unions by virtue of already having worked professionally—have jobs at any given time. Most performers pay the rent by working as salespersons, in restaurants, as stock clerks, in secretarial positions and in other jobs that provide them a living but are easy to leave at a moment's notice in case the break comes. Some highly talented performers spend 20 or more years of their lives waiting on tables, never or hardly ever working in their profession, in television. It is estimated that some 80% of AFTRA and SAG members, the bona fide professionals, make less than $2,000 a year in their chosen professions, as performers. Yet, there is the handful who make it big, and for most young people who wish to be performers, the dream is always there.

Salaries vary greatly. From $1 million a year for a superstar newscaster and interviewer on a national network to less than $10,000 a year for a combined newscaster and interviewer and board operator and time salesperson in a small local station. Newspersons in middle market America have salaries in the $10,000 to $20,000 range. Big cities pay $40,000 to $50,000 for some news anchorpersons. New York City and a few very large markets put some newscasters in the $100,000 category. The networks pay more for top-flight personalities. If the TV station invests in your promotion (billboards, news stories, cross-plugs), you know they consider you a money-maker and will pay you accordingly. Many dramatic and entertainment stars earn in the hundreds of thousands and millions and many who are not so well known but who work regularly earn a good living. But remember that competition is intense and that success is the exception rather than the rule.

Locally originated programming is primarily of the news and information genre. It is relatively stable and good income employment. Local entertainment is produced primarily during times of high station income and is therefore unstable, infrequent and low-paid. Major programs, including nationally distributed shows and most regionally distributed shows, whether for network or syndication use, are produced in Los Angeles or New York. Commercials are produced in additional places such as Chicago, Cincinnati, Dallas and Atlanta. Local commercials are usually produced locally. If you are interested in freelance performing, as opposed to staff jobs with stations, you will have to establish yourself in those cities where the kinds of programs you might be on are produced. Most performers now live in either Los Angeles or New York, with the successful ones maintaining residences in both places.

Assess yourself. What is there within you that can make a unique contribution to television? Introspection to find the nature of your own being is extremely difficult. It can be painful and contrary to peer group identification and acceptance. It can be inconsistent with one's personal and private psyche. A TV performer who makes it is, at least in public, different, and must accept that special place to maintain recognition and success.

Bibliography

Duerr, Edwin, *Radio and Television Acting*. Westport, Conn.: Greenwood, 1972 (reprint of 1950 edition).

Ewing, Sam, *You're On the Air*. Blue Ridge Summit, Penna.: TAB Books, 1972.

Hawes, William, *The Performer in Mass Media*. New York: Hastings House, 1978.

Hyde, Stuart W., *Television and Radio Announcing*. Boston: Houghton Mifflin, 1971. 2nd edition.

Lewis, Bruce, *The Technique of Television Announcing*. New York: Hastings House, 1966.

Aspiring performers, particularly dramatic actors and actresses, should consult works on acting techniques for the stage. A theatre coach or drama professor will help you choose appropriate books from the hundreds published and the dozens likely to be found in the card catalogue of even a modest library.

GERTRUDE L. BARNSTONE

● Gertrude Barnstone has been the producer of "Sundown's Treehouse," a children's program, and Director of Community Relations for KPRC-TV, the NBC affiliate in Houston, has been a consultant on minority group liaison and producer-planner of children's programs for a Houston cable television system, and has taught public broadcasting at the University of Houston. She has produced and conducted a "Texans in Washington" interview series and an interview-talk show on Houston radio stations. She has also served as a member of the Federal Communications Commission's national Committee for the Instructional Television Fixed Service.

Her other communications work includes service as a member of the Executive Board of the Texas Film Commission and as producer of a film on rehabilitation of handicapped children. She has been a consultant on the development of educational, artistic, cultural and recreational facilities for a "new town" in Texas and served as director of development for the Institute for Storm Research in Houston.

As elected member of the Houston School Board from 1964 to 1969, she was credited with the leadership in providing the first equal educational opportunities for all children in a large city in the south. She has also been chairperson of the State of Texas Women's Equity Action League, vice-chairperson of the Houston chapter of the American Civil Liberties Union, and board member of a number of social service and minority rights organizations.

As a painter and sculptress, her works are in a number of private collections and as part of public and private buildings in the Houston area. She has also worked as a welder in industry. She is the recipient of awards from ethnic, interracial, educational and social organizations. She is a graduate of Rice University.

8

ALTERNATIVE SYSTEMS

BY WILLIAM HAWES AND
GERTRUDE L. BARNSTONE

ALTHOUGH PUBLIC ATTENTION has been devoted primarily to open circuit or broadcast television, alternative systems have become important in their own right and are steadily growing in number and impact. Some alternative systems distribute their signals solely or principally by coaxial cable (wire), some through microwave, and some use combinations of two or more methods. Some systems are closed circuit, others are a combination of both open and closed circuit. Principal alternative systems are community antenna or cable television (CATV), closed circuit television (CCTV), Instructional Television Fixed Service (ITFS), Multipoint Distribution Service (MDS) and satellites.

BACKGROUND

Although many American families live in markets served by only one or two TV stations, "ideally each American home should have access to a minimum of five stations—affiliates of the three national commercial TV networks, at least one educational station, and one independent commercial station. The normal coverage pattern of conventional broadcasting networks, stations and translators simply cannot provide this choice of service in all areas."[1] *CATV*, a direct receiver-to-home type of distribution, was developed to meet this need. Originally, CATV brought a full range of program services including broadcast

319

channels, local origination programs and other services into remote areas of the country such as mountainous regions where broadcasting through the airwaves was difficult or impossible.[2] CATV began to grow about the same time as did commercial television broadcasting. "By 1948, there were 108 authorized television stations. But, at that point, unanticipated problems in picture reception resulting from electrical interference prompted the Commission to put a freeze on further station construction while it reexamined assumptions about the minimum distances necessary between transmitters. This freeze lasted from 1948 to 1952 and it was then that cable systems got started. It was expected that cable would be strictly a short-term proposition and that with the lifting of the freeze, and the growth of new stations, the demand for cable would drop off."[3] CATV was not driven out by the spread of new broadcasting stations; instead, cable systems began using microwave radio equipment to bring in program material from distant cities, and repeater-type broadcast stations called translators were developed. CATV continued to develop relatively unregulated but without vast audiences and, consequently, without vast advertising revenues for support. Gradually CATV moved into the suburbs and finally into the top 100 markets of the nation where, frequently, reflection, blanketing and electrical noise from tall buildings make ideal reception difficult or impossible. By 1978 CATV had enrolled over 12 million subscribers in the 50 states served by over 3,800 operating cable systems in more than 8,500 communities. CATV's steady growth indicates that by the mid-1980s cable may serve at least one out of every four homes.

A communication *satellite* is a spacecraft placed in orbit synchronous with the earth's rotation and which receives and transmits communication between earth stations. It is possible to have direct satellite-to-home reception which could perform some of the functions of CATV: radio and TV programs, computer data, radio-telephone calls, news information and photographs. The first satellite relays—Telstar (1962), Syncom (1963), Early Bird (1965)—depended upon expensive ground-station equipment. Although the standard costs are drastically reduced, satellite-to-home rebroadcasting raises complex economic and political problems because of its potential effect on existing investments and impact on international publics.[4] Homeowners would also have to invest in special antenna and converter equipment. Another problem is that satellites cannot provide local TV services. Those would have to come from local stations or systems like CATV.

"When a CATV company originates its own program material and sends it via cable to subscriber homes, it becomes an example of a *closed-circuit* distribution system. In closed-circuit systems, wire or cable connects the originating and receiving points, leaving no radio (open) links in the communications circuit."[5]

CCTV developed concurrently with broadcasting and serves many needs, from highly developed systems in education, medicine and government to the automated TV used for observation in banks, offices, stores, factories, elevators and similar places. In 1978 about 2,000 school systems were using CCTV. It is estimated that by the mid-1980s American business will be spending $1.5 billion for its CCTV and other audio-visual systems. Unlike CATV, satellites, ITFS and MDS, closed circuit television is not regulated by the government.

Instructional Television Fixed Service has been called an "on-the-air closed circuit system" because it combines features of both. In July, 1963 the FCC opened 31 channels in the 2500-2690 megahertz frequency range for use by educational institutions and organizations. According to FCC *Rules and Regulations* (Section 74.901), ITFS is a fixed station operated by an educational organization and used primarily for the transmission of visual and aural instructional, cultural, and other types of educational material to one or more fixed receiving locations. An applicant may be licensed for as many as four channels to serve a single area. The FCC rules further provide that ITFS signals be limited in power so they can be received only at locations which are a relatively short distance from the transmitting site. ITFS is a distribution system in which preselected receiving points are connected by radio signals. Transmissions are not intended for direct home reception by the general public. Therefore, ITFS is neither a broadcast (open-circuit) system nor a closed-circuit system in the sense of wired (cable) installations. In addition to serving school and college classrooms, ITFS has immense potential for continuing education with tailored-to-the-area programming going into inner city churches, community centers and prisons from nearby educational institutions. In 1969 the FCC authorized ITFS systems to use low-power response stations using voice transmissions at remote classrooms to allow two-way verbal exchange between students and their instructors. This was later expanded to include the transmission of data signals on these talk-back channels so that data processing techniques could be utilized. In 1971 the FCC regularized the ITFS service and at the same time designated the top three channels in the band for Operational Fixed purposes. These are licensed to business and industry for a variety of purposes, including field communication and surveillance. Operational fixed channels are used principally by oil companies. They may also be used by local government.

Multipoint Distribution Service is transmitted at 2150 MHz, and is similar to ITFS except that it is used for commercial purposes. The first application for an MDS license was in 1971 by Taft Broadcasting Company, Houston. Within four years there were over 400 applications on file at the FCC with several systems in operation. A common carrier system, an MDS transmitter installation costs about $65,000. A user pays an installation fee plus time costs when the service is used—similar to the use and payment of long-distance phone service. The Taft system has been principally used during conventions to disseminate advertising and information to groups at the convention. MDS licensees see a broad use of the service, including video distribution of film libraries to branch schools, diocese-wide programming of theological instruction, training the unemployed, verifying fraudulent checks, viewing police lineups, industry training programs and business conferences. Hotels use MDS to distribute news, weather, time, temperature, financial and other information to guests. By 1976 a growing use of MDS was as a distribution system for "Pay-TV."

Cable and CCTV systems are gradually becoming major consumers of TV equipment and, as employers, are offering new areas for creative talent, especially for the young and inexperienced. Schools once devoted exclusively to traditional broadcasting curricula are now giving some consideration to these alternative systems of television. The material that follows offers some approaches for the student and the new professional in the areas of Cable, Closed Circuit Television, Instructional Television Fixed Service and Multipoint Distribution Service.

OPERATING THE SYSTEMS

Administration

The complex administration of an alternative TV system concerns itself with organization, legal requirements, personnel, funding and development, and technical operations. Each of these areas will be briefly sketched here with references for further study. Special attention is given to CATV revenues and costs and technical operations.

Organization. Tables of organization for alternative systems resemble those of broadcast stations. (See Fig. 1.) At the top is the board of directors representing the broad policies and financial interests of the TV operation. Under it is the chief officer of the organization—the CATV manager or director of media (titles vary)—who has the principal responsibility for making decisions and spending money wisely on a day-to-day basis. Next are the department heads. A few department heads cover many tasks for cable and CCTV. Some departments such as sales may be excluded from a tax- or privately-supported CCTV operation. Reporting to each department head is a staff which varies greatly in size. An alternative TV system usually has fewer people than a broadcast station; however, some CATV or CCTV operations may have as large a staff as some of the smaller TV stations. In one large urban market the smallest staff at a network affiliated TV station is 97 fulltime employees. A nearby cable system serving a tiny fraction of the same market has 40 fulltime employees.

Legal Requirements. CATV is franchised by local governments to citizen groups. A franchise is an agreement between the owners and local officials stating the services to be provided, the schedule for completion, citizen participation, use of public facilities, taxation, violation fees and technical details. In addition, CATV is regulated by the FCC, and new systems must obtain an FCC certificate of compliance. ITFS and MDS use microwave and are licensed by the FCC to educational organizations and private operating companies, respectively. Satellites are regulated by the Communications Satellite Act, the President, the National Aeronautics and Space Administration (NASA) and the

SAMPLE TABLES OF ORGANIZATION

Community Antenna Television (CATV)

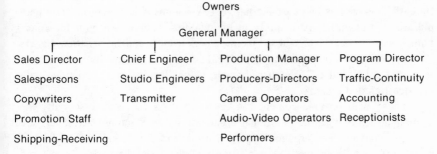

Owners

General Manager

Sales Director	Chief Engineer	Production Manager	Program Director
Salespersons	Studio Engineers	Producers-Directors	Traffic-Continuity
Copywriters	Transmitter	Camera Operators	Accounting
Promotion Staff		Audio-Video Operators	Receptionists
Shipping-Receiving		Performers	

Closed Circuit Television (CCTV)

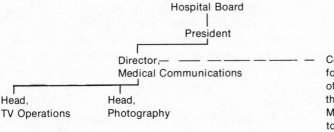

Hospital Board

President

Director,— —— ——— —— ——- — Coordinator
Medical Communications   for Distribution
                                          of Medical Information
Head,   Head,   throughout Hospital,
TV Operations Photography   Medical Center or
                                          to Several Centers

Instructional Television Fixed Service (ITFS)

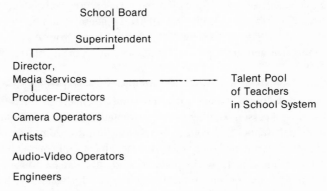

School Board

Superintendent

Director,
Media Services —— —— ——- —— Talent Pool
                              of Teachers
Producer-Directors   in School System

Camera Operators

Artists

Audio-Video Operators

Engineers

Fig. 1

FCC. Although closed circuit TV does not use the airways and is not federally regulated or franchised by local authorities, it must comply, as do all alternative TV systems, with appropriate federal, state and local laws concerning copyrights, hiring practices and contracts.

Personnel. Managers, sales people, communications lawyers, engineers, installers, repair persons and manufacturers are among the personnel required by CATV as well as by other alternative TV systems. Capable production people are also essential, particularly in major cities where many non-TV entertainments (sports, stage, clubs, cinemas, parks, etc.) and information centers (lecture halls, schools, museums, newspapers, etc.) compete for audience attention. CATV and CCTV must compete in quality, diversity and price with broadcasting and cinema.

Those who provide content for CATV and CCTV need essentially the same qualifications as the traditional broadcast-TV production staff. There are some differences. The production person needs to be multi-talented and to do many different things well. A good grasp of the capabilities of miniaturized equipment is essential. He or she is often inexperienced but eager to learn and optimistic about the future of alternative media, and, in many cases, willing to work for less money than one would earn in broadcasting, at least at first. One needs to know how to scrounge and reuse materials. One frequently has to work long hours, overtime and unattractive schedules. Until the cable industry finds an adequate means of financial support, such relative hardships will continue for those seeking positions in production. CCTV and CATV can in many ways be compared with embryonic commercial TV in the late 1930s and post-World War II 1940s. With broadcast TV now virtually impossible to break into for a newcomer, aspiring entertainers, newscasters and production personnel—producers, directors, switchers, audio operators, camera operators, staging crews—will find these growing industries more likely places in which to find jobs. For example, in the mid-1970s the average number of resident audio visual specialists reported by 276 industrial firms from AT&T to Xerox was between five and eight persons, with several reporting staffs of between 10 and 20.[6]

Keeping in mind that the administrative and technical personnel, that is, non-production personnel, may constitute as many as three-fourths of the employees, a person wanting to take advantage of these opportunities should combine high school and college courses in business administration, law, marketing, engineering and other related areas, along with courses in communications. Those who want to be in production should pursue courses in the fine arts, languages, history, government, sociology and psychology. Inasmuch as media experience is highly desirable, a student should participate in co-curricular activities such as plays, music, dance, sports, school newspapers, art displays, speech contests and writing competitions as well as the school's radio and TV stations or systems in an attempt to gain experience and recognition.

Funding and Development. Public and private investments in alternative

TV equipment and programs are in the billions of dollars. Obsolescence is fairly rapid, especially for the less expensive gear, and indications are that this factor will continue to be high. Many educational institutions and industries are presently storing TV equipment that they do not use and cannot economically repair. We often hear teachers say: "I cannot fix our videotape recorder. Even if I can get our contract repair shop to pick it up soon, it will probably be out of service three or four weeks." Distribution of new equipment has far outdistanced an ability to maintain it. Nevertheless, costs for many alternative TV systems are quite modest compared to broadcast operations. For example, an initial investment for a citizens' group that wants to improve its knowledge of media may be $2,500 for a portable videotape camera and playback unit; $5,000 to $10,000 may provide sufficient CCTV equipment for a small privately owned clinic where a physician wants to videotape and observe patients undergoing therapy in several treatment rooms.

Prior to the 1970s alternate TV systems were mainly black and white, but by the mid-'70s many systems had converted to color. A basic ITFS system could be put in operation for as little as $50,000. On the other hand, one ITFS installation built in the early 1970s invested $250,000 for the plant (a wing of an existing building) and $500,000 for color equipment. (See the section on "Production Facilities.")

Cable Revenues and Costs

As has commercial broadcasting, CATV has developed through private enterprise. A businessperson or several of them put up sufficient capital from their own resources or from bank loans to hire the personnel, build the facilities, wire the location and establish the programs. Many commercial broadcasters and newspaper owners have CATV companies, except in the largest markets where FCC rules prohibit them from doing so. There are four principal sources of income for cable: subscriber fees, advertising, leased channels and pay television.

Subscriber Fees. The most obvious source of income for CATV is a fee, usually paid monthly. In 1977 the general range was $6 to $9 per month. The average cable system had about 3,130 subscribers, with Pennsylvania having the most systems (over 400) and California the most subscribers (over 1.5 million). Some cable systems have less than 100 subscribers; Teleprompter in 1977 was the largest multi-system owner (MSO) with over one million subscribers. Multiplication shows that the average cable system charging its 3,130 subscribers $6.00 a month would gross only $18,780. The amount would not cover expenses, much less programming. Nevertheless, the potential is there if the number of subscribers is increased. Outside salespeople frequently go from door to door explaining the benefits of cable and signing up customers.

A CATV system may also charge an installation fee, averaging about $15. This fee is often waived by a system initially, so that subscribers will be encouraged to take the service. There is a slight additional initial hook-up fee and monthly subscription fee for each additional TV set in a subscriber's home.

Advertising. Over 200 CATV systems have advertising as a second source of income, with rates from $5 to $200 per minute. Small businesses which do not feel they can afford spots on commercial TV stations frequently buy spots and programs on cable systems which reach an audience in the immediate vicinity of the businesses. In general, however, advertising on a local origination channel is minimal, totaling about $3.5 million in 1977 industry-wide. Cable, with its fragmented small audiences, has not been able to compete with on-air TV for advertising revenues, although these figures are nearly double the revenues for 1973.[7]

Leased Channels. A CATV system may lease channels or time on a given channel as a source of income. Users include professional and public interest groups as well as business and industry. For example, medical specialists in teaching hospitals could inform practitioners in the field how to perform certain treatments; organizations of architects, educators or lawyers might wish to distribute information on an exclusive basis to their membership. "Women in Cable," in Memphis, Tennessee, leased and operated a channel oriented to a "total concept of women and their use of the new communications," including specific materials such as how to set up a model day care center.[8]

Pay Television. Just as some people are willing to pay for live entertainment, a certain number are willing to pay for viewing special TV programs. Pay TV has been in an experimental stage for many years, but recently has sought to become a viable competitor to "free" (advertising supported) TV. Major points of disagreement have arisen between broadcasters and cablecasters. According to the Special Committee on Pay TV of the National Association of Broadcasters, the cost of pay TV would be considerable. First, a person would have to pay for cable service and, second, would have to pay additional fees for movies and sports events—presumably the very movies and sports events one now sees free on broadcast TV. In the average American home, TV is on 5¾ hours a day, and the figure is higher in lower-income homes, where people depend on free TV for most of their recreation. Obviously, it would be a hardship on millions of families to have to pay to see movies or sports on their own TV sets.[9] Nevertheless, Pay-TV's future cannot be denied. An "Analysis of Consumer Demand for Pay Television," prepared by the Office of Telecommunications Policy by Stanford Research Institute, Menlo Park, California, predicts that pay cable subscribers would increase from 100,000 in 1974 to 14.7 million in 1985, and over-the-air pay TV subscribers, from zero to 1.5 million. And it showed revenues for the two services jumping from $8 million to some $1.9 billion over that time span. The study contends that 20 per cent of the nation's households will subscribe to a pay service by 1985.[10]

CATV Costs. Like most businesses, CATV is usually a losing proposition until the system is established. During the initial stages management keeps costs as low as possible. The expenses of installation, distribution and facilities of CATV are substantial. Cost of laying cable in rural areas in the mid-1970s was about $10,000 a mile; in urban areas such as New York City the cost could reach $80,000 per mile. The average system consisted of 100 to 200 miles of cable. The high cost of installation and maintenance has forced some cable operators to be late in fulfilling their franchise agreements. In an address to the International Radio and Television Society's Faculty-Industry Conference in 1974 the Chairman and Chief Executive Office of Warner Cable Corporation, Alfred R. Stern, said: "While all of us realized that urban cable systems would be vastly more expensive to construct and much harder to penetrate, we nevertheless faced the future fairly confident that all types of sophisticated new services, offering opportunities for added revenues, would be ready and waiting to help finance the higher costs and help lure the urban subscriber. Well, we were wrong. The hardware isn't there and the software isn't there—at least not at an economically viable cost nor in a problem-free form."

Rates charged by the CATV owner are subject to the conditions of the city or local government franchise and cannot be raised without permission of the local government. CATV company costs sometimes included in a franchise are cable connection and disconnection fees, requirements to pre-wire multiple dwellings, and compulsory reduced rates for preferential classes of users such as senior citizens or the disabled. Some franchises may require the CATV owner to provide studio facilities and airtime for public access programming.

Despite problems, the industry continues to grow. In the mid-1970s emphasis seemed to be not as much on gaining new franchises as on achieving greater penetration where CATV is already in operation.[11]

Technical Aspects. All TV systems are means of distributing information and entertainment via the airwaves or wire. Alternative TV systems are essentially closed circuit or are combined with limited open circuit microwaving within special frequency ranges established by the FCC. CATV is principally wire; ITFS and MDS use microwave; CCTV is principally wire; satellites principally use open-circuit and microwave. All of these signals go to predetermined receiving points. (As this is written, satellite-to-home broadcasting is not yet in operation.) Figure 2 shows CATV sources of programming, such as existing commercial and educational stations, remote sports events and community activities. These are either picked up from the airwaves by a master antenna complex, from greater distances and with higher quality than by a home antenna, or originated as studio programming sent via closed circuit to a common distribution point called the headend. The signals are electronically improved and *re*distributed over the various channels to subscribers wired into the coaxial cable. This cable is sometimes laid in underground conduits, though usually attached to existing utility poles. This method of distribution necessitates payment to the utility company for pole use and franchising by the operative governmental unit—city, township, county—for use of the easement. A drop line goes from that wire into the individual subscriber's home, where any number of TV sets can be wired. When the first cable system was built in

FORMS OF DISTRIBUTION

CATV DISTRIBUTION

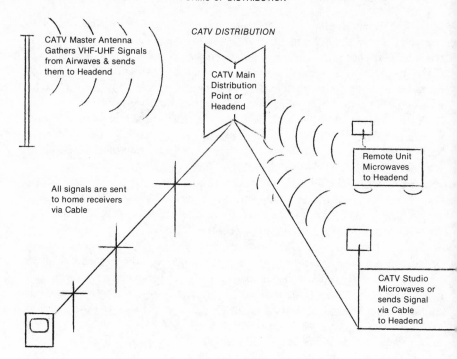

CATV Master Antenna Gathers VHF-UHF Signals from Airwaves & sends them to Headend

CATV Main Distribution Point or Headend

Remote Unit Microwaves to Headend

All signals are sent to home receivers via Cable

CATV Studio Microwaves or sends Signal via Cable to Headend

CLOSED CIRCUIT DISTRIBUTION

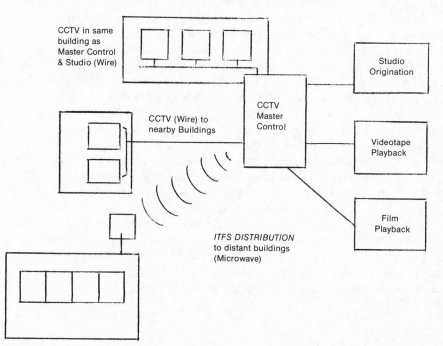

CCTV in same building as Master Control & Studio (Wire)

CCTV (Wire) to nearby Buildings

CCTV Master Control

Studio Origination

Videotape Playback

Film Playback

ITFS DISTRIBUTION to distant buildings (Microwave)

Fig. 2

1949, it had the capacity for only one channel. The state of technology has since developed through the years, where most systems have 6 to 12 channels with a potential of 30 or more depending upon cable configuration. FCC rules had required that all systems would have to have at least 20-channel capacity by 1977, but in 1976 the FCC gave systems until 1986 to meet this requirement.

Satellites are adding a new dimension to TV distribution systems. Information can be sent from a ground transmitter in one location via satellite to another ground receiver thousands of miles away which distributes the signal over traditional broadcasting stations, CATV, CCTV, specially equipped home antennas or unaugmented home receivers. Feasibility of such transmission for unaugmented home receivers is not expected until the mid-1980s however. In 1977 ten Intelsat IV and Intelsat IVA satellites were in orbit with the Intelsat V series to follow in 1979–80, and about 135 earth stations were in operation around the world in some 78 countries. In 1977 use was being made in the United States of ATS (Applications Technology Satellites) 1, 3 and 6 and of Canada's CTS (Communications Technology Satellite). PBS, the Public Broadcasting Service, had arranged to use part of Western Union's "Westar" satellite and expected to have 162 earth stations serving 270 public television transmitters in operation by the end of 1978.

A number of organizations were developed to promote the use of satellites. Among the noncommercial groups is the PSSC, Public Service Satellite Corsortium, composed principally of educational and public broadcasting entities, and the Public Interest Satellite Association, composed primarily of public interest, minority and women's groups.

The potential for the utilization of satellites to geographically link isolated areas of the world was dramatically illustrated by the launching of the ATS-6:

A recent example is the launching of the Applications Technology Satellite-6 (ATS-6) into equatorial orbit by the National Aeronautics and Space Administration. ATS-6 was initially located at 94 degrees west longitude over the Galapagos Islands in view of the continental United States. The ATS-6 was used, among other things, for the Health Education Telecommunications experiment conducted by the Department of Health, Education and Welfare and the Corporation for Public Broadcasting. This involved direct broadcasting of educational and two-way medical teleconferences through ground receiving units placed in geographically large and remote regions, such as the Rocky Mountain region, the Applalachian states and the states of Washington and Alaska. This spacecraft has been used in connection with the ATS-1 and ATS-3, already in orbit. In preparation for this experiment NASA contracted with the General Electric Company and Stanford University to design a low cost receiver-converter permitting receipt of satellite signals and their conversion to a form used by a standard UHF television receiver. Thus, the equipment for each of approximately 300 sites consisted of a conventional television set, a simple antenna, and the special converter, which would service either a single community receiver or perform in conjunction with public broadcasting microwave or cable television systems in operation.

ATS-6 has the capacity to relay two separate color television signals with each signal accompanied by four voice channels. Programs can be transmitted in several languages simultaneously.

The spacecraft was recently relocated over Kenya, East Africa so that the Indian government would use it for the broadcast of daily television programs to 5,000 villages and cities in that country. Programming will involve school instruction and teacher education, better agricultural techniques, family planning and hygiene, and occupational skills.

It is the advent of this type of communications satellite, with capabilities much greater than geostationary spacecrafts previously orbited, that clears the path for educational television and other information transmission systems of the future.[12]

Production Facilities

The keynote to production facilities for alternative systems is miniaturization. Central to this idea is the use of lightweight, transistorized, single tube color cameras instead of broadcasting's bulkier, heavier plumbicon or image orthicon cameras, and the use of narrow gauge videotape of one-half, three-fourths and one-inch instead of broadcasting's two-inch videotape. The problem for manufacturers has been to produce reliable, low cost miniature equipment that would be compatible and compare favorably in quality with standard broadcasting equipment. The challenge is being met, but the state of development and lack of standards leave a number of rough spots. So much new equipment has come into the miniaturization field that buyers are confused as to quality, price and even utilization. Only now are endurance data and preferences for models and manufacturers being documented by pioneer users of alternative systems. Obsolescence, constant repair and adjustment, and incompatibility have cost unnecessary millions of dollars. A simple comparison of miniaturized and broadcast equipment costs may be illustrated by examining a system's most common unit—the camera:

Industrial Grade Camera: less than $15,000 each. Has fewer refinements, less flexibility, more difficult to maintain, shorter life, less brilliance to picture, less sharpness, more distortion. Greater mobility.

Medium Grade Camera: between $15,000 and $35,000 each. Has refinements comparable with expensive cameras, easier to maintain and service than higher or lower cost cameras, picture quality can be as good or better than high-priced cameras with use of time-base corrector. Reasonable mobility.

Broadcast Grade Camera: more than $50,000 each. Has all refinements and accessory options described in earlier chapters, requires constant maintenance. Limited mobility.

Program origination facilities may be described as (1) fixed, (2) mobile and (3) studio. (Figure 3 shows sample floor plans for production facilities for different alternative systems.)

Fixed Facilities. The simplest use of TV is a vidicon camera and a receiver in fixed position. The TV camera is unnoticed, mounted to a wall or ceiling bracket, capable of scanning a wide area because of its wide angle lens. The vidicon camera may be automated to the extent that it pans right or left, up or down. Video information is viewed on a receiver or on tape within the camera. A microphone is not necessary. These cameras, used mainly for surveillance, can be seen in many public buildings. Under somewhat more elaborate circumstances information may be picked up by a camera in fixed position and sent to a TV control room where it is recorded, read or redistributed throughout the system. For instance, news information from a wire service machine, weather reports, stock market quotations, sports scores and a TV program schedule could all be sent silently and continuously on various channels of a cable TV operation. In education the video learning carrel has come into prominence. The carrel is designed as an individual learning center. A person has a telephone and a keyboard connected to a computer. He or she may receive on a TV screen responses from the computer when the keyboard is activated or may view video information by telephone request. Such carrels are ideal for independent study and have found considerable applicability in medical schools where busy interns can pursue their studies on demand.

Essential to static facilities in addition to small vidicon cameras and receivers is narrow-width videotape. CATV and CCTV facilities use relatively inexpensive small reels of videotape. In the mid-1970s ¾-inch videotape was emerging as a standard gauge in the United States, principally because of large purchases by the government. However, much equipment is purchased from Japan where ½-inch videotape is standard. All widths can be saved, stored, erased, reused and duplicated in various gauges as needed.

An example of fixed facilities is the University of Arizona's "Micro-campus," which offers full-credit instruction at remote locations on videotape and videocassettes. The programs are taped in classrooms with fixed camera and videotape facilities and are then distributed on videocassettes. A description of the fixed facilities follows:

The first step was to equip the video classroom. For $20,000, four Sony AVC-3210 cameras were acquired, along with two 25-inch monitors, a Sony control console, including an audio mixer and special effects generator, and five recorders. Three of the recorders are Sony AV-3650

PRODUCTION FACILITIES

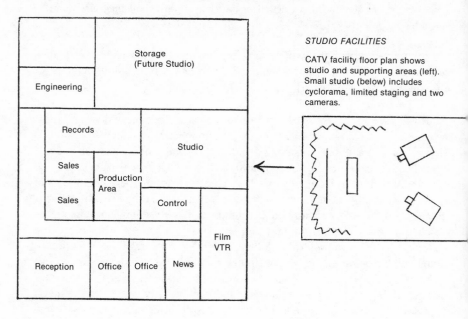

STUDIO FACILITIES

CATV facility floor plan shows studio and supporting areas (left). Small studio (below) includes cyclorama, limited staging and two cameras.

FIXED FACILITIES

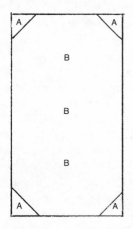

MOBILE FACILITIES

Portable camera picks up program (left) which is recorded on videotape (center) and played back on TV receiver (right).

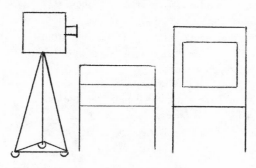

Units are moved from classroom to classroom to distribute programs on demand.

A closed circuit classroom with cameras in fixed positions (A) and a fixed hanging microphone (B).

Fig. 3

half-inch reel-to-reel units, while the other two are VO-1600 three-quarter inch U-Matic videocassette models.

One of the cameras is used in the control room for titling, but also serves as a backup for the others. One of the three classroom cameras is mounted above the ceiling. Through a small cutout, its 15 to 75mm zoom lens looks directly down upon the instructor's desk. It can record a full newspaper page or fill the screen with an enlargement of a four-by-six inch card.

Besides printed materials and diagrams, the overhead camera can also produce displays on the classroom monitors of such things as printed circuit boards, which would otherwise have to be passed from hand to hand. While necessary for the Microcampus production, this capability also enhances the real-time learning environment.

The remaining two cameras are mounted in the control room and look out on the classroom from cutouts in the back wall. All of the cameras are remote-controlled from the console. The audio is picked up by six microphones mounted in the classroom ceiling.[13]

Mobile Facilities. In broadcasting, a familiar unit for picking up a program from a non-studio or remote location is usually a huge van, truck or, in the case of newsfilm camera operators, a car. CATV has pioneered the use of these vehicles scaled down for its lighter and smaller cameras. CCTV, essentially an internal service, has less frequent use for such equipment. In one instance a church owns a remote unit for the purpose of videotaping Sunday services. During the week the truck is available for public service projects at nominal cost. Programs for cable and CCTV are recorded on location and disseminated later. The extreme in miniaturization is the camera-videotape unit which resembles a motion picture camera. It is so lightweight, flexible and inexpensive that it is available to nearly every group or individual who wants one, thus making every neighborhood in the community a potential studio.

A dramatic turn has taken place in recent years in production and distribution, suggesting that portable miniaturized cameras will not only replace large traditional broadcasting cameras and, perhaps, film cameras as well—the mini-cam is already doing this—but that videocassettes and videodiscs will strongly compete with traditional forms of distribution. A portable TV camera, video-tape recorder-playback and receiver is a very inexpensive way of distributing information for "in-house" use. ". . . it is likely that by the late 1970s we will see the advent of truly lightweight, non-umbilical, entirely self-contained video recording systems. These systems will be the size of today's Super 8 cameras, but will feature some form of mini-cartridge which will fit into the side of the camera for total handheld operation."[14] One manufacturer of oil drilling equipment uses videocassettes to record programs of the latest equipment actually working on the site. These videocassettes are then taken by an instructor to various oil installations throughout the world where they are played on compatible receivers. The instructor adds supplementary information and answers questions, thereby keeping those in the field continually up-to-date.

Studio Facilities. The main considerations when planning a TV studio are location, size, equipment, maintenance, convenience to storage areas and future requirements. Size depends upon individual uses and needs, but, in general, studios for alternate media origination are small-to-medium in size—from 900 to 1,200 square feet. The studio complex includes a performance area, control room containing video and audio controls, racks of electronic equipment, videotape machines, film chain(s), a workshop and storage. Readily accessible storage areas for scenery, props, display and graphic materials and spare parts are often inadequate but necessary, and so is a 6- by 8-foot (minimum) service door with similarly proportioned access areas. Recommended are a 14-foot (minimum) grid height on which to hang lights, at least six dimmer-controlled lights, a cloth cyclorama (not a hard one) continuing around the studio and made of light gray or natural fiber of 60 per cent reflectance value, and a smooth, level floor of poured concrete. The studio should be sound proof—free from exterior noise (hallways and streets) and interior noise (air conditioning, plumbing and reverberation from its own walls).[15] Preferences for various brands of equipment depend on the objectives of those who use and maintain it. A few brands frequently mentioned by engineers are noted below. An engineer as well as a production staff should be in on the development of a facility. Generally speaking, trends indicate that inflation will keep equipment prices on the rise, but technological innovations will make it more reliable and easier to maintain in the long run, offsetting price increases. The following sample list of equipment comprises a quality two-camera production and/or instructional alternative TV facility priced in the mid-range (keep in mind that the costs listed here are 1976 figures and, depending on inflationary trends, may be of value to you principally as comparison guides):

Studio Cameras (2)	*Estimated Unit Price*	*Total*
Norelco color camera, 3-tube, with complete chain	$32,000	$64,000
or		
Shibaden color camera, 3-tube, with complete chain	25,000	50,000
or		
Hitachi color camera, FPC-1000P	17,000	34,000

Film Chain

16 mm film package including multiplexer ($2,500), pick-up camera ($17,000), slide projector ($500), neutral density filter ($1,400), super-8 projector ($300), remote control ($150), optical track and related equipment		24,000

Videotape Recorder-Playback

2 1-inch VTRs complete with editing capability	24,000	48,000
2 ¾-inch VTR with record and playback	1,900	3,800

Picture Control (Switcher and Engineering)

Switcher complete with chroma key (price range $6,000 to $35,000)	11,500	11,500
Switcher rack	250	250
5 Black and white monitors (minimum requirement)	500	2,500
Color monitor	625	625
*Time Base corrector (for converting signal for cable distribution; price range: $10,000 to $14,000)	10,000	10,000
*Sync generator (price range: $3,000 to $6,000)	3,000	3,000
Engineer's monitor	500	500
Engineer's rack	250	250
Vectorscope (for matching cameras)	3,050	3,050
Passive mechanical switchers (3 recommended)	110	330
*Image enhancer 8000 (makes picture sharp)	10,000	10,000
Lighting in studio, including dimmer board, light package ($5,000), installation of grid ($1,000 to $15,000)	30,000	30,000

Distribution

Video distribution (for keeping cameras in phase)	2,000	2,000
Audio distribution	1,000	1,000

Audio Equipment

Audio console including turntable ($400), reel to reel audiotape recorder ($500), 2 cartridge machines with playback		5,000
Microphone (six recommended as minimum; price range: $125 to $500 each)	125	750

Maintenance

*Parts inventory, installation contingency (a complete spare camera should be available for parts)		15,000
Studio A total with Norelco cameras		$237,855
with Shibaden cameras		223,855
with Hitachi cameras		207,855
Studio B total with Norelco cameras (less $38,000 from Studio A, so marked *)		199,855
Total cost for Studio A & B		$436,710

Other Costs

Closed-circuit. A simple closed-circuit system can be developed for only a few thousand dollars: inexpensive cameras and playback units, such as one buys for home use, additional monitors as necessary, and wire to connect the receiving points in a given building with the distribution source. As shown above, however, any alternative system, including closed-circuit, can have a great range in cost, depending on the need for sophistication and, of course, on the available budget.

ITFS. ITFS costs are considerably lower than those for broadcast instructional TV. An ITFS transmitter, which is about the size of a four-drawer filing cabinet and may be installed virtually anywhere, costs as little as $20,000. Using vidicon equipment for minimal studio facilities plus about $1,000 for receiving antenna and downconverter for each receiving site, an ITFS system can be installed, reaching up to a dozen schools in a district, for about $50,000. More sophisticated systems cost more. A four-channel color system in the Houston, Texas, Spring Branch School District, reaching 40 schools, cost $1.5 million, with about $11,250 per year production and maintenance at each channel.

UTILIZATION OF THE SYSTEMS

Whether the alternative TV system is CATV, CCTV, ITFS or MDS, the physical layout, equipment and procedures for producing locally originated programs are similar. Although production approaches for these systems resemble those of broadcast television, there are some important differences based largely on several philosophical concepts and corollaries: specialized audiences versus mass audiences, sustained continuity, hometown credibility versus Madison Avenue professionalism, and programs on demand versus scheduled programs.

Specialized Audiences versus Mass Audiences. Traditional broadcasting measures the audience acceptance of its programs by means of ratings—that is, how many viewers were seeing a program or commercial at a given time. Top rated programs are retained, lower rated programs are cancelled, even though the latter may be viewed by millions of people. Alternative TV audiences generally are small. Forty-channel reception is bound to fractionalize the viewing audience. Serving a few people with specific needs thoroughly and well may yet prove to be the hallmark of success in television.

Sustained Continuity versus Interrupted Continuity. How many times have you said, "If only I could see this movie uninterrupted by commercials!"? Alternative TV frequently offers feature films, sports events and other entertainment without interruption. This is largely through leased channels serving commercial centers (theaters, hotels, conference centers), through pay TV and through CATV origination channels.

Hometown Credibility versus Madison Avenue Professionalism. As Madison Avenue goes, so goes the nation and the world. Undoubtedly, advertising has changed the world. The good life as defined by motion pictures and television is fast, exciting, abundant—that is, geared to the products the programs are designed to sell—and largely unrealistic. Alternative TV systems, even if principally out of economic necessity, frequently present local programming that is more direct and believable. Many CATV public access programs, for example, emphasize remote input from "neighborhood" studios throughout the city, going into the community seeking people in their natural environment rather than creating a setting in the studio. It means using mobile cameras and verité techniques to express life as it is. CATV consultant Del Jack has said: "In general, it is important that cable find a different way to use what money there is and not try to compete with network production. In other words, don't worry about production mistakes but be concerned about the statement, the honesty, and let a new form fitting new circumstances develop."

Programs On Demand versus Scheduled Programs. A major inconvenience of traditional broadcasting is that the viewer must watch a program in accordance with the schedule devised by the network or station. Station programmers try to pick the hours most people are likely to see a program. Sometimes the program is rerun so that more viewers will see it. Cable TV with its numerous channels offers more selections at any given time, but does not offer direct viewer control over the schedule. A computerized system whereby the viewer can dial in a request for a specific program which can be seen at home or school, and a videocassette system of distribution whereby the viewer owns or leases programs that can be played on privately owned equipment are developing in the mid-1970s. In instruction, ITFS and CCTV provide multiple-channel flexible scheduling of ITV programs not possible on public television stations.

Producing

Programs for alternative systems are developed the same way as are programs for commercial television, with varying application of the philosophical differences just mentioned.

Idea Origination. A producer at the CATV facility, business, medical center or educational institution recognizes a need for a certain program or series. The producer discusses this idea with the potential producing, financing and distributing sources. Usually the producer has spent a great deal of time writing up the proposal in the form of outlines or scripts. If the manager of the production and/or distribution facility thinks the idea has merit, the idea will then be passed along to the production chief and others who estimate how much the program will cost. After a dollar estimate is reached by the production facility, the producer approaches the potential financiers.

Budget. The producer's budget estimate should be as firm as possible. This is especially true for close-budgeted CATV and CCTV programs where literally "every cent counts." Many alternative TV programs depend principally on donors, grants from government and foundations, trade out agreements with merchants, educational institutions and, in the case of cable television, commercial options as mentioned earlier.

Program Production. A cue sheet or simple outline may provide a sufficient script for most programs. Some programs do require a complete script; for example, a physician's lecture may require precise audio-visual cues for slides, films, charts, boardwork and three-dimensional setups. The cue sheet is given to the camera operator, talent and other assistants. The alternative TV facility frequently is so compact that a producer-director may even engineer the program and perform as talent. Some alternative TV systems have fulltime or part-time production staffs. Some producer-performers are already paid: teachers by school districts, doctors by hospitals, ministers by churches, executives by companies. Some performers are hired by the TV system on a fee basis and others, usually citizens in the community, contribute their talents free.

The Playback. Programs are videotaped for playback on various channels at optimum viewing hours and are frequently repeated. Some programs or series are saved and syndicated by the individual producers or by CATV and media distributors. Alternative media still do many "live" programs. These systems have almost immediate feedback from their local audiences by phone and mail. This response is of as much interest to alternate TV services as ratings are to broadcasters. Dialogue between the alternate system and the viewer is on-going. Two-way audio and video transmission is being used more frequently, particularly in instructional, business conference and "new town" situations.

Directing

The director's responsibility is to assemble the program elements artistically.

Planning. A director takes the raw materials and assembles them into a program or series of programs. The director must keep in mind that the purpose of many alternate media programs is to inform, and to use a direct style of directing with minimal dependence on special electronic effects. The studio is usually small and camera movement is therefore limited. In fact, cameras may be simply "placed" in the best positions for getting shots with a zoom lens. Sometimes a single camera will do the job, the director repositioning the camera after cutting to slides or film. Studio distances being short, directors commonly adjust lights, move cameras, signal talent and cue up films while taping the program. Programs are also typically completed after the first or second "take," except in some situations where directors enhance programs with sophisticated editing. While these limitations may appear to restrict a director, the result may be quite the contrary, for in such situations a director frequently substitutes greater artistic imagination for mechanical and electronic facilities.

Staging. In many alternative media situations the studio is small. The set may be an exercise barre in front of a bare wall or cyclorama; a desk or lectern in front of a window or bookcase flat; an empty space with pools of patterned light; a single hanging drape; a front or rear screen projection and two chairs on a riser; a half-dozen large boxes serving as seats. Lighting, similarly, is frequently limited to basics. Sets are often reused for different types of programs. Limits on floor space sometimes require that sets be struck and reassembled each time, necessitating simple construction. On the other hand, some ITFS, cable and CCTV facilities have studios and equipment comparable to opulent commercial facilities.

Rehearsal. Much alternate media programming is extemporaneous; that is, turning cameras on talent and shooting, without scripts or rehearsal. This sometimes results in extremely poor programs, as well as, sometimes, unexpected excitement. Except for remote actuality programming, rehearsal is important, whether for an entertainment presentation or for a teacher presenting instructional materials. In instruction, particularly, it is important to eliminate the "talking head." Even in extemporaneous discussion shows, there should be orientation of the participants to the format, content outline and procedure of the program.

Videotape or Live Production. Almost all programs are videotaped. Videocassettes are revolutionizing education. All materials on alternative media do not have re-use value, however, and the producer should carefully select which programs to save and which to erase. In some alternative TV studios with limited equipment the reverse is true: the lack of a videotaping machine results in a one-time presentation only of a live program that may have turned out to be good enough to be re-used.

Performing

Although alternative TV systems sometimes use professional performers for originating programs, as well as showing professionals in programs from other sources, many performers are drawn from other professions: teachers, physicians, ministers, lawyers, politicians and other citizens. Many of these non-professional and sometimes volunteer performers obviously need more assistance than do professionals. Basically, these non-professionals should try to seem natural, move little, sit and stand straight, be well prepared and organized, check clothes style and colors with the director, and use the least make-up possible.

Many performers donate their services for personal experience or community prestige. The quality of volunteer performers varies greatly, principally because they cannot or will not spend enough time to sufficiently research material or rehearse. Token fees are sometimes paid, depending on the availability of funds for the program. Instructional program performers are usually under contract to the school system or for that particular series. Alternate media make a good entry point for beginners who want media experience as performers.

PROGRAM TYPES

Children's Programs

In developing a cable TV program for children one can be simple, direct and use the community for talent and as a studio, rather than try to rival the expensive productions of broadcast television.

Decide what age group you want to reach. Child development people in public schools and colleges usually are pleased to advise and offer guidance on what is most meaningful to which age group. Reach into the community for children—not performers. Keep in mind the pluralistic nature of our society and be sure to involve children of every ethnic group.

The approach can be simple, such as giving the youngsters a camera and a free rein to shoot whatever and however they want, providing technical advice and support as needed. There can be news of and by youngsters; utilization of talents of children who perform musically; a "how to" program with children adept at skills and crafts such as macramé, weaving or blowing a horn.

It is important to involve the youngsters themselves in the development of the concept and ideas. The program will flow more naturally and children viewing the program will relate more readily to programs other young people have helped to develop. Through cable TV children in one part of a city can share what is unique and individual about their section of the community with children in another area of the city.

Seek inexpensive activities. For example, try folk tales—African, early American, or stories made up by the children—as roller drawings. Using strips of brown Kraft paper, draw the story from beginning to end and pull this through a cardboard box, one side of which has an opening—a proscenium—revealing the drawings. The children narrate the story in their own words as they pull it through. You will find added ideas and resources in community agencies such as mental health groups, nutritionists, drama organizations and others. These groups usually are willing to give assistance and materials for children's programs. For example, in Anderson, Indiana, General Electric Cablevision produces *Kid Stuff,* a weekly half-hour program with a two-fold emphasis: what is available for children to do in Anderson and what local children are doing. The program is taped for the most part outside of the studios, going to parks, children's library, classrooms, shopping centers, skating rinks and private homes. Guests are often pet owners, model builders, singers and theater groups. Another cable operation, LVO Cable Louisiana, in Lake Charles, each week conducts a lesson in TV broadcasting for a scout troop. Instruction in all phases of production is under supervision of cable personnel, and the children's productions are cablecast.

An example of how a typical—great need, no budget—program series evolves is the experience of two seniors in the Department of Communications at the University of Houston who produced 10 half-hour children's programs for CCTV distribution at Texas Children's Hospital.

A minister at the hospital asked that programs be produced for confined children of all ages. He indicated that live programs could originate from fixed facilities located in the chapel at the hospital. The chapel is equipped with three stationary vidicon cameras with fixed focal length lenses, one vidicon with a zoom lens, one portable vidicon with a fixed lens mounted to a tripod on wheels, an audiotape recorder, a few non-technical lights and some stationary microphones. In addition, a modest second production studio facility was available at a local high school. This studio has three vidicon cameras, four 5,000-watt lights and an assortment of smaller ones, various microphones, audio and videotape recorders, a film-slide chain, a small switcher with a special effects generator, and a Sony "Rover" (hand-held or tripod mounted) camera using half-inch videotape. Equipment at both facilities was black and white.

With these facilities in mind, the producers began developing scripts listing the segments they could present live or on videotape. The first script featured a bi-lingual story and folk songs; the second was a tour of a popcorn supply company, a film of hot air ballooning, and a videotape of a gorilla at the zoo; the third script added a demonstration on how to make American Indian masks from paper bags, construction paper and paper plates; the fourth included a taped segment on blimps and a puppet show; the fifth had a drawing lesson. The remaining five programs featured variations on the ideas already mentioned.

During the production period the producers learned several useful lessons. They found that willing, talented people rarely want to perform for free, and even if they do, they are not always dependable and often do not show up at the studio. As a result, the producers tended to perform a great deal themselves. The producers concluded that in order to keep studio time to a minimum, everyone must know exactly what he or she is doing in advance through discussions and rehearsals without equipment. Further, unless well functioning editing equipment is available, video editing can be extremely time consuming and frustrating, thus making a live production easier in the long run. Generally, they agreed that the more complicated the production, the more people it takes to produce it, with the quality of any show being directly proportional to the amount of time and, in most cases, the number of capable people involved in it. "It is possible to produce a half-hour children's show with no money in about two hours of studio time but you've got to really have your act together." [16] When it came to the playback, the producers were discouraged to learn that many children did not see the programs because of insufficient publicity.

Educational Programs

Some 2,000 school systems throughout the country use CCTV programs for the regular curriculum, special courses and services, professional teachers meetings, in-service training sessions and adult supplementary education.

The simplest use in the individual classroom consists of having students view materials on a portable receiver fed by a videotape player. An example of more sophisticated use is the introduction of wired learning carrels. At one school, a teacher who is the Learning Center Coordinator and a student assistant teach the youngsters how to use the equipment, and tapes are produced by students and teachers for self evaluation in dramatic productions; students use a Sony Porta-Pak to record activities on location; field trips are taped for viewing by students unable to go.

Colleges and universities are frequent users of closed circuit television equipment. Some universities have found it difficult to keep track of the proliferation of installations; thus, the systems on a given campus—in the colleges of business administration for computer data, engineering for laboratory experiments, law for observation of mock trials, education for the improvement of teacher training, arts and sciences for animal research, architecture for the study of building designs—may not even be technically compatible. Adult education is making more and more use of CCTV. Classes stressing performance, such as teaching and acting, frequently use portable videotape cameras to record exercises which are then played back for the participants.

The first ITFS systems began in 1964 in the Mineola, Long Island and Parma, Ohio school systems. In late 1977 there were 186 systems with 500 channels in operation. It is estimated that more than 7 million children receive some part of their instruction through ITFS.

An interesting example of cooperative utilization of ITFS is The Association for Graduate Education and Research (TAGER), composed of seven private and two public colleges in the Dallas-Fort Worth area of Texas. Its purposes: "Providing the necessary planning to develop cooperative programs, enhancing higher education and opening avenues to obtain optimum utilization of faculties and other academic resources; providing greatest benefits to students and participating institutions of the North Texas area." The network includes six industrial plant receiving locations and has involved a total enrollment of about 25,000 students sharing over 1,500 courses. Undergraduate courses in non-technical areas such as foreign language, theology, history, sociology are presented as well as graduate offerings in engineering, science, mathematics and business. TAGER has both full enrollment students and auditors, with a complete system of fees, registration, examination, seminars and lectures. The system allows each participating institution to contribute its professional talent and courses already in the curriculum and saves receiving institutions the cost of initiating new programs on each campus. Courses are also offered for the benefit of students at remote locations.

A number of Catholic Archdioceses and Dioceses are using ITFS for networking instructional materials among several cities, and have credited ITFS, in some instances, with preserving their parochial school systems through this economically efficient distribution of educational materials.

Stanford University pioneered courses to industry employees who enrolled for credit and received instruction through ITFS at their office or plant sites within reach of the signal from Palo Alto, California. Stanford also developed the audio response system which permits these students to communicate with the instructor during the lessons.

The producer of ITFS programming must keep in mind the learning goals, alert not to allow the entertainment element to overshadow the educational. Timing is important; the pace must be slow enough for the class to keep up. Programs longer than 20 or 30 minutes tend to diminish interest. In contrast to the constant pressure of commercial television, ITFS productions can be paced throughout the year. There is increasing use of duplication in order to accommodate class scheduling. Masters may be put on two-inch tape, then dubbed down to cassette for broadcast through use of one time-based corrector per channel. ITFS systems usually combine in-house productions with material purchased or rented from producers of instructional films and from distributors of educational series.

Medical Programs

The main purposes for medical TV facilities within hospitals and colleges of continuing education are in-service training for doctors and nurses, diagnosis, and orientation for patients (acquainting the latter with the hospital services and procedures in an attempt to allay fears). Hospital and medical staffs serve as subject-matter specialists for TV productions. Some medical schools are giving their students basic TV production training so that graduates have some understanding of TV and will be better able to utilize the medium.

Typical of the developing use of TV in hospitals and medical centers is the Medical Community TV System at the Texas Medical Center in Houston. This system distributes tapes and film via cable from the facility in the library basement on four closed-circuit TV channels to 18 hospitals at the medical center, and by microwave to four hospitals up to 10 miles away. In addition, the system's staff gives general technical assistance to nine of the 22 hospitals which have production studios. Programs are scheduled in advance, usually in response to requests. They are produced in local hospitals, obtained without charge from pharmaceutical houses, or are rented from the Network for Continuing Medical Education in New York. The same schedule of programs runs for two weeks so that every doctor has a chance to see them.

One of the production studios at the Center, at M. D. Anderson Hospital, has a color system with two IVC 500 cameras, a film chain, a master recorder IVC 960 and IVC 870 for editing. Its major daily distribution and delivery system is videocassette, with the cassette machine brought into the classroom or conference room. The studio is 40 feet by 20 feet with a well equipped control room, including chroma key and special effects, a special still camera, a camera for photographing the back of the eye, and a camera for attaching to a microscope to photograph inside the stomach. The cost of equipment totals more than $300,000. The CCTV staff includes a supervisor, three program directors who do everything from producing to switching and directing, one motion picture camera operator, a cinematographer, three engineers with first class FCC licenses and one electronic technician. As part of the total medical communications activities of the hospital, the TV studio has access to all support facilities—graphics, audio-visual library, still photography, needed resources for production. As is often the case in educational and industrial TV systems, this medical system does not always hire experienced TV people, but frequently employs people with related talents and backgrounds and trains them.

Through television, not only are professionals in hospitals, students in medical, dental and nursing schools and physicians at home being served, but para-medical personnel and other persons in health areas in communities are being provided with information and assistance in both preventive and curative health care methods. The ATS-6 satellite experiment which ended in 1975 provided medical and health services to parts of Alaska and other isolated areas of the United States that otherwise would have received little, if any. In the mid-1970s networking hospital communications began to grow as a means of avoiding duplication, obtaining desired materials more easily and cheaply, and providing quicker diagnosis and information exchange. The five largest medical TV systems, in Los Angeles, San Francisco, Dallas, Chicago and Houston, are considering linking their resources through satellite and microwave.

Industry Use

Surveillance is a common use of automated TV in industry. Other uses include protection for banks and all-night grocery stores, observation of experiments in progress such as molten metals and radio active materials, flights to outer space, retrieval systems scanning data in libraries, law enforcement for criminal identification and airline flight schedules. An extensive use is for in-house exhibition of new products such as automobiles and fashions and for the international sale of antiques and art objects.

A 1976 survey showed 76 private videotape networks in existence carrying company-originated programming to six or more locations on a regular basis. The survey also showed that 90 per cent of the nearly 300 companies reporting used audiocassette, slide and 16 mm film projectors. Overhead and filmstrip projectors were being utilized by 60 per cent, while only 15 per cent used Super 8 mm format. Training, information-news, management-employee and marketing communications videotapes are being produced on broadcast quality equipment by such companies as AT&T, Mutual of Omaha and Sears. The tapes are then duped onto one-half and three-quarter-inch formats for distribution. Approximately 65 to 70 per cent of the respondents own at least one videocassette player and about 40 to 50 per cent have in-house reel-to-reel videotape machines. Only 20 to 30 per cent of this group has established closed-circuit TV systems for internal information distribution.[17]

In another study Douglas and Judith Brush found that "It is now possible for a business executive in the course of one day to view in his office an overseas economic report taped the day before, an update of a company field operation, a management development program on the emerging role of women in business, and, in the company lunchroom, an employee news program. After lunch he may attend a live, nationwide televised sales meeting using large-screen projection and later assist his company president in making a videotaped report for security analysts. . . . Private television has become a management medium to a greater extent than any other audio-visual system. In at least two-thirds of the companies surveyed, the chief executive officer appears regularly in company produced programming. He may be no Johnny Carson, but people tend to pay attention.''[18] In 40 per cent of the organizations using video, TV operations are administered by the training director; in another 40 per cent, direct supervision of TV is in sales, marketing or public relations departments.[19] The programs typically include slide shows, moving pictures, video-tape or combinations of all three. Videotape with its instant replay facility is utilized to train supervisors as they role-play anything from talking to sales personnel about lagging sales to problems of racial prejudice. A typical studio setup, in one company, consists of two wall-mounted remote control cameras with special effects generators, including fading and split screen capability. The latter is especially useful in taping supervisors and groups. There are also two floor cameras, two large and two small monitors. There is little or no editing. A Sony 3650 is used.

Many companies have developed sophisticated training programs and equipment which excel those of most educational institutions. For example, Holiday Inn University in Memphis, Tennessee has a CCTV training program which extends the classroom day by feeding one or two channels in the evening into 200 students' rooms. A large color TV studio equipped with two color cameras, a color film chain and a 1-inch videotape recorder is in nearly continuous operation. Production procedures are similar to those in commercial studios. There are no live productions and no specific time frame. A program is as long or as short as needed to do the job. Subjects include an introduction to machine training (i.e., cash registers), the reservation system, the Holidex terminal codes for confirmed reservations, waitress training, principles of management and innkeeper maintenance.

In another example, combining aspects of industry, medicine and education, First National City Bank in New York City discovered that CCTV effectively communicates medical health care information. The health care program was shown to about 10,000 employees in three of the company's largest office buildings. Topics included ''The Sun and Your Skin,'' ''Basic First Aid'' and ''Dental Care.'' They were produced in part on location with portable equipment: two one-half inch black-and-white Sony Rovers, a quick set tripod, three Colortran (quartz) lights, a Shire audio mixer, four Sony lavaliere microphones, two Electrovoice 635A microphones, earphones, a Sony AC adapter, a 12-V battery and a broad light. A cart enables the operators to move the equipment from the bank premises to a skin cancer clinic in New York University Hospital. Original half-inch black-and-white tape is transferred to one-inch with all editing done electronically.[20]

A further example of videotaped in-house industry use is that of an engineering company that trains its recent college graduates in its own particular construction methods. Over 200 training tapes are used, viewed on-the-job on a television set or at large meetings through video-beam projector on a wide screen. This particular operation is done completely by one person. This video director prepares a script, goes to a job site with a back pack and several 20-minute ¾-inch tapes. The results of eight hours of shooting are edited down to a 20- or 30-minute tape. The video director also edits tapes sent in from the company's overseas operations. In addition to this type of training, tapes are made of the progress of particular projects to show clients, and executives deliver speeches before the camera in order to critique themselves.

One advantage of industry video production over standard television requirements is that there are not the usual rigid time strictures; industrial tapes and films can be as short or as long as needed.

Minorities, Women and Other Special Groups

Segments of the population largely overlooked and tokenly acknowledged by standard broadcast media—Blacks, Hispanics, Native Americans, Asian-Americans, women, the aged, the handicapped and other groups—see cable TV as a possible way of presenting material of special value as well as a possible avenue of increased opportunity for employment, creative outlet and business advancement.

Charles Tate, director of the Booker T. Washington Foundation and its affiliate communications group, the Cable Communications Resource Center, in Washington, D.C., sees a tremendous potential in cable for technological, economic and sociological progress. He notes that while the average family in the United States watches television about six hours a day, Blacks and the poor watch about seven-and-one-half hours per day. In the context of the long struggle of Blacks for survival, liberation and equal opportunity, Tate sees cable offering great opportunities by way of ownership and as a medium bringing needed information, opportunities for self-help and a sense of community. "Blacks are addicted to television," Tate says, "and according to several surveys view it as the most creditable source of information among all media. Yet we have almost nothing to do with program content and have almost no access to the airwaves as a means of information dissemination by Black people. Black ownership of cable systems is a most practical and effective way to liberate our communities from these conditions."

"On the positive side," Tate adds, "cable television offers the opportunity for Blacks to aggregate their human and external resources in the construction and long term operation of these new telecommunications systems in their communities. Entrepreneurs, lawyers, engineers, technicians, salespeople, managers, program producers and investors are all needed to build modern cable systems," He believes that once having gained "solid credentials," these professionals would not have to remain in Black systems, but could enter the broader marketplace. Most Black leaders agree that cable ownership or high level control through broad-based community corporations would provide for the meaningful delivery of needed health, education and social services. In late 1977 cable franchises were held by Blacks in 30 communities, with seven of them operational, mainly in small, medium and rural markets.

Representatives of groups which are multi-lingual or whose members speak primarily a non-English language recognize the special value of cable in potentially providing channels dedicated to a particular foreign language. Through this kind of unifying media experience, cable can also, according to many minority leaders, provide the kind of education that can lead to more sophisticated political participation, particularly when another potential facet of cable is employed: two-way communication.

Leonel Castillo, Commissioner of the U.S. Immigration and Naturalization Service, the former Controller of the City of Houston and a leader of minorities' communications projects, sees cable as an instrument for including people largely excluded by broadcast television: "The unique, most exciting feature of cable is the 'dialogue' capability. The communication flow can be two-way. Can you imagine the impact when programs, delivered in a familiar language that not only provides critical information on the what, where and when of community events such as City Council meetings, political developments and school board meetings, also provide an opportunity for instant citizen feedback? The implications, in terms of the potential for inclusion in the political decision-making process, are far-reaching. And this applies to all ethnic groups."

"Educational programs tailored to the needs of specific groups," Castillo adds, "should have significant impact. Undoubtedly, some will have historical and cultural focus that strengthen self-image, sense of identity and feeling of community; others will be more pragmatic, teaching practical skills in home improvements, sewing, budgeting, first-aid, child-rearing, nutritional cooking, income tax filing, test taking, application form filling and other essential areas. When programs of this type are coupled with others which explain laws, civil rights, how the legal system operates, how and where to apply for legal, social or municipal services—and what to do and who to contact if rights are violated or services not rendered—you should see impressive changes."

There are two basic production approaches to the direct involvement of the community in such programming: to bring representatives of the community into the studio for a discussion or other kind of presentation, and to take station or community-owned video equipment into the community and tape programs or do live carriage of meetings and other events of concern to the community.

Women, although comprising 51 per cent of the population of the United States, are a decided minority in terms of programming and employment in television broadcasting—as in most fields. Representation of women in television programs is still principally as wife-servants to husbands and as sex objects. Although in the mid-1970s the pressures of feminist groups resulted in some employment gains for women, they filled relatively few executive positions and virtually all clerical and typist jobs.

Janice Blue, a leader in feminist communications efforts, believes that cable offers hope for equal portrayal and job opportunity for women, but feels that it has not yet begun to fulfill its potential: "The local cable versions of the 'Coffee With Connie' programs show little imagination. Most of them deal with the conventional how-to's—how to make the perfect piecrust or how to update last year's wardrobe—while ignoring the serious need of women to learn the how-to's of changing their lives—how to run for office or how to apply for everything from graduate school to real estate loans to food stamps. These are the unmet needs on our commercial and public television stations, needs that cable television could meet. If women, city by city, had an access channel and developed their own local programming and then established a network of programming, every woman would have a greater opportunity to emerge from the stereotyped, partial existence that most women are in and become a whole human being. Women should participate as managers, engineers, salespersons, producers, directors, camera and sound operators, writers, anchors, reporters and subjects on the programs."

The requirements of cable for women are similar to the potential uses for minority groups, including the dissemination of information and the creation of a community of awareness and purpose.

Cable and other alternate television systems have shown special potential in meeting the needs of the aged and the handicapped. For example, in Reading, Pennsylvania deaf groups have been trained in the use of portable video equipment to develop programming in sign language about schools, conferences and other matters of interest. The Deafness Research and Training Center of New York University some years ago established a National Cable Television Production Cooperative to promote captioned television programming for deaf audiences. They have also worked with cable access projects whereby deaf people, by making videotapes, can talk with each other over long distances.[21] A number of cable systems have established forums for the aged, featuring discussions on nutrition, jobs for the elderly and other issues not frequently treated by broadcast TV stations. Two-way cable has opened new doors for isolated people, including the aged, by providing two-person activities such as chess and similar games and joint arts and crafts work.

Public Access on CATV

With the growing realization that communications is the most powerful force in society for influencing people, many groups and individuals in the 1950s and 1960s began to seek access to the communications media. The value of reaching large masses at once with a statement of needs and ideas was of particular value to minority, women and special-need groups, such as those discussed above, who had been effectively barred from the communications mainstream. Citizen groups interested in social and political affairs sought access to the media. Educators and local governments became aware of the importance of wide, immediate outreach. The broadcast media, including television stations, provided little if any access for these groups. With the surge of cable television and its multiple channel capacity, a new and viable access means was available. In 1972 the Federal Communications Commission prescribed that all new CATV systems were obligated to provide three free access channels in each community served: one for public access, one for educational use and one for local government. Existing systems had to meet these requirements by 1977.

Use of the access channels varied, depending on the particular community and on the efforts of the cable system to involve the public.[22] Some systems provided special studio space and equipment for program production and, in a few instances, even a percentage of their profits to fund public access programming. Some hired an access coordinator to work with the public. For example, one such coordinator in Schenectady, New York worked with a Community Access Group of 100 members representing 20 organizations who were provided by the cable system with two Porta Paks to produce 25 to 30 hours of programming each week. Other systems, however, provided neither assistance nor incentive for use of the access channels and, when confronted with the FCC rules, provided time grudgingly, frequently successfully discouraging any public access channel use in that community.

In some areas citizen organizations, school boards and/or municipal offices developed detailed plans for effective use of cable access channels. For example, in 1973 the Boston Consumers' Council reported to Mayor Kevin White on the five major uses of access channels by cities: 1) special programming services for the deaf, senior citizens, non-English speaking groups, teachers, doctors and others; 2) home instruction for children and others who are confined to their homes, for working people who want an opportunity to take college courses and for people in need of vocational training; 3) community programming, including meetings, neighborhood news shows and ethnic programs; 4) commercial uses, including computer communications (freeing phone lines), banking services, meter reading, marketing research, transportation control, credit information checks, security systems and employee training; and 5) official communications such as fire and police needs, street surveillance, tele-medicine and public transportation control.

The expected use of cable access channels did not materialize as thought, however, and while there was extensive use in some markets, there was no use in others. In 1976 the Federal Communications Commission deleted the requirements for access channels for all cable systems with fewer than 3,500 subscribers, for systems which do not have sufficient channels to provide access outlets, and where demand for full time use has not been made. Where access channels will still be available, the FCC ruled that only one such channel would be required per system even if that system serves more than one community. The initiative for seeking access to cable television now seems to be totally that of individual community organizations. In the mid-1970s the dreams of utilizing CATV for public access remained far from reality and were still a sporadic local and experimental enterprise.

Future Alternative Systems

Among the technological developments showing most promise for future television systems are satellites and holography. Satellite experimentation began in the early 1970s with a concentration on education and health needs. Holography (a laser beam system) in the late 1970s was still in its early experimental stages, but offered the most dramatic change possibilities.

Lasers figure in two major developing television applications. A laser beam's capacity to carry multiple channels far exceeds that of pre-laser technology. Laser beams provide the base for holography. They illuminate the subject in what is basically wave front reconstruction photography to provide a highly exact reproduction in three dimensions. A hologram can be recorded on the photosensitive surface of the television camera as readily as on photographic emulsion. The hologram data can then be transmitted and reconstructed on a receiver.[23] Imagine the ultimate reality of being in a training, education or entertainment chamber surrounded on all sides, floor-walls-ceiling, by holography receivers in which your television experience will be totally three dimensional!

We must always keep in mind, however, that the end goal is not technological perfection, but, hopefully, the use of television technology to achieve humanistic growth, to achieve through the use of the power of television an equal opportunity for self-realization for all people.

NOTES

Unless otherwise indicated, sources for 1976 statistics are *Broadcasting,* A.C. Nielsen Company, National Cable Television Association or *Television Factbook.*

[1] Sydney W. Head, *Broadcasting in America.* Boston: Houghton Mifflin Company, 1972, p. 88.

[2] The top ten CATV states ranked by CATV percentage of penetration shows Wyoming (45.7%), West Virginia (40.8), Montana (36.0), Vermont (34.5), Delaware (31.8), New Hampshire (27.0), Pennsylvania (24.0), New Mexico (23.7), Idaho (21.6), Mississippi (20.5). A.C. Nielsen Company, U.S. Television Ownership Estimates, September, 1975.

[3] Head, *op. cit.*

[4] See also Richard K. Doan, "Turn Off That Satellite," *TV Guide,* Vol. 22, No. 11, March 16, 1974, p. 6.

[5] Head, *op. cit.,* 89.

[6] "The AV Industry's First Corporate Communications Centers Guide," *Audio-Visual Communications,* February, 1976, p. 8–17.

[7] NCTA Local Origination Directory, 1975, and 1977 Cable Services Directory. Available from the National Cable Television Association, 918 Sixteenth Street, N.W., Washington, D.C. 20006.

[8] *TV Communications,* July, 1974, p. 60.

[9] See also Arthur R. Taylor, "Does the American Family Need Another Mouth to Feed?" New York: CBS, 1974.

[10] *Broadcasting,* May 10, 1976, p. 58.

[11] The top ten CATV states ranked by number of CATV households in 1976 were California, Pennsylvania, New York,

Texas, Ohio, Florida, Illinois, West Virginia, Washington, Michigan.

[12] Richard W. Rappaport, "Satellite Communications, Cable Television Systems, and the Advent of the International Communications Grid," *Communications/Engineering Digest*, Vol. 1, No. 3 (December, 1975), 33–4.

[13] "University of Arizona Microcampus Permits Students to Study Anywhere at Anytime," Sony Application Bulletin, 1973.

[14] Doug Sheer, "Video: Entering an Era of Video Instamatics," *Audio-Visual Communications*, December, 1975, p. 9.

[15] E. Carlton Winkler, "Cable Origination Studio Design," *TV Communications*, July, 1974.

[16] Charles O'Brien and Emily L. Proctor, "The Making of Fun Factory." Houston: Unpublished special project report, 1975.

[17] "The AV Industry's First Corporate Communications Centers Guide," *op. cit.*, 8.

[18] *Multicast*, February 26, 1974.

[19] *Ibid*.

[20] Eugene Marlow, "Preventive Health Care via TV," *Educational Broadcasting*, Vol. 7, No. 4 (July–August, 1976), pp. 28–32.

[21] *Cablecasting Guidebook*. Washington, D.C.: The National Cable Television Association, 1973. Unpaged.

[22] According to NCTA's *Local Origination Directory*, published in November, 1975, 329 cable TV systems or 69 percent of the respondents indicated that they were providing their local origination channels to individuals and community groups.

[23] Emmet N. Leith and Juris Upatnieks, "Photography by Laser," in *Lasers and Light*. San Francisco: W. H. Freeman & Co., 1969, pp. 347–8.

BIBLIOGRAPHY/RESOURCES

Bermingham, Alan and others. *The Small TV Studio (Media Manuals)*. New York: Hastings House, 1974. An in-depth look at the features and amenities that typify the small studio (1600 sq. ft. or less).

Cable Sourcebook 19—. Washington, D.C.: Broadcasting Publications, Inc. Yearly. Listing of all systems, by State.

Cable Television. Santa Monica, California: the Rand Corporation, 1973. Many consider this series of publications central to any study of cable TV. It is especially useful to citizen groups and educators.

Cable Television and Education. Washington, D.C.: The National Cable Television Association, March, 1973.

Feldman, Nathaniel E., *Interconnecting Cable Television Systems by Satellite: An Introduction to the Issues*. Santa Monica, California: The Rand Corporation, 1973. A short report on the principal issues.

ITFS Instructional Television Fixed Service (2500 Megahertz) What It Is . . . How to Plan. Washington, D.C.: National Education Association, Publications-Sales Section, 1967. Introductory information.

LeDuc, Don R., *Cable Television and the FCC*. Philadelphia, Pennsylvania: Temple University Press, 1974. A history of government regulation of cable.

Millerson, Gerald. *Basic TV Staging (Media Manuals)*. New York: Hastings House, 1974. Basic principles demonstrating labor-saving approaches for small-budget productions.

Quick, John and Herbert Wolff. *Small-Studio Video Tape Production*. Reading, Mass.: Addison-Wesley Publishing

Co., 2nd ed., 1976. Especially useful for those in cable and in closed-circuit television.

Recommendations for the Establishment of Community Antenna Television (CATV) in the City of Houston, Texas. Houston: University of Houston, 1974. Includes a draft of a model ordinance for a large city.

Seiden, Martin H., Cable Television USA: An Analysis of Government Policy. New York: Praeger Special Studies, 1972.

Smith, Ralph Lee, The Wired Nation; Cable TV: The Electronic Communications Highway. New York: Harper & Row, 1972. Introductory material.

Television and the Wired City: A Study of the Implications of a Change in the Mode of Transmission. Washington, D.C.: National Association of Broadcasters, August, 1968. A Herman W. Land Associates report prepared for the President's Task Force on Communications Policy.

University at Home. Montreal, Canada: Les Dossiers de la Vice-Presidence sux Communications, 1972. An international symposium evaluating the university at home organized by the University of Quebec and Radio-Quebec.

"White Paper," Television Digest, January 21, 1974. Includes the report of the Cabinet Committee on Cable Communications under Clay T. Whitehead.

Periodicals

Audio-Visual Communications, 750 Third Ave., New York, New York 10017.

Cable Sourcebook, Broadcasting, 1735 DeSales St., N.W., Washington, D.C. The standard directory to the industry.

Communications/Engineering Digest, 1300 Army-Navy Dr., Arlington, Virginia 22202.

Community Antenna Television Journal, 4209 N.W. 23rd St., Suite 106, Oklahoma City, Oklahoma 73107.

CATV Newsweekly of Cable Television, CATV, 1900 West Yale, Englewood, Colorado 80111.

Educational & Industrial Television, 607 Main St., Ridgefield, Connecticutt 06877.

Educational Broadcasting, 825 S. Barrington Ave., Los Angeles, California 90049.

Hope Reports, 919 S. Winton Rd., Rochester, New York 14618.

NCTA Bulletin, National Cable Television Association, Inc., 918 Sixteenth St., N.W., Washington, D.C. 20006.

The Originator, Broadband Communications Networks, Inc., P.O. Box 416, Malvern, Pennsylvania.

TV Communications, CATV, 1900 West Yale, Englewood, Colorado 80110.

Video & Audio-visual Review, Link House, Dingwall Ave., Croydon CR9 2TA, England.

Videocassette and CATV Newsletter, Martin Roberts & Associates, Box 525 N, Beverly Hills, California 90210.

Videoplayer, Suite 213, 13273 Ventura Blvd., Studio City, California 91604.

Organizations

Cable Communications Resource Center, 2000 K. Street, N.W., Washington, D.C. 20006

Cable Television Information Center, Urban Institute, 2100 M St., N.W., Washington, D.C. 20036.

Community Antenna Television Information Service, Massachusetts Institute of Technology, Building E40, Cambridge, Massachusetts. 02139.

Publi-Cable, c/o Television Office, National Education Association, 1201 16th St., N.W., Washington, D.C. 20036.

Public Interest Satellite Association, 55 West 44th Street, New York, N.Y. 10036

Public Service Satellite Consortium, 4040 Sorrento Valley Blvd., San Diego, California 92121

INDEX

353

358

INDEX

Lazarsfeld, Paul, 95
Leavitt, Susan, 161
Lekolite, 288
Lettering for graphic cards, 291, 292
Liberace, 178
Library, film and tape, 109
Lighting, 76-77, 274, 284-90, 335; application of, 289-90; background, 286-87; backlight, 287, 289, 290; and "barndoor" device, 287, 290; controllable factors in, 287, 289; dimmer for controlling intensity of, 287, 289, 290, 335; equipment for, 76-77; eye, 286; for facial modeling, 285, 286; fill, 286, 289, 290; functions of, 284-85; and illusion of reality, creating, 285; and inverted Y, 289; key, 286, 289, 290; kicker, 286; for modeling, 285, 286; and mood, 285; motivated, 285; for performer, 285, 290; quality of, 286, 289; scenery, 286-87; from scoop, 286, 287, 288, 289, 290; for settings, 274; and shadows, elimination of, 286, 287; silhouette effects created by, 286, 287; special effects achieved with, 290; from spotlight, 286, 287, 288, 289, 290; types of, 286-87; visibility function of, 284-85
Log, station, 85, 256
Long shot (LS), 147, 218, 220, 231, 258
Lowe, Russ, 194
LVO Cable Louisiana, 340

McClay, Eileen, quoted, 196, 197
McGraw-Hill Company, 14
Magazine program, 125
Magnetic press, 292
"Magnificent Marble Machine, The," 282
Make-up, 295-96, 301
Marconi, Guglielmo, 6
Martinez, Palma, 194
Mass Culture, the Popular Arts in America (Rosenberg and Manning, eds.), 95
Maxwell, James Clerk, 5
May, Andrew, 6
MDS (Multipoint Distribution Service), 16, 319, 321-22, 327
Mead, Margaret, 113

Medical Community TV System, 343
Medical program, 343-44
Medium shot (MS), 147, 220, 258
"Meet the Press," 282
"Meet the Public," 250, 251
Merton, Robert K., 95
Metromedia, Inc., 14
Metropolitan Pittsburgh Public Broadcasting, Inc., 21
Microcam, 58
Microcampus, 331, 333
Microphone, 72-76, 149, 260, 335; back-to-back electrostatic, 73; bi-directional, 72, 73; boom, 74-76, 287, 313; cardioid, 73, 74; condenser, 72, 75; double-element, 73; hypercardioid, 73; lavalier, 74, 76, 313; omni-directional, 72, 73, 313; with radio transmitter, 76; reflector, 74; ribbon, 72, 73; rifle, 74; selection of, for program type, 74-76; slung, 76; tie-tack, 74, 76; uni-directional, 72, 73, 74, 75
Microwave, 16, 17, 320, 322, 327
Miniaturization, 330
MINI-CAMS, 51, 57, 58, 64; accessories to, 58-59
Minnelli, Liza, 301
Minority program, 191, 192, 193, 194, 346-47
Misiaszek, Loraine, 193
Mist, staging effect of, 280-81
Monitor, camera, 51, 79, 85, 232, 233, 292, 335
Monroe, Early D., Jr., 48
Multiple system owners (MSOs), 17
Multi-way clean feed system, 83
Music: for commercial, 157; cues for, 259; for drama program, 124; and producer, 99, 102-03
Music program, 178; techniques of writing, 179
Mutual of Omaha Insurance Company, 344

"Name That Tune," 282
"Narcotizing dysfunction," 95
National Aeronautics and Space Administration (NASA), 322, 329